CONTENTS IN BRIEF

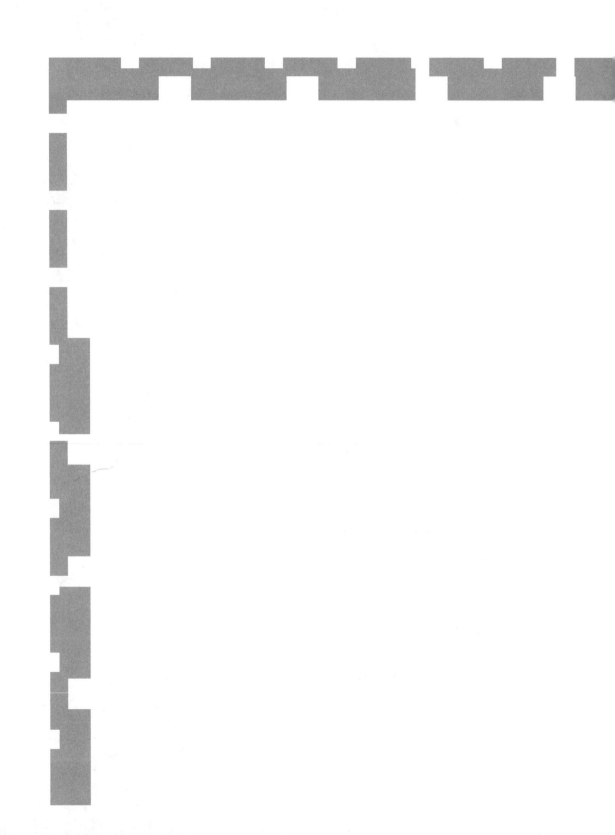

EXTENDED TABLE OF CONTENTS

PREFACE

As we entered the new millennium, retailing, like so many other fields, was rapidly changing. The lifestyles of today's consumers have changed enormously since retailing was in its infancy. Today's consumers demand that merchants address their shopping needs in new ways. Those retailers who don't will more than likely fall by the wayside, like companies such as Bonwit Teller, B. Altman & Company, Gimbel's, Montgomery Ward, Sterns, and others that were once marquee players in the industry. They didn't change with the times, and ultimately lost their customer bases.

Retailing today is a new arena that offers shoppers purchasing alternatives to the traditional brick-and-mortar in-store experiences. E-tailing, for example, is moving very quickly to capture an increasing share of the market. Catalog offerings continue to explode in record numbers, and the sales being generated by the home-shopping networks grow larger each and every day.

While traditional retailers continue to merchandise their facilities with well-known labels, more and more are embracing the private label phenomenon. Some retailers, such as Gap and Banana Republic, have taken this concept to new heights by focusing their businesses on the store-is-the-brand concept, which exclusively utilizes their own brands.

Many specialty retailers, once focused on a single merchandise classification, have expanded their offerings to other product lines. Banana Republic, for example, now features products for the home alongside of apparel, and Eddie Bauer does likewise with bedding in addition to its traditional offerings.

Supermarkets are no longer the typical food stores that simply feature standard canned goods, produce, and other related items. Progressive companies like the North Carolina-based Harris Teeter and Publix are emporiums that feature sushi bars, large fresh flower sections, and bakeries that turn out large assortments of fresh baked goods. Others are adding large sections that feature CDs and some apparel. Their decors are no longer the typical lackluster configurations, but environments that motivate purchasing and make shopping a pleasure.

Shopping centers are fast becoming arenas where entertainment is part of the landscape. New Roc City, a mall in New Rochelle, New York, features an amusement park ride on its roof, two skating rinks, a sports bar and pool hall, an IMAX movie theater, and a huge arcade. The concept simulates a type of Disney Main Street. Of course, a variety of stores are also in abundance.

Store themes continue to become more prominent. Environments are being designed to simulate sports facilities, jungle atmospheres, and the like. Niketowns provide shoppers an opportunity to live in sports arenas; The World Golf Village gives the golfer the feeling of being on a golf course, Rainforest Café simulates a tropical environment replete with rare birds and magnificent foliage; and the NBA stores provide simulated basketball arenas. These and other themed facilities have proven to motivate shoppers to buy in larger quantities.

Retailers are moving in the direction of "scent and sound" environments. With the air punctuated with refreshing scents and sounds that put shoppers in a better buying mood, it is expected that selling will be easier to accomplish.

These are but a few of the concepts that are making headlines in retailing for the new millennium. Numerous others are also gaining in importance and will be examined throughout the text.

There are several pedagogical features that are unique to this text including one that focuses on a major retailer and the direction that the company takes in regard to the running of the operation. Stein Mart, a principal U.S. off-price chain, has been selected to show the reader how it involves itself in the important aspects of retailing such as store location, merchandising decisions, visual merchandising, and so forth. It will show how retailers dovetail their operations to make their businesses prosper. Each chapter will feature a segment of **The Stein Mart Story** that relates to the material in the chapter.

An Ethical Consideration appears in each chapter in the text. It focuses on the need for ethics in the retailing community and many of the areas in which some merchants do not subscribe to ethical behavior.

Also in the text are numerous **Focuses** that feature a variety of companies that provide innovative approaches to the industry. Each chapter presents several of them.

Additional pedagogical aspects of the text are numerous and include:

- **Learning Objectives** which alert the student to what he or she will be able to master.
- **Trends for the New Millennium** that examine the latest in retail innovation.
- **Chapter Highlights** that give an overview of the important points in the chapter.
- **Important Retail Terms**, that when mastered, will prepare the student with a vocabulary that is used in day-to-day retailing.
- **Review Questions** that require the reader to recall the materials that have been presented in the chapter.
- **An Internet Activity** which requires the use of the Internet for its solution.
- **Exercises and Projects** which necessitate some form of industry contact such as company visits, interviews, or observations.
- **Case Problems** that focus on individual businesses facing the challenge of solving problems that are related to the chapter material.

An instructor's guide is also provided. It offers teaching methodology for each chapter along with the answers to the review questions and case problems. A test bank that includes objective examinations and essays is also provided. The guide includes listings of related videos, prepared by the authors, that can be used with this text. A PowerPoint presentation and supplementary readings are available on two CDs to instructors who adopt the text.

Additionally, a wealth of photographs and charts are incorporated throughout the text. Web sites have also been highlighted throughout, not only to show their importance to today's retail environment, but also to serve as a tool for students to learn more about the industry.

Whether the reader of this book is one who is merely interested in learning about the exciting field of retailing or is graduating from a two- or four-year educational institution, and wishes to pursue a career in retailing or a parallel field, this text will provide the information necessary to satisfy those needs. It is not meant merely to focus on the upper levels of management and the theories that govern those positions, but also to present an overall picture of the industry and the mid-management levels which the vast majority of students will eventually reach.

ACKNOWLEDGMENTS

We wish to thank the following people and organizations for their invaluable help in the writing of this textbook:

Allan Ellinger, Marketing Management Group; Steve Goodman, Graj + Gustavsen; Marcy Goldstein, JGA Inc.; Donna Lombardo and Steve Kelly, Belk's Department Store; The Doneger Group; Michael Stewart, Rootstein; Susan Edelman, Stein Mart; Ellen Diamond, photographer; Gigi Farrow, fashion consultant; Amy Meadows, Marshall Field's; Tim Wisgerhoff, Saks Fifth Avenue; Manoel Renha, Lord & Taylor; Proffitt's; FRCH; Federated Department Stores; Sensormatic Electronics Corp.; International Council of Shopping Centers (ICSC); The Mills Corporation; Claritas, Inc.; Beth Terrell, Lizden Industries; Billie Scott, Simon Property Group; David Spaeth, Spaeth Design.

Reviewers selected by the publisher were very helpful in writing this book. They include Cindi Baker, University of Wisconsin and Madison Area Technical; Evonne Bowling, Scottsdale Community College; P. Renee Foster, Delta State University; Naomi Gross, Fashion Institute of Technology; Diane Minger, Cedar Valley College; Gail Schmidt, Briarwood College; and Deborah Weinger, Katherine Gibbs School.

Jay Diamond
Sheri Litt

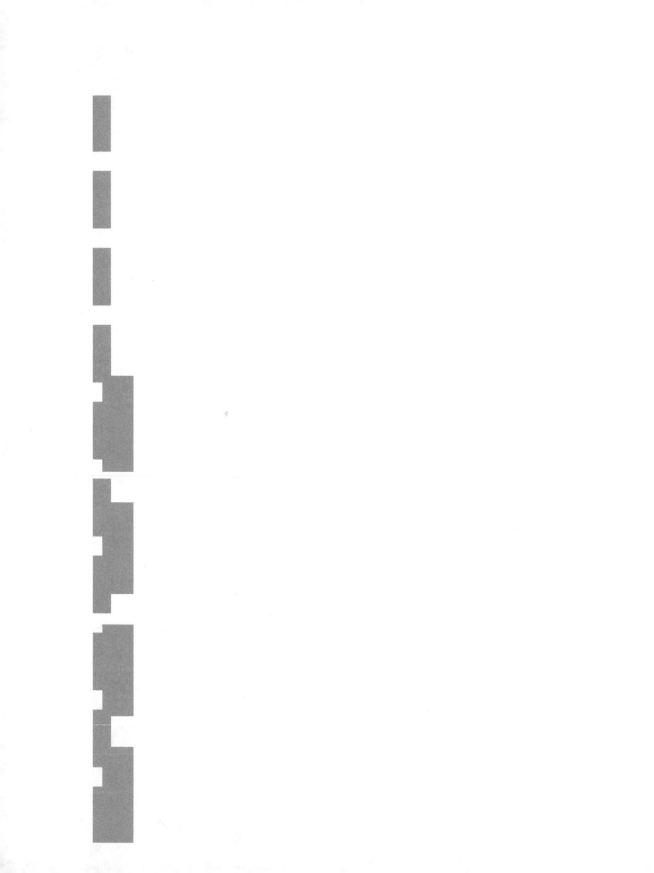

PART ONE

Introduction to Retailing

Retailing, as we know it today, is vastly different from what it was in the past. Consumers, more than ever before, have avenues for purchasing that are not restricted to the traditional stores and handful of catalogs that not too long ago were the only games in town. Consumers can now satisfy their needs with a wealth of merchandise in creative brick-and-mortar environments that run the gamut from department stores to unique specialty stores, from a never-ending number of catalogs that feature every conceivable type of product, from Web sites that offer the shopper just about any consumer goods that have ever been made, and from home shopping networks that feature a wealth of products around the clock. No, retailing is no longer what it once was, a somewhat limited industry with somewhat limited shopping choices, but an exciting, multifaceted arena that affords shoppers unlimited merchandise choices from around the world.

No one can properly explore the present landscape of retailing or its future without a look at the past. In Chapter 1, a historical look at the industry begins with the peddlers who were once the only way in which consumers could get their merchandise and traces the evolution that has taken place since then.

In Chapter 2, the various types of brick-and-mortars throughout the United States and abroad are featured, including the traditional department stores and specialty organizations as well as the newer "store is the brand" merchants, subspecialty retailers, and franchisers.

Off-site retailing has gained such significant momentum that it is thought by industry professionals to pose somewhat of a threat to the traditional means of purchasing. Along with an unparalleled number of catalogs to fit every lifestyle, an expansion of home shopping outlets on television, and e-tailing that seems to be taking the nation by storm, the shopper has countless ways in which to spend his or her money. These comparatively new retail entries are extensively examined in Chapter 3.

Rounding out the first section of the book, Chapter 4 offers a close inspection of modern consumers, and how they are motivated in terms of purchasing.

In each chapter, an overview of the trends that apply to the topics of discussion is presented to give the reader an insight into the latest industry developments.

CHAPTER 1

Retailing from Its Early Days to the Present

After you have completed this chapter, you should be able to discuss

- ▸ The early days of retailing in the United States and how early retailers differ from today's businesses.
- ▸ The similarities and differences between department stores and chain organizations.
- ▸ How two value retail operations—discount operations and off-price stores—differ.
- ▸ The characteristics of major retailing capitals around the world and how they differ from one another.
- ▸ Methods employed by retailers for global expansion.
- ▸ Reasons why retailers are entering foreign markets as part of their expansion programs.
- ▸ Pitfalls of overseas expansion.
- ▸ The importance of ethics in retailing.
- ▸ Career opportunities in today's retail marketplace.

At this very beginning of the new millennium, retailers are facing challenges that never confronted them before. New retailing outlets such as the Internet Web sites, vast numbers of global merchandise resource centers, and rapid changes in technology are just some of the issues that merchants must assess in order to make certain that their companies will maintain their competitive edge.

To better understand the new retail environment, it is beneficial to understand how retailing in America has evolved since its infancy and has made necessary transitions to meet the needs of the consuming public.

A look at the history of American retailing, beginning in the sixteenth century, will provide the framework for the principles and practices of modern day retail businesses.

RETAILING IN AMERICA: A HISTORICAL OVERVIEW OF THE INDUSTRY

In the early years of colonial America, retailers had few avenues through which to reach the market. Practices were primitive, available merchandise was severely limited, and the needs of the customers were extremely basic.

Trading Posts

In the early days of retailing in America, stores as we know them today were not part of the landscape. The American colonies were dealing with the many struggles that developing communities must face. While the needs of the early settlers were minimal in comparison to those of today's consumers, some products were essential to their everyday lives. The first American retail institution, the **trading post**, was established in the early sixteenth century to satisfy these needs. Products manufactured in Europe were available at these outposts along with agricultural products supplied by farmers and pelts supplied by trappers. Currency was not used in the negotiation; instead, goods were traded for other goods in a bartering system. While this primitive form of retailing is virtually nonexistent today, it is considered to be the forerunner of flea markets. Of course, flea markets in the twenty-first century are not places where bartering is the means of selling, but a place where cash and credit cards are used for purchasing. While many of today's flea markets are actually big business arenas and show no resemblance to the trading posts of the past, there are still some remnants of the old trading posts or swap shops in rural areas where the locals come to buy and sell used items, home-made goods, and farm products.

Peddlers

In extremely remote, rural areas, where there were no trading posts, the settlers resorted to buying goods from **peddlers** who went from place to place hawking their wares. They sold such necessities as pots and pans, tools, knives, and foodstuffs, including coffee and tea, that weren't grown by the farmers. As at the trading posts, much of the goods were bartered because the people didn't have the currency for outright purchases. The peddlers took a variety of produce and crudely made furniture in exchange for their goods.

In addition to bringing various much-needed items to the farmers, the peddlers also carried eagerly awaited news from the settlements and from Europe. In fact, the peddlers were one of the few ways by which these new Americans could learn about their homelands.

While the merchandise and information peddlers brought to the farmers was imperative to their happiness and meager existence, it often came at a dear price. Without competition to serve as a check on prices, many peddlers took advantage of their customers and charged them unfair prices. With the profits they realized from these ventures, some peddlers went on to open stores, and some became major retailing entrepreneurs.

The trading posts flourished for many years, as did the businesses of the peddlers.

General Stores

It wasn't until the early eighteenth century that the first real, permanent retailing establishments came into existence. They were known as **general stores** because their inventory was extremely varied and included goods ranging from food to fabrics. Unlike their predecessors, general stores were operated primarily on a cash basis, although those with good credit were allowed to run up bills that they would pay periodically. Farmers, for example, would get some of their supplies from the general stores and be allowed to pay for them when the crops were harvested and sold. This practice was actually the forerunner to the formal charge accounts that came later.

The physical arrangement of inventory was something of a hodgepodge. Nothing had a set place in the store; as the goods came in, they were put wherever room could be found. The stores also housed the post office and places where people would congregate to exchange news and gossip or just pass the time.

Much like the peddlers who came before them, the general store merchants charged prices that were higher than might be considered fair. With the lack of competition and the population dependent on the general store, these merchants could set their own prices and some became the wealthiest people in town. As goods from overseas became more plentiful, and American-made goods were becoming more available, the stores were able to carry a wider assortment of merchandise. The general store didn't face any competition until early in the nineteenth century when a variety of merchandise became even more plentiful. It was this abundance of merchandise that led to the beginning of specialization in retailing. Although the limited-line or specialty store became popular at this time, the general store remained a business venture, especially in the far-flung areas where other retail businesses didn't open more modern facilities. Even today, in the most rural parts of the South, some general stores are still in operation.

Limited-Line Stores

By the mid 1850s, merchants started to open **limited-line stores** or **specialty stores** that restricted their offerings to one classification or line. The industrial revolution was now in full steam, and a wealth of goods never seen before was available. Reacting to this abundance of products, and the consumers' need to have them, retailers opened limited-line

Abercrombie & Fitch is an example of a limited-line store.

stores in record numbers. Unlike the general store, this new type of store featured a wide variety of goods in one product line, such as shoes, food, hardware, clothing, or millinery, so that customers had an assortment with both breadth and depth to choose from.

The success of the limited-line store has carried over until today. In fact, it is fast becoming the most important segment of the retail industry.

Chain Organizations

Chain store organizations developed shortly after limited-line stores, with the first chain—the Great Atlantic & Pacific Tea Co.—beginning operations in 1859. When the specialty store merchants found success in one geographical area, some expanded their operations to other locations. When these new outlets succeeded, retailers opened still more units. These retailers were "inventing" the **chain store organization**. Simply defined a

Crate & Barrel is one of the fastest expanding home product chain organizations.

chain store organization is a retail business with four or more units, similar in nature, and having common ownership. Chains may specialize in any merchandise category, such as soft goods, home, food, pharmaceuticals, video rentals, music, and so forth. They continue to spread quickly throughout the United States and abroad. Chains like The Limited, Gap, Toys "R" Us, Crate & Barrel, CVS, Pottery Barn, and Abercrombie & Fitch are expanding in record numbers. Not only do they continue to open stores under their company's origi-

nal name, but many have also established new entities under different names, featuring other merchandise mixes targeted to new market segments.

A case in point is Limited Brands with several thousand stores. Under the Limited umbrella, chains stores like Express, Victoria's Secret, Bath & Body Works, Express Man, Limited Too, and others, are achieving significant success.

Department Stores

In the mid-nineteenth century the concept of selling a wide assortment of merchandise under one roof was revived in a new form, the **department store**. Unlike general stores, with their haphazard arrangement of goods, department stores had carefully structured layouts that stocked each merchandise classification in a specific area. Shoppers looking for shoes, for example, could find an assortment of them in an area that had *only* shoes. Unlike their competition—specialty stores—department stores offered a wide variety of both hard goods and soft goods. A customer could buy a dress, a handbag, bedding, and table linens without having to leave the store. It was **one-stop shopping** at its best. Essentially, the department store is the bringing together of many different specialty stores in a single environment.

The department store format was an immediate success. Companies like Macy's and Marshall Field's soon began to expand their operations much as their specialty store counterparts had. The additional units they opened were smaller versions of the original main stores, or **flagship stores**, and were called **branch stores**. Department store companies developed an organizational structure with central control of management and merchandising philosophies. Thus, the branches were merely selling outlets. All decisions were made at the flagship, which established the rules and regulations to be followed by the branches.

Mail-Order Retailers

At about the same time that the department store was achieving success, yet another retailing venture was under way: **mail-order selling**, through which retailers brought merchandise directly to the consumer. Great numbers of Americans lived too far away from stores to patronize them, yet, they needed a variety of products. Direct-mail retailers served those needs. Montgomery Ward & Co. published the first mail-order catalog in 1872. Sears Roebuck & Co. followed suit in 1896. These catalogs featured numerous products in a variety of classifications that rural families could choose from for delivery via U.S. mail. Year after year, with the success of mail-order retailing, these two companies expanded their catalogs until they became **big books** of several hundred pages and contained every conceivable type of merchandise. Although their successes continued well into the twentieth century,

Giant retailer Sears Roebuck & Co. began with a single small location in 1887 and published its first catalog, limited to watches and jewelry, in 1888.

both companies eventually disbanded these operations. While sales volume remained stable, the cost of doing business with these enormous books was too high, and thus became unprofitable.

Although the huge Spiegel catalog is still a mainstay in American retailing, the trend in catalog selling has been toward issuing smaller catalogs numerous times throughout the year. Every department store, most specialty chains, and numerous companies that use only direct selling methods are crowding mail boxes with scores of catalogs that offer a wealth of products. Another change in recent years has to do with how customers place their orders.

While the term *mail order* is still used informally for this type of merchandising, the vast majority of purchases are made over the telephone. *Catalog selling* is therefore a more appropriate term for this type of retailing.

Supermarkets

Large departmentalized food stores, or **supermarkets**, came on the scene in the early 1930s. Until that time, people shopped for food at grocers, butchers, and bakers. The Great Atlantic & Pacific Tea Co. is credited with developing the supermarket concept, with it's A & P stores. Other early supermarket chains were Grand Union and Kroger. The notion of one-stop food shopping quickly caught fire, and the race was on for other foods merchants to enter this form of retailing. By the 1950s the supermarket became the dominant force in

The Whole Foods supermarket chain features a wide variety of fine food products.

food sales, forcing many small grocers, butchers, and bakeries to go out of business. So successful were these ventures that more and more units were opened in neighborhoods all across the United States. With their low prices, self-service format, and wide selection of products, supermarkets became *the way* Americans shopped for food.

It wasn't long before supermarkets expanded their inventory into nonfood items, enabling shoppers to purchase many products that once required separate stops at specialty stores such as pharmacies, books stores, hardware stores, and the like. The availability of nonfood items not only satisfied the needs of the store's customers, but also gave the companies a profit advantage. Traditionally, food carries a comparatively low markup, and thus a small profit margin. On the other hand, nonfood items enjoy higher markups, thus returning more profit per item to the store.

More and more nonfood items continue to be added to supermarket inventories every day. Greeting cards, paperback books, stationery products, a host of health-care items, plants, hosiery, cosmetics, and tools are commonplace in these stores. Sales for these products continue to increase and help make supermarket retailing a profitable venture.

Discount Operations

In the years immediately following World War II, a new type of retail store was born: the **discount store**, where shoppers could find appliances, cameras, and many other hard goods at prices substantially lower than those charged in the traditional department and specialty stores. The first major discounter, E.J. Korvettes, thrived for many years, but has now gone out of business. The discount stores people shop at today are its direct descendents.

The discount concept is simple. Stores would lack the usual amenities, featuring instead plain pipe racks and basic counters, and they would provide very few services. In exchange for putting up with the stripped-down environment and lack of services they had been accustomed to else-where, customers were offered lower prices. Clearly marked tags with the regular price and the discounted price made it clear to customers that they were getting a bargain.

Best Buy is a discount operation specializing in electronics.

Today, discount retailing is big business. Companies like Kmart, Wal-Mart, and Target generate an enormous volume of business. These modern discount stores are not only selling hard goods as their predecessors did, but a large variety of clothing, accessories, shoes, food, stationery, records, and garden products—all at discounted prices.

One significant change from their early counterparts is that contemporary discounters offer pleasant shopping surroundings and a host of customer conveniences. The significant volume they achieve enables them to operate in this manner and still turn a profit.

Off-Price Stores

A new type of retail store, the **off-price store**, made its debut on a grand scale in the early 1980s. Frieda Loehmann, founder of the now popular Loehmann's stores is credited with introducing off-price selling. She began her business on a very limited scale in the 1920s in her home in the Bronx, New York. Each day, Loehmann would go to the Garment Center in Manhattan, where she would buy a few items at greatly reduced prices. She paid cash for the merchandise and was therefore readily welcomed by fashion's top manu-facturers. Because she paid low prices and because she had such low overhead, she was able to sell the goods at less than the usual retail price. Day in and day out she followed the same routine. It wasn't long before she opened a store near her home that became a

Marshalls is one of the leading off-price merchants in the United States.

magnet for budget-concious and fashion-concious women throughout the metropolitan area. Like the discount stores, Loehmann's and later off-price stores lacked the amenities of full-price retail outlets.

Today, off-price retailing is a major force in the industry. Along with the Loehmann's chain, companies like Syms, Burlington Coat Factory, Marshalls, T. J. Maxx, and the Men's Wearhouse have outlets all across the country. They are major purchasers in wholesale markets throughout the world, always ready to buy "opportunistically" so that they can satisfy the needs of those seeking bargains. Designer labels and manufacturer brands such as DKNY, Ralph Lauren, Calvin Klein, Liz Claiborne, Guess, and others are mainstays in the off-price merchant's premises.

Manufacturers sell to the off-price retailers as a way to dispose of merchandise that has been left after the traditional store buyers have finished purchasing for the season.

The Stein Mart Story
A Historical Perspective

WHAT COULD BE CALLED THE PROTOTYPICAL AMERICAN DREAM began in 1905 when Sam Stein, a young immigrant, walked across Europe to board a ship to the United States in search of a new life. After landing at Ellis Island, he found his way to Greenville, Mississippi, where he began selling notions and piece goods door-to-door, calling on wealthy cotton planters and tenant farmers alike. As the business grew, he traded his horse and cart for a small store in Greenville, which ultimately grew to fill an entire city block.

In 1949, while liquidating his stock in order to move into a new location, Sam's son Jake realized that by discounting prices they could draw from a different, untapped customer base. It was in this new location that Jay Stein, recently retired chief executive officer, working with his father Jake, began to develop a more upscale business through special buys on designer and better merchandise. In 1977, Stein Mart opened a branch in Memphis, Tennessee, a city much larger than Greenville. The response was overwhelming.

In 1984, the company relocated to Jacksonville, Florida, where it opened the corporate offices for its ever-growing chain. Today, it is a premier off-price retail venture, with more than 250 stores in 35 states and with plans to expand to 550 stores.

Stein Mart is a unique operation that combines a conventional specialty store approach with discount prices.

The Stein Mart story, which will continue in later chapters, serves as a model for those who hope to achieve the American Dream of entrepreneurship.

Warehouse Clubs

In the 1980s, the **warehouse clubs** concept was born and began opening in huge, industrial type spaces. Such clubs, where goods are sold at large discounts, were originally established for union members and other large organizations. Today, anyone who pays an annual fee of about $40 can shop at these stores.

Companies like Sam's Club, Costco, Pace, and BJ's are among the largest warehouse clubs, with stores located throughout the country. They offer a vast and ever-changing merchandise assortment. While the food inventory, which constitutes the largest part of the warehouse club business, is made up of the same product categories throughout the year, buyers can never count on finding the specific brands and products they want. The availability of goods is based upon the buyers' ability to buy at favorable prices. That is, they buy opportunistically.

In addition to foods, warehouse stores carry automotive goods, electronics, outdoor furniture, books, apparel, stationery supplies, cameras, jewelry, and a host of other products. The availability of each merchandise classification at a given time depends on whether the stores' buyers can make deals that will allow them to sell at bargain prices. Another way warehouse clubs keep costs down is by accepting only cash payments; however, some stores, including Sam's Club, do take Discover Card which has a very low fee.

Unlike other retailing ventures, warehouse clubs sell the products only in bulk. Soft drinks, for example, are usually packaged in 24-unit cases; film in 6-packs; and cereals in double packages. To promote food items, as many as a dozen demonstrators prepare samples of hot and cold food at cooking stations on the sales floor.

Warehouse clubs can be extremely profitable despite their low prices because of the money brought in by membership fees. If one considers the huge number of consumers who join these clubs—and pay their dues annually—it is simple to understand their profitability. Thus, unlike other retail ventures where markups need to be high enough to cover overhead expenses and bring in a profit, these retailers need not have high price margins to succeed.

The warehouse clubs continues to thrive and grow, opening new outlets across the United States and in many foreign countries.

Manufacturer-Owned Retail Outlets

At about the same time as off-price retailing and warehouse clubs were in their infancy, consumers were introduced to another new retail operation, the **manufacturer-owned outlet**. With bargain merchandise as the primary draw, shoppers quickly took to these shopping environments.

Manufacturers began to open their own outlets as a way to dispose of unwanted merchandise. Even after selling their leftover inventories to the off-pricers, many still had large quantities of goods in their warehouses. By opening their own stores, designers and manufacturers could "clean out" their inventories to make room for the next season's offerings. Since it is fashion items that quickly change from season to season, it is wearing apparel that led the way in this area of retailing.

Today, all across the country, numerous outlet centers—usually either outdoor or indoor malls—house the outlets of numerous major designers and manufacturers in a single location. These outlet centers have become favorite destinations for price-conscious consumers. Retail companies that produce their own goods such as Gap and Banana Republic are found alongside manufacturers such as Jones New York, Coach, Dooney & Burke, Mikasa, Nine West, Gucci, Perry Ellis, and Liz Claiborne.

Maine Gate Outlet Center is typical of outdoor malls that feature many manufacturers' outlets.

Visitors to these outlets find bargain merchandise, often priced as much as 50 percent lower than the traditional retailers, in vast assortments; however the items they find are primarily last season's goods.

So successful are these ventures that many manufacturers are using their left-over fabrics and other materials to produce products especially for these stores.

Flea Markets

Flea markets have their roots in gatherings called *swap shops* or *swapmeets* where people bartered their unwanted household items. Swap shops generally took place in rural areas for one day over the weekend. They had no formal structures or continuity. In fact, once someone's goods were sold out, that "retailer" went out of business.

In the early 1980s, the **flea market** took on a new meaning. In parking lots of racetracks, drive-in movies, and other locations that were easily accessible to consumers, vendors began to set up shop with a host of goods that they purchased from manufacturers and sold at very low markups. They were able to market their goods at these attractive prices because their overheads were minimal. Individual spaces cost as little as $40 for the day, with none of the usual expenses for electricity, telephone, insurance, and so forth. The flea market environment is festive and fun, making it a place to bring the whole family. Merchandise offerings included a wealth of items from clothing and foods to household goods and electronics. Many of the markets featured entertainment, fun food, and other enticements.

The flea market concept quickly caught on and flea markets eventually became a regular part of people's shopping routines, not only because of the bargain pries but also for the interesting merchandise assortment. Some flea market vendors carried designer jeans, nationally advertised brands, and other products that could be found—at higher prices—in traditional retail operations. Many flea markets also operate in conjunction with farmers' markets and attract food shoppers with the freshness of their produce.

So successful were these ventures that many of the stall operators opened units at many different flea markets, actually becoming chain operations. At many flea markets, the temporary quarters available in the early years, have been replaced by permanent structures. In Sunrise Florida, a suburb of Ft. Lauderdale, for example, more than 1,000 vendors hawk their merchandise in permanent buildings as well as outdoor stalls. A wealth of fashion merchandise, expensive jewelry and watches, electronics and other items fill the shelves and racks. Open every day of the week, the market draws large crowds of shoppers. Another location, operating under the same owners in San Jose, California, is even larger. In each of these environments, entertainment helps to attract the crowds. In the Sunrise Swap Shop, its name taken from the early flea market days, a circus performs several times a day, and such big name acts as Willie Nelson and the Gatlin Brothers have appeared. No doubt, when the family has had its fill of entertainment, they head to the vendors to shop.

Boutiques

Catering to affluent men and women, **boutiques** have become a favorite shopping places for those seeking high fashion and individuality. Also in the 1980s, just as others were seeking bargains in flea markets and off-price stores, a very small portion of the population headed to these very specialized stores to buy their fashion merchandise. Exclusive apparel and accessories and excellent personal service were the key to the boutiques' success. They can now be found in affluent areas all over the country.

Kiosks

Originating in festival marketplaces like Quincy Market in Boston and South Street Seaport in New York City, the **kiosk** immediately gained favor with the consuming public.

Kiosks were like mini stores placed in the aisles and open areas of these marketplaces, where vendors would sell such wares as sunglasses, tee shirts, and other small items from attractive displays.

Today, kiosks are found in the large indoor malls as well as at festival marketplaces. Many do such a thriving business that they have moved into regular retail stores. Lids, a company that sells sports caps with the logos of just about every team in every popular sport, is one company that made the move from kiosk to store.

Kiosks have spread rapidly and are found today in malls, airports, and festival marketplaces.

Category Killers

Another phenomenon that appeared on the scene in the 1980s is the **category killer**. Category killers are extremely large operations that offer enormous selections of merchandise in one classification at discounted prices. Their assortments are so huge that shoppers are almost certain to find the products that meet their particular needs. Examples of such companies are Toys "R" Us, Kids "R" Us, and Best Buy.

RETAILING TODAY: A GLOBAL INDUSTRY

Today's retail landscape is broader than ever before and spans every part of the globe. While the majority of retail businesses stay within the trading areas of specific countries, many American merchants are expanding their operations into foreign countries and, conversely, many European and Asian retailers are coming to our and each other's shores. The **global retailing** landscape is without parameters.

Companies that seek to expand into international markets must address numerous considerations. A retailer's success in one country does not guarantee success in another. Too often, even the largest, most solidly established store in one country meets disaster when it opens foreign branches. Galeries Lafayette, for example, the renowned French department store failed in its attempt to bring its business to New York City. Even with what was considered to be a prime location, the company never quite adapted to the needs of Americans. On the other hand, Benetton, the Italian-based retailer met with considerable success when it expanded throughout the United States. Before long it had more than 800 franchised outlets in the United States. Its product mix had great appeal to American consumers, and it quickly became a household name. Although it enjoyed considerable success for many years, increased competition cut into its profits, and it had to retrench. Its difficulties, however, were the same as many American retailers were experiencing, and they did not lead to abandoning the U.S. market. Benetton, finding it still has great appeal in the United States, is refocusing its operations in this country to try to recapture its initial success. Other companies that expanded into international markets have met with better fortune than these two. Toys "R" Us, for example, has become a popular shopping experience in many parts of the world.

International Retailing Centers

All over the world, retail expansion is reaching unparalleled heights. New businesses are regularly joining those that have existed for many years, and the mainstays of the industry are regularly opening new units in areas that they had not previously entered. Throughout North America, Europe, and Asia, in particular, the growth of retailing has been unprecedented. Retailing has grown most extensively in certain dominant countries on each continent.

The United States

As we learned earlier in the chapter, American retailing has evolved from very basic roots to become a complex industry made up of a wide assortment of different types of organizations. Today, the United States has more retail companies that any other country. The industry's geographical range spreads from coast to coast, with many of its companies well represented in every region—the north, south, east, west, and central United States. The major retailing centers are New York City, Chicago, Atlanta, Miami, Dallas, Houston, and Los Angeles.

The United States is a vast retailing empire. Within its borders numerous department store groups, chain organizations, and independent retailers offer vastly different merchandising concepts. It encompasses giants like Sears and Wal-Mart, midsize marquee names like Federated's Macy's and Bloomingdale's, somewhat smaller companies like Office Depot, and the numerous relatively unknown retailers that operate in a limited trading area.

Although its population is small in comparison to those of some other nations such as China, its retail presence is dominant worldwide. It is no wonder that the United States, with the latest in technology, communication systems, public and private transportation capabilities, has become the world leader in this segment of the business community.

In addition to the factors already mentioned, others have also contributed to American dominance. They include few government regulations, the ability to transfer goods effectively from production points to the consumptions points, the retailers' ability to produce their own private label goods, and the availability of a large number of permanent wholesale markets within the buyers' reach. Many retailers have joint programs with their suppliers to keep track of inventory, engage in cooperative advertising and promotion, and allow **chargebacks** to vendors when retailers must reduce prices to move inventory. No other country enjoys all these benefits.

No other part of the international marketplace offers the diversity of shopping options that Americans enjoy: higher-priced, specialty venues with exclusive merchandise and personal service for the upscale market; no-frills retailers for those seeking bargain-priced value merchandise; and a vast middle ground of retailers ready and able to satisfy every type of customer. As we will learn later, this depth and breadth of retail offerings is without parallel in any other region of the world.

Of course, domestic retailing is made up of more than **brick-and-mortar stores**. It is also made up of a rapidly growing number of catalog operations and Web sites. Nowhere in the world is off-site retailing nearly as abundant. In addition to those businesses that operate exclusively as off-site retailers, brick-and-mortar companies also have off-site retailing divisions.

The top ten U.S. retailers are listed in Table 1.1. Some of them are store-only merchants while others have catalog divisions, and are either actively involved in **e-tailing** or getting ready to make entry into the field. The majority of the top ten operate under only one name (Wal-Mart, for example); others are made up a number of divisions each with a different name (for example, Target, Inc., operates Target, Mervyn's, and Marshall Field's).

Although they are all headquartered in the United States and the majority of their business is in this country, many have revenue-producing units all over the globe. The companies in the top ten include discounters, department stores, specialty stores, supermarkets, and warehouse clubs, and they offer merchandise mixes that range from being extremely restricted (supermarkets like Kroger and Safeway for example) to being extremely diverse (as is the case of Target).

Chapter 2, Brick-and-Mortar Retailing, and Chapter 3, Off-Site Retailing: E-Tailing,

Catalogs, and Home-Shopping Networks, contain in-depth discussions of these major retailing formats.

TABLE 1.1		
TOP TEN U.S. RETAILERS BY VOLUME		
COMPANY	**HEADQUARTERS**	**NUMBER OF UNITS**
Wal-Mart	Bentonville, AR	4,190
Kroger	Cincinnati, OH	3,660
Sears	Hoffman Estates, IL	1,134
Home Depot	Atlanta, GA	2,960
Albertson's	Boise, ID	2,150
Kmart	Troy, MI	2,533
Target	Minneapolis, MN	1,307
JCPenney	Plano, TX	3,725
Safeway	Pleasanton, CA	335
Costco	Issaquah, WA	1,688

Source: *Stores*, July 2001. © Copyright 2001 NRF Enterprises, Inc. Used with permission.

The United Kingdom

The United Kingdom which is England, Scotland, Wales, and Northern Ireland, is the only nation in Europe that is not on the continent. As in the United States, retailers there include department stores, specialty chains, mail-order houses, and food emporiums. Unlike in the United States, where off-pricers and discount operations are plentiful, most retailers in the United Kingdom have a traditional pricing policy. The United Kingdom also has one type of American retailer not found in the United States: **mixed-merchandise stores** that sell combinations of products such as foods, soft goods, and books.

The food halls at Harrod's, the premier retailer in the United Kingdom, are famous throughout the world.

Department stores range from perhaps the best-known store in the world, Harrods, with its wide assortment of upscale, unusual offerings, including antiquities and gourmet foods, to the House of Frasier, a company that operates stores selling mainstream goods under several different names in the same way that Target does. Many of the department stores contain **leased departments**, which are spaces rented out to private merchants who determine their own merchandise mixes.

Specialty chains flourish in the United Kingdom. For example, Body Shop, an important store in the United States, is actually a British company and is one of that nation's more successful nonfood chains.

The mail-order businesses, which continue to grow in volume, is primarily based on big-book catalogs, similar in size to the ones produced in the United States by Sears and Montgomery Ward. Unlike those operations, however, the vast majority of the merchandise is not sold directly to the consumer but through **agent order takers**. The agent order takers show the catalogs to prospective customers, many of whom are members of their own families, and place the orders for them. In return for the service they provide, they are paid a small commission. Great University Stores, which sells mostly apparel, is the largest mail-order company.

A major reason consumers buy mail-order goods from agent order takers is that they can buy on credit and pay their bills over time, in the same way as U.S. consumers make use of the credit plan retailers offer. Of course, credit costs money, and the considerable finance charges substantially increase the cost of the goods.

Smaller catalogs are becoming more popular in the United Kingdom. These books often number fewer than 100 pages and feature a more specialized, branded merchandise assortment. Unlike the big books, these catalogs use the direct channel of distribution. That is, buyers receive the catalogs directly, and order without the aid of a middleman.

Traditional merchants that previously sold goods only in their stores are also entering the mail-order retailing field. Marks & Spencer, a household name in U.K. retailing entered the fray with a catalog that featured a wealth of housewares and clothing in 1996.

Of course, the mail-order business is small in comparison to the United States, and only time will tell if these off-site ventures will gain in popularity.

Led by Tesco and J. Sainsbury, food retailing is big business in the United Kingdom. Service and innovation, rather than price competition, is the focus of these and other giant food stores. They aim to create customer loyalty with "loyalty cards" that give their regular customers a small discount for their patronage. Other promotions have centered on community outreach—providing computers to schools, for example. Their successes have led them to acquire other food retailers in different parts of the world, thus becoming international purveyors of foods. Tesco's international expansion has centered on numerous European countries, while Sainsbury's has entered the U.S. market by acquiring Shaws, a supermarket chain.

Rounding out the major retail categories are the mixed-merchandise stores. Perhaps the most famous such company is Marks & Spencer. The vast majority of its inventory is in food and soft goods lines such as clothing for the family, housewares, and cosmetics. Others in this retail classification include Storehouse, the WH Smith Group, and the Boots Company. Each has its own merchandising specialty and has wide appeal to the British consumer.

Retailers from other nations have opened branches in the United Kingdom. Expansions *into* the country include Sears, Blockbuster, and Toys "R" Us from the United States; IKEA,

One of France's major retailers is the Samartaine department store group.

from Sweden; and Benetton from Italy. Conversely, British companies such as Laura Ashley, Body Shop, and Tie Rack have had major success in America.

France

Retailing in France occurs in a variety of venues, with department stores being one of the major ones. Paris alone is home to 12 department stores. The leaders are Galeries Lafayette, Printemp, Samaritaine, and Bon Marche, headquartered in Paris, with branches located throughout the country. They carry a wide assortment of merchandise, as do the American department stores, with fashion as the leader.

The most fashionable, upscale operation is Galeries Lafayette. Although hard times had fallen on this French institution, it is making a tremendous turnaround with a $60 million facelift of its flagship alone. Aside from its significant attention to the brick-and-mortar operation, the company is taking a major plunge into e-tailing.

 Focus on . . .
Galeries Lafayette

WITH ITS FLAGSHIP LOCATED ON BOULEVARD HAUSSMANN, Paris's leading street for fashion retailing, Galeries Lafayette is easily accessible for the French as well as visitors from around the world. It has long been a department store mainstay, but has had recent competition from the shopping centers that have cropped up outside of the city. Not ready to throw in the towel, the company embarked on a two-tiered program, one a renovation of the store and the other an upgrading of its Web site, in the hope that these investments would lead to a more profitable future.

The first phase of the redevelopment took place in the flagship store. The facelift addressed all of the company's trouble spots and soon achieved a doubling of sales for designer label merchandise. One of the strategies that gained immediate approval was to use the concept of grouping merchandise according to lifestyle rather than price. Higher-priced labels such as Commes des Garçons are placed alongside lower-priced lines that meet the same needs, giving the shopper a choice of different price ranges. It was a daring move that paid off. So successful has the concept been that brands such as Lanvin, Chloe, Prada, and Anna Sui have agreed to become part of the "new" Galeries Lafayette. Also dominant in the new store design is the use of more in-store shops. Shopping in these smaller boutiquelike shops is more like visiting a specialty store than being in a large department store.

Its top-to-bottom renovation is not the only change in the company's flagship. Customer service has also been vastly improved. Like many other retailers around the world, Galeries Lafayette recognizes that—in addition to the merchandise selection—service is key to maintaining customer loyalty, and hence, higher profits, in the face of ever-increasing competition. To this end, several improvements are in place. A "hostess" at the escalator landing on each floor directs clients to the areas that will best serve their needs. In these days, when time is of the essence, many shoppers appreciate the time saved by such guidance. Large numbers of personal shoppers are ready to assist with merchandise selections and make certain that every customer need is satisfied. This service is a way to increase the average size of the sale, and cut down on returns as well as to win customer loyalty.

The renovation also makes the store a more comfortable place to shop. The size of the dressing rooms has been increased by as much as 30 percent; rest areas with comfortable upholstered furniture where beverages are served are available on fashion floors; and a new branch of the upscale Parisian food chain, Lina's, has been added to cater to the hungry customer.

The second phase of Galeries Lafayette's improvement involves the Internet. The company incorporated virtual mannequins and personal shopping into the existing Web site, which in the past was used only for informational purposes. It was the first Web site in France to offer a system that allows shoppers to see an image of their own bodies in the merchandise as well as online purchasing. (Such *virtual try-ons* will be discussed in Chapter 3.) It takes the customer less than one minute to design a customized virtual mannequin with exact measurements, face shape, skin and hair color, and hairstyle. The shopper is shown a variety of items that can be "dragged" to the newly created form, on which the entire outfit, along with selected accessories, is displayed. Since many women take their friends along on shopping sprees for advice, the new system is capable of transmitting the pictures to their friends via e-mail so that they can give the same input as they would if they were actually in the store together.

Galeries Lafayette hopes that after using the new technology customers will eventually patronize the store for a wider variety of merchandise.

The company prides itself on these improvements, where shopping is simpler and more pleasurable for its clientele, and expects to remain one of France's leading fashion emporiums.

• •

Shoppers can also find fashion merchandise in such specialty stores as Cime-camiaeu, Etam, and Yves Rocher. These French companies must also compete against branches of such foreign chains as the Gap (United States) and Marks & Spencer (United Kingdom). These and other specialty stores are popular because of the short time needed to make purchases and the concentration of their offerings.

When visitors think of French fashion, they think of exclusive designers like Christian LaCroix, Missoni, Claude Montana, Valentino, and others, who sell their clothing from the boutiques that bear their names. These shops offer both *couture* (custom-made) or *prêt-à-porter* (ready-to-wear) fashions. Although only the extremely affluent can afford to buy at these boutiques, they are the best places to see the latest fashion innovations.

The **hypermarket** is another type of retailing operation in France. Selling other product lines in addition to food, these giant markets turn a better profit than food stores because nonfood items have higher markups. These stores sell foods along with other items. Carrefour is the leading hypermarket in terms of sales, and it has gained international acclaim by opening units in Spain and South America.

Japan

Retailers in Japan have a different kind of relationship with their suppliers than U.S. retailers have. It is more of a partnership in which suppliers take responsibility for inventory replenishment. Sales associates, who are employees of the vendors and are paid by them, provide their managers with information about product requests at the retail level and other information that would affect decisions about what inventory the retailer should carry. Often the vendors actually refurbish the stock and share in visual merchandising and other store promotions. In many cases, unsold merchandise can be returnable to the supplier.

Japanese department stores are an outgrowth of the **kimono stores**, which sold fabrics to be tailored into garments, and the **terminal stores**, which were located in railroad terminals and sold convenience goods. Little by little, many of these merchants expanded their operations into department stores. One of the oldest, Takashimaya, has expanded into international markets and now has stores in New York City and elsewhere.

Other major department store retailers are Mitsukoshi, based in Tokyo, Hankyu, based in Osaka, and Seibu, also in Tokyo. They sell general merchandise to customers from every age group, and unlike in U.S. department stores, food occupies a large area in every store. The stores are very service oriented, providing everything from information about the products they sell to assistance with party planning.

More important than department stores in terms of size are the supermarkets and superstores. While both types of stores carry a wide assortment of products, the former leans more toward food and the latter carries more general merchandise. The largest stores in these categories are Daiei, which is the largest retailer in Japan, and Ito-Yokado.

Convenience stores are comparatively new in this country. Their inventories range from prepared foods to books and magazines. They are considerably smaller than the department and superstores, operate many hours of the day, and are welcomed by the vast majority of Japanese as places where they can satisfy most of their basic needs. The largest store in this group is the Seven-Eleven Japan Co.

China

Now that China is moving toward becoming a **market economy** it is one of the fastest-growing retail arenas. Retailers from all over the world are focusing their attention on the major cities of Beijing and Shanghai, where stores like Burberry are becoming popular with tourists and residents alike. Government-owned establishments, called *Friendship Stores* also account for much of the country's retail sales. However, more and more Chinese are starting their own retailing ventures, selling everything from foods to household products.

When Hong Kong reverted back to China in 1997, after many years of British rule, it was feared that this great venue for shopping would take a new direction. On the contrary, Hong Kong still remains a shopper's paradise. It is one of the world's greatest shopping environments for every type of merchandise— ready-to-wear, watches and jewelry, custom-made clothing, electronics, fine household furnishings, and so forth. Most world-renowned retailers and designers have a significant presence in Hong Kong along with the local department and specialty

Hong Kong is home to retailing and manufacturing from all over the world.

stores. The city also boasts one of the world's largest shopping centers, Harbour City, where 600 shops and 50 restaurants serve Hong Kong residents and foreign visitors.

Other Major Retail Centers

Along with these major retail centers, other nations around the globe also have important retailing industries. Canada and Mexico in North America and Germany, Italy, and Greece in Europe, all have their share of department stores, supermarkets, and other retail entities.

While many of the retail operations in these countries are home-grown, many others are branches of companies from other countries. In Mexico, for example, the U.S. giant, Sears, has a major presence, along with France's Carrefour. They successfully coexist with Mexican chains like Sanborns, which features a variety of products along with eateries in each of its units.

The trend is for stores all over the world to enter new markets outside of their own countries. Many of these merchants such as Wal-Mart, are achieving considerable success, while others, such as Galeries Lafayette, have not been able to make the transition successfully.

▭▭▭ Foreign Expansion Arrangements

When companies that are headquartered in one country want to expand into other parts of the globe, they can use any one of a number of approaches that have proved to be successful in domestic expansion. They include franchises, licenses, joint ventures, and wholly owned subsidiaries.

Franchising and Licensing

Under a **franchising** arrangement, the franchiser gives the franchisee the right to open a store that bears the franchiser's name. The franchiser usually provides the merchandise to the franchisee, trains the new business "partner," and provides other components necessary for making the franchise a success. In exchange, the franchiser receives a fee, a percentage of the sales, or commission on the merchandise sold. This arrangement enables a company to gain an international presence and maintaining control over its image without actually owning the new units.

Benetton, the Italian manufacturer and retailer, has expanded into many parts of the world through franchising. With more than 2,000 units in their own country, Benetton has franchised more than 3,000 additional units in the United States, France, and Asian countries. Others that have used this approach are America's Athlete's Foot, with units in Canada and Australia, Spain's Mango, with stores in Greece, Portugal, and France, and Canada's Mad Science Group, with units in the United States.

With **licensing**, the retailer offers the company's name and expertise for a payment that generally takes the form of a fee or royalty. Typically, the licensee purchases merchandise from the licensor, but this is not always the case. While this arrangement does give the licensor overseas exposure, it may be risky because the licensee might not properly operate the business and thus cause image problems for the licensor.

Saks Fifth Avenue, one of America's high-image, fashion retailers, has entered the Saudi Arabia market with a licensed store in Riyadh. Saks believes that the country is an ideal choice for a Saks Fifth Avenue store because a segment of its population is exceptionally wealthy. This venture is a test of international expansion for the company. If it is as successful, as management believes it will be, it will serve as a model for expansion into Europe.

Joint Ventures

In a **joint venture**, two or more retailers act as partners for the purpose of starting a new business. By entering into a joint venture with a native business, a company from another country can avoid many of the risks of international expansion. For example, a retailer that is successful in one country might not have the necessary knowledge of consumer preferences and governmental requirements in the other country to succeed there. With the foreign retailer's capital and technical know-how and the local retailer's understanding of what is needed for success in its country, the foreign operation has a good chance to succeed.

Some of the international retail joint ventures include France's Printemp department stores in Taiwan, America's Wal-Mart in Mexico, Japan's Sogo in Taiwan, the Netherlands' Makro in Beijing, and America's McDonalds all over the globe.

WHEN THE WALTONS OPENED THEIR FIRST STORE, a five-and-ten in Bentonville, Arkansas, in 1962, little did they or anyone else imagine that the family business would become one of the most important parts of the fabric of American retailing. Not only has Wal-Mart become the largest retailer in the United States, their non–U.S. sales in 2001 exceeded $33 billion. And according to reports from their international management team, they haven't even scratched the surface! In order to understand fully their joint ventures outside of the United States, it is perhaps best to have a globe close at hand.

First on the list for significant expansion is China. Wal-Mart currently has six stores in China, but, according to John Menzer, president and chief executive of the company's international division, "China is the country of the future. Wal-Mart could double its size with just expansion in China, but it may take 20 to 30 years." With China virtually an untapped market by current-day retailers, Wal-Mart executives are spending countless hours building strong government and public relations there. One of the keys to Wal-Mart's joint venture successes China is its development of local relationships. Before they begin any venture, they make certain that they have national and provincial approval concerning store sites.

Although Wal-Mart has a brief history in global markets, it has no competition in sales volume. The international division was launched in 1991 with a joint venture in Mexico, and now has a variety of retail outlets including Sam's Clubs, supercenters, grocery stores, and suburbia apparel stores and restaurants in that country. With the more than half of Mexico's population under twenty-one, it is one of the company's favorite markets. Other markets that are considered to be strong growth areas are Puerto Rico, which has nine Wal-Marts and six Sam's Clubs, Argentina, with ten supercenters, Brazil, with nine supercenters and six Sam's Clubs, and Korea, which has a total of five units. On the horizon are joint ventures in Germany, which is described as a "work in progress" by the international division's CEO, and Turkey.

Wal-Mart is busy developing the numerous unused factories and other real estate it owns in many foreign countries as retail centers. It has even gone underground in China, building a subterranean unit below a soccer field and stadium.

Wal-Mart's insight into foreign expansion has made it a successful international business. It pays strict attention to the different merchandising demands of the various overseas markets, rather than using just one concept globally, an approach that takes particular advantage of their joint venture partnerships.

Wholly Owned Subsidiaries

Many retailers create a **wholly owned subsidiary** in order to open a store in a foreign country. With this approach, companies avoid establishing any formal affiliations with other businesses. In this way they assume complete control and all risks associated with the venture, and they are able to maximize profits. Some retailers take this approach because they do not have to divulge their practices to partners. Of course, some nations forbid foreign businesses to be soul owners of companies within their borders. In such circumstances, joint ventures are the only way to have a presence in that country.

Reasons for Overseas Expansion

More and more retailers are currently expanding into foreign lands than ever before. Having made their initial successes at home, they can find themselves ready to break into foreign markets for a number of different reasons. These reasons include the amount of competition at home, a ready market of international travelers, having a unique product, and potential for increasing profits.

Competition

When competition in a specific country is particularly stiff, it may inhibit retailers from expanding operations. In the United Sates, for example, competition is keen in almost

The Gap is an example of a U.S. retailer that has expanded into the Canadian market.

every part of the country. While many American companies succeed despite the competition, their profits are lower because of it. By entering less-saturated retail venues where competition is minimal, the chances for acceptance and ultimate profitability are greater.

Canada is one of many countries that foreign retailers are entering aggressively. According to Richard Talbot of Talbot Thomas Consultants International, Canada is "under-retailed compared to the U.S." Using the analysis by this group, as well as those of other consulting organizations, American retailers including the Gap, Banana Republic, Wal-Mart, and many others have opened Canadian branches. Soon to follow are J. Crew, Old Navy, Pacific Sunwear, Abercrombie & Fitch, and G & G Retail. These companies are betting that their operations will be profitable because of lower retail saturation in Canada than in the United States.

International Travel

People from virtually every part of the world regularly leave their countries and travel to other regions. Many are business executives whose work takes them to many foreign countries; others are tourists who are seeking to experience the excitement afforded by overseas travel.

Some cities such as New York, Paris, Rome, Hong Kong, and London are international destinations for world travelers. During these trips, the vast majority of visitors head for stores to bring back remembrances of their adventures. Each city has its own high-profile retailers, which those from other countries seek out during their visits. Bloomingdale's, in the United States, Au Printemp in Paris, and Harrods in London are just a few retailers that have reputations outside of their own countries. Chain stores like the Gap, Victoria's Secret, and Banana Republic in the United States, French Connection and Nicole Farhi in France, and Benetton in Italy also attract a great deal of attention from tourists. Knowing that they already have name recognition and a strong image abroad can motivate companies to open stores around the world. With business travel and tourism at an all-time high, it is a safe bet that global expansion will continue to escalate.

A Unique Product

The fashion industry is one segment of retailing in which products are unique. Designers world over have captivated international audiences with their imaginative—and unique—styles. The collections they offer to the ultimate consumer clientele are singular combinations of silhouettes, color harmonies, textures, and construction details. Individuality is the key to these designers' successes, leading fashion devotees around the globe to seek out their creations.

To capture a share of the international fashion market, designers such as Fendi, Yves St. Laurent, Giorgio Armani, Claude Montana, Jil Sanders, Ralph Lauren, and Calvin Klein have established networks of boutiques outside of their native countries. The trend for this type of retailing venture is growing everyday, as designers open shop at most fashionable addresses in the world.

As a result of its unique products, Hugo Boss has successfully captured a share of the international market.

Profitability

The key to success in business is its profitability. When domestic markets are significantly saturated, companies in that market segment are less able to increase profits unless they seek out new markets. Thus, it may be time for overseas expansion. In order to expand their horizons, many businesses, retailers included, look elsewhere to establish new units. Underserved countries such as China, for example, are promising venues in which to seek increased financial rewards. With fewer existing outlets in these nations, retailers have the space they need to grow and ultimately increase profits.

Pitfalls of Globalization

Even the most carefully conceived plans for growth do not always bear fruit. Many merchants have learned that international expansion does not always result in success. The successful American retailer Barney's had a rude awakening when its Asian endeavor resulted in failure. Galeries Lafayette met with extreme losses when it chose to establish a unit in the United States. Kmart's overseas expansion was a failure and caused considerable losses for the company. These are just a few of the retailers whose overseas plans resulted in unexpected losses.

Some of the pitfalls of globalization include the following:

Economic Downturns

It is very difficult to foresee the future direction of the economy. Recessions are always a possibility anywhere in the world, and expansion during these times plays havoc with the best-laid plans. The following are just two examples of what can occur. Analysts were taken by surprise in 1998 when Asian capitals had serious business declines that significantly affected American retail interests. When Mexico devalued the peso in 1994, it was a nightmare for companies such as Wal-Mart that had high hopes for retailing units. Since currency devaluation is a rare occurrence, businesses were not prepared to handle the ensuing crises.

Consumer Differences

Peoples needs, tastes, and habits often differ from country to country. What might have satisfied the retailer's consumer clientele at home might not satisfy potential customers abroad. Food preferences, for example, are not uniform throughout the world. If close attention isn't paid to these details, success might turn into failure.

Local Competition

Sometimes retailers try to expand their operations into other countries without carefully assessing the domestic operations that could seriously hurt their plans. When Galeries Lafayette opened in New York City, it found itself in an overly saturated retail environment with no room for another competitor. Knowing that the new store would be surrounded by such stellar performers as Macy's, Bloomingdale's, Lord & Taylor, and Saks Fifth Avenue, the company should have been able to predict that it would fail. Their shortsightedness and inability to recognize the competitive forces that faced them led them to disaster.

Similarly, Benetton, which made an early splash into American retailing but had short-lived success, did not have the staying power to compete with such companies as the Gap and The Limited. These merchants better understood what U.S. consumers' needs were and were able to address them quickly. Unable to withstand the competition from the locals, Benetton's popularity soon faded.

ETHICS IN RETAILING

All retailers, no matter where they are based or how many countries they do business in, need to adhere to high ethical standards to ensure their consumers are treated fairly. If a

TABLE 1.2
TOP 20 GLOBAL RETAILERS[1]

COMPANY	COUNTRY OF ORIGIN	PRIMARY FORMATS
Wal-Mart	United States	Discount, Warehouse
Carrefour	France	Cash & Carry, Convenience, Discount, Hypermarket, Supermarket
Kroger	United States	Convenience, Department, Drug, Specialty, Supermarket
Home Depot	United States	DIY[2], Specialty
Metro	Germany	Department, DIY, Supermarket, Mail Order, Specialty, Supermarket, Warehouse
Ahold	Netherlands	Cash & Carry, Convenience, Discount, Drug, Hypermarket, Specialty, Supermarket
Kmart	United States	Discount
Albertson's	United States	Drug, Supermarket
Sears	United States	Department, Mail Order, Specialty
Target (Dayton Hudson)	United States	Department, Discount
Safeway	United States	Supermarket
JCPenney	United States	Department, Drug, Mail Order
Tesco	United Kingdom	Convenience, Hypermarket, Supermarket
Costco	United States	Warehouse
Rewe	Germany	Cash & Carry, Convenience, Department, Discount, DIY, Hypermarket, Specialty, Supermarket
Intermarche	France	Convenience, Discount, SIY, Hypermarket, Restaurant, Specialty, Supermarket
Auchan	France	Convenience, DIY, Hypermarket, Restaurant, Specialty, Supermarket
Edeka/AVA	Germany	Convenience, Discount, DIY, Supermarket, Hypermarket
Ito-Yokado	Japan	Convenience, Department, Discount, Hypermarket, Restaurant, Specialty, Supermarket
J. Sainsbury	United Kingdom	Convenience, Hypermarket, Supermarket

[1]These rankings are subject to change as many companies are poised for acquisitions.

[2]Do-it-yourself

Source: Deloitte Touche Tohmatsu in conjunction with *Stores*.

company's practices are not ethical, customers will stop patronizing it, and the result will be lower profits.

Some companies have established their own guidelines to maintain or improve their ethical practices. Many nations have laws aimed at eliminating certain unethical practices.

Whether through self-regulation or government intervention, it is a necessity for retailers to "do the right thing" if they are to remain in business.

Unethical business practices often occur in advertising, pricing, and conflicts of interest. Therefore these areas are often subject to regulation.

Advertising

One of the ways in which some retailers motivate consumers to purchase their goods is with advertisments that claim their prices are lower than those of the competition. They use such terms as *value* or *comparable value* in their ads and state that these items would cost more at other stores. In many cases, the "comparable prices" are made up, and the merchandise is no more expensive at other stores or the higher-priced merchandise is not identical to what the advertiser is selling.

Some local governments, particularly in the United States, require that if such terms are used, the retailer must be able to verify that the identical goods are sold at the higher prices at another store. Such regulations reduce considerably the number of ads that use the ambiguous terminology.

Price Gouging

One unethical practice is to raise prices of goods during emergencies. For example, when a hurricane is about to strike, merchants of such a product as lumber, which is needed to protect windows, will quickly raise their prices. Such price gouging is against the law in many states. In these states, retailers that price gouge may be fined. Even in places where it is not against the law, price gouging is unfair to consumers, and retailers who do it may lose customers.

Price Fixing

It is unethical for two or more retailers in a competitive environment to conspire to charge the same prices. From time to time, for example, competing supermarkets have been found to fix milk prices. Price fixing is against the law in most areas and is punishable by heavy fines.

Conflicts of Interest

All too often, retailers and their vendors will engage in forms of deal making that are unethical. It was once commonplace, for example, for buyers to expect vendors to give them gifts that are actually bribes. When buying decisions are made on the basis of such gifts, the quality and price of goods offered to consumers are compromised. This unethical practice is also unfair to honest vendors.

In an attempt to overcome this unethical practice, most merchants have made it clear to their employees that receiving gifts from vendors will not be tolerated. The following Conflict of Interest Policy at the Stein Mart organization is typical of how retailers expect their employees to remain ethical.

Conflict of Interests Policy

The Company expects that its Associates will conduct themselves in a professional manner at all times and that they will discharge their assigned responsibilities without entering into any type of situation that would result in a conflict of interest.

A conflict of interest would exist if, in the course of employment, a Stein Mart Associate's judgments or decisions were influenced or could be perceived as having been influenced, by the acceptance of goods, services or gifts for personal gain or benefit.

Stein Mart Associates will abide by the following guidelines to help reduce the chances of facing a conflict of interest in all Stein Mart related business dealings.

Relationships with vendors and suppliers—Stein Mart Associates are responsible for conducting business on behalf of the company in an honest and ethical manner. This responsibility has been and will continue to be upheld by awarding business solely on the basis of price, quality, service and need. Therefore, Associates and members of their families may not accept cash payments, loans, gifts greater than nominal value ($50.00), services or non-local entertainment from vendors, suppliers or individuals doing or seeking to do business with Stein Mart. Any gifts received that are judged to exceed these guidelines will be returned to the sender.

Participating in business related functions, including the acceptance of lunches or other meals, or accepting invitations to attend local sporting or entertainment events with suppliers, customers or competitors on occasion, is a normal and permissible business practice. Associates will exercise caution to avoid a cumulative effect of accepting and participating in even these types of business-related functions on a regular basis so as to avoid the appearance of a conflict.

Stein Mart's conflict of interest policy helps to instill a code of ethics for its employees.

CAREER OPPORTUNITIES IN TODAY'S RETAIL MARKETPLACE

The nature of retailing today is unlike anything in the past. With the coupling of brick-and-mortar operations with off-site ventures such as catalog sales and e-tailing, the opportunities for a successful career have never been better. Not only are opportunities for lifelong careers in retailing to be found in just about any city and town, but with the expansion taking place across the United States and in major retail centers throughout the world, the choices available in retailing are unrivaled in most other industries.

It is a growth industry with positions at all levels available to both men and women. There are no glass ceilings to hold women back from moving into upper management as there is in many other industries. A close inspection of the retailing industry verifies that if the ability is there, anyone can reach the top.

It should also be noted that what was once a comparatively low-paying field now offers competitive salaries. Unlike other industries, retailing is an arena that allows for quick advancement for these who show promise. Most retail organizations do not require that employees must be in a given position for a given length of time before being promoted.

In the retailing industry, women have every opportunity for advancement.

The career opportunities are vast and varied and are waiting to be filled by those who show a willingness to work hard and have the drive necessary for success. A complete overview of the opportunities that await candidates for retailing positions and how to go about securing them is found in the Appendix, Careers in Retailing and Related Fields, where topics such as interviewing, writing resumes and cover letters, and postinterview practices are covered.

TRENDS FOR THE NEW MILLENNIUM

- A few of the many types of retailing operations already in existence will have a significant place in the industry's future. The most vital of the brick-and-mortar companies will continue to thrive.
- Value operations will continue to grow with more and more consumers turning to these stores.
- The globalization of retailing will continue to expand. Not only will American enterprises such as Wal-Mart and the Gap make greater inroads in foreign markets, but overseas retailers will also gain greater international prominence. The French based retailer, Carrefour, for example, will continue its aggressive presence in other European markets as well as in South America and Asia. On the fashion front, the Swedish retailer of chic bargains, Hennes & Mauritz, or H&M, which operates more than 700 stores in 12 countries, has invaded the United States. Sephora, the European beauty giant, continues on its international expansion program with more than 50 U.S. stores. These global expansions are just the tip of the iceberg, with the overseas invasions growing considerably.
- Career opportunities will continue to soar with salaries and opportunities reaching new heights in every phase of the business.

CHAPTER HIGHLIGHTS

- During the colonial period and the early years of the United States, retailing was primitive and trading posts, peddlers, and general stores were the only methods of purchasing available to consumers.
- The limited-line or specialty store is the only form of early retailing that remains important in today's marketplace.
- Department stores were the first retail organizations to feature a wide assortment of both hard and soft goods in an orderly fashion.
- The mail-order businesses, initiated by companies like Sears and Montgomery Ward, were the forerunners of today's catalog operations.
- Off-price operations, discounters, and warehouse clubs are organizations that provide value shopping for the public.
- Global retailing is growing rapidly as companies all over the world are opening units in foreign markets.
- Overseas expansion does not guarantee success. Many retailers such as France's Galeries Lafayette have failed when they attempted to open stores in other countries.
- Retailing practices in other countries are often different from those at home; therefore, it is necessary to research locations before undertaking new ventures.
- Most overseas expansion is accomplished through joint ventures in which a retailer from outside the country joins forces with a partner in the "host" country.
- Companies expand internationally because of such factors as competition at home, international travel, product uniqueness, and profitability.
- Expansion abroad sometimes fails because of eco-

nomic downturns, consumer differences, and competition from local businesses.

• Retailing is a field that offers seemingly unlimited opportunity for both men and women.

IMPORTANT RETAILING TERMS

trading post

peddler

general store

limited-line store

specialty store

chain store organization

department store

one-stop shopping

flagship store

branch store

mail-order retailer

big book

supermarket

discount store

off-price store

warehouse club

manufacturer-owned retail outlet

flea market

boutique

kiosk

category killer

global retailing

chargebacks

brick-and-mortar stores

e-tailing

mixed-merchandise store

leased department

agent order takers

hypermarket

kimono stores

terminal stores

market economy

franchising

licensing

joint venture

wholly owned subsidiary

FOR REVIEW

1. What was the earliest form of retailing in America? How is it different from today's retail operations?

2. In what ways are department stores like trading posts? In what ways are they different?

3. What are some characteristics of a chain store organization?

4. In what ways has catalog selling changed since it was first introduced in the late nineteenth century?

5. What is the difference between an off-price merchant and a discounter.

6. What is a warehouse club? How does it achieve a high level of profits?

7. How did manufacturers open their own stores?

8. Why are kiosks a method of operation favored by many new companies that want to enter retailing?

9. What are the similarities and differences between retailers in the United States and in the United Kingdom?

10. Describe at least three steps Galeries Lafayette has taken to restore the flagship store to a favorable position.

11. What are some ways in which merchandising in Japan differs from merchandising in the United States?

12. What organizational structures are commonly used by merchants when they open foreign units?

13. List the four main reasons for the global expansion of retailing.

14. Why do some foreign retail ventures fail?

15. What is the outlook for those wanting careers in retailing?

AN INTERNET ACTIVITY

Use an Internet search engine such as Yahoo to find out about one of the world's major retailers (a U.S. chain operation or a French department store, for example, or any other retail entry). Use what you learn to write a research paper no longer than three pages. The report should include the following:

- History of the company
- Size of the operation in terms of units.
- Domestic and overseas presence.
- Merchandise assortment.
- Methods of doing business with its clientele.

    The paper should be typed, double spaced.

EXERCISES AND PROJECTS

1. Write to a warehouse club to obtain information about its operation. Prepare a brief, double-spaced report, of no more than two pages. Include the following information:
    - The size of the company in terms of dollar volume.
    - The scope of its product line.
    - The membership fee.
    - The locations served by the company.
    - Its plans for overseas expansion.

2. Prepare a report on retail franchising in the United States. The library houses such periodicals as The Franchise Annual that offers a wealth of information on the subject. Include in the report the following:
    - The size of franchising in the United States
    - The most typical types of retail operations that are franchised
    - Franchiser restrictions on franchisees
    - Advantages and disadvantages of franchising
    - The outlook for franchising

The paper should be no more than three, double-spaced, typed pages.

THE CASE OF THE INTERNATIONAL EXPANSION DILEMMA

One of the older women's clothing chains in the United States, Gallop & Company, has been in business since 1935. Beginning as a modest one-unit company, its continued success has resulted in a retail operation of 825

stores. Although its headquarters is still in Lexington, Kentucky, the location of its first store, Gallop & Company is now a coast-to-coast operation. Now the women's clothing market in the United States has become oversaturated, limiting further U.S. expansion. More specifically, better-known companies such as The Limited, their chief competitor, have already claimed much of the prime retail real estate across the country, leaving little room for Gallop & Company to pursue further domestic expansion.

Gallop's aggressive management team wants the company to continue to grow and has decided to look outside the United States for expansion opportunities. Those responsible for the expansion program are in agreement that Mexico would be the best place to begin. However, there is some disagreement as to which organizational structure to use. The president and CEO of the company, John Gallop, a third-generation chief executive, believes that the best road to take would be to set up a joint venture with a high-profile business in Mexico City. The second in command, Helen Avidon, disagrees. She firmly believes that with their expertise a wholly owned subsidiary would be ideal. Yet another opinion came from the company's chief financial officer, Marc Litt, who thinks they should expand through some form of licensing.

While all economic indicators suggest that the time is ripe to begin global expansion, the management team has yet to come to a decision concerning the best method to employ. Each member of the executive team has given several plausible reasons for his or her recommendation.

With time being of the essence in order to preempt any other competitor from making the first strike in Mexico, it is imperative that a final decision be made.

Questions

1. List the pros and cons of each form of expansion: joint venture, wholly owned subsidiary, and franchising.

2. Which approach do you believe would best serve the interests of the company? Defend your answer with facts and analysis.

CHAPTER 2

Brick-and-Mortar Retailing

After you have completed this chapter, you should be able to discuss

- ► The present status of brick-and-mortar retailing.
- ► The different types of retailers that fall within the traditional classifications.
- ► The reasons for the success of branch stores in the United States.
- ► Why retail chain organizations are considered to be the most important retail category in the United States.
- ► The different classifications that comprise value-oriented retailing.
- ► The differences between discount operations and off-price retailers.
- ► Why many manufacturers have opened their own outlet centers.
- ► Reasons for the success of the retail clearance centers across the United States.

Day after day, consumers encounter what seems to be an endless barrage of news reports and advertising extolling the benefits of buying on the Internet. With editorials in newspapers and magazines about the growth and importance of e-tailing and ads for Web sites in print media and television or radio underscoring the ease and satisfaction of making this type of purchase, we are often lead to believe that traditional retail stores, with the brick-and-mortar operations that they are known by, have outlived the time when they thrived as the major retail outlets.

However, when we look at the actual amount of money spent making purchases on the Internet it pales in comparison to what is spent in stores. The most recent figures indicate that only 1 percent of retail transactions come as the result of Web site buying. Perhaps, future generations will see a significant rise in e-tailing, but while it holds the promise of becoming a viable method of retail selling, its time has not yet come.

Catalog shopping, another form of **direct selling** is also growing in importance. Many brick-and-mortar operations use catalogs to augment their in-store sales, and other companies are exclusively catalog merchants; but the percentage of retail sales they represent is minimal when compared to buying in stores.

Even with new sources of competition, brick-and-mortar retailers are experiencing enormous growth. Department stores are expanding with the opening of numerous branches, chain stores are extending their reach domestically and overseas, and value-oriented stores such as discounters and off-pricers are finding their way into every region of the United States.

Thus, while the picture presented by some gives the impression that the time when brick-and-mortar retailers could expect significant growth is past, the sales volumes belie such an impression. Sales have never been greater!

Included in the overall brick-and-mortar classification is a wealth of different types of operations. They include traditional retail operations such as department and chain stores and the more recent value-oriented outlets.

TRADITIONAL RETAILERS

Best known among the **traditional retailers** are department stores and specialty chain organizations. They are among the largest retail classifications both here and abroad. Each type serves a specific merchandising need, with the former offering a wide array of products and the latter a more narrower range of merchandise. Every classification of consumer products, ranging from apparel to foods, is available through one of these two types of retailers.

Department Stores

As you learned in Chapter 1, the department store dates back to the end of the eighteenth century. It is still a viable form of retailing, with major companies based in the United States and numerous foreign countries. Many department stores enjoy marquee recognition not only close to home, but also at great distances from their headquarters. In America, Macy's and Bloomingdale's enjoy instant recognition all over the country as well as on foreign shores. Similarly, Harrods, in London, is world-renowned and is visited by tourists from every part of the globe. These and other department stores have become "institutions" in their immediate marketplaces and to the tourists who visit the cities they are in.

There are two types of department stores: the full-line department stores and the specialized department stores.

While both types of department stores remain viable forces in retailing, they now face a great deal of competition from the chain organizations (described later in this chapter). With so many women in the workforce and the ever-growing demands of careers, people have less time to spend scouring huge department stores to find the items they need. The smaller chain units enable customers to move through the store quickly and make the necessary purchases in a short time.

For the same reasons, catalogs and e-tail Web sites have taken some business away from department stores. To meet this competition, many brick-and-mortar stores have created their own mail-order divisions and Web sites to make sure that overall company sales volume continues to climb.

Many of today's department stores, be they full-line or specialized, have embraced the concept of the **store within a store**. That is, they build small shops that feature just one type of merchandise. For example, a designer shop might feature only Ralph Lauren or Chanel or a boutique might sell only upscale intimate apparel. The store-within-a-store concept is that it "feels like" a specialty store, a place where shoppers can go knowing that it stocks the type of goods they want without looking through endless store aisles to find it. This allows customers to complete their shopping more quickly. As a walk through any major department store demonstrates, more and more of these shops are popping up to replace the traditional store layout with one oversized department after another, many of which might need to be scoured before shoppers find what they want.

TABLE 2.1
TOP TEN U.S. DEPARTMENT STORE CORPORATIONS RANKED BY SALES VOLUME

COMPANY	TYPE	HEADQUARTERS
Sears	Full-line	Hoffman Estates, IL
Federated[1]	Full-line	Cincinnati, OH
J.C. Penney	Full-line	Plano, TX
May[2]	Full-line and specialized	St. Louis, MO
Dillard's	Specialized	Little Rock, AR
Saks	Specialized	New York, NY
Kohl's	Specialized	Menomonee Falls, WI
Nordstrom	Specialized	Seattle, WA
Neiman Marcus[3]	Specialized	Chestnut Hill, MA
Belks	Department store	Charlotte, NC

[1]Owns Macy's, Bloomingdale's, and many other department stores.

[2]Owns Filene's, Lord & Taylor, Famous-Barr, and many other department stores.

[3]Owns Neiman Marcus and Bergdorf Goodman.

Source: *Stores,* July 2001 and updated. © Copyright 2001 NRF Enterprises, Inc. Used with permission.

The majority of today's department stores are parts of groups, such as the Federated Department Stores, which owns Macy's, Bloomingadale's, and Rich's and Target, which has on its roster Mervyn's and Marshall Field's. Other retail operations have only one name for all their department stores; these include J.C. Penney and Sears.

The ten largest department store organizations in the United States are listed in Table 2.1.

Full-Line Department Stores

Originally, the department store was meant to provide one-stop shopping for consumers. The merchandise assortments featured on the selling floors included a wide variety of both hard goods and soft goods. Patrons could shop for apparel and wearable accessories, move on to sections where furniture was sold, make selections of tableware, and shop for both large and small appliances they might need. Companies like Macy's, Marshall Field's, Bloomingdale's, and Carson Pirie Scott made their reputations as hard and soft goods merchants. To this day, they stock inventories with a variety of products, much the same as they did in their early days of retailing.

While product diversity is still the forte of the **full-line department store**, many have taken new paths in terms of the product mixes or merchandise assortments. The vast majority of today's department store merchants are concentrating on soft goods and accessories, with less emphasis on hard goods. In department after department, shelves and racks are filled with apparel for the family and a wealth of wearable accessories such as shoes, jewelry, handbags, and the like. Next in importance for most of these retailers are products for the home such as dinnerware, glassware, flatware, bedding, and other items. With the designers who have made their reputations in the apparel field feverishly entering the home furnishings market, these products are gaining a larger share of department store sales. Furniture has remained an important part of the department store's overall inventory for some companies. Bloomingdale's, Marshall Field's and Macy's, for example, still rely upon their furniture sales to bring in profits to their companies.

Bloomingdale's is a member of Federated Stores, the major department store organization in the United States.

Missing from most department store inventories are major appliances. Except at Sears, refrigerators, washers, dryers, and ranges are no longer to be found in major full-line department stores. Now that these products are marketed more successfully at discount chains throughout the country, their profitability for department stores has decreased. Small appliances, such as microwave ovens and food processors and housewares, have taken their place. Many department stores also stock their inventories with a variety of electronics.

.¦. **Focus on . . .**
Federated Department Stores

WITH MORE THAN 400 DEPARTMENT STORE LOCATIONS IN 33 STATES, Federated is considered by most industry professionals to be the premier department store organization. Its roster of stores boasts such headline names as Bloomingdale's, Macy's, Burdines, Lazarus, The Bon Marche, Goldsmith's, Rich's, and a catalog division, Fingerhut. Each division operates independently and serves the needs of a specific region. While it had been one of the major retail players in the industry, Federated didn't reach the status it enjoys today until the mid 1990s when it acquired Macy's and Broadway Stores, Inc.

Key to the success of Federated's organization is the merchandising approaches it takes. Through continued research, it makes certain that its product mix is appropriate for its targeted consumers. A mix of high-profile brands such as Ralph Lauren, Liz Claiborne, and Calvin Klein; new designer collections; manufacturer lines that regularly bring profits; and a roster of private-label offerings fill the stores. It is the emphasis on private labels and brands that has given rise to Federated's recent success.

An in-house division, the Federated Merchandising Group, conceptualizes, designs and sources its own merchandise, merchandise that is by definition exclusive to the company. Shoppers do not see only the same "me-too" products that are available at most competitors; they also find unique offerings that are available only at Federated. All the private labels are created for the entire organization except for Bloomingdales, which carries only some of these lines. Private brands like Alfani, I.N.C., Charter Club, Club Room, and Souson continue to provide enormous sales volume to the company, often outperforming the manufacturer labels displayed alongside them.

Customer service is also a priority at the Federated Stores. Many stores have added seating areas in which shoppers can relax, new food services that address different palates, and in-house computer kiosks that can be used by shoppers to places orders for merchandise which might not be at that branch and which can be shipped within a matter of hours. They also continue to offer traditional services such as private shoppers.

The organization also prides itself on its commitment to employee diversity. Of its total workforce, 75 percent are women and 42 percent belong to racial and ethnic minority groups. Among managers, 67 percent are women and 21 percent are minorities. These numbers have earned the company a place on *Latina* magazine's list of the 50 Best Companies for Latinas to Work for in the U.S., and *Black Collegian*'s list of Top 100 Employers.

While Federated recognizes the importance of *bricks-and-clicks retailing*, a mix of in-store and electronic retailing, it is its brick-and-mortar stores that are moving ahead most vigorously. Of course, it is the company's hope that its e-tailing investment will pay off in increased sales and ultimately bring customers from the Web site into the stores.

Specialized Department Stores

Today, many merchants engaged in department store retailing restrict their inventories rather than carry full lines. Some sell mostly apparel and wearable accessories, while others focus on home furnishings. Saks Fifth Avenue, Neiman Marcus, and Nordstrom specialize in apparel and accessories, while Fortunoff is primarily a home furnishings store.

While specialized department stores and specialty chains both sell narrow assortments of merchandise, the two types of stores are quite different. A specialty chain might have as many as a thousand units or even more. Each unit is generally a one-story facility with limited floor space. A **specialized department store** usually occupies a multilevel facility with floor space that rivals many full-line operations, and it stocks a vast assortment of goods.

 Focus on . . .
Proffitt's

MOST FASHION-CONSCIOUS CONSUMERS AND RETAIL PROFESSIONALS know about the major department store organizations that are the retailing headliners. Outside of the industry professionals, however, few have heard of a company called Proffitt's. Up until a few years ago, Proffitt's was a small, family-owned, five-unit department store chain specializing in women's clothing based in Tennessee. It served a tiny trading area in comparison to other chains. Then the company was sold to Brad Martin, and with significant financial backing, what was once a "David" of the retailing industry has become a Goliath.

Proffitt's purchased what was to be its marquee division, Saks Fifth Avenue, in 1998. Soon after, Proffitt's changed its corporate name to Saks, Inc., underscoring the importance of the jewel in its crown. The empire, which became a $7 billion conglomerate and numbered more than 350 stores, also included Carson Pirie Scott, Herberger's, Younkers, McRae's, Parisian, Bergner's, Boston Store, and its original company, Proffitt's. Each store in the group approaches retailing in the manner that best suits the trading area it serves.

The retailing business environment as a whole has been in a state of flux in recent years, and the same has been true of the Proffitt's or Saks group. Never accepted as a "good fit" by industry analysts, Saks Fifth Avenue was spun off after just two years in the Proffitt's family. It became part of Saks Fifth Enterprises, a separate, independent, publicly owned company.

The divisions that remain continue to serve the needs of their customers. Carson Pirie Scott, for example, a Chicago-based department store with branches in the Midwest, is a full-line merchandise operation, featuring both hard goods and soft goods that appeal to the middle-income market; Younkers operates 53 stores in the Midwest; and McRae's serves the Southeast with 30 stores; Parisian's business is in the Southeast and Midwest; Herberger's focuses on the Midwest and Great Plains; and the group's pioneering founder, Proffitt's, has 31 units, most of which are in Tennessee.

After the spinoff, the remaining stores comprised the Saks Department Store Group, a division within Saks Incorporated Enterprises. The group remains among the top ten department store groups in the United States, even without Saks Fifth Avenue.

Recognizing that steady gains in in-store traffic is no longer only achieved through advertising, the Saks Department Store Group has taken to other means to increase customers' store visits. One of the key approaches has been through the Internet. Many consumers are motivated to use electronic commerce for their needs because of limited time or a liking for this relatively new concept, and of course, sales that come directly from a shopper browsing the Saks Department Store Group Web site are greatly welcomed. The Saks Department Store Group organization, like other major retailers, hopes for something beyond an electronic sale, however; it hopes that satisfaction with the Web site will encourage trips to the store and the purchase of products not available through e-tailing. While the Internet offers some merchandise, the assortment pales in comparison to the store's offerings. The company expects that once they are tempted to make a visit to the brick-and-mortar store, they will become regular patrons.

The company is also renovating stores in ways it hopes will encourage continued visits to them. Carson Pirie Scott, in Chicago, has renovated its shoe salons to make them more exciting for their customers. Similarly, the other stores in the group are making considerable in-store changes to attract more shoppers.

Brick-and-mortar expansion is also a goal for the company. With its numerous new branches, the Saks Department Store Group is betting on the notion that shoppers, although fascinated with e-tailing and catalogs, will begin to return to the stores in record numbers.

Like many other department store giants, the Saks Department Store Group has set out to make its brick-and-mortar stores the heralded places they once were, and to give them an even greater presence in the retailing landscape.

Branch Stores

When vast numbers of Americans started to leave major cities across the country for the suburbs, many department stores took it as an opportunity for expansion. Stores like Macy's, Bloomingdale's, Carson Pirie Scott, Marshall Field's, and Dayton's seized the moment and opened replicas of their flagship stores. The branches became the salvation of these companies, many of which were seeing business fall off sharply at the main stores.

Today, every mall in the country is home to such branch stores. They are the **anchor stores** in these vast shopping arenas and serve as the attractions that bring in shoppers. Smaller malls have two or more anchor branches, while the majors have as many as six. Old Orchard in suburban Chicago, for example, boasts branches of such stores as Nordstrom, Lord & Taylor, Saks Fifth Avenue, Marshall Field's and Bloomingdale's.

The sizes of the branches vary depending on the trading areas they serve and the anticipated needs of the people in that area. Some are small operations while others are nearly as large as the flagships they represent. In general, merchandise offerings fall into the same categories as at the main stores, but the selections are pared down based on the size of the branch and expected sales volume. However, each department store group must decide the proper road to take for branch expansion, and must alter its merchandising philosophy to customer demand. Some companies might even eliminate certain departments completely if the re-

search shows that they will not fare successfully in the branches. In some cases, different merchandising approaches are used in different branches within the same company. Bloomingdale's, for example, in its New York City flagship, gives a great deal of floor space to its furniture department because this store's success derives in part from this merchandise classification. Many branches, however, lack sufficient space to stock such inventory, and customers' need for it is not as great, so they feature their inventories in fashion and wearable accessories instead.

Old Orchard, a shopping center located in a Chicago suburb, is home to many of America's branch stores.

The organizational structures of branch stores is worth noting. Unlike the flagship stores where all of the major decision making takes place, the branch is primarily a selling arena. Executives based at the flagship stores oversee merchandising, advertising, special events, store operations, and the like, and determine the policies that govern the entire organization. Branch store managers and their subordinates follow these edicts. So very little decision making takes place at the branches. The decisions made there usually involve hiring people in lower-level positions, such as sales associates, determining employee schedules, and so forth. The branch's goal is to turn a profit for the company and leave the steering of the organization to the management team at the flagship.

The health of branch stores, in general, is excellent; more and more of these units are being opened in malls and downtown areas wherever the need arises.

 The Stein Mart Story
Maintaining Market Share in the Competitive Retail Arena:
Brick-and-Mortar Expansion

WHILE THE MAJORITY OF ORGANIZATIONS IN THE RETAILING ARENA are pursuing off-site ventures through Web sites and catalog expansion, Stein Mart is moving in the opposite direction. That is, while it does participate somewhat in e-tailing and catalog selling, its forte continues to be and—according to corporate executives—for the near future at least, will remain the brick-and-mortar outlets.

They made this decision because they believe that their customers are people who prefer to "feel the goods" and make their purchasing decisions in the store. They seem to be correct. During the year 2000, 22 stores opened and only one closed. The size of the company's sales has quadrupled since its public offering in 1992, and sales at the end of 2000 were at $1.2 billion!

The expansion has been greatest in Texas and Florida, with the number of stores at the end of 2000 reaching 43 in Texas and 32 in Florida.

Until management decides the time is ripe for off-site expansion at this off-price giant—which they don't think will be anytime soon—the brick-and-mortar expansion will continue.

Chain Organizations

In spite of the fact that e-tailing is capturing retail headlines, it is the chain organizations that are fulfilling the needs of the consumer, as shown by their record sales. The chains' concentration on specialized merchandise inventories in small spaces seems to fit the needs of today's shopper. With the vast majority of women working outside the home, the once favorite pastime of many has been abandoned. Instead, people buy only when the need arises, and at places where it is quick and efficient to do so. With the continued expansion of such companies and the significant growth in sales attributed to them, it is obvious that the chain organization is the place for retail action and profitability.

By definition, a chain is an organization that has two or more units and is centrally operated and managed. Of course, the chains that most consumers are familiar with are those that have significantly greater numbers of units, with some comprising several thousand stores. Their greatest presence is in women's apparel; men's wear; children's clothing; wearable accessories such as jewelry, handbags, and shoes; home furnishings; toys; electronics; food; drugstores; books; pet products; office supplies; computer products; and sporting goods.

Walgreens is the largest drugstore chain in the United States.

Chain organizations are big business. Many companies are opening several new units every month. Others are expanding their operations through acquisition. In the drugstore arena, for example, both approaches have been popular. Walgreens, the industry leader, has followed the expansion route in a grand manner. At the present time, the company has over 3,000 units, with plans to open a new store every day. In the next decade it expects to have 6,000 stores. On the other hand, CVS and Rite Aid have grown through acquisition. CVS increased the number of outlets by acquiring Revco and Arbor Drug; and Rite Aid has grown with the acquisition of Thrifty/Payless, Marco, and K&B stores. These two patterns of growth are evident in just about every type of chain operation.

It should be noted that the expansion of chains is not restricted to the domestic market. Many American and foreign companies are vigorously entering overseas venues. At the head of the American list is Wal-Mart, with major growth initiatives in Asia, especially China and South Korea. Wal-Mart is also eyeing Europe. In Germany, it purchased the hypermarket Wertkauf, and it is planning for future expansions in that and other European countries.

TABLE 2.2		
TOP U.S. CHAIN ORGANIZATIONS[1] BY SALES VOLUME		
COMPANY	SPECIALTY	HEADQUARTERS
Wal-Mart	Food, household items	Bentonville, AR
Sears, Roebuck & Co.	Clothing, appliances, furniture	Hoffman Estates, IL
Kmart	Housewares, apparel, etc.	Troy, MI
Home Depot	Household products	Atlanta, GA
Kroger	Food	Cincinnati, OH
Safeway	Food	Pleasanton, CA
Costco	Food, household items	Issaquah, WA
Ahold USA	Food, variety	Atlanta, GA
Albertsons	Food	Boise, ID
Walgreen	Drugs	Deerfield, IL
CVS	Drugs	Woonsocket, RI
Winn-Dixie	Food	Jacksonville, Fl
Rite Aid	Drugs	Camp Hill, PA
Lowe's	Housewares	North Wilkesboro, NC
Publix	Food	Lakeland, Fl
Toys "R" Us	Toys	Paramus, NJ
Circuit City	Electronics	Richmond, VA
Food Lion	Food	Salisbury, NC
A & P	Food	Montvale, NJ
Best Buy	Electronics	Minneapolis, MN
Limited	Apparel	Columbus, OH
Gap	Apparel	San Francisco, CA
Office Depot	Office supplies	Delray Beach, FL
TJX	Off-price apparel	Framingham, MA
7 Eleven	Convenience foods	Dallas, TX

[1]Many of the major chains offer a variety of products. Some are specialized chains, while others offer a more diverse merchandise assortment. A number of these chains have divisions that use names other than the corporate name. Gap, for example, has divisions called Gap, GapKids, BabyGap, Banana Republic, and Old Navy.

Source: Adapted from *Stores*, July 2001. © Copyright 2001 NRF Enterprises, Inc. Used with permission.

While chains, by definition, have specific merchandising and management similarities, they are classified in different ways. They may be categorized by their merchandise assortment or by their pricing policy, as traditional chains or value-oriented chains (off-price stores and discounters). Traditional chains and their product assortments are discussed first.

Traditional Chains

Retailers that buy first-quality goods to sell at standard industry markups are classified here as **traditional chains**. In order of volume, supermarket chains are at the top, followed by drugstores, with home centers and apparel merchants following. Not too far behind are booksellers, computer stores, and toy merchants. Each category is continuously growing in terms of overall units and is showing consumer confidence by virtue of sales increases.

SUPERMARKETS

With three of the top ten retailers in the United States **supermarket** chains, it is quite evident that Americans prefer to do their food shopping in these venues. Although competition from warehouse clubs like Sam's Club and Costco is heating up, and the entry of online grocers like Peapod and Webvan is drawing away some business, supermarkets are far and away the largest group in the country's top 100 retailers. For all of the hoopla attributed to the Internet, it is certainly not having an impact on brick-and-mortar grocers.

The consolidation of supermarket chains is also a major trend in the industry. Delhaize America, for example, has acquired Hannaford Bros., the largest supermarket chain in New England. Ahold USA, the nation's eleventh largest retailer bought U.S. Foodservice, a company that sells prepared foods to supermarkets. Not every attempted acquisition is successful. Royal Ahold's offer to purchase the Pathmark chain, for example, was stopped by the **Federal Trade Commission**. Nonetheless, most industry analysts predict that many more industry takeovers will occur.

The **product mix** at the supermarkets continues to change. While packaged food still accounts for the majority of the inventory, other food and nonfood items play a significant role in overall sales. Publix, for example, offers freshly prepared sushi in its stores, and Har-

ris Teeter features a full selection of freshly prepared foods. At many markets, more and more space is being used for in-store baked goods, as well as specialty counters that offer a variety of gourmet food items. The inclusion of these foods provides the shopper with more variety to choose from. In addition, the merchant can add a greater markup to these items than what is added to the packaged items traditionally found in supermarkets. Markups on packaged foods are limited because the majority of

Harris Teeter is a supermarket chain noted for its prepared foods.

them are available in any food store. The baked goods and gourmet items, however, are exclusive to the particular stores and can be priced accordingly.

The nonfood and food-related categories include a host of items that help increase over-all store sales and result in better profits. Products such as greeting cards, paperback books, stationery, tools, fresh flowers, and other **impulse items** that customers buy without ad-vance planning are usually marked up more than the foods are. More and more super-market chains are increasing the space for such goods to bolster their bottom lines.

TABLE 2.3		
TOP FIVE SUPERMARKET CHAINS IN THE UNITED STATES		
COMPANY	**HEADQUARTERS**	**2000 SALES**
Kroger	Cincinnati, Ohio	$49,000,400
Albertson's	Boise, Idaho	36,762,200
Safeway	Pleasanton, California	31,976,900
Ahold USA	Chantilly, Virginia	27,757,000
Publix	Lakeland, FL	14,600,000

Source: *Stores,* July 2001. © Copyright 2001 NRF Enterprises, Inc. Used with permission.

DRUGSTORES

The retail drugstore industry is lead by Walgreens, CVS, Rite Aid, and Longs. A J.C. Pen-ney subsidiary, Eckerd, has also become a major player. The field, which once was domi-nated by small independent druggists, has grown into a $12 billion industry, and the local druggist has become a distant memory.

The merchandise mix at retail drugstores features a wealth of products that complement the packaged drug and drug related items and the pharmacy stations that dispense pre-scription drugs. A visit to any of these emporiums immediately reveals a wealth of food products, stationery, books, greeting cards, cosmetics, photographic equipment, in-house photography developing services, and seasonal merchandise. The expansion into these lines not only helped to increase overall sales, but also made the operations more profitable because markups on many of these items can be greater than on over-the-counter and pre-scription drugs. Thus they have a positive effect on the bottom line.

One current trend in the drugstore industry is the opening of freestanding stores located at corners where converging roads bring heavy traffic, and thus potential customers. Wal-greens has led the way in this movement, and Eckerd, a competitor to Walgreens in many areas, has followed suit. Thus, the corner drugstore is returning in a new form.

HOME CENTERS

When Home Depot came onto the scene in 1978, it revolutionized the retail segment that caters to do-it-your-selfers. With its prime competitor, Lowe's, right behind, it domi-nates an industry once made up of independent hardware stores. Of course, there are smaller entries in this field such as Menard and 84 Lumber.

Consumers are attracted to **home centers** by the wealth of merchandise found under one cavernous roof and by the low prices that defy competition. A shopper looking for lighting fixtures, tools, machinery, flooring, paint, bathroom accessories, doors, or lumber will find wide assortments to fit their needs. And these operations have now added garden centers to further satisfy the needs of home owners and increase the stores' profits.

Not only do home centers serve the needs of the individual home owners, but they also supply wares to commercial contractors. With separate service areas catering to contractors and vast on-hand inventories, home centers have become the contractors' primary source for building supplies.

The vast majority of the home centers' product mix is made up of practical merchandise. To meet the needs of do-it-yourselfers more concerned with home decorating than home improvement, Home Depot has opened Expo Design Centers. These stores feature up-scale assortments of home decor items that appeal to more affluent consumers. Interior designers and individual consumers alike have made these stores regular stops.

The small neighborhood hardware store has virtually disappeared from this retailing sector. The warehouselike home centers have taken their places and have run with the ball.

Home Depot is the United States' leading home center.

APPAREL SHOPS

Who hasn't heard of or visited Gap, Old Navy, Banana Republic, American Eagle Outfitters, Abercrombie & Fitch, or one of the other apparel chains? Each of the merchants in this classification tries to distinguish itself by product differentiation. While many still rely upon purchasing their goods from a variety of vendors in the hope that they will carry these goods exclusively within their trading areas, the larger chains carry only private-label products. This approach is often referred to as **the store-is-the-brand retailing.** By using this approach and developing their own products, the chains are certain that they will have a unique identity.

Expansion by apparel chains is occurring at a very rapid pace. Whenever a new mall opens, it is certain to house a variety of stores under Limited's umbrella, The Limited and Express, for example; and Gap spin-offs such as GapKids, and BabyGap as well as other Gap divisions such as Banana Republic. When malls expand or are restructured, it is certain that these companies will occupy more space than they did originally.

Companies such as Ann Taylor and Talbots are also making major inroads in the fiercely competitive field, though on a smaller scale than The Limited and Gap. They are opening spin-offs in order to capture new segments of the market. Ann Taylor, for example, has pursued the value market with its Ann Taylor Loft stores, and Talbots has started to cater to apparel **subclassification** with the introduction of Talbot Petites.

An indication of the enormous success of the apparel specialty chains is their 26 percent share of the marketplace, making them the biggest channel of distribution for such merchandise. This success has led manufacturers and designers to enter this arena directly. Recognizing that many of them have loyal consumer followers, they have established retail divisions alongside of their wholesale operations. By having their own retail spaces, they can showcase their entire collections, and not be restricted by the purchasing budgets of their traditional retail accounts. When a shopper visits a department store, for example, only a fraction of the designer or manufacturer's offerings are featured.

Old Navy, a division of the Gap organization, continues to expand its apparel offerings.

Many of the **marquee labels**, such as Ralph Lauren, Liz Claiborne, Levi Strauss, Calvin Klein, and others, have had considerable success with retail outlets. They continue to open a large number of stores, so it is certain that many consumers are buying directly from them.

Focus on . . .
Gap, Inc.

ONE OF THE MOST VISIBLE AND HIGHLY SUCCESSFUL CHAIN OPERATIONS is Gap, Inc., which sells through a number of different stores that feature the corporate name as well as others such as Banana Republic and Old Navy. The organization has grown from a company that was composed of only Gap stores into the giant that it is today. It is the fourth largest of the specialty store organizations headquartered in the United States, with more than 3,000 stores and with sales greater than any other chain employing traditional prices.

First, the company expanded its operation by opening divisions that used the Gap name (GapKids and BabyGap, for example), which were designed to satisfy the needs of the shoppers who bought Gap merchandise for themselves. These newer entries immediately found success by using the same merchandising philosophy that brought such acclaim to the original Gap stores where parents bought their own clothes. A walk through most malls in the United States finds outlets from these three units within a few yards of each other, an approach that has enabled Gap to become one of the few retailers to be successful in outfitting the entire family.

Gap stores are not only thriving in the United States, but also in many overseas markets where they have a significant presence.

Two of the newer entries in the Gap organization are Banana Republic and Old Navy. Gap acquired Banana Republic more than a decade ago, and it launched Old Navy in 1994. Each unit has won significant acceptance throughout the country.

Banana Republic originally marketed itself with a "safari and khaki" image. The stores were like stage sets of the outback, with bamboo, netting, pith helmets, and worn, rustic jeeps used to foster its environments. Not a trace of that concept is visible any longer. Instead, the company repositioned itself into a marketer of casual, professional, and elegant apparel. As is the case with the Gap stores, Banana Republic carries only products that are created especially for it. No designer labels here, only Banana Republic labels. It is the epitome of the store-is-the-brand retailing. The prices are moderate when compared to those of designer labels, but more expensive than the Gap stores. While some items do resemble the styles of such high-profile designers as Prada, the similarity is said to be only a coincidence. The product developers at the company have a complete understanding of the market it serves and create items that will best serve its customers' needs.

Its customer base is the successful young male and female business executive who wants to purchase sophisticated clothing suitable for casual, daytime, and evening dress.

With more than 300 units, many of which are two- and three-story facilities, the company's expansion plans are making it one of the more visible apparel chains in the country.

At the other end of the Gap spectrum is Old Navy. The newest of the company's divisions, it is making one of the loudest splashes in apparel chain history. Since its inception, it has regularly pumped up profits for the corporation. The merchandise, which is intended to appeal to families, bears the lowest prices in the organization. The product mix includes apparel for men, women, and children. The unit has extremely broad appeal and counts as its customers everyone from inner-city teens to baby boomers. Its image is a mix of fun and nostalgia.

After starting in San Francisco with a single unit near Gap headquarters, Old Navy has grown into a major retailer with more than 400 stores. Each is a cavernous space with huge assortments of private-label merchandise in a wide array of colors piled up on tables or hung on plain racks. The stores' decor features retro graphics and antique trucks.

Gap continues to open Old Navy units that are huge for apparel chain stores. The Old Navy store on 34th Street in New York City for example, has 150,000 square feet of floor space. The size is not unique to New York City; San Francisco's flagship store occupies 100,000 square feet. Old Navy assesses sites of out-of-business retailers in prime locations in an effort to gain high visibility to shoppers.

Aggressive advertising has been one factor in Old Navy's success. On television, viewers are treated to quirky advertising campaigns such as those that featured the fashion guru Carrie Donovan before her death in 2001. Such promotions gave Old Navy a fashion connection even though its prices are far below those typical of the fashions in the magazines—*Vogue* and *Harper's Bazaar*—of which she had previously been an editor. Old Navy has become a company that is sought after by mall operators everywhere because, as some put it, it has the ability to bring as much traffic as the anchor department stores.

With these successes in its group, Gap, Inc., continues to be the nation's premier retail apparel chain.

● ●

BOOKSTORES

Once a very small part of the retail market, booksellers have reinvented themselves and have become a major force in retailing. Companies like Borders and Barnes & Noble continue to expand with stores that resemble anything but the prototypes of the past.

These stores feature not only a wealth of books in every conceivable category, but also lounge areas with comfortable chairs where shoppers can examine their selections before purchasing them, coffee bars where customers can sample a cappuccino and a pastry, and open spaces where entertainers such as storytellers, guitarists, and singers perform. These bookstores have become recreational destinations for families.

Bookstores like Transitions have become gathering places to examine books while sipping a cappuccino.

Unlike most retail operations that close no later than 9:30 P.M., these stores keep their doors open until 11: 00 P.M. It is not unusual to see a great number of people sipping their favorite beverages in the coffee bar and then standing in line to make their purchases at this late hour.

It should be noted that while a good deal of book purchasing is accomplished through the Internet, the social nature of the newly created atmosphere in this new type of retail space has made the brick-and-mortar bookstores a profitable venture.

MISCELLANEOUS CHAINS

Many traditional chain store companies specialize in other merchandise classifications such as shoes, eyeglasses, home accessories, jewelry, handbags, toys, museum reproductions, pet supplies, records, and tapes. Some are large chains with many units, while others are smaller chains with only a few units.

As is true with the chain retailers mentioned previously, these retailers are also experiencing considerable growth. Most of them are enjoying success in the malls throughout the country and in freestanding units as well.

VALUE-ORIENTED RETAILERS

A steady area of growth in American retailing has been within the segment that provides value to shoppers. While **value retailing** is not a recent phenomenon, the downturn in the economy that came late in the 1980s added extra incentive for value retailers to expand and other merchants to enter the field. After several years of conspicuous, free spending, the recession of the 1980s caused many consumers to rethink their buying habits. In particular, the *yuppies* (young urban professionals) who had come of age in a time of plenty, awakened to learn that easy wealth was not the norm.

Capitalizing on the economic downturn, merchants that already catered to the value shopper quickly began to expand their operations with hundreds of new outlets. Joining them were new retailers that wanted to ride this new wave of value merchandising. At the outset of the new millennium, thousands of brick-and-mortar stores of every type were opening everywhere, with value retailers at the head of the pack. Out front were

TABLE 2.4 TOP U.S. VALUE RETAILERS[1] BY SALES VOLUME		
COMPANY	**PRODUCT LINES**	**HEADQUARTERS**
Best Buy	Consumer electronics	Minneapolis, MN
Circuit City Group	Consumer electronics	Richmond, VI
Office Depot	Office supplies, electronics	Delray Beach, FL
Toys "R" Us	Toys, children's products	Paramus, NJ
Staples	Office supplies, electronics	Framingham, MA
TJX	Apparel	Framingham, MA
CompUSA	Computers	Dallas, TX
OfficeMax	Office supplies, electronics	Cleveland, OH
AutoZone	Auto products	Memphis, TN
Payless ShoeSource	Shoes	Topeka, KS
Ross Stores	Apparel	Newark, CA
Pep Boys	Auto supplies	Philadelphia, PA
Bed Bath & Beyond	Home products	Union, NJ
Burlington Coat Factory	Apparel, linens	Burlington, NJ
PETsMART	Pet products	Phoenix, AZ
K-B Toys	Toys, children's products	Avon, MA
Linens 'n Things	Home products	Clifton, NJ
Service Merchandise	Home products, jewelry	Nashville, TN
CSK Auto	Auto products	Phoenix, AZ
Tower Records	CDs, audiocassettes	Sacramento, CA

[1]Includes discounters and off-price merchants.

Source: *Stores*, August 2001. © Copyright 2001 NRF Enterprises, Inc. Used with permission.

discounters such as Wal-Mart, the nations largest retailer, and Target; off-price merchants such as TJX, with their T.J.Maxx and Marshalls divisions, and category killers such as Toys "R" Us, Best Buy, and Circuit City; manufacturer closeout stores; and retail clearance centers.

Unlike the traditional retailers, which are primarily located in major shopping malls and downtown central districts, value-oriented retailers are more likely to be found in **power centers** or **outlet malls**.

A close inspection of the top retailers in the United States shows that the majority of them are value-oriented. Circuit City, Best Buy and Toys "R" Us, all three discounters, head the list of specialty retailers. In fact, of the top ten in this category, eight are value stores; only Gap and The Limited are traditional retailers.

In addition, the vast majority of the top retailing of all types are ones that offer discounted merchandise.

U.S. value-oriented retailers have also been successful abroad. TJX operates Winners outlets in Canada, Sam's Club units are found in Mexico, and Toys "R" Us has a presence in the United Kingdom. While value retailing has not been an important trend in other countries, the successful entry of these and other companies into foreign markets indicates that this type of merchandising can be profitable worldwide.

Discounters

As explained in Chapter 1, a discount operation purchases merchandise at full price from vendors but sells it a price lower than that charged by the traditional retailers. They buy early in the season as do traditional retailers, but they discount goods in the hope that the greater volume will make up for the lower per-unit profit. With discounters like Wal-Mart and Target continuing to increase their market shares, it is obvious that discounting is a major form of retailing in the United States.

Discounting is not limited to one merchandise classification. The giants mentioned above stock a wealth of different items including apparel, small appliances, household products, electronics, and so forth. Others, such as Best Buy, restrict their offerings to electronics, appliances, and other related items. Still others specialize in soft goods.

A 2000 Triversity survey of top chains shows that the office supplies group is one of the fastest growing segments in discounting. Of the top U.S. Value Retailers, Office Depot is third, Staples fifth, and OfficeMax eighth. These companies have virtually erased the local stationery supply store from memory.

Electronics discounters are among the most important value retailers. At the top of discounters are Circuit City and Best Buy, where computers, television receivers, and stereo systems are featured in tremendous assortments. Pricing and selection are their fortes.

Rounding out the discount group are the auto supply shops such as AutoZone and Pep Boys, the home furnishing centers like Bed Bath & Beyond and Linens 'n Things; music shops, with Tower Records as a leader; toys, headed by Toys "R" Us and K-B Toys, and pet products, sold by such giants as PETsMart.

Off-Price Retailers

Often confused by the public with discounters, the off-price retailers are also value-oriented organizations, but they have a different approach to merchandising. Instead of buying at full prices, these merchandise practice **opportunistic buying**. That is, whenever wholesale prices fall, they are there to scoop up the bargains. For example, the fashion industry is a seasonal business, and manufacturers must make room for their new collections to satisfy the needs of their accounts retailers that must constantly revise their inventories. Even

Stein Mart is a fast growing U.S. off-price retailer.

in the most successful companies like Liz Claiborne, Calvin Klein, DKNY, Ralph Lauren, and Tommy Hilfiger, merchandise is always left over at season's end. The only way in which these companies can quickly dispose of such items is by offering them at reduced prices. This creates the opportunity for the off-price merchants to buy quality goods at lower prices.

By making only low-cost purchases, off-price retailers are able to offer their customers well-known labels at reduced prices. They buy for less, and thus sell for less. Unlike the discounters, which take lower markups, the off-price retailers take markups that are comparable to the traditionalists. It s their ability to "buy right" that allows them to use this pricing structure.

Off-price retailers must operate in a number of ways that are different from other retailers' practices, including the following:

- They cannot get merchandise as early as traditional merchants. Since price is their main consideration, they must wait until the manufacturer deems it necessary to rid itself of the goods. Early purchasing, at full price, enables traditional stores to be the first to receive the goods. The off-price retailers' customers are willing to get the merchandise later in the season in exchange for the lower prices they pay.

- They cannot locate stores alongside those of traditional retailers in major malls and downtown shopping districts. These prime locations purposely exclude off-price retailers because their price structure would result in unfair competition to the traditional department stores and chain organizations that buy at full price and charge their customers full price.

- Off-price retailers are generally forbidden to mention the names of their vendors in their advertising programs. Instead, they use headlines such as "Closeout of Famous Designer," or "Designer Swimsuits at 40% Less Than Regular Prices" in their ads. In this way traditional department stores and specialty chains will not be hurt directly if they feature the same items at higher prices.

The major merchandise category of off-price retailers groups are those that are apparel oriented, followed by wearable accessories. The constant changes of style direction and the seasonal nature of apparel retailing mean that these products must be disposed of quickly by vendors. The out-of-season lines are generally sold as **closeouts**. The merchandise offered as closeouts usually consists of incomplete assortments of colors and sizes, which buyers who represent the off-price retailers must settle for. But there is a tradeoff: the prices they pay are well below the original wholesale prices.

Heading the list of off-price retailers is TJX, with its Marshalls and T.J. Maxx divisions. Collectively, these stores account for approximately half of the off-price retailing business. Others in this category include Stein Mart, Loehmann's, Burlington Coat Factory, Ross Stores, and Syms.

With value shopping on the rise, the outlook for off-price retailing is extremely favorable.

Manufacturer Closeout Stores

Although many manufacturers dispose of their leftover items to off-price retailers, the number of such remaining items may be so great that complete disposal through only these outlets is not practicle. Manufacturers' selling these goods directly began modestly in the late 1970s at locations like North Conway, New Hampshire, and Secaucus, New Jersey. The practice has now grown into a rapidly expanding industry, **manufacturer closeout stores**. All over the United States, nationally recognized manufacturers and designers have opened their own outlets to dispose of slow-selling merchandise. Many of these stores are clustered in such centers as outlet malls. DKNY, Ralph Lauren, Calvin Klein, Liz Claiborne, Nine West, Dooney & Bourke, Mikasa, Gucci, and Geoffrey Beene are among the designers that have outlets in such centers. The advantage to manufacturers and designers of owning their own closeout stores is that they can increase their profit by selling directly to the consumer instead of through an off-price retailer.

The importance of this form of retailing can be best understood by examining some of the different centers that house these stores and clearance centers, which are discussed below. Heading the list of outlet mall managers is the organization that owns a group of malls known as the Mills. Sawgrass Mills, the largest of the group, is located in a suburb of Fort Lauderdale, Florida. It boasts more than two miles of selling space, all under one roof. Featured are closeout stores for Ralph Lauren, DKNY, Nine West, Tahari, Wedgwood, Mikasa, and other brand names.

Rehoboth Outlets on the Delaware shore features manufacturer closeout stores. Its three separate but neighboring malls are managed by Charter Oak Partners, the largest privately owned outlet developer in the United States.

So successful has this venture been that entertainment areas and major restaurants such as the Cheesecake Factory, Rain Forest Café, and Wolfgang Puck have opened branches. Other successful outlet malls are Woodbury Commons in upstate New York, a center for upscale fashion designers; Belz Outlet Centers in St. Augustine and Orlando, Florida; and Freeport, Maine, an outdoor center that boasts many streets lined with designer outlets.

Because of the price structuring of outlet malls, they cannot be located within close proximity to traditional malls or downtown central districts. They are purposely built sufficiently far from traditional shopping locations so they will not compete with them. If the manufacturers opened outlets too close to traditional retailers, they would jeopardize the wholesale operations they depend on, which in turn depend on business from department stores and full-price specialty chain organizations.

Retail Clearance Centers

As discussed earlier, department stores and specialty chains sell merchandise to consumers at regular prices, offering them a wealth of services that justify such prices. Even with the best possible planning, these merchants are likely to be left with unsold merchandise at the end of the season, even after initial markdowns have been taken. With shelf space often limited, retailers must move merchandise as quickly as possible to make space on the selling floor for new items. One salvation for retailers left with slow-selling items is the **retail clearance center**.

Specialty stores like Gap have entered the retail clearance arena.

Major department stores such as Saks Fifth Avenue, Neiman Marcus, Nordstrom, and Lord & Taylor; specialty stores like the Gap, Banana Republic, and Ann Taylor; and catalog companies like Spiegel have all entered this arena. Outlets such as Saks' Off-Fifth and Last Call by Neiman Marcus are ringing up record sales. Not only are they disposing of the slow sellers from their regular stores at the clearance centers, but in spite of the lower prices being charged, they are turning a profit because of the high turnover.

In spite of all of the hoopla regarding off-site selling, brick-and-mortar retailing is alive and well and making progress on both the traditional and value-oriented fronts.

An Ethical Consideration

WHILE THE WHOLE AREA OF VALUE SHOPPING CONTINUES TO GROW, some unethical practices exist that give a bad name to this industry segment. In particular, many stores that are known as the off-price retailers do not always fairly represent the prices that they charge for their merchandise. Many proprietors mislead shoppers by leading them to believe that their prices are much lower than the regular selling price. This is sometimes true when the merchandise is "last season's," damaged goods, or a manufacturer's closeout. However, much of the merchandise in value stores is actually produced for these outlets and not part of regular designer or manufacturer's collections, as the consumer is lead to believe. Merchants of this sort would better serve the public if they were to make customers aware that their low prices are not always for merchandise that is identical to items sold elsewhere.

TRENDS FOR THE NEW MILLENNIUM

- The outlook for brick-and-mortar retailing is exceptionally favorable in both the traditional and value categories. The major companies will continue to open outlets wherever consumer demand is positive.
- The lead among the chain organizations will continue to be held by those stores that offer discount prices. With Wal-mart, Kmart, Home Depot and Costco among the top ten in U.S. chains; and given the expansion programs of these companies, discounting will continue to play a major role in retailing.
- Supermarkets will offer even greater product diversity by adding new types of merchandise. More prepared foods, cosmetics offerings, and home products will vie for the shelf space now given to the store's staples.
- Manufacturer closeout stores will be more visible all over the country, opening newer and larger units to serve bargain shoppers. More and more designers and manufacturers will stock these units with goods produced especially for the bargain seekers in addition to the leftovers goods from previous seasons.
- Retail clearance centers will continue to proliferate because of the demand by the vendors.

CHAPTER HIGHLIGHTS

- Brick-and-mortar retailers are the most important segment of the retailing industry in terms of overall sales.
- The best known of the traditional retailers are department stores and specialty chains.
- Department stores are classified as either full-line operations or specialized companies.
- Many traditional department store companies have expanded their organizations through acquisitions.
- Department stores started operating branches because of population shifts to the suburbs across the nation.
- The drugstore retail segment is now dominated by a few giants such as Walgreens and CVS, and the vast majority of small druggists have closed their doors.
- Bookstores have become entertainment centers where live performances and cafes share space with the book inventory.
- The greatest movement in retail sales has been away from traditional retailers to value-oriented retailers.
- Off-price merchants, discounters, manufacturer closeout stores, and retail clearance centers are the components of the value retailing.
- One of the fastest-growing segments of the discount chain category is office supplies retailers.
- Because of the nature of their price structure, off-price retailers must locate their stores away from traditional shopping malls.
- Major companies like Saks Fifth Avenue, Neiman Marcus, and Nordstrom have had enormous success in selling excess inventory at their own clearance centers.

IMPORTANT RETAILING TERMS

direct selling

traditional retailers

store within a store

full-line department store

specialized department store

anchor store

traditional chain

supermarket

Federal Trade Commission

product mix

impulse item

home center

the store-is-the-brand retailing

subclassification

marquee labels

value retailing

power center

outlet mall

opportunistic buying

closeouts

manufacturer closeout store

retail clearance center

FOR REVIEW

1. What does the term *brick-and-mortar retailing* mean?

2. In what way do the two department store types differ?

3. Why was the department store concept so successful when it was introduced to American consumers?

4. Why have most department stores discontinued their appliance departments?

5. Define the *store-within-a-store* concept used by department stores. Why has it achieved such success?

6. Identify the department store company discussed in this chapter that started as a small operation and has grown to be a major player through acquisition route. What are some of the divisions within that organization, today?

7. What trend led department stores to expand by opening branch stores?

8. Why have the specialty chains become the most successful of today's brick-and-mortar operations?

9. Describe one method supermarkets have used to increase their overall profits.

10. What does the term *the store is the brand* mean?

11. Name one method stores like the Gap and Banana Republic have used to differentiate their merchandise from that of other retailers.

12. Discuss some features bookstores have added to make the stores more exciting for their clienteles?

13. What are the major differences between the discount operations and the off-price retail outlets?

14. Why don't discounters and off-pricers locate their stores in traditional shopping malls?

15. What does the term *manufacturer closeout store* mean?

AN INTERNET ACTIVITY

Select five of your favorite brick-and-mortar retailers. Make certain that you are very familiar with the merchandise in the stores you choose. See if these retailers have Web sites. Go to the Web sites to find out what merchandise is available.

Develop a table with the following column headings:

- The name of the store

- Major merchandise categories in stores

- Merchandise available on Web site

Compare the merchandise available at the brick-and-morter stores with the merchandise available through the Web site. Prepare a double-spaced report.

EXERCISES AND PROJECTS

1. Write to or visit the public relations department in a full-line or specialized department store organization to learn about the topics listed below. Use the information to write a two-page, double-spaced report.

   Topics:

   - The company's history

   - The merchandise mix it offers its clientele

- The store's target market
- Other means of transacting business, such as catalogs and a Web site
- Potential for overseas expansion

2. Visit an off-price outlet store to find out what nationally advertised manufacturer and designer brands it stocks. Prepare a chart with headings as shown below to record the information. List at least ten brands. Price tags usually show the regular price along with the price at the off-price store.

Store _____

Location _____

Brand	Regular Price	Outlet Price

THE CASE OF THE OFF-PRICE COMPETITOR

Clements Department Store has been successfully operating five traditional stores in the South for many years. It opened its first unit in 1945, and subsequently expanded to four other locations, each within a radius of two hundred miles of the flagship store. The company is a family business with four generations involved at present. Until recently, it did not have any direct competition, an unusual position for a department store to be in. Of course, there were specialty stores in the area, and households could make purchases from the many catalogs they received regularly. Many families also have begun to make purchases over the Internet. When all is said and done, however, the majority of the customers were faithful to the company, calling upon it for most of their buying needs. The merchandise assortment was substantial for the trading area, and the clientele was sufficiently satisfied to pay the prices asked.

Last year, the situation at Clements changed. What was once the perfect retailing situation was changed by the opening of highly visible new operation, The Smart Shopper, an off-price venture that sold merchandise bearing many of the same labels carried by Clements, but at lower prices. While the merchandise offered at the new company wasn't generally available at the same time as at Clements, nor were the size and color assortments complete, the brand-name merchandise was still there for the taking.

The new venture was located within the same radius as the five Clements stores and adjacent to a major highway, making it within easy reach of the customers who frequented any of the Clements stores. The Smart Shopper immediately became a destination for the curious shoppers who wanted to learn what bargains might be found. Sales began to fall at each of the Clements' stores.

Each member of the Clements family in the management team reacted differently. Steve Clements, its founder, felt that once their curiosities were satisfied loyal customers would return, and that no changes should be made. His daughter, Julia, senior vice president, felt that playing the waiting game was dangerous and that the results would be harmful to the company. She believed an aggressive advertising campaign was necessary to bring the shoppers back to the stores. Bill Reilly, Julia's husband and general merchandise manager felt an aggressive approach would be necessary to meet the new competition. His plan was to play The Smart Shopper's game and introduce off-price merchandise.

As sales begin to slip even more, the three are still trying to come up with a solution to the problem.

Questions

1. With whom do you agree?
2. What other approaches should the company take to bring the customers back to them?

CHAPTER 3

Off-Site Retailing: E-Tailing, Catalogs, and Home-Shopping Networks

After you have completed this chapter, you should be able to discuss

- ▶ The effects of the three major off-site retailing classifications on brick-and-mortar retailing.
- ▶ The fundamental components that must be addressed when starting a Web site.
- ▶ The multimedia approach to retailing.
- ▶ The ways in which interactive e-tailing better serves the needs of the customers.
- ▶ Why catalog shopping continues to appeal to consumers.
- ▶ Ways in which businesses that were formerly catalog companies are expanding their businesses.
- ▶ Why home-shopping channels continue to experience record sales.

Among modern retail professionals all across the United States, a topic of interest is the recent increase in customer spending in venues other than the brick-and-mortar stores. More and more shoppers are choosing to make purchases electronically, through catalogs, and via the numerous home-shopping networks on television. While these retail outlets are making significant gains in their share of the consumer dollar, it is too early to tell if their presence will result in the demise of brick-and-mortar stores. At this time, the percentage of off-site consumer spending pales in comparison with in-store shopping. However, with the considerable efforts of countless businesses now embracing **off-site purchasing** as a means to satisfy consumer needs and bring a profit to their companies, it is obvious that this trend will not only continue but also gain momentum.

During the past few years, with the advent of **electronic retailing**, a new language has been created. Consumers have come to hear and use new words, words that hadn't existed in the recent past. The new terminology includes such terms as *dot-com*, *search engine*, *Web site*, and *e-tailing*, and its use has become commonplace on the lips of industry professionals and consumers alike. Whenever discussions about retailing in the new millennium take place, these terms are included.

While e-tailing has generated a great deal of excitement and enthusiasm in the industry, the verdict is still out on its actual long-term success and on where it will lead future generations of retailing.

Long before anyone dreamed of electronically filled orders for consumer goods, those unable or unwilling to go to stores took care of their buying needs through catalogs. Although the granddaddy of them all, the Sears catalog, has ceased publication, catalogs are alive and well in the United States and are bringing in record sales. Major department stores are constantly expanding their direct marketing efforts, and catalog-only companies are featuring merchandise heretofore rarely found in catalogs. Whether it is the traditional merchandise offerings such as apparel and housewares or unusual items such as original artwork and rare plants, an abundance of goods can be found in catalogs. American households today are regularly bombarded with unsolicited catalogs; and the catalog business is certain to gain even greater momentum than it has already realized.

Rounding out the off-site retailing are the television "programs" that sell a variety of products to consumers. Cable channels devoted to shopping programs include QVC; HSN, the television shopping network; and Shop at Home. The variety is not as great as at other off-site ventures, with jewelry being the most common offering, followed by women's apparel. Day by day and hour by hour, customers are placing orders in record numbers, making these programs a viable outlet for some vendors. Akin to the shopping programs is the **infomercial**, a form of advertising that reports the virtues of a particular product such as a cooking device or workout equipment in a time block—such as a half hour—more usually associated with entertainment programs. Although limited somewhat to specific types of merchandise, it too has had considerable success in selling its wares via television.

Through these off-site selling shopping venues, retailers are able to offer consumers many alternative methods of making purchases.

E-TAILING

With the vast majority of American households owning computers, and the major proportion of them having access to the Internet, electronic retailing, or "e-tailing," as it is generally called, is a natural medium for selling merchandise to consumers. Retailers run multimillion dollar advertising campaigns to bring shoppers to particular Web sites to look for the products they need. Retailers hope they will find what they want, buy it, and return again and again for additional purchases. As in any fledgling industry, the proliferation of e-tailers has been enormous. The number of entries in this retailing format is without rival among retailing venues. Not a day goes by without another Web site, or **e-tail address** being launched. As in the case of brick-and-mortar organizations, the fittest survive, and the others fail.

The e-tailing industry is divided into two parts: those that do business on-line exclusively, **Web site-only retailers**, and those that are divisions of either brick-and-mortar retailer or catalog operations. Each type of operation will be discussed in terms of the benefits of its approach to e-tailing and likely future directions of the concept.

Connecting to the Internet

No exploration of e-tailing would be complete without a discussion of the Internet and the way in which its users access it.

Accessing the Internet begins with the selection of an Internet service provider that enables individuals to reach the sites they want to explore. Some of the better-known providers are America Online, AT&T Worldnet, and MSN. For a fee, users are entitled to "log on" to the Internet. The servers usually come with browsers that allow one to reach specific Web sites, or search for sites with information he or she seeks, such as weather conditions, stock quotations, and products and services available for sale.

Internet Explorer and Netscape are the two most widely used browsers. If the user does not know a particular Web site he or she wants, a *search engine* can help find pages in the particular area of interest. Some search engines that are especially helpful when shopping online are Yahoo.com, iWon.com and Snap.com. After logging on to any of these or other search engines, the shopper keys in the product he or she is looking for and is given a selection of sites to choose from. The vast assortment of products offered online run the gamut from electronics, books, and CDs to a host of apparel items and wearable accessories for every member of the family.

The ideal situation for a Web site owner is for users to access it directly without having to search for it. Users can do this when they know the Web site's "address." To reach

America Online is the leading U.S. Internet service provider.

the site, they merely have to key in this address. The screen quickly brings up the specific sites introductory page, or home page. The Web site address is much like the old-fashioned address or telephone number we use to locate a company. As people come to remember their favorite store's location, it is easy for them to make a trip to it. Getting users to remember a Web site's address is very important to e-tailers for two reasons. First, it minimizes competition from other e-tailers by bypassing search engines, which supply the Web addresses of a variety of vendors. Second, it brings the shopper to the Web site quickly.

A look at the print and broadcast advertisements for Web sites shows just how important e-tailers think it is that consumers know their Web addresses. The name of the Web site is featured prominently in each such advertising messages. In this way, e-tailers make sure that those who are interested in exploring its offerings can head directly to the Web site.

iWon.com is a major search engine for Internet shoppers.

The Fundamentals of Starting a Web Site

The investment needed to start a Web site varies considerably. It might be as little as a few hundred dollars to design and post a page on an existing site that charges e-tailers a small monthly fee for the service. In contrast, the costs may amount to enormous sums to design a unique site that is attractive and easy to use, making it easy for shoppers to find and buy the products they want. Of course, a complex, multilayered site featuring a large number of products will need to pay a hefty monthly fee in addition to the initial costs.

Entrepreneurs with dreams of building their own companies are starting e-tailing ventures in vast numbers. Thousands upon thousands of these hopefuls are filling the Internet with art galleries, craft outlets, apparel shops, and the like in the hope that they will gain the kind of consumer recognition that is almost impossible to achieve with a brick-and-mortar store in today's overcrowded marketplace. While the initial investment in starting up a Web site is minimal in comparison to opening a store, the competition is fierce. Who can buck the competitive edge of such household names as Amazon.com and eBay.com?

Merchandise Assortments

Those wishing to enter the fray must begin with a product or service to sell. If the company Web site is a division of a brick-and-mortar retailer or a catalog business that aims to expand its sales, the retail concept might be in place. Even for such ventures, it is often necessary to narrow the product offering to those that have the widest appeal in order to display it in the limited space typically available on Web sites. New companies must first develop a merchandise plan or service program that will have appeal to Internet users. **Me-too merchandise** should be avoided. Such merchandise merely replicates other companies' offerings and the duplication might result in oversaturating the market. Once the merchandise plan or service program is in place, the next step is to design the Web site.

Web Site Design

Having an attractice and original **Web site design** is essential to attract potential customers. As with the print and broadcast ads, it is the unusual that stands out and captures the consumer's attention. A mundane and lackluster Web site will not motivate the sites' visitor to explore it. To make certain that the Web site is as attractive as possible, e-tailers employ specialists in Web site design for this task. As the need for Web site designers increases, more and more people are specializing in this new area. Care should be exercised before hiring a designer to create a Web site. Make sure to find someone whose skills and talent are equal to the task and whose design ideas are compatible with the desired image for the site. It is essential to look at the potential designer's portfolio before deciding to hire him or her. Once the designer has been selected, it is time for the next step: deciding on the scope of the venture.

The Scope and Size of the Web Site

A look at a sampling of the multitude of Web sites that fill the Internet reveals a wealth of different approaches. Some are merely single pages that tell visitors the best way in which to contact the company to learn about specific products or whet the prospective customer's appetite with a special offer. Such sites are more like advertisements than genuine e-tailers, since they do not actually accommodate sales transaction. At the other end of the spectrum are Web sites that feature page after page of specific offerings, complete with methods for ordering. It is the latter approach that brings the best results to the merchant on the Web.

Probably the highest Internet profile belongs to Amazon.com. Its Web site addresses all of the basics to ensure a significant merchandise assortment and good customer service. When the Web site comes up on the screen, the viewer immediately finds his or her name prominently displayed. This tends to give the shopper the

Amazon.com is the highest profile merchandise Web site in the country.

feeling he or she is getting the kind of personalized service that more and more brick-and-mortar retailers are giving their customers. Thus, the visitor feels good about the shopping experience from the onset. This initial screen also lists the different product classifications available and allows the visitors to reach them by pointing and clicking on the category names. By scrolling down, visitors can see the wealth of items available in the selected category. If the visitor decides to buy an item, he or she is lead through a series of steps to complete the sale.

The Lands' End Web site is even more personalized. On its first page, along with an attractive representation of a featured product the visitor finds several choices that allow him or her to select the type of shopping "adventure" he or she prefers. "Lands' End Live" makes it possible to speak with a service representative; "Personal Model" shows how a specific item will look on the customer's own figure; and "Orient Express" assists with the selection of the product to fit the clients needs. While the merchandise at Lands' End might not be particularly unusual, the approach to selling with its emphasis on **interactive shopping**, makes a difference.

Of course, Amazon.com and Lands' End are both high-profile merchants. With enormous budgets and large talent pools to create their Web sites, they are able to continually refine the site design to address new circumstances that arise, thereby making their Web sites more and more productive. Smaller companies and those with limited financial resources must keep their Web sites fairly simple to stay within their means. With careful planning they will be able to eliminate unnecessary expenses without sacrificing those features most needed for their purposes.

Types of E-Tailers

Exploring the many retailer sites on the Web, reveals three basic types of companies: organizations that use the Internet exclusively to conduct all of their business, catalog companies that use the Internet to bring additional sales, and the brick-and-mortar operations that use a multimedia approach which includes a Web site to augment its sales.

Web Site-Only Retailers

Many companies began their operations as exclusively e-tailing businesses. These Web site-only retailers, or **e-commerce businesses**, use neither stores nor catalogs for the sale of their merchandise. Some of these businesses feature a wealth of products that surpass those available at the largest department stores, while others restrict their offerings to one or two merchandise classifications.

One of the better known global Web site-only operations is eBay.com. The concept behind eBay is to host electronic auctions in which registered members bid for a vast number of products that are put up for sale by other members. The Web site boasts more than 4 million different items up for sale at any given time. Not only has it become an American institution, but its is also achieving international marketing recognition through eBay Australia, eBay Japan, and others divisions. Potential purchasers scan the various offerings within a chosen category, make a bid, and learn whether or not the bid has been accepted. Its attractive format has led to worldwide acceptance by consumers.

Designeroutlet.com is one of the first companies to sell fashion merchandise at deeply discounted prices on the Internet. The site was started by a few fashion executives with more than 50 years of combined experience in the fashion industry. It offers overstocked merchandise from most major designers, including such internationally recognized labels as Ralph Lauren, Prada, Dolce & Gabbana, Fendi, Adolfo, and Nicole Miller at prices far below the original retail prices.

Ebay.com is a global Web site operation where products are bought and sold exclusively through the Internet.

TABLE 3.1
TOP 15 U.S. INTERNET RETAILERS[1], 1999

COMPANY	WEB SITE	PRIMARY PRODUCT OR SERVICE
eBay	ebay.com	Auction venue
Amazon.com	amazon.com	Books/media
Dell	dell.com	Computers/software
buy.com	buy.com	Computers/media
Egghead.com	Egghead.com, onsale.com (formerly)	Computers/software
Gateway	gateway.com	Computers/software
Quixtar	quixtar.com	Broad selection
uBid	ubid.com	Auction venue
Barnes & Noble	bn.com	Books/media
Cyberian Outpost	outpost.com	Computers/software
MicroWarehouse	microwarehouse.com	Computers/software
Office Depot	officedepot.com, vikingop.com	Office supplies
eToys.com	etoys.com	Toys
Lands' End	landsend.com	Apparel
The Spiegel Group	spiegel.com, eddiebauer.com, newport-news.com	Apparel

[1]Companies for which E-commerce is the primary business.

Note: The rankings are subject to change because of the volatility of this market.

Source: *Stores*, September 2000. © Copyright 2000 NRF Enterprises, Inc. Used with permission.

The offerings are updated every two weeks, making it worthwhile for fashion-conscious shoppers to make frequent, repeat visits. Each item is shown in full color so customers feel they know what they're getting. Once customers select an item, it goes into a shopping basket, where it remains until the purchaser is ready to check out. A final look at the selections allows customers to change their orders up to the last minute. The company accepts returned merchandise, making it a safe place in which to shop.

With fashion enthusiasts often too busy to visit the many off-price fashion retailers in person, the designeroutlet.com Web site fills an important need, allowing the target shoppers to buy fashion goods in their limited spare time and in the comfort of their homes.

Because it is anything but a me-too operation, it has become the Internet destination for those wishing to take advantage of its discounted fashion merchandise.

Table 3.1 lists the top 15 Web site-only or e-commerce businesses.

Catalogers with E-Tailing Operations

As most consumers know, numerous retail operations specialize in direct marketing via catalogs, including such major companies as Spiegel, Fingerhut, and Lands' End. They market to

L.L.Bean is a high profile catalog company with e-tailing exposure.

consumers who either have limited time for shopping, do not live within easy reach of the major shopping centers, or prefer the convenience of shopping from home. By providing quality merchandise and excellent customer service, many catalog companies have developed large numbers of loyal clients. While some of these companies operate closeout centers, the basis of their business is to serve their customers through catalogs, which are updated periodically.

In the new era of electronic retailing, the vast majority of these companies have augmented their catalog sales with Web sites. While the products offered for sale on the Web sites pale in comparison to that of some Web site-only retailers, the sales results have been promising enough to merit further on-line expansion. Spiegel.com offers items ranging from wearing apparel for the family to electronics. Lands' End is limited in the range of its offerings to casual clothing. Recently Sears acquired Lands' End in order to expand its own presence in this segment of the apparel market.

Today most retailing professionals agree that adding a Web site to the mix is necessary to remain competitive. With buying more and more in the hands of young consumers who are very comfortable with buying on the Internet, it is essential for the catalogers to embrace this selling venue. Not only that, but other market segments are beginning to feel at home surfing the net. Senior citizens who were not receptive of the computer at first are now beginning to understand its benefits and are turning to the Internet as a means of keeping up with the world. Many of these seniors first went online for the latest news and financial information, but are now using the Internet to buy goods. While many continue to use catalogs for shopping, they are finding that the Web can more quickly satisfy their needs.

Other segments of our population, not just those mentioned above have within them catalog shoppers who have now turned to the Internet for many of their purchases.

Table 3.2 lists the top ten e-tailing divisions of catalog companies.

TABLE 3.2
TOP TEN E-TAIL DIVISIONS OF U.S. CATALOG COMPANIES

WEB SITE	PRIMARY MERCHANDISE	ANNUAL MEAN INTERNET SALES PER HOUSEHOLD
landsend.com	Apparel	$207
microwarehouse.com	Computers	186
spiegel.com	Apparel	1,067
llbean.com	Apparel	308
bhphoto.com	Photo, video, and audio equipment	2,700
abcdistributing.com	Gifts	257
harborfreight.com	Tools	228
cameraworld.com	Cameras, camera accessories	813
hammacherschlemmer.com	Broad selection	436
jcwhitney.com	Auto parts	600

Bricks and Clicks

A fairly new entry in the changing jargon of the new millennium is **bricks and clicks**. The term is used for brick-and-mortar stores that have developed Web sites as an added means of reaching consumers. *Bricks*, of course, refers to the physical store and *Clicks* to the simple task of clicking the computer's mouse to order the desired goods.

The roster of retailers that have developed Web sites is staggering. Full-line department stores like Macy's and Marshall Field's, more specialized department stores like Saks Fifth

In a variation on e-tailing, shoppers at a self-checkout kiosk in a Giant Eagle supermarket buy their purchases online within the brick-and-mortar store.

Avenue, and apparel chains like Gap are just a few of the many that have recognized the need to become e-tailers.

The breadth and depth of the merchandise mix is miniscule in comparison to what is available in the stores. However, the actual sales that result from the Web site are one purpose of these endeavors, but not the only one. Most merchants believe that electronic exposure will motivate satisfied shoppers to visit the store to make future purchases. So in a sense, one of the drawbacks to shopping at brick-and-mortar retailers' Web sites—that they offer only a limited number of products—is a strength for the company. Customers will come to the store to select from the wider assortment of goods.

Another purpose is to extend the company's reach beyond its geographical area. The Internet reaches consumers in areas without physical access to stores. Many retailers are using their Web sites to build a market in areas where they might open additional "physical" units in the future—if data from the Web site indicates enough consumer interest. The level of interest is easy to measure through analysis of the Internet sales, using the zip codes of Web purchasers.

Table 3.3 lists major brick-and-mortar retailers that now augment store sales with e-tailing.

TABLE 3.3
INTERNET SALES BY BRICK-AND-MORTAR RETAILERS

STORE	PRIMARY OFFERINGS	AVERAGE ANNUAL SALES PER HOUSEHOLD
Barnes & Noble	Books, media	$126
Gap	Apparel	375
Wal-Mart	Broad selection	454
JCPenney	Broad selection	219
CompUSA	Computers, software	586
Borders	Books, media	89
REI	Recreational equipment	575
Sears	Tools, appliances	310
Nordstrom	Apparel, accessories	272
Macy's	Broad selection	132

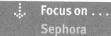
Focus on . . .
Sephora

IN JUST A FEW SHORT YEARS, SEPHORA HAS BECOME a major player in the vastly profitable cosmetics industry. Industry professionals and consumers alike are heralding its presence. Rarely has a company made such an immediate impact all over the globe.

Formed in 1993, Sephora was acquired as a division of Moët Hennessey Louis Vuitton (LVMH), the world's leading luxury products group in 1997. With the LVMH empire including such internationally recognized names as Christian Lacroix, Givenchy, Kenzo, Louis Vuitton, and Guerlain, Sephora is a good fit. Sephora benefits not only from its association with such a stellar roster but also from the fact that the parent company is extraordinarily well funded and is ready to make significant investments to assure the division's future success. Sephora is currently the leading chain of perfume and cosmetics stores in France and the second largest in Europe with stores in Luxembourg, Spain, Italy, Poland, Germany, and the United Kingdom. In Asia it is represented with outlets in Japan and is now opening new stores across the Asia–Pacific region. The Sephora retail concept arrived in the United States in 1998 with the opening of its 21,000-square-foot flagship store in New York City and a second store in Miami. The Flagship store has caused great concern to its neighbor, Saks Fifth Avenue, which has long been the premiere purveyor of luxury cosmetics in New York.

The Sephora stores are distinctively different from their competitors. It merchandises a complete line of international fragrances, cosmetics, and "well-being" products, arranged alphabetically to provide the browser with an

Sephora is a rising star in the bricks-and-clicks arena; customers can shop its products on the computer or in a store.

easy way to discover what is available for sale without having to undertake a time-consuming search for a given brand. With such innovations as the Top Ten Fragrance Wall; a Fragrance Organ, where shoppers can test and compare fragrances; the Cultural Gallery, a section that features exhibits related to beauty; a Treatment Library, which showcases a variety of products to meet any special care needs; the Lipstick Rainbow, a display of 365 shades; the Nail & Polish Spectrum, an array of 150 shades packaged in practical miniature bottles; it is truly the "temple of beauty."

Launched in October 1999, Sephora.com extends the Sephora retail beauty concept to a wider audience. Through this e-tail venture, the company hopes to create a haven of unique beauty and knowledge for the whole world to share. The company spends many millions in advertising campaigns to ensure that its presence on the Web will gain immediate attention. By the use of two of fashion's superstars, Kate Moss and Carmen Kass, in the print media campaigns, the company attaches recognizable faces to its image.

Since the Web site's launch, it has met with overwhelming success, averaging one million "hits" a day. Often, the site is so busy that would-be customers find it difficult to access. To make Sephora.com an even bigger player in the crowded Internet beauty arena, the upscale e-tailer has entered into a broad-based alliance with Yahoo, the medium's most heavily trafficked Web site. With Yahoo reporting more than 47 million site visits each month, it is a place where Sephora will be able to maximize its exposure.

Multichannel Retailing

In this day of highly competitive retailing, it is essential that merchants expand their operations and take advantage of the different consumer channels available to them. Each of the channels offers a different opportunity for shopping. Store visits are time-consuming, but for most types of merchandise large segments of the population still favor this way of making their purchases. Catalogs provide a leisurely means of shopping without having to travel to stores or be limited by store hours. The Internet can be accessed from the workplace as well as in the home, providing even more convenience to shoppers.

Thus, the way a company can achieve the greatest retailing exposure is by becoming a **multichannel retailer.** To do so, it must have brick-and-mortar outlets, a catalog division, and an Internet Web site. Most typically, a brick-and-mortar retailer embraces first catalog selling and then e-tailing. This is not always the case, however, American Girl, one of America's most visible retailers of specialized dolls and accessories, was first and foremost a catalog operation. It then spread its wings with a flagship store in Chicago and a Web site.

American Girl has made great sales gains as a multichannel retailer, first selling products through a catalog and later expanding to a flagship store and online shopping.

An analysis of July 2000 data in the *Wall Street Journal* shows that while on-line sales have escalated in all categories, it is the multichannel retailers that are getting most of these dollars. In fact, the difference in online sales by multi-channel retailers and online sales by Internet-only retailers is staggering. In all but three classifications, the multichannel retailers have far outperformed the Web site-only companies. In product classifications such as "event tickets," "computer hardware/software," "apparel/sporting," and "flowers/cards/gifts," the multichannel merchants had an edge of at least 80 percent.

Although the Internet will most certainly remain an active channel for selling directly to consumers, by itself it does not yet have enough power to compete with the multichannel retailers.

The Stein Mart Story
Its Role in Off-Site Retailing

JUST LIKE MOST OTHER RETAILERS, STEIN MART is always analyzing methods of improving market share besides in-store selling. However, unlike the vast majority of the major players in the industry, it has not pursued other retail channels with much vigor.

While the company maintains a Web site that features a history of the company, a look at its merchandise offerings, a corporate profile, locations of its stores, and other pertinent information to prospective consumers and vendors, it does not do any e-tailing. Company spokespeople cite the limited profitability of such ventures as the main reason for this decision. Of course, if in the future on-line selling becomes necessary, Stein Mart will join the fray.

The purpose of the company Web site is to "drive people to the stores." It hopes that featuring current print advertising and offering to notify customers of upcoming sales will motivate people to come to the stores.

While other retailers are moving full-speed ahead into catalog selling, Stein Mart is inching into this channel slowly. Stein Mart publishes advertising inserts in newspapers that are, in effect, mini catalogs. These inserts have had positive results, bringing in enough nonstore sales to make them worthwhile. Once in a while, the store does direct-mail advertising, but not on a regular basis.

Stein Mart believes in doing business the old-fashioned way, and it will remain with that concept until it identifies a need to use other avenues to improve market share.

Virtual Catalogs

The next section is about real catalogs that you can hold in your hand. Not surprisingly e-tailers have borrowed the concept to introduce the **virtual catalog**, which simulates a printed catalog to show products on the Internet.

America Online is a major player in the virtual catalog business. Its Shop@AOL Web site is filled with selected items from AOL's merchant partners, including Macy's.com, Gap.com, Bluefly.com, eBags.com, JCPenney.com, and other high-profile retailers. Shop@AOL brings together a wealth of products and makes purchasing easier for the shopper than if he or she had to examine each and every catalog or Web site of the individual merchants. An AOL Web site/virtual catalog simply called *The Basics* offers women guidance in building a wardrobe and features the merchandise needed to carry out this task, including apparel and accessories that can be coordinated to create a complete wardrobe. If shoppers need additional information about the goods shown, they can access the Web sites of the particular stores through a link at the AOL site.

Interactive E-Tailing

While Internet sales continue to spiral upwardly in many classifications, some e-tailers in the fashion arena are experiencing growing pains. Unlike product information available online for books, CDs, and computer software, information for apparel is not sufficient to motivate shoppers to buy; they want to feel the texture of the fabric, try on the item, examine how it is made, and perhaps even consult an expert. Of course, for jeans and other basic apparel products, little selling effort is needed to make the sale. For fashion-forward apparel such as designer clothes, customers seem to feel the lack of real-time communication with a "live" fashion consultant.

Shopping Consultants

Many e-tailers are finding solutions to this problem that involve making their Web sites more interactive. LandsEnd.com, for example, offers two interactive services. One makes it possible to interact online with a company representative. The other allows the customer to speak to a customer service representative through a voice telephone connection. Since the offerings at Lands' End are rather basic, the communication needed to make purchasing decisions is rather straightforward, and both modes of communication appear to address customers' concerns.

More and more dot-coms are adding interactive sections to their Web sites so that shoppers in every merchandise classification will be able to buy with greater ease and have less reason to return the products that they have chosen.

Virtual Try-Ons

When shoppers buy apparel in a store, they have the opportunity to try it on before making a final decision. When they shop for apparel online they do not have that opportunity and must make a buying decision based on an imagined "picture" of how the outfit will fit and how it will flatter the figure.

Or at least that used to be the situation. Now, many e-tailers have solved the problem by adding virtual mannequins that correspond to the shopper's actual figure. The shopper creates his or her likeness by entering his or her measurements, and once the personalized mannequin is created, he or she can "try on" any item the e-tailer sells.

Such companies as Lands' End and Macy's in the United States and Galeries Lafayette in France now provide such **virtual try-ons**. At Macy's.com, the model is first constructed on either a CD-ROM or its Web site. To create the model, the customer enters dozens of measurements. The more measurements entered, the more accurate the representation will be. In addition, the customer may scan in a photograph to see his or her own face on the accurately proportioned model "trying on" the selected item. The shopper can browse through a variety of styles, try each on, and select the most becoming ones. Once the customer makes a decision to buy, one click takes him or her directly to the checkout page to complete the transaction.

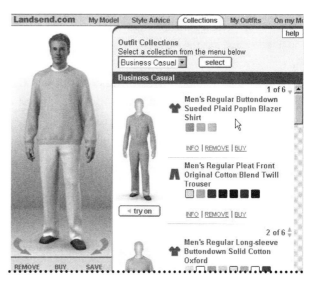

Land's End was one of the first retailers to offer a virtual try-on service.

Internet Fraud

One reason many potential purchasers do not buy online is that they are not certain that the transaction will be secure; that is, they fear that computer hackers will break in and learn credit cards numbers and other personal information required for e-tail transactions and use this information to make purchases—or even "steal" their identities. While some say security is not a major problem, estimates indicate that nearly 10 percent of online sales involve the fraudulent use of credit cards or debit cards. At Beyond.com, a company that was one of the earliest online sellers of compute software, the matter was significantly worse. Nearly half of the retailer's sales were made to people using fake or stolen credit card numbers!

Today, new technologies are being introduced to fight fraud and make consumers more comfortable about making Internet purchases. This development is absolutely essential for an industry that is expected to reach more than 40 million households in the United States, producing $108 billion in revenue, and accounting for 6 percent of all consumer spending according to a study in 2000 by Forrester Research of Cambridge, Massachusetts.

One of the leaders in developing this new technology is CyberSource in San Jose, California. CyberSource systems assist merchants in screening out fraudulent transactions by calculating risk factors. They examine 150 features of a potential sale to determine the relative risk involved. The process takes less than 10 seconds and cuts the losses from fraud to less than 1 percent.

While it is virtually impossible to eliminate all online purchasing fraud, just as it is impossible to do so at the brick-and-mortar retailers, experts agree that some simple steps can reduce the risk even further. NEWrageous, a marketing service company in Olney,

Maryland, has developed a list of prevention tips on preventing fraud for e-tailers. They include the following:

- Be wary of orders with different bill-to and ship-to addresses.
- Be cautious about orders that are larger than the typical purchases.
- Be cautious about orders that indicate next-day delivery.
- Be careful about international orders.
- Whenever there is a doubt, telephone the customer for additional information.

One of the ways in which the industry is hoping to reduce credit card fraud is by accepting checks, just as it is done at brick-and-mortar stores. By using one of the many check-guarantee companies that are in the business of taking the risk out of accepting checks, many Web sites are exploring ways of allowing customers to pay by check instead of charging their purchases.

CATALOGS

When the early catalog pioneers such as Sears and Montgomery Ward first introduced their big books it was for the purpose of reaching people who were not in close proximity to stores. Today, Sears is no longer in the direct-mail business and Montgomery Ward is no longer in business at all. This abandonment on the part of the industry's founders has not led other companies to close their direct marketing divisions. The likes of Spiegel and Fingerhut are reaching households in record numbers with big books and a wealth of smaller, more specialized catalogs, proving that catalog retailing is alive and well and here to stay. There are many reasons for the popularity of catalog buying, including the following:

- First and foremost, catalog shopping is easy, while in-store shopping has become more time-consuming than ever before. Department stores, for example, continue to increase their merchandise inventories at the same time as they are reducing the number of sales associates. With so much to see and so little personal attention available, the once pleasurable event of a shopping expedition has become a time-consuming chore.
- The difficulty of shopping at brick-and-mortar retailers is more of a problem because women are working outside the home. They are in record numbers actually performing two jobs, one in their place of business and the other at home tending to their family's needs. This situation gives them less time to visit the stores, requiring them to find alternative ways to make purchases.
- Catalogs' visual presentations have become more and more sophisticated, and the quality of the merchandise offered is getting better and better. Shoppers are now able to evaluate each offering easily and shop with confidence.

- Catalog shopping is not limited by store hours; it may be done at any time, at home at the end of the day, for example, or during the lunch break at work.
- Ordering is simple. With most ordering possible 24 hours a day, and the availability of knowledgeable company representatives ready to answer questions, purchases are easily made.
- Specialized datalogs are available to meet individual shoppers' particular needs. Literally hundreds upon hundreds of catalogs routinely bring consumers offerings that are difficult to find at the brick-and-mortar stores. One catalog might feature only natural fibers, another offer a vast assortment of writing implements, and so forth, for virtually any other product classification.
- Catalog sellers have generous return policies, so buyers can feel safe that they will not be "stuck" with merchandise that does not live up to their expectations.

The catalog industry is divided into three categories: catalog operations with little or no other outlets, catalog companies that also sell through brick-and-mortar stores and/or on-line, and brick-and-mortar organizations with catalog divisions.

As discussed earlier in the chapter, most retailers today use a multichannel approach, combining brick-and-mortar outlets, Web sites, and catalog selling. The following divides catalog companies according to their primary means of doing business.

Lillian Vernon is still considered by many to be a catalog-only retailer, despite its having launched a Web site.

Catalog-Only Retailers

With the Internet such an integral part of retailing, it is unlikely that any business that relies exclusively on direct marketing will be able to compete. Spiegel, Lillian Vernon, and Fingerhut, all of which used to be strictly catalog companies, for example, are operating Web sites. While their Web sites do bring sales, the companies are still classified as catalog companies.

Nonprofessionals have come to believe that with online purchasing becoming more and more popular, the catalog company is heading for extinction. However, Internet sales currently account for less than 1 percent of all retail sales, and those businesses that are exclusively online operations are less likely to compete in today's retailing arena than those that have other outlets as well.

Table 3.4 lists retailers that use catalogs as their means of reaching consumers.

TABLE 3.4
TOP TEN U.S. CATALOGS-ONLY RETAILERS[1]

COMPANY	MAJOR OFFERINGS
Lands' End	Men's and women's apparel
Micro Warehouse	Computers
L.L. Bean	Apparel, camping equipment
BH Photo and Video	Photo, video, audio equipment
ABC Distributing	Gifts
Fingerhut	Apparel and home products
Harbor Freight	Tools
Camera World	Cameras and camera accessories
Hammacher Schlemmer	Unique items
JC Whitney	Auto parts

[1]Many of these companies also sell through stores and/or on Web sites, but their primary distribution channel is catalog.

Catalogers with Brick-and-Mortar Outlets

Many companies began as catalog operations, fully intending to remain exclusively in that retailing segment. They believed they could achieve their goal of reaching a certain segment of the population in just about any trading area without opening stores.

Now, however, several of these catalog companies are also increasingly opening up stores to sell their goods. One such venture is The American Girl, a division of Pleasant Company.

Focus on . . .
The American Girl

IN 1986, PLEASANT COMPANY INTRODUCED THE WORLD to its exciting new concept of dolls by mailing its first consumer catalog to a selected market. Joining the dolls in the catalog a year later were historical fashions for the dolls to wear. With the wide acceptance of the catalog, the company introduced a magazine that was filled with stories about their collections. Year after year, new additions were made to the line, and business continued to boom. The catalog was its only means of transacting business until 1998 when American Girl Place, a store that featured the entire collection of dolls and accessories, opened in Chicago, Illinois.

This new brick-and-mortar retail division was an immediate success. The multistory brick-and-mortar outlet is actually a combination sales arena and entertainment center. It is a place where little girls could come not only to make purchases but also to spend a few hours being entertained. The store has a tearoom with "high chairs" for the dolls so they could share the refreshments with the girls, and a theater with live productions.

Crowds are so large that customers must wait in lines that snake around the building, to gain entrance to the store, just like at Disney World. Little girls, with their dolls and parents in tow, wait patiently for a chance to visit the store. At peak periods, such as Saturdays and holidays, the sight of several hundred people on line is commonplace.

In addition to the catalog, magazine, and American Girl Place store, the company also publishes and markets American Girl books, promotes special charity events, and features a Web site for access by those wanting to purchase online.

It is the store, however, that has become the centerpiece of the retailing empire. It enables new customers to learn the American Girl concept firsthand and old customers to play out their fantasies through their on-site adventures with their dolls.

Recognizing that their loyal clientele is constantly aging, with many early devotees now in their adolescent years, a "Daughters" newsletter was introduced in 1999 for parents of this age group. It aims to help parents understand the growing pains of their adolescent children and make meaningful decisions concerning their upbringing.

Now a subsidiary of Mattel, Inc., Pleasant Company continues to operate all its divisions, including the American Girl, independently.

• •

Other companies that started as catalog operations are also expanding their operations with brick-and-mortar stores. Patagonia, a company that specializes in ski apparel and accessories, has opened full-price and outlet stores in many parts of the country, J. Jill, a women's apparel specialty catalog, has a growing number of mall stores, and J.Crew, now has a wealth of stores across the United States in addition to its catalogs.

One reason these direct-mail companies are opening stores is that retail stores can show an even greater selection of the goods than catalogs can. By exposing shoppers to a wider selection, they hope to increase the average number of sales per customer.

▨ Brick-and-Mortar Catalog Divisions

It is hard to find a store anywhere in the United States that doesn't send out a catalog. Perhaps the only remaining members of the store-only category are small, independent merchants that feature limited assortments and appeal to very small market segments in limited trading areas. Most other retail institutions have embraced catalog merchandising, with department stores and specialty chains leading the way. Early on, the direct-mail retailers sent out catalogs only during a few peak selling periods such as Christmas, Easter, late summer (back-to-school), and so forth. Today department stores such as Macy's, Lord & Taylor, Marshall Field's, Belk, and Dillard's each send more than 30 catalogs through the

SPRING 2002
bloomingdale's|bymail

Bloomingdale's by mail is the company's catalog division.

year. Chain stores also use direct mail extensively, and their numerous catalogs reach consumer households in record numbers. Some even issue catalogs that offer totally different merchandise from the store. Victoria's Secret's stores, for example, specialize in *innerware*. Its catalogs, by contrast, feature a more diverse product line.

While most brick-and-mortar operations would prefer in-store visits, they have come to recognize that catalog selling not only brings sales to the company, but can motivate off-site shoppers to make a trip to the store where more merchandise is available. The larger selection can in turn lead to larger purchases.

Retailers often find that a catalog that replicates the merchandising concept of the store may not be on target for the direct-mail customer. As a result, more and more of them are creating independent divisions to address the special needs of their direct-mail clientele.

Focus on . . .
Macy's by Mail

EVER SINCE MACY'S ENTERED THE RETAILING FRAY IN 1857, it has been one of America's most visible brick-and-mortar organizations. A large number of visitors to New York City make that shopping emporium a must on their sight-seeing list along with such attractions as the Empire State Building and the United Nations. Of course, those who live within close proximity to its Herald Square flagship or other units of the company that dot the United States go to Macy's whenever they need to replenish their wardrobes or buy merchandise for their homes. In Macy's management's idea of a perfect "retailing society," these regular store visits would be *the* way *all* customers filled their everyday shopping needs. Recognizing that catalog shopping has become a way of life even for those within reach of the stores, and a necessity for those without sufficient time to shop, Macy's entered the direct-mail business as a way to meet its clientele's needs.

Macy's by Mail was established in 1999 to better serve this market. As a member of the Federated family, it is able to tap that organizations database of 58 million customers, and another database of 31 million from another Federated direct-mail division, Fingerhut. Using both of these sources, Macy's by Mail has been able target a significant part of the American population. The catalog is mailed to 50 states, 29 of which do not have Macy's stores. This gives the company exposure far outside of its normal trading area.

As with any new venture, changes are constantly being made to better serve the direct-mail clientele. Initially the company thought that what was right for the stores would be right for the catalog. It would simply be a matter of selecting from the store's assortment to make up the catalog's offerings. They were wrong. Duplication of the store in a catalog didn't address the needs of the segment of the population that bought through direct mail. So, after just one year in business, the merchandise mix in the catalog changed. Research indicated that the merchandise in the catalog needed to fall in a lower price range to capture this market and that the high-profile collections of Ralph Lauren, Donna Karan, and Tommy Hilfiger, the store's mainstays, did not sell well to catalog shoppers. It also revealed that specific products were more important than specific brands. After its initial year in operation, Macy's by Mail reduced its nationally branded and private label merchandise from 70 percent to just 33 1/3 percent.

With its own buyers and product developers, Macy's by Mail is achieving an independence from the brick-and-mortar stores. Unlike Macy's brick-and-mortar operation, with its trendsetter image, Macy's by Mail moved more to the middle. Offering a selection that appeals to mainstream America in terms of style, attitude, and lifestyle has made the company's direct-mail approach more profitable. It has also determined that it can better serve this clientele by offering items not found in the stores.

With a 25 percent improvement in response rate since its launch, Macy's by Mail is on target for achieving its goals.

HOME-SHOPPING CHANNELS

At any hour of the day or night shoppers can tune into a variety of television "programs" through which they can buy merchandise comfortably and conveniently. **Home-shopping channels**, such as HSN, the television shopping network; QVC; and Shop-at-Home, fill TV screens with a wealth of merchandise ranging from jewelry and apparel to sporting goods and products for the home. It is an industry that continues to achieve record sales by catering to a segment of the population that responds quickly to "bargain" prices.

Today, home-shopping channels are more sophisticated than they once were. By and large, the items are developed primarily for the programs. They are produced with the audience in mind and marketed in a way that motivates quick purchases. One of the on-screen devices shopping channels use is an inset that changes rapidly to show the quantity of an item that are available, how many remain unsold, and how quickly they are selling. Shoppers wishing to avoid being closed out respond to this "selling" message.

Of significant importance to these shopping arenas are the celebrities who appear to sell their own products or those of other producers. With our society smitten by celebrities and

Item 508-561
Hunter 52"
Westbury
Remote Control
Ceiling Fan
Light / Brushed
Nickel Finish

Retail Value $159.90
HSN Price
$118.00
S&H $17.95
FLEXPAY 2 x $59.00

Chat Live W/ Lou at 8PM on HSN.com
1-800-284-3100   hsn.com
HSN

HSN, the television shopping network, allows people to shop without leaving their homes for products they see on television.

"sold" by their endorsements, this marketing approach works. Whenever a well-known individual makes an appearance sales grow.

Another reason for this medium's success is its interactive format. Callers may speak directly to anyone making the sales pitch—including a celebrity. Other shoppers listen in on the conversations and are often motivated to buy the items being discussed.

The home-shopping-channel format had already reached unprecedented heights, when these organizations began their own Web sites which feature the same products. With this innovation the medium has become even more important. Many shoppers feel more comfortable making Internet purchases, and regular viewers can avail themselves of the merchandise when they are away from the home since a TV is not necessary. Users may quickly log-on to their favorite home shopping Web site from work during the lunch break, for example.

Focus on . . .
HSN, the Television Shopping Network

SINCE ITS INCEPTION AS THE PIONEER OF HOME SHOPPING programming in 1977, HSN, the television shopping network has maintained its leadership position. First introduced to a small audience in 1977, the company's programming has achieved enormous success in the market it serves. Today, HSN is on the air 24 hours a day. It reaches more than 70 million households in the United States and countless others through affiliation with shopping channels in Germany and Japan. Recognizing the potential of the enormous Spanish-speaking market, it now produces Home Shopping en Español.

In an effort to direct its viewers to specific merchandise, the cable channel features a schedule of the times when each product classification will appear. In this way, potential customers may plan to watch during the period when the desired merchandise is sold.

The company's ability to sign celebrity "partners" who appear live to market their products has been extremely beneficial. Susan Lucci, the actress best known to television audiences as Erica Kane on *All My Children*, has become an HSN beauty *maven*. The company took Lucci on board in an exclusive arrangement to sell her own line of quality hair and fragrance products, which are not available elsewhere. Because of her star status, the line sells in record numbers.

HSN has also joined forces with *Marie Claire* to create Home Fashion Network (HFN), a channel that features affordable, fashionable clothing. *Marie Claire* is a fashion magazine, founded in 1937 by French industrialist Jean Prouvost, published in 26 countries and read by more than 15 million people worldwide. So well known is the publication that women everywhere have heralded its inclusion as part of HFN. Its first entry on the cable resulted in unprecedented sales for apparel: the entire collection sold out in a record two hours.

The HFN show regularly introduces new collections to its viewing audience. Some of these private-label collections were designed by top U.S. product developers; others were created with the assistance of the celebrities. Items are specifically tailored to fit the audience's needs in terms of fashion appropriateness and pricing.

HSN has also entered the electronic arena with its own Web site, which has been instrumental in bringing unparalleled sales figures to the company. The organization generated $1.2 billion in sales from television and the Internet in 1999, had more than 68 million sales and customer service telephone calls, and shipped more than 34 million packages.

A recent deal between HSN and Excite@Home, the Internet's fifth most visited Web site, makes HSN an even more important player. The new format allows cyberspace shoppers to view live broadcasts of HSN-TV and simultaneously interact with Excite.com via cable. Also available to users—a first for this type of retailing—is a host of interactive capabilities, such as online interaction with HSN hosts, participation in real-time chats, live product polls, contests, and the ability to shop online simultaneous with family and friends.

The unique shopping experience has no rivals in the home-shopping industry.

An Ethical Consideration

WHILE THE AUDIENCE FOR THE HOME-SHOPPING NETWORKS continues to grow, these ventures are often less than forthcoming with the multitude of viewers who regularly frequent their programs. Too often, the viewer is presented with merchandise that has a "regular retail price" that is higher than the price at which the home-shopping network offers it for sale. Where does this "regular" price merchandise exist? Can it be found in a store or on a Web site? Or is it just a marketing device to make the consumer believe he or she is getting a bargain? Since most of the merchandise is developed especially for the programs, the supposed regular price generally comes from the vendor's imagination and is not based on fact. Another unethical practice is sometimes used to sell "precious" jewelry. By flashing a word similar to *diamond* on the screen the merchant leads the shopper to believe that the stone shown is a diamond. As a result, an unsuspecting shopper may purchase a "gem" that is actually not a precious stone. This is deceptive selling.

TRENDS FOR THE NEW MILLENNIUM

- While the e-tailing phenomenon will continue, many of today's e-tailers will not be able to remain in business.
- More and more brick-and-mortar organizations are making heavy investments in e-tailing, with the likelihood that they will be more profitable than online-only companies.
- Multichannel retailing will become the most prevalent approach in the industry.
- Catalogs are becoming more and more specialized to appeal to narrower, better-defined market segments.

CHAPTER HIGHLIGHTS

- Before launching a new e-tail business, the e-tailer must determine the merchandise assortment to be offered for sale and design a Web site of the size and scope to fit its needs.
- The three categories of e-tailing ventures are Web site-only e-tailers, brick-and-click companies that have both stores and Web sites, and catalog companies that augment their sales with Web sites.
- In order to remain competitive, more and more retailers are using a multichannel approach.
- Many brick-and-mortar merchants expect their off-site operations to result in more customers' shopping at their stores.
- The present overabundance of retailers on the Internet will probably be reversed as many Web site operators are forced to abandon their businesses.
- Interactive e-tailing, which enables the customer to have questions directly answered, is becoming more and more popular.
- Internet fraud remains a problem in the industry and accounts for significant losses.

- Some early catalogers such as Sears and Montgomery Ward have ceased to publish their big books.
- Home-shopping channels, many of which have added Web sites, continue to increase their sales volumes.

IMPORTANT RETAILING TERMS

off-site purchasing
electronic retailing
infomercial
e-tail address
Web site-only retailers
me-too merchandise
Web site design
interactive shopping
e-commerce businesses
bricks and clicks
multichannel retailer
virtual catalog
virtual try-on
home-shopping channels

FOR REVIEW

1. Describe the role search engines play in e-tailing.
2. What is the first decision that must be made by the merchant that is planning a Web site?
3. Why have many e-tailers added interactive features to their Web sites?
4. With their catalog operations so successful, why have such giants as Spiegel and Fingerhut added Web sites to their businesses?
5. Define the term *bricks-and-clicks*.
6. Explain how multichannel retailing has helped merchants expand their sales volumes.

7. What is a virtual catalog?

8. What are virtual try-ons? How do they benefit consumers?

9. What can e-tailers do to reduce fraud on their Web sites?

10. Describe the difference between big books and the catalogs most retailers now use to reach their clienteles.

11. How extensive are the catalog divisions of most major department store organizations?

12. Describe how the Home Shopping Network has expanded its Internet operation.

AN INTERNET ACTIVITY

Explore three Web sites that are divisions of major retailers such as department store chains or organizations. Determine the following for each site:

- The depth and breadth of its offerings.
- The types of visuals used.
- What, if any, interactive devices are used.
- Whether it is possible to create a virtual mannequin.
- If the Web site is affiliated with any other Web site.

Arrange the information in a three-column table as follows:

	Store A[1]	Store B[1]	Store C[1]
Merchandise			
Visuals			
Interaction			
Virtual Mannequins			
Web site Affiliation			

[1]Insert name of store.

EXERCISES AND PROJECTS

1. Compare the merchandise assortments and formats of five catalogs mailed to your home. Focus on the following:

   - The breadth and depth of the offerings.

- The quality of the illustrations.
- The clarity of the order form.
- Any tie-ins with other retailing channels such as Web sites.
- Any warranties.

Write summaries of your findings. Each summary should be typed, double space, on a separate sheet of paper.

2. Compare the operations of two home-shopping channels. Show your findings on a table as follows:

	Channel A[1]	Channel B[1]
Product Mix		
Shopper Interaction		
Celebrity Presence		

[1]Insert name of home-shopping channel.

THE CASE OF A CATALOGER'S POTENTIAL FOR EXPANSION

The last 50 years has seen significant growth in the catalog operation of Dreams for the Home, Inc. When it first began operation, the merchandise mix was a simple assortment of home accessories, such as lamps, mirrors, framed prints, and throw pillows. As their years in business brought a continuous increase in business and customer requests for new items, the company's product assortment increased. New merchandise classifications, such as table linens and bedding, were added, bringing even greater sales to Dreams for the Home. Today, in addition to these product categories, some decorator furnishings, such as wine racks, accent tables, ready-made draperies, statuary, and other items, have been added to the collection.

Last year the company was less successful than in the past. For the first time, sales leveled off. While this might be a fluke, management believes it might be time to consider multichannel retailing. Their thoughts have centered on entering the Internet with a Web site devoted to all of the company's catalog offerings, starting a brick-

and-mortar operation, or using a combination of all three channels to reach its market. Session after session has been concluded without any definitive decision about the future direction for Dreams for the Home.

Questions

1. Should the company rest on its laurels and continue to sell exclusively by catalog?

2. What are pros and cons of opening a brick-and-mortar stores?

3. Is the Internet a viable option for the company?

CHAPTER 4
Identification, Analysis, and Research of Consumer Groups

After you have completed this chapter, you should be able to discuss:

- ▸ The importance of consumer research and analysis for today's retail organizations.
- ▸ How the study of demographics helps retailers better understand the needs of the consumer.
- ▸ How the characteristics of geographic region affect inventory decisions.
- ▸ Why it is necessary for retailers to study various age classifications and how these groups make purchases.
- ▸ How lifestyles affect the shopping requirements of consumers.
- ▸ How different social classes approach their purchases.
- ▸ The importance of understanding the family life cycle to preparing merchandise assortments.
- ▸ The difference between rational and emotional buying motives.
- ▸ The importance of the patronage motive to retailers.
- ▸ The manner in which Maslow's Hierarchy of Needs affects consumer spending.
- ▸ The different approaches retailers take to consumer research.

Whenever a shopper walks into a store, logs on to a Web site, or peruses the pages of a catalog in search of something he or she needs, a sale seems to be within easy reach. If, however, the individual can't find what he or she is looking for, it is likely that the merchant didn't work hard enough when planning the available assortment. How many times have consumers who were eager to buy come away from in-store or off-site venues disappointed? Is it merely the mood of the shopper that prevents purchasing, or is it the retailer's poor planning that results in a lost sale? Or, is it the fault of the manufacturers that developed products without regard to consumer preferences that led the retailer to stock merchandise that never really had a chance to sell?

The educated merchant who toils in today's highly competitive retail arena must carefully investigate the forces that motivate consumers' buying behavior. Taking chances without understanding the real needs of potential customers often leads to losses rather than profits. A walk through any store filled with markdown racks immediately signals that the merchant failed to identify the likes and dislikes of the clientele. Of course, there is no such thing as perfect planning. Retailers, no matter how carefully they have planned, will always be left with broken sizes, colors that didn't catch the shopper's fancy, or a few items that simply didn't catch fire. While some of this is to be expected, it should not be a dominant part of the retailer's selling experience. In order to maximize profits, every merchant, no matter what product classification is being offered, must pay strict attention to his or her consumer market. Guesswork must be eliminated and replaced with educated decision making. The age old axiom that the customer is king (or queen for that matter) still applies today. By understanding the concepts of consumer behavior, and more specifically, the patterns of motivation and habits, a retailer is likely to address customer needs and thereby maximize profits.

The merchant has at hand a variety of different tools to safeguard against unfortunate merchandising errors. These tools include a host of traditional, fundamental concepts concerning consumer motivation and behavior, such as demographic analysis, Maslow's Hierarchy of Needs, motive assessments—which are both rational and emotional—class structures, and lifestyle categories. Knowing the details of each, and properly applying them to the company's specific situation, will more than likely prove to be a fruitful experience.

ASSESSMENT OF CONSUMER GROUPS

Every educated retailer understands that it is virtually impossible to satisfy the needs of everyone in his or her trading area. No matter how attractive the merchandise might be, how value-oriented the product mix is or how complete the assortment might be, it is simply a matter of fact that not everyone will be motivated to buy in one store, through one catalog, or on one Web site. Different age groups, for example, will respond differently to a company's product mix, as will people with different lifestyles. Reality teaches us that retailers must appeal to specific segments or groups in order to achieve success.

> **The Stein Mart Story**
> Maintaining Market Share in the Competitive Retail Arena:
> Investigating Consumer Needs

UNLIKE MANY OF TODAY'S RETAILERS WHO FOCUS ON younger generations, Stein Mart targets primarily females aged 35 to 60. Even in the men's wear departments, it is women who make the majority of the purchases for their significant others. Stein Mart's aim is to respond to the aging baby boomer. It believes that this is the market with money to spend but that these customers want value for their dollar. As an off-price player with marquee labels such as Ralph Lauren, Claiborne, Calvin Klein, and others, Stein Mart is the store with a great deal of potential in this area.

Stein Mart keeps tabs on its customers through a customer loyalty program that spells out individual characteristics. From this information, shopper profiles can continuously be updated. When the customer signs up at the register for the loyalty program, the UPC-code on the items she has bought is used to analyze her preferences and project future purchases.

This in-house data has revealed that less is being spent on juniors and more merchandise is needed for special sizes. In response, Stein Mart has started to minimize its smaller size offerings and expanded its larger sizes. Even in the miss departments, where others stores end assortments at size 12, Stein Mart has found that a good assortment of 12 through 16 is necessary to satisfy its customers' needs.

Like most other retailers, Stein Mart relies on census figures and other surveys to indicate trends that are forthcoming in the industry.

• •

Demographics

Briefly defined, **demographics** are the study of various characteristics of the population such as size, geographic concentration, age, occupation, education, lifestyle categories, and income. Retailers can learn about their consumer market by carefully studying the demographic elements. Although generalizations about the typical customer in the trading area cannot be assumed to apply to each individual shopper, demographic information helps retailers predict the kinds of merchandise that will sell well within their market. By and large, most brick-and-mortar organizations need not explore the population in its entirety unless they are the giants in the industry, like Wal-Mart and Sears, with what seems to be boundless trading areas. Catalogers and e-tailers also have the potential to sell just about anywhere. With the world potentially their trading area, they should know the specifics of the makeup of the entire population. Most stores, however, need to concentrate only on the trading areas they serve.

Sales potential is based upon the size of the population served by the business. In addition to studying current population figures, it is imperative to determine popluation trends, that is, whether the numbers are growing or declining. In this way, merchandise plans for the future will more accurately address the needs of the retailer's changing consumer base.

Retailers can obtain a wealth of figures from the federal government, trade associations, such as the **National Retail Federation**, or, if funds are available, from any one of the many marketing research firms in the United States.

Geographic Location and Climate

Where people live is also an important factor in determining what they will buy. This is particularly essential in assessing the specific apparel needs for the family. In the southern tier of the United States, consumers have greater year round needs for swimwear and other warm weather clothing based on that part of the country's climate. If the company has the majority of units in such a region, these purchasing needs are easy to assess. If, however, the retailer is a brick-and-mortar one whose outlets stretch into numerous geographic regions, more of an in-depth study must be done. Gap, for example, with stores located from coast to coast and abroad, must tailor its merchandise mix according to the regions in which the stores are located. While jeans are a principal product for every unit in the chain at all times, winter-weight outerwear would be required inventory for the northern-based stores, while lighter outerwear would be more suitable for stores in warmer climates.

Population Concentration

Consumers who live in densely populated cities have different needs from those in suburban areas, who, in turn, seek different merchandise from rural populations. Even supermarket retailers must carefully address consumer needs based upon population density. Stores in major metropolitan areas, for example, tend to have a greater affinity for gourmet foods, while stores in outlying regions require greater emphasis on staples. City dwellers, who typically live closer to their favorite supermarket than do suburbanites or rural populations, often make smaller, more frequent purchases rather than stock up on a weekly grocery shopping trip.

In the case of the off-site ventures, geographic concentration is generally widespread. Of course, in cases where the products are oriented to more selective areas such as lawn and garden products, the efforts generally focus on suburban regions. If direct-mail pieces, for example, were targeted to just about any region, those reaching inner city dwellers would bring virtually no sales.

Each merchant must study different regions and determine which ones have the greatest sales potential. By using only today's figures on geographic concentrations, the retailer will not have sufficient information for future merchandise planning. It is imperative that projection analysis be utilized for future years to see if the immediate geographical findings are heading for change.

Age Classifications

The merchandise needs of one age group are by no means identical to that of the others. While food is a constant in every household, it is obvious that there are numerous differences in the requirements of each group. Cereal for example, is generally a staple in all age categories, but the type preferred by each one varies considerably. The sugar varieties are naturally targeted to children, while the more health-oriented, are directed to more mature audiences.

Apparel is another merchandise classification that requires analysis by age group. While both teenage girls and their mothers wear skirts, the styles and hemlines worn by each group differ. The younger set is usually more taken with the trendy silhouettes. If the fashions of the time indicate one trend, this group is ready to buy. On the other hand, the moms generally take a more middle-of-the-road approach.

In these and most other product groupings, age plays a major role in consumer acceptance. It is therefore necessary to study these age classifications to make the proper merchandise decisions.

Age groups are segmented in a variety of ways. Some classify the groups with the use of such designations as **baby boomers** (born between 1945 and 1959), **generation X** and **generation Y** (ages 18–34 at the turn of the century) to study their differences. The United States Department of Commerce uses a more traditional breakdown segmenting the groups into children, teenagers, young adults, young middle-aged, older middle-aged, and elderly. It should be noted that each methodology offers a good deal of information for the retailer. The study of each one will provide research that is sometimes overlapping but it still benefits decision making.

Information on these classifications is regularly updated by the Department of Commerce and is easy to obtain from the federal government.

CHILDREN

Those from birth to age 13 comprise the children category. Knowing whether the trading area contains large numbers of families with children is important to retailers in establishing their overall merchandising policy. Although the needs are different for infants and pre-teens, there is a great deal of similarity in the general needs of each group. If more detailed data is needed to make better merchandise judgments, it might be appropriate to confer with trade organizations, such as the National Retail Federation, or to employ the services of a market research firm.

In general, the younger members of the group have neither buying nor decision-making power when it

This Pottery Barn Kids catalog underscores the importance of children as consumers, leading companies like Pottery Barn to focus on them.

comes to purchasing. However, there is a tendency for the children to influence the purchases that are being made for them.

Specific foods such as the aforementioned sweetened cereals, frozen pizza, and a host of soft drinks are part of the likes of the young. Since television targets the young with a wealth of advertising, it is imperative that the food retailer stock these products in great breadth and depth.

Clothing is no longer relegated to the basics. Children are influenced by what they see on television and in the preteen magazines. The styles are more fashion-oriented and the colors no longer remain within the staple range.

Stores like Kids "R" Us, GapKids, and Limited Too have focused on this age group. From the expansion of these companies, it is evident that the children's market is constantly growing.

TEENAGERS

Retailers who specialize in trendy clothing regularly target their wares to the teenage market, the 13- to 19-year-olds. No other age classification presents quite the same interest in this merchandise. Avid followers of the trends depicted in publications such as *Seventeen* magazine, teenagers purchase just about anything that is new. The price points they are attracted to are at the lower end of the scale, enabling them to buy more items, and they prefer to buy at specialty stores such as Wet Seal.

A large portion of this age group also makes shopping treks to stores like Gap, American Eagle, and Old Navy for clothing. Unlike the trendy merchants, these retailers provide the teenager with a wealth of jeans, T-shirts, sweats, khakis, and other items that are central to their wardrobes.

In addition to being great consumers of apparel, teenagers are the largest purchasers of compact discs. As loyal fans of the ever-growing number of rock groups around the world, they buy just about any recordings that these musicians offer. A visit to stores like Tower Records, Best Buy, and Borders immediately reveals that the vast majority of the CD inventory is aimed at the teenage market.

With more and more teenagers working after school, their purchasing power continues to increase.

YOUNG ADULTS

The vast majority of those in the 20-to 34-year-old age group are interested in fashion merchandise. They are either finishing college and heading for the work world or are already employed in a full-time career. Their apparel needs are divided into three categories: career clothing, special occasion apparel, and leisure attire. With incomes relatively high, this group is able to afford more expensive merchandise than those in the same age group years ago.

The favorite places to shop for apparel and accessories are Banana Republic, Gap, Ann Taylor, J. Crew, and The Limited.

Home furnishings have also become extremely important to this age group. Whether they are unmarried and live alone, share with other singles, or are married, they have significant home furnishing needs. The places where they shop are unlike the places where people in past generations shopped for these needs. Instead of the traditional stores that their parents frequented, this group heads for more contemporary merchants, such as Crate & Barrel, IKEA, Pottery Barn, Pier 1 Imports, and Restoration Hardware. In addition to the enormous selections available at these stores, delivery is generally immediate. People in this age group often want their purchasers right away and don't want to wait months for delivery. By responding to these needs, the present-day home furnishings retailers have replaced many of the old-timers like W.J. Sloane.

Young adults are the primary market for stores such as J. Crew because of their normally high incomes and need for a variety of clothing types.

 Focus on . . .
Pottery Barn

ONE OF THE MAJOR SUCCESSES IN THE HOME FURNISHINGS' ARENA is Pottery Barn. It was established as a single unit store in lower Manhattan in 1949. Its goal was to offer home furnishings that were exceptional in comfort, style, and quality at affordable prices. Unlike other home furnishing retailers, who bought their inventories from numerous vendors, Pottery Barn's approach was to sell merchandise that was designed exclusively for its needs by an in-house creative team. Its formula for success was at once embraced by a large number of New Yorkers seeking to find more exciting products for their homes that were generally unavailable at the traditional retailers.

After success with its first unit, the company continued to expand. Not only did the expansion focus on adding stores from coast to coast, but it also focused on expanding the product offerings. Originally concentrating on small items such as picture frames, glassware, dinnerware, decorative accessories, and gift items, the merchandise mix now incorporates all items necessary to furnish a home.

On the selling floor, through catalogs, and on its Web site, Pottery Barn features a whole host of furniture for every room in the house. These items are accessorized with lamps, rugs, wall hangings, artwork, candles, paper flowers, and all of the products that were introduced in the store's original concept.

For those with limited time to shop, the company's Web site exquisitely presents decorated rooms that are replete with everything needed to make them a comfortable setting. The room designs change with each season. Not only is an overview of a room featured, but the shopper can also zero in on an item for closer inspection with a mere click of the mouse. The Web site is also arranged in a manner that allows the Pottery Barn catalog shopper to get a closer look at the items featured in the book.

Pottery Barn is a company that has achieved success by tailoring its products to the needs of an ever growing segment of the home furnishings market.

. . . .

Young adults are also very important to physical fitness apparel and outdoor retailers. Workout clothing and running shoes, for example, rank among this group's top purchasing needs. Stores like Sports Authority and catalogs like L.L.Bean cater to this group.

Finally, members of this group are also major purchasers of computer products, frequenting such stores as Office Depot, CompUSA, Best Buy, and Staples.

YOUNG MIDDLE-AGED

The 35–49 age group represents a great deal of spending power America. Those with careers in such areas as investment banking, computer engineering, e-commerce, law, and

medicine have paid off their college loans and are ready to enjoy the rewards of their labors. They are now able to purchase a host of expensive products. Luxury automobiles, high fashion apparel, precious jewelry, original art, and exotic travel are just a few of the areas this group indulges in.

Stores like Saks Fifth Avenue, Neiman Marcus, Bloomingdale's, and a host of others are regular haunts for this group. With many of them having limited time to shop, they have become one of the major segments of the e-tail community. Shopping on line is second nature to many in this age classification.

The Polo Ralph Lauren stores are regular haunts for young middle-aged shoppers.

This group is also likely to dine in the most fashionable restaurants. This has resulted in an enormous increase in upscale dining establishments.

OLDER MIDDLE-AGED

Like their counterparts in the previous age segment, they too are able to afford the luxuries of life. Many have reached the pinnacle of success and continue to enjoy their accomplishments by making extravagant purchases. Of course, a large number in this group are retired and armed with significant sums of money.

Those with significant affluence patronize the luxury emporiums of the world. Not only are American merchants beneficiaries of their wealth, but so also are many global merchants. Extensive travel to foreign shores brings them within reach of the British, French, and Italian designers. They too frequent the posh dining establishments and treat themselves to everything and anything they want. The explosion of upscale retailing is evident in many of America's fashionable shopping areas. New York City, for example, has witnessed the opening of numerous world famous designer boutiques to cater to the city's affluent residents as well as to tourists.

Of course, not everyone in this age classification is privileged. Many are middle income wage earners and retirees who spend more cautiously. Value shopping is clearly what motivates many in this group. The off-price retailers such as Marshalls, T.J. Maxx, Syms, and Stein Mart all cater to this class. Especially for those on restricted budgets, these stores offer great values on high profile manufacturer goods and marquee labels. Discounters such as Target, Wal-Mart, and Kmart are regular stops on their buying jaunts. This is also the age classification that regularly visits clearance centers across the country to make purchases.

ELDERLY

Most in this age group are retirees. The "gray heads," as they are known, spend rather cautiously. Many relocate into retirement communities. Fashion is not generally a must for them. They seek more functional purchases. They spend a great deal on health products, making them the major markets for companies like

World famous boutiques like Hermès have opened units in fashionable shopping areas to cater to affluent older middle-aged clientele.

Walgreen's and CVS. Typically, the elderly are cautious shoppers, buying only what they deem to be the necessities of life. Even those with more wealth than they ever imagined tend to become careful spenders. As a group, the elderly are considered to be difficult shoppers.

This group dines out a lot, but value restaurants are their usual destinations. Travel is prevalent in this age group, but again, value is important.

Occupations

A very important part of today's purchasing decisions involves the consumers' occupations and where they spend their time carrying them out. It is obvious that the investment banking community and those that make up the various trades have different needs, especially when clothing needs are considered. Those retailers who target the former group must concentrate on suits and accessories such as business shirts, ties, and dress shoes.

In today's work environment, changes in appropriate dress have caused many retailers to refocus their inventories. **Casual Friday**, when the business suit is left home, has in many firms spilled over into other days of the week. The emphasis on proper dress, even in the legal profession, has given way to more relaxed business casual clothing all week. Merchants who cater to this group must adjust the inventory levels of more formal attire and begin to stock sports coats, contrasting trousers, open collared shirts, and slip-ons to serve the needs of male clientele and pantsuits and casual dresses for working women in order to maximize sales.

Many companies permit employees to "dress down" at least once a week. As this employee goes about her normal job, she is also functioning as a model for the casual apparel that her employer sells.

Another phenomenon that has affected retailers in terms of career clothing needs has been the continuous increase of those working at home. Many millions of consumers spend their days at computers in home offices rather than in traditional workplaces. Jeans and T-shirts and even sleepwear have become standard dress for these people since they need not interface with others. Because of this ever growing trend of at-home employment, many restaurants must readdress their markets. Office furniture suppliers are finding a greater need for scaled-down desks and chairs to fit the home offices and many have built bigger businesses because of this new business environment. An examination of retailers such as Staples and Office Depot reveal a significant expansion of the home office departments.

Even in major department stores, the last bastions of proper dress in retailing, the dress code has changed. Selling floor personnel were once relegated to wearing basic colors and traditional apparel. Now, just about anything goes as long as it epitomizes good taste.

Merchants must continually reevaluate their consumer markets based on the changing needs of their occupations. Inventories must then be adjusted to satisfy those needs.

Lifestyle Profiles

A great deal of research has been undertaken to examine people's attitudes and lifestyles and how these affect their purchases. While studies that categorize attitudes and lifestyles regularly surface, none have had as great an impact on retailing as the VALS™ study.

VALS, SRI Consulting Business Intelligence's psychographic segmentation system, has become the most widely used segmentation system employed by all segments of the marketing community. It is regularly updated through surveys that investigate consumer attitudes and motivations. Specifically, the use of VALS assists retailers in:

- Identifying their target markets
- Uncovering what the target group buys and does in their lives
- Locating the areas in which the largest segments of the target market lives
- Identifying the best ways in which to communicate with the target groups
- Gaining insight into why the target group acts the way it does

The concept categorizes consumers into eight specific profiles. They are *Actualizers, Fulfilleds, Achievers, Experiencers, Believers, Strivers, Makers,* and *Strugglers.* Each classification represents a different set of interests, motivations, and habits for those in the group. For example, the Achievers collectively are attracted to premium products, such as innovative electronics, purchase a variety of self-help publications, and are avid readers of business periodicals. Strivers are image focused, spend a great deal on clothing and personal care products, carry a large credit card balance and are avid television watchers. Strugglers, or those with the least amount of financial resources, are loyal brand shoppers, readers of the scandal tabloids, and clip coupons for purchases.

Through the understanding of these psychographic categories and by singling out those that relate to their client base and potential markets, the retailer is better able to determine such factors as location expansion, merchandise assortments, price points, advertising formats, and media consideration.

A greater detailing of the VALS concept is available on the Web at www.sric-bi.com/VALS, and in the following diagram.

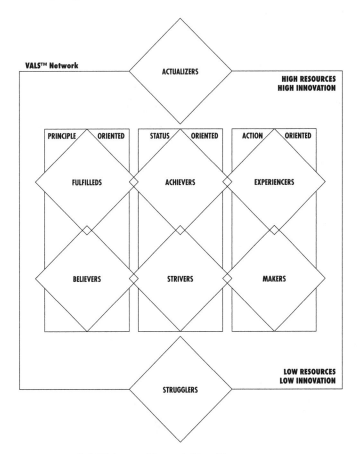

American consumers generally fall into one of these eight profiles.

Income

Although many of the preceding classifications indicate personal consumer preferences based upon such characteristics as lifestyle, age, and occupation, it is an individual's income that ultimately plays the most significant part in whether or not a purchase can be made.

While one might like to purchase a Mercedes Benz, wealth plays an important role regarding the purchase. Similarly, individuals often are motivated by the fashion advertisements in *Elle* magazine. But, while the styles are exciting, many must opt for lower-costing apparel that would fit their budgets. Even when food is the product in question, income may play an important role. For example, with so many women out in the workforce, there is less time for food preparation. A good alternative would be to buy freshly prepared dinners. Of course, many of these items are pricey, and therefore limited to those with greater resources. The frozen dinner alternative might be the answer for those with smaller disposable incomes. Brochures that stimulate thinking of vacationing in exotic, far away shores make many consumers consider taking the plunge. Of course, once costs are examined, it is the affluent that actually take the trip.

Education

Whatever a person's income, his or her level of education may also make a difference in purchasing decisions. The more formally educated one is, the more likely it is that he or she will come to recognize the need for specific products. For example, advanced degrees provide entry into such fields as law and investment banking. This individual is required to dress a certain way. Politicians and advertising executives, for example, often patronize stores like Brooks Brothers for their clothing.

Additionally, the educated market more likely purchases a variety of books. With so many in this class at the upper levels of employment, they find their time too limited to visit bookstores. Instead, the online approach is utilized. Such Web sites as Amazon.com and BarnesandNoble.com are the beneficiaries of the educated market.

With more and more students graduating from college, and the number going on to graduate and professional schools increasing, the need for retailers to appeal to these groups continues to increase.

Social Class

All over the world, the various nations' populations are divided into separate **social classes**. The distinctions, as we know them in the United States, are based upon such factors as income, goals, education, attitudes, and sometimes birthright. Being born into significant wealth and ongoing social standing that has passed from generation to generation, for example, immediately places the offspring in the upper-upper class.

By studying each of the traditional groups that make up class structure, the retailer is able to get a better look at the specific goods and services generally required by them. He or she can then set up a merchandising and management plan that will have the potential for success.

The American class structure is made up of the upper, middle, and lower classes. Each of these three classifications can be further divided into two subcategories.

Upper Class

This group represents the wealthiest in America. It accounts for approximately 3 percent of the population, and tends to be wealthier today than at any other time in history. With the evolution of new technology toward the end of the twentieth century, more citizens have reached billionaire status. Microsoft's Bill Gates, for example, with an estimated wealth of $60 billion, rose from the lower-upper class to achieve this status.

UPPER-UPPER CLASS

This segment of the upper class accounts for about 1 percent of the population. In order to be counted as a member of this group, one's wealth must be inherited. They are the socially elite families in American society. Purchasing is often understated. There is an emphasis on quality and cost is never a factor. They live in the most affluent enclaves, such as on Park Avenue in New York City, South Hampton, New York, and Palm Beach, Florida. Travel is to exotic global destinations, where they often have their own vacation homes. Education is taken at the elite schools at home and abroad. Couture labels, fabulous jewelry, and anything they desire is there for the taking. They are members of country clubs that are restricted to families with considerable prestigious backgrounds.

One retailer favored by the upper-upper class is Tiffany & Co.

LOWER-UPPER CLASS

While they do not have the credentials of the upper-upper class, such as family history, they are often wealthier. They are the **nouveau riche** of our society, having come upon their fortunes through hard work. Rock stars, investment bankers, and business tycoons are part of their group. Their purchases are often extravagant, and rarely understated. They are the buyers of couture clothing, luxury automobiles, and lavish travel. Many in this class reveal their successes by indulging themselves in purchases that are obvious to the world. They belong to the wealthiest country clubs, but not those reserved for the upper-upper class families. They have homes in many prestigious locales such as East Hampton, New York and Beverly Hills, California. They frequent retailers like Bergdorf Goodman and Saks Fifth

Avenue, the couture houses abroad, and Harry Winston for their jewels. Travel is taken in places not frequented by the masses, where they often own their own vacation villas. They are considered to be **conspicuous spenders**.

Middle Class

Grouped together, these two subclasses account for approximately 42 percent of the population. Although they comprise a single classification, the two segments are distinctively different in terms of their shopping needs.

UPPER-MIDDLE CLASS

They are considered by many retailers to be the best consumer market in the country. They are concerned with education and often send their children to private schools. They are always trying to gain upward mobility to the lower-upper class. While their financial resources are not unlimited, they do tend to spend a great deal on expensive, tasteful merchandise. They are the purchasers of luxury cars, designer clothing—albeit not the couture variety—and a host of services. Designer labels such as DKNY, Ralph Lauren, and Calvin Klein are among their favorites, with shopping undertaken at major department stores like Bloomingdale's. The are considered to be excellent shoppers and often turn to the closeout centers of Neiman Marcus and Saks Fifth Avenue to buy the headline labels at a fraction of the original costs. They are members of country clubs, travel extensively, and spend considerable leisure time on the golf course.

LOWER-MIDDLE CLASS

Distinctly different from those at the upper spectrum of this group, the lower middle has a more modest income and is more cautious about spending. They purchase automobiles that provide them with economy and durability, have a strong sense of value, and are the frequent purchasers at stores like Target, Wal-Mart, and Kmart. Off-price centers are also their favorite destinations because they can get more for their dollar. They are the do-it-yourself crowd and flock regularly to stores like Home Depot for their household needs. While they do travel somewhat, the mode is usually by car to more localized areas. They are loyal sports enthusiasts and attend the games of their favorite teams.

The lower-middle class frequents value merchants such as Wal-Mart and Sam's.

Lower Class

At the time of this writing, the economy has given many households greater income than ever before; however, the majority is still in the lower class category. With approximately 55 percent of the population, they account for more than one-half of the consumers in the United States.

UPPER-LOWER CLASS

Without question, price is the most important consideration for this group. Whether it is apparel, home furnishings, food, or anything else, price is first and foremost. They regularly scout the discount outlets and off-price centers for bargains, and most often choose the major chains such as Wal-Mart, Target, and Kmart in which to shop. The wholesale clubs such as Sam's, Costco, and BJ's are other destinations they are likely to patronize for a major portion of their everyday needs. Instead of utilizing the Internet and catalogs as alternatives to the brick-and-mortar retailers, many turn to cable television. They are in fact the targeted market for the home shopping channels.

LOWER-LOWER CLASS

Shopping needs other than those necessary for survival are unimportant to this group. They will buy clothing only as needed, and then it must be serviceable items. Secondhand and thrift shops are the arenas for many of their purchases.

An Ethical Consideration

GIVEN THE FACT THAT THOSE WHO MAKE UP THE LOWER-LOWER CLASS of the population are not privy to the merchandise that people in other classes are, there is still a need for them to be able to satisfy their needs with merchandise that is fairly marked. Often times, the very same items available in their communities sell for less elsewhere. In particular, grocery items sell for more than in other locations. This practice occurs because many in the lower-lower class do not have access to cars and cannot take costly public transportation to bring them into more competitive shopping arenas where the prices are lower.

Merchants who exploit this segment of the population are doing so at the expense of those incapable of finding their goods elsewhere. Even well-known supermarkets that deal in zone pricing are often culprits in this practice.

Family Life Cycle

Another type of methodology that retailers use in assessing their markets is the **family life cycle**. The concept is based upon the premise that families can be grouped according to the age and family status of the heads of households. Specifically, it addresses the composition of families and how the specific family units affect such purchases as clothing, accessories, home furnishings, food, automobiles, pharmaceuticals, housing, physical fitness equipment, travel, and recreation.

The classifications within the family life cycle have changed throughout the years. Unlike early in the 20th century, when households were more traditionally comprised, today's categories feature unconventional segments.

Childless Singles under Age 45

This group represents an excellent market for many retailers. Collectively, they are a group that has a great deal of discretionary income since they support only themselves. After the rent and utilities have been paid for, the remainder of purchasing generally concentrates on clothing, cosmetics, physical fitness products and memberships, recreation, entertainment, dining in restaurants, automobiles, and travel. Those at the upper end of the income scale are generally fashion conscious and often choose marquee designers such as Ralph Lauren, Joseph Abboud, Calvin Klein, Donna Karan, and the wealth of new fashion creators that grace the pages of *Women's Wear Daily* and *DNR*. They generally take their meals in better restaurants, join upscale fitness centers, purchase the latest cosmetics by cosmetologists such as Bobbi Brown, and travel to the famous clubs around the world that cater to singles. Value and bargain shopping is not their preoccupation, but instead choose brick-and-mortar merchants or convenient off-site retailers. In terms of automobiles, many fancy BMW's, other foreign cars, and a host of SUVs.

Of course, not everyone in this group is enjoying the financial resources that enable "frivolous" spending. While they need only to concern themselves with their own needs, his or her approach to shopping is more cautious. They head for Banana Republic and Gap as well as stores like Ann Taylor. They patronize department stores, as well as specialty stores, and frequent less expensive restaurants. Automobiles might more likely be American made sports cars.

Childless Singles 45 and Over

This has become a very large segment of the population with more and more individuals opting to remain single. Many maintain their own premises, while others participate in shared households, a classification known as **multiple-member/shared households**.

Much like their counterparts who are under age 45, they too live exciting lifestyles without the responsibility of dependents. Many in this group are employed in the new technology fields, are self-employed, and are well represented in the legal, investment banking, and medical professions. They spend in a manner that is similar to those in the preceding group and frequent many of the same retail institutions. Of course, as they age, their purchases tend to become more conservative. They are the drivers of the Mercedes Benz automobiles. They take numerous vacations and generally spend money on whatever pleases them. Those with less prosperity are still the targets of many merchants because their purchases are only for themselves.

Single Parents

The significant increase in the divorce rate in the United States and the number of unmarried mothers have made this group one that is constantly growing. Members of this group have the task of supporting themselves and children who may or may not live with them. They are often the ones who have considerable stress in making their incomes last beyond the next paycheck. Women, in particular, find their discretionary purchasing power eroding. Typically earning less than their male counterparts and burdened with the rearing of children without the benefit of a mate, they find making ends meet a difficult task. Thus, they are the value shoppers who frequent the discounters such as Wal-Mart and Target, and the off-price merchants such as T.J. Maxx, Burlington Coat Factory, and Marshalls. They generally eat at home and only dine out for special occasions. They purchase modestly priced cars and take limited, less costly vacations. A small segment of the single mother group has better incomes and can therefore spend without as much caution.

Single fathers have similar problems. Unless they are in the high-income group, they are saddled with child support payments and sometimes spousal support, both of which render them unlikely to spend on anything but essentials.

Multiple-Member/Shared Households

This is a fast-growing stage in the family life cycle. With the cost of living spiraling upward, more and more people are choosing to live with others with whom there is no marital or family connection. In the big cities like New York, Chicago, and San Francisco, where apartment rentals are soaring, several people sharing a single residence has become commonplace. With the exception of those with incomes above the average range, this has become the new household.

This is a diverse group that includes singles who live together, eventually planning marriage; members of same-sex relationships, members of the opposite sex without any amorous connections; and two or more sets of single parents whose children reside with them. They are of no particular age group.

Given the diversity of those in this classification, their purchasing characteristics vary considerably. Singles who live together with the intention of marrying, for example, often have considerable disposable income because of their shared expenses for housing. The arrangement leaves plenty of cash for necessities as well as luxury items. Even more buying potential is at the hands of members of long-term same-sex relationships. They have dual incomes and typically have no plans for child rearing, a situation that can eventually cost a great deal. Those in this arrangement often buy cars like the BMW Z3, wear the best clothing from stores like Barney's, take lavish vacations, and in general, are the dream customers for upscale merchants. Of course, spending by the two single-parent families that share common living facilities is usually restricted, making them less attractive to merchants.

Single-Earner Couples with Children

This classification has shown the most radical drop in recent years. Except for those with young children of preschool age, most couples have dual incomes. Even those with young children are opting for day care so that the family income can be maximized. Unless the single earner has a professional career or is in some high paying arena such as investment banking or new technologies, the income generated doesn't allow for many luxuries. Not only must they provide for themselves, they must address the needs of their offspring.

Those with limited budgets choose their purchases carefully and patronize the retailers that offer value. Discount outlets, off-price stores, and warehouse clubs are main venues for much of their needs. Once the children are of school age, the situation tends to change with the marital partner returning to work.

For the smaller number of affluent single earner families, their disposable incomes enable them to buy from traditional retailers where price doesn't play a major role.

Dual-Earner Married Couples with Children

Apparel retailers such as Eddie Bauer are expanding into home products to appeal to young families.

Depending on the ages of the children, these couples have different buying needs and spend their dollars in many different ways. Those with children at home have significant expenses. Some choose preschool programs for their children while some elect for private schooling once the offspring reaches the kindergarten age. The vast majority, of course, utilizes public education.

By comparison with the preceding classification, this group is better off financially and is far more appealing to retailers. With a dual income and one household they are generally able to satisfy their needs. The more affluent may shop at Banana Republic and Gap, while their lower-income counterparts may have to settle for Old Navy.

Two cars are typical for many of these families. They eat out more than those families that preceded them in earlier generations, spend money on family vacations, and often buy on the Internet and from catalogs since their days are filled.

Many in this group are funding their children's college education or are looking to do so in the future. In either case, with the escalating costs of higher education, these families are often termed *cash poor*. College tuition takes a big bite out of their incomes, leaving them less to spend on items other than the basics.

Childless Married Couples

The age groupings in this category range from the young to the elderly. Typically, these couples are better off than those with children since they generally have two incomes and have little responsibility other than themselves. In every age grouping, clothing expenditures, food requirements, automobile choices, entertainment preferences, travel, and home furnishings are of little consequence, albeit tastes will undoubtedly differ. They are usually the purchasers of luxury products and shop at traditional retailers.

Travel is particularly extensive for the older members of this group. A look at the numerous extended cruise itineraries, for example, indicates that there is a need for this type of venture. These couples have the financial capacity and, since they are often retired, the time to enjoy themselves.

Automobiles for most in this group are in the luxury class with the younger consumers generally choosing foreign makes, such as Audi and BMW. Their older counterparts elect full-sized American cars, such as Cadillac and Lincoln.

Empty Nesters

As couples age and their children grow up and move out, many couples enjoy the **empty nester** status. Expenses for this group are minimized and purchasing needs maximized. They often choose to purchase products and services that they couldn't afford in years past. Some families continue to earn dual incomes, making them even more likely to be free spenders, and others are single income families, with one spouse retiring.

As the group ages its needs begin to change. Often smaller residences are chosen, country clubs are joined, and travel becomes more extensive. They are still in need of clothing, except that their choices might be of a more conservative nature.

With the size of this market constantly growing, more and more vendors are coming to recognize them as a viable segment and are producing goods specifically to meet their needs. Prescription medication is not their only need. There is also a host of goods and services that are still relevant to their lives. Many, for example, are still willing and able to buy fashionable merchandise, except that the size requirements may have changed. Liz Claiborne, a collection that features a wealth of different styles aimed at middle-aged women, also produces a larger-sized line for the more mature female. By concentrating on this market, they are able to satisfy their loyal customers who have moved into a new grouping.

It should be noted that people move in and out of these lifestyle classifications many times during their lives. As incomes change, so do the needs of their families. No group has members with exactly the same characteristics as we have discussed. It is therefore imperative for retailers to carefully examine each group in terms of their differences and utilize other market assessment tools to determine appropriate product mixes.

CONSUMER BEHAVIOR

In addition to examining the demographics of their markets, retailers must consider consumer buying motives and behavior. By undertaking this investigation, they will be better able to appeal to their client base and prospective clienteles.

Buying Motives

What motivates consumers to purchase? Is it price? Is it to gain a social advantage? Is it quality? Is it for safety reasons? The answer to all of these questions is yes! Is each purchase product based upon a single buying motive? This answer is no! In the case of the purchase of a Jeep Grand Cherokee, for example, some might consider purchasing it because it is practical. Others might be motivated to buy because of the status it provides. These are both viable motives for buying. But different people purchase the same product for different reasons. Buying the jeep for practical reasons is known as a **rational motive**. Purchasing the jeep for the purpose of status is known as an **emotional motive**.

Rational Motives

Such factors as practicality, quality, price, durability, serviceability, care, adaptability, and warranties constitute rational buying motives. The very essence of value shopping is based upon the idea that consumers are looking for merchandise that offers many of these qualities. Discounters like Wal-Mart and Target have built enormous retail empires by providing their customers with items that are competitively priced, provide serviceability, and feature quality. Similarly, the off-pricers such as Marshalls and T.J. Maxx offer their customers prices that cannot be duplicated elsewhere. By utilizing the rational approach, these merchants are finding that their sales volume is soaring.

While rational purchasing has been a constant in many consumer product groups, it hasn't always played as important a role in apparel as it does today. In the 1980s, the **yuppies** (a word regularly used to describe young urban professionals with large incomes) were often called conspicuous spenders. Price was rarely a consideration in their purchasing habits. They bought anything that satisfied their egos and brought status to them. The economic recession at the close of the 1980s dealt a blow to this group, and was considered responsible for a more rational approach to shopping. Today's young executives, having faced a similar boom-and-bust economy, typically spends more wisely. A large number, although able to afford higher-priced merchandise, may be seen shopping in stores like Old Navy, where fashion and value are featured.

Other goods that are purchased based on rational motives include computers, electronics, packaged food, and home office equipment and supplies. Stores like Office Depot, Office Max, Staples, Circuit City, and Best Buy have built mega-retail operations based on rational purchasing principles.

Emotional Motives

Many retailers use emotional motives to target their customers. Merchants realize that by appealing to their customers desire for prestige and status, they can gain significant profits.

In the case of automobiles, there is a segment of the population that is motivated by status to purchase certain models. A Lexus, Mercedes, or BMW may receive a high performance rating, but it is often the name on the car that drives such a purchase.

Apparel and wearable accessories are other merchandise classifications where prestige often takes the forefront. Would the sales for Ralph Lauren's Polo products be as high if the insignia was removed from the outside of the garments? How successful would the signature bags of Louis Vuitton be if the ever-present logos were taken off the bags? These are vinyl handbags that bring large profits to the company. Similarly, the fabrics, embellishments, handwork, and limited production that make up famous couture creations don't really account for the costs of the garments or their popularity with consumers. It is often the prestige of attending the couture collection openings in Paris, Milan, and London and the chance to be seen by the press that motivates purchases.

Dining in certain restaurants is also a prestigious event. It is often difficult to obtain a reservation at a globally famous restaurant even though the cost of a meal is outrageous. Being seen in such a venue brings enough prestige to the patrons to make the eating expense worthwhile.

Today, retailers all over the world are creating excitement in their stores by adding home furnishing lines that bear the signatures of famous worldwide apparel designers. Names like Ralph Lauren, Versace, Calvin Klein, and Bill Blass are helping these retailers generate sales in departments like bedding and housewares. It should be mentioned that many industry professionals attribute the birth of the prestige label to Pierre Cardin. By capturing the public's attention with his revolutionary bubble dress in the 1950s, he was quickly catapulted into fame. Through his ingenuity, he transformed his business into a fashion empire via the licensing route. It wasn't long before everything from watches and sunglasses to household furnishings bore his signature. Status was now available in more modestly priced merchandise that the masses could afford. By combining rational and emotional purchasing motives, some retailers have been able to appeal to a segment of the population that insists on value, but also is motivated to buy merchandise that offers them prestige and status.

Patronage Motives

Patronage motives address where consumers shop. There are numerous factors that make up this motive classification. They include convenience, service, price, salesperson availability, liberal exchange policies, and merchandise assortment. When a merchant offers any or all of these, the merchant is appealing to the clientele and has established a level of comfort for them. When this comfort level becomes expected by shoppers and the company provides it, the end result is customer loyalty. Knowing exactly what to expect each time they shop, the customers return again and again. This is the dream for every merchant.

Not only are brick-and-mortar retailers satisfying their customers with positive shopping experiences, but so are many of the off-site merchants. With the latter group trying to capture a share of the consumer market that doesn't have the time to visit the stores, service has become an important part of the purchasing decision. Shoppers not only want the convenience of shopping online or in catalogs, but they also expect speedy delivery. Slow delivery, especially at peak selling periods like the Christmas season, has made many consumers anything but satisfied shoppers.

It is up to each merchant, whether it is a brick-and-mortar operation or off-site company, to determine the consumer's needs and provide them with a level of service that makes them a loyal customer.

Maslow's Hierarchy of Needs

An American psychologist, Abraham Maslow, conceived a major theory on motivation. His concept, known as **Maslow's Hierarchy of Needs**, has been widely accepted by retailers and other marketers. Maslow theorizes that people attempt to satisfy five levels of needs beginning with the most important (physiological needs) and ending with the least important (self-actualization needs). As individuals reach each level, the next level in the hierarchy is likely to be fulfilled.

Thought of in a pyramid, the most basic of the levels—at the bottom of the pyramid—are the **physiological needs** addressing such requirements as food, water, shelter, clothing, and sexual satisfaction. Retailers attempt to cash in on these requirements by stocking a host of products to satisfy them.

The next level incorporates the **safety needs**. Automobile salesmen point out the value of air bags to a potential customer. Similarly, life insurance agents underscore the importance of policies that provide for loved ones.

Continuing upward are **social needs**, which merchants address through advertising. Ads that show the benefits of cosmetics, jewelry that makes the wearer more socially appealing, and cars that will affect the social status of the driver all fall into this classification.

At the next level are the **esteem needs**. It is this segment that sells the consumer on the such purchases as first-class travel, belonging to upscale, prestigious health clubs, and cars that will make one the envy of others such as Mercedes Benz.

The pinnacle of the scale addresses **self-actualization needs**. The retailer concentrates on products and services that show how individuals may maximize their potential. Education, symphony subscriptions, and self-employment workshops are part of this level.

It should be noted that the bottom level of Maslow's Hierarchy of Needs is the broadest and most attainable. Each subsequent stage becomes narrower, indicating that the higher needs are more difficult to attain.

CONSUMER RESEARCH

With all of the these theories available for retailers to study their target markets, there is often a need to examine research studies that address the potential customers. Major trade associations, such as the National Retail Federation, often undertake these studies. When a major retailer wants to find specific information regarding their own potential customers, the services of an outside agency is often employed, or the research is conducted in-house.

Trade Associations and Organizations

There are numerous trade groups serving the needs of retailers with research studies. These organizations address a host of subjects, the scope of which is dependent on their missions. The National Retail Federation (NRF) is the largest retail organization in the world. Its goal is to serve its membership in every aspect of retailing. Among their many endeavors is research. Studies are regularly conducted and made available to its members which include some of the largest merchants in the world. By subscribing to the organization, merchants are able to obtain any studies NRF has conducted. By logging on to NRF's Web site, www.nrf.com, would-be members can assess the group's offerings.

Other more specifically oriented trade groups include the Institute of Store Planners (www.ispo.org), the National Association of Sales Professionals (www.nasp.com), the International Mass Retail Association (www.imra.org), and the Fashion Group International (www.fgi.org).

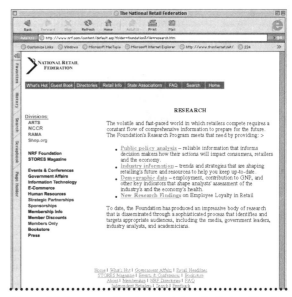

The world's largest retail trade association, the National Retail Federation, provides research studies for members.

Governmental Resources

Each level of the United States government conducts research involving endless subjects. Included are studies that deliver factual information on consumers. The federal government, through the Census Bureau, provides a wealth of information on population, an area that retailers need to examine regarding their consumer bases. A great number of important charts, tables, and graphs that concern the population are easily available at the Census Bureau Web site (www.census.gov). An excellent hard source is the Statistical Abstract of the United States, which features the same information.

Market Research Groups

There are numerous research organizations dedicated to conducting studies that provide consumer motivation and behavior information. Among the better known are SRI International, a consulting firm that specializes in market segmentation systems (www.sri.com), the Gallup organization, that among other things, offers consumer measurement study (www.gallup.com), and ACNielsen, the world's largest provider of market research (www.acnielsen.com).

Focus on . . .
ACNielsen

THE ACNIELSEN CORPORATION is a globally structured organization that represents more than 9,000 clients in more than 100 countries. Their expertise lies in the measurement of competitive marketplace dynamics, understanding consumer attitudes and behavior, and developing advanced analytical insights that generate increased sales and profits.

Retail measurement by the organization provides continuous tracking of consumer purchases at the point of sale through scanning technology and through in-store audits. Clients that subscribe to its services receive detailed information on actual purchases, market shares, distribution, pricing, merchandising, and promotional activities—all of which are vital to the success of any retail organization. The company also offers consumer panel services that provide detailed information on actual purchases made by household members, as well as their retail shopping patterns and demographic profiles. Specifically, the data is culled from 126,000 households in 18 countries.

In addition to the general studies that the company produces, it also engages in customized research. This service includes quantitative and qualitative studies that deliver information and insights into consumer attitudes and purchasing behavior, both of which are vital to the success of any retail operation. The company believes that taking what consumers say at face value is insufficient. By reading between the lines and grasping the subtle nuances of what is said—or often left unsaid—the analysis is more meaningful for problem solving. Additionally, the company conducts studies that measure customer satisfaction and brand awareness, which is important to the success of private labels utilized by most major retailers. In the case of private label merchandise, AC-Neilsen provides test marketing services that launch new products or reposition existing brands. Its overall service helps retail managers to gauge product penetration, evaluate overall product performance, and analyze the effectiveness of promotional endeavors. The company also engages in research that measures a retailer's own brand versus competitive brands.

● ●

In-House Research

Many of the retail giants have their own **in-house research** departments. These departments investigate a wide range of areas for the company including consumer research. Identifying potential customers and addressing the problems involved in appealing to them is of paramount importance to any in-house team. Once the problem has been defined and identified, the team is ready to begin the gathering of data. Like their outside counterparts, in-house teams they utilize many different tools to find solutions to the problems they are charged to investigate. Among these tools are:

Questionnaires

The researchers determine the list of questions. Once each question has been carefully developed, they are arranged in sequential order. The formats used in questionnaires include personal interviews, telephone, mail, and the Internet. The intended audience dictates what format is used. For example, although the Internet is gaining in popularity for consumer research, it is not used when the target market is an older generation. Many senior citizens are either computer illiterate or disinterested in the technology. Therefore, this tool probably wouldn't bring the sufficient number of responses necessary to make the survey reliable.

Observations

This technique involves watching people and recording their actions. If a retailer was trying to determine the effectiveness of a new type of visual presentation in the store, he or she would use **observation research**. Someone would record the number of individuals who have shown interest in the presentation.

Personal interviews are an important way of gathering consumer information in-house.

Focus Groups

The **focus group**, or consumer panel as it is sometimes referred to, is a technique in which a retailer invites a small representative group of customers to assemble and answer questions about such areas of concern as merchandise assortments, price points, service, visual presentations, and advertising. These panels are either formed sporadically or on a regular basis. More and more merchants are using the latter format in that it gives them regular feedback on the store.

Research Samples

In order to make any study a meaningful one, it is imperative to select a **research sample** or representative group of the body of people being investigated. There is no need to elicit information from each and every customer, but from a fraction of those in the targeted group. It is very much like the polls used to predict political elections. In the election for President, for example, the sample used might merely be 1,000 individuals. If the sample is carefully chosen, then the predicted results will prove to be right.

Once the sample has been selected, and the data has been collected by the chosen methodology, it is time for processing and analysis. It is the analysis that is extremely important. If the data is properly used, the retailer is able to make the necessary adjustments to his or her company that will better serve the needs of the consumer and make the business more profitable.

The power of the consumer is such that he or she will either make or break the retailer's opportunity for success. The wealth of competition in retailing gives the shopper what seems like unlimited venues for their selections. If not satisfied by one company, there are many others to choose from until a level of satisfaction is achieved.

TRENDS FOR THE NEW MILLENNIUM

- Because of the increased amount of competition in retailing today, retailers will be carefully studying their markets to determine how to best get their fair shares.
- The baby boomers will continue to get significant attention in terms of their product needs since they are generally better off than the generation that preceded them. Studies show that these individuals are less satisfied with the typical retiree products and are opting for less traditional purchases.
- Although the family life cycle has been studied for many years by market researchers, nontraditional families are becoming more and more important. For example, multiple-member/shared households are more prevalent, so retailers will be paying more attention to them.
- Focus groups will play an even greater role in helping the retail community determine whether or not they are making the right purchasing decisions to serve their clienteles.

CHAPTER HIGHLIGHTS

- The study of demographics provides retailers will a wealth of information that helps them address their customers' needs.
- Since different geographic locations dictate different shopper needs, it is important to understand the specifics of the communities served by the retailers. For example, colder climates will certainly have different merchandise requirements than warmer climates.
- The study of age groups is imperative to determine what the specific needs of each group are. Except for a limited number of products, different ages have different needs.
- Lifestyles generally play an important role in assessing consumer needs. While an investment banker and a farmer might have the same annual income of $100,000, each will spend his money differently.
- The multiple-member/shared household category is one of the fastest growing segments of the family life cycle.
- Consumers make their buying decisions on rational or emotional motives. The retailer must determine which plays the more important part in the purchase of his or her goods.
- The retailer must study Maslow's Hierarchy of Needs so that he or she can better serve the needs of the potential market.
- Consumer research is accomplished in many different ways, including the use of in-house staffing, outside marketing research firms, or trade associations.
- The vast majority of consumer research is accomplished through the use of questionnaires, observations, and focus groups.

IMPORTANT RETAILING TERMS

demographics

National Retail Federation

baby boomers

generation X

generation Y

casual Friday

social class

nouveau riche

conspicuous spenders

family life cycle

multiple-member/shared households

empty nesters

rational motive

emotional motive

patronage motives

yuppies

Maslow's Hierarchy of Needs

physiological needs

safety needs

social needs

esteem needs

self-actualization needs

in-house research

observation research

focus group

research sample

FOR REVIEW

1. Is it possible for the retailer to plan so perfectly that there will not be any merchandise left for markdowns? If so, how can this be accomplished?

2. What is meant by the term *demographics*?

3. What source might a retailer use first to find out general information about the portion of the U.S. population that might affect his or her business?

4. Why is it important for Web site retailers to learn about the different geographic concentrations in the United States?

5. How important is it for merchants to study the needs of different age classifications in his or her trading area?

6. In what ways did companies like Pottery Barn change the nature of home furnishing retailing?

7. How has Casual Friday changed the merchandising philosophies at some major retailers?

8. Why is the study of lifestyles so important for the retailer to understand?

9. Explain the VALS 2 concept and how it helps retailers with their merchandise planning.

10. Are there any other factors besides income that are needed to determine the type of products that a consumer will be likely to purchase?

11. How does the lower-upper class differ from the upper-upper class in their purchasing habits?

12. Which social class is considered to be the conspicuous spenders in our society?

13. Which social class makes up the vast majority of the population in the United States?

14. What is meant by the classification, "Multiple-member/shared households"?

15. Differentiate between rational and emotional motives.

16. Can the same product be influenced by both an emotional and rational motivation?

17. What does the term patronage motive mean?

18. According to Maslow, which needs must be first satisfied before one can move on to the next stage?

AN INTERNET ACTIVITY

Select one of the Web sites listed in the Consumer Research section of this chapter and determine what type of service is provided to the retailer. After you have logged onto the Web site of your choice, prepare a paper that addresses the following:

• the overall mission of the Web site

• the cost, if any, to gather information from the site

• the different types of information provided

• the depth of the information available

• your impression of the Web sites' assistance in providing research information

Your response should be not more than three double-spaced typed pages.

EXERCISES AND PROJECTS

1. Prepare a list of questions that could be used in a survey to determine whether a ladies' clothing retailer in your community should expand into menswear. An actual questionnaire takes a great deal of refining and input from more than one individual, however, your assignment is only to write the questions that might be used. Include ten questions that you consider important to the survey. Each should be multiple choice, giving the respondent three or four options to choose from.

2. Select a retailer in your community and determine to which social class or classes it is appealing.

Construct a chart and record the following information: name of store, location, type of store, merchandise assortment, and price lines. In a summary statement, include which social class or classes are being targeted and discuss your reasons for this conclusion.

THE CASE OF PRICE REPOSITIONING

Sibena is a 15-unit ladies' specialty chain located in Nebraska. Headquartered in Omaha, with the remainder of the stores within a two hundred mile radius, it opened its doors 25 years ago and has been a successful venture. Throughout the years, the customer base has been extremely loyal. Sibena provides excellent customer service and merchandise assortments that have always satisfied the needs of the clientele, resulting in excellent profits for its owners. The price points for the company are generally moderate, with a smattering of higher priced merchandise in each of its classifications. For example, the bulk of the sweater inventory features items priced from $30 to $50, with just a few items marked as high as $75.

This region of the country has begun to realize greater prosperity. Sales have never been stronger. During the semiannual analysis of the sales figures, the buyers recognized a fast turnover of the higher priced items. Merchandise at the upper price points had begun to check out even faster than the bulk of the inventory.

At the semiannual meeting of the management team, a new merchandising approach was introduced. Beverly Nadler, the general merchandising manager, offered a plan that would change the price structure at Sibena. The new concept eliminated the lower price points and featured a much more expensive line of merchandise. Some agreed to the repositioning of price points; however, the general consensus was to tread slowly. After considerable discussion, the idea was tabled until the new concept could be further studied.

Questions

1. Should the company desert its present pricing structure in favor of the new idea? Why or why not?

2. How should the management team go about determining if the plan would be successful?

PART TWO

ORGANIZATION, MANAGEMENT, AND OPERATIONAL CONTROLS

Before any business can operate successfully and return a profit to its investors, it must establish an organizational structure that will enable it to carry out its goals in the most efficient manner. The most talented individuals must be selected to manage the functions that have been outlined in the structure. Once these two areas have been carefully addressed, a number of different operational controls must be put in place. Specifically, the speedy distribution of the merchandise, and its safeguarding, are imperative to achieving the levels of success that were established during the formation of the organization.

In Chapter 5, Organizational Structures, a host of different organizational approaches for retail operations are examined. A look at retailing history reveals that some of the aspects of earlier structures are still in use today.

Throughout Chapter 6, Human Resources Management, the role of human resources managers and their staffs are explored, underscoring their importance to the retail organization. The various roles of these managers are explored in detail.

One of the major obstacles plaguing merchants of every size and classification is shoplifting and internal theft. In Chapter 7, Loss Prevention, these problems are addressed, as are the ways in which today's merchants are coping with them.

In Chapter 8, Logistical Merchandise Distribution, discussion centers on the all important manner in which the merchandise that has been ordered by the buyers and merchandisers reach the selling floors.

Once each of these managerial endeavors and operational controls have been carefully accounted for and are working satisfactorily within the developed organizational structure, the company is able to deal with the challenges of operating a retail business in the new millennium's competitive environment.

CHAPTER 5
Organizational Structures

After you have completed this chapter, you should be able to discuss:

- ▸ Reasons why all retailers, no matter their size, need organizational structures.
- ▸ How a retailer determines the exact table of organization necessary for his or her company.
- ▸ The major divisions or functions of most retailers, and why they are vital to the operation.
- ▸ Why the merchandising division is considered the lifeblood of any retail organization.
- ▸ The difference between line and line and staff tables.
- ▸ The major features of the Mazur Plan, and its relevance to department store structures in the United States.
- ▸ Why the centralization of chain store functions has played such an important role in the organization's success.
- ▸ The reasons why many chains have embraced some form of decentralization in their organizations.

Whether a shopper enters a store, peruses a catalog, logs onto a Web site, or turns to any of the cable channels that sell a host of different items, he or she is generally unaware of the complexity of the retail organization being patronized. The shopper is simply using any number of means to purchase items. To those in the industry, however, the task of making the different retail channels accessible to the consuming public is a formidable one. Behind the scenes of every retail operation is a management team that structures the organization so that it will be a viable shopping experience for its customers, while maximizing the company's profits.

In the not too distant past, the matter was less complicated. Retailers were either brick-and-mortar companies, which also had catalog divisions, or direct merchants who gained all sales via the mail or telephone. Today, the retail arena has changed considerably. The playing field, except for the small, independent entrepreneur, is replete with operations that subscribe to multichannel retailing. Their involvement in stores, catalogs, and Web sites has changed their organizational structures. Should these retailers have separate structures for each of their channels or should they simply develop one overall plan, placing each channel under one large umbrella? As we will learn in this chapter, there is no correct answer.

No matter how large or small a retail operation is, it still needs to organize itself in a manner that will help it flourish. The operator of a single unit gourmet food store and the CEO of an industrial giant are both faced with the challenge of developing a specific organizational structure that best suits their operational needs.

In this chapter, attention will focus on the various functions of a retail organization, the different concepts utilized in organizational structures, and a historical look at structures of the past and how they have shaped today's retail environment.

ESTABLISHING THE STRUCTURE

Before a company can embark on any tasks, such as merchandising or promotional activities, it must develop a structure that encompasses all of its functions. This structure, its **table of organization** or **organization chart**, must focus on the needs of the target market and the employees who will fulfill these needs. The **organizational structure** must be segmented into a format that allows for upper level management, mid-managers, and all of the other employees of the company to satisfactorily interface with each other. Only then will the operation perform smoothly and achieve the ultimate goal of maximum profitability.

Before such a table of organization can be established, it is necessary to determine the various activities essential to the operation of the retail venture. While each business has its own goals and parameters for doing business, there are certain basic areas that must be addressed in each of them. The degree to which each of these activities is utilized in the company is dependent upon its size. The major retailers, because of the nature and scope of their businesses employ huge staffs to carry out the functions of the company, while their smaller counterparts rely on just a few people to perform a variety of tasks. In either case the functions that must be embodied in a table of organization are basically the same.

Retailers usually segment their activities into five different areas or **divisions**, merchandising, promotion, operations, human resources, and control. Before these different **functions** may be set into the company's organizational structure, each must be carefully examined. Although some businesses place more emphasis on one function than another, all bases must be sufficiently covered to assure that the operation will run smoothly and efficiently.

The Stein Mart Story
Organizing for Growth

LIKE EVERY MAJOR RETAILER, STEIN MART is always seeking to improve its operation. One way it does this is to tailor its organizational structure to meet the demands of its day-to-day functioning. Although, Stein Mart has grown from a small independently run company, it now embraces the organizational structure that best fits its present size and future expansion plans.

The company utilizes a four-division plan that has at its head the chairman and CEO. It is interesting to note that the CEO, Jay Stein, is the same family member who took the company from infancy to its current status. This arrangement makes it possible for the store to keep a family focus, while ascending into the areas of big business. Directly under the CEO is the president and Chief Operating Officer (COO) who reports directly to the CEO. The four division heads report to the COO.

The four division heads are chief merchandising officer (CMO), chief financial officer (CFO), executive vice-president for stores, and senior vice-president for human relations. Each has a number of subordinates, whose responsibilities are divided according to the needs of the organization. For example, the CMO has three general merchandise managers, each specializing in a particular merchandise classification.

In addition to its own management control, Stein Mart uses the leased department approach to run its shoe division. Its experience shows that an outside company is better suited to bring greater profits to the store through this arrangement.

The company is always ready to tailor its organization to fit its needs.

Merchandising

The **merchandising division** is considered by many to be the lifeblood of any retail operation. It should be understood that merchandise procurement is a formidable task—one that necessitates a great deal of planning and ultimate execution by a number of different people at different management levels.

Some of the activities that the merchandising division handles include:

Merchandisers regularly communicate with their resources to learn about the latest product offerings.

- Buying the merchandise from resources that are domestically or globally based.
- Product development for the purpose of providing label exclusivity to the customers.

- Pricing goods in a manner that considers profitability, while at the same time addresses the competitive nature of retailing today.
- Developing a mix between nationally branded and privately branded lines.
- Determining the price points that will bring the greatest sales potential to the company.
- Negotiating the best terms with vendors so that profit margins will be maximized.
- Establishing sound relationships with vendors.
- Securing advertising and promotional allowances from vendors that help offset the high costs of promotion.
- Interfacing with market consultants in order to learn about industry trends in terms of style, fabrication, and color.

An Ethical Consideration

WHILE THE PROCUREMENT OF THE BEST POSSIBLE MERCHANDISE should be a primary focus in retailing, sometimes, the best is overlooked so that the buyer will be the recipient of gifts that pass from the vendor. In actual practice, there are some buyers, much to the dismay of their employers, who either buy items that are not the best available, pay more than the product is worth, or pass on some promotional allowances for personal gains.

While most companies have policies regarding these unethical practices, as shown by the Stein Mart policy in the first chapter, some buyers and merchandisers still line their pockets by resorting to these unscrupulous means. For example, instead of purchasing 100 pieces of an item, a buyer purchases 200, resulting in potential markdowns and an adverse effect on the company's bottom line. (Of course, the personal rewards never justify the buyer's greed.)

Professional buyers must always think of the needs of their company and customers first. If unethical buying practices continue, the stores' profit picture will be likely to suffer and, perhaps, cause the demise of the organization.

Promotion

Never before in the history of retailing has there been a climate that features such a wealth of players. Brick-and-mortar-based retailers are not only competing with each other, but they are also constantly dueling with catalogs and Internet Web sites to capture their fair share of the market. In this mix there are the traditionalists and numerous value retailers that add even greater competition.

To make certain that retail organizations are getting their names and products noticed by the public, a wealth of responsibilities are entrusted to the organization's **promotion divisions**, including:

- Selecting the appropriate advertising media for the organization.
- Establishing an advertising signature that is immediately recognized by the consumer.
- Creating advertising materials that are timely and best exemplify the merchandise that is being sold by the company.
- Choosing an advertising agency that best represents the company.
- Creating promotional activities that can capture the attention of the consumer audience.
- Establishing good relationships with the press.
- Developing and executing visual presentations that will motivate people to buy.

Commercial artists who work in the promotion division are responsible for creating eye-catching ads.

Operations

Sometimes referred to as the store management division, the **operations division** cuts across many different functions. The operations division overseas physical maintenance of the facility, management of workrooms, store security and loss prevention, delivery and receiving of goods, and customer services.

In addition, employees in this division are involved in the following tasks:

- Establishing a plan that will safeguard the operation from employee theft and shoplifting.
- Maintaining workrooms that handle merchandise alterations.
- Developing a customer service system that will address the needs of the customer.
- Overseeing the physical plant and making certain that is up to the highest standards.
- Purchasing equipment and supplies that are necessary to keep the operation functioning.
- Planning and developing plans to improve the physical environment of the store.

Human Resources

Staffing the organization with capable employees and carrying out a program that evaluates performance are the primary responsibilities of the **human resources** division. Without the best people employed in every store position, the profitability of the company is threatened. Whether the individual is a behind-the-scenes player, such as a buyer, or a floor sales associate, his or her role is essential to company's success. This division must make certain that its hiring choices and recommendations are sound.

Some the specific functions that the human resources division is responsible for include:

- Selecting recruitment resources that will bring well-trained personnel to the company.
- Establishing an interview process that adequately screens applicants.
- Training new employees and retraining current employees with new procedures.
- Developing a compensation plan that makes the company competitive with other retailers and motivates employees to work to their maximum potential.
- Establishing a benefits package that addresses the needs of employees.
- Organizing a labor relations program that carefully considers the employees as well as management.

Control

Safeguarding the company's assets is the role of the **control division**. Employees working in this division of the company are responsible for accounting functions, expense and budget control, and customer credit. In order for the company to turn a profit, it is imperative for this group to carefully assess any expenditures that are being considered and determine if they are appropriate for the functioning of the operation.

Specific tasks of this division include:

- The establishment of a general accounting procedure that involves account payables and receivables.
- Inventory planning and supervision.
- Preparing reports for use in-house and by governmental agencies.
- Development of merchandise and statistical reports.
- Preparing sales audits.
- Establishing a credit program for customers that addresses short-term and long-term credit.
- Conducting credit interviews that will help determine credit risks.

Organizational Models

Once these areas have been examined, it is time for the company's chief executive officer and his or her management team to focus on the establishment of an organizational structure that is best suited to carry out its functions and achieve its goals. It should be remembered that there is no single plan that is universally used. There are a number of models that may be adjusted to fit the company's needs. Most retail operations are structured as either **line** or **line and staff organizations**.

Line Organizations

Those people who produce revenue for the company or are the **decision makers** are considered to be line employees. Their activities directly involve making such decisions as buying the merchandise, planning advertisement, and managing the store. Sales associates are also considered to be line personnel because they sell the merchandise that produces income for the company. Thus, they are **producers of revenue**.

Most small retail operations are line organizations. Each person employed by the company is involved in some way as a decision maker or producer.

Line and Staff Organizations

As the size of a retail operation grows, it is commonplace to add personnel to the company who are neither producers nor decision makers. These are staff people. They are **advisory personnel** who assist the line people with their decision-making tasks. A store's fashion director, for example, doesn't buy the merchandise but scouts the market and notes the trends for the buyers and merchandisers. A store's research department studies problems and makes recommendations to management as to how the problems should be solved. Many of the individuals who fill the staff positions are highly paid and vital to the success of the operation.

As a company continues to expand, it is likely that more and more staff positions will be added to its employee roster.

THE ORGANIZATION CHART

Once the details of the structure have been established, it is essential to present it in a format that is easily examined by all members of the organization. This not only gives an overall picture of the company's operation in terms of functions, but also outlines the relationship of one division to another. The organization chart, as it is called, is based upon a hierarchy of positions. It clearly depicts the **reporting structure** of the company, indicating who reports to whom. The size of the company and its numerous functions dictate the type of chart that will be utilized.

Small Store Organizations

Although many small retailers fail to develop an actual organization chart, they still function in a way that allows certain tasks to be performed by certain personnel. Since there may be as few as two or three employees in a small company, each one understands his or her responsibilities and role. Boutiques, single-unit specialty stores, and small grocery stores are typical small retail organizations. A formal chart for such a business would use a format similar the following one:

In the above example, the operation consists of seven people—the owner, manager, three sales associates, a tailor, and a stock person. It is a line organization since everyone in the company is either a decision maker or one who produces revenue for the business. At the helm is the owner who, by virtue of the fact of his or her investment, has the general

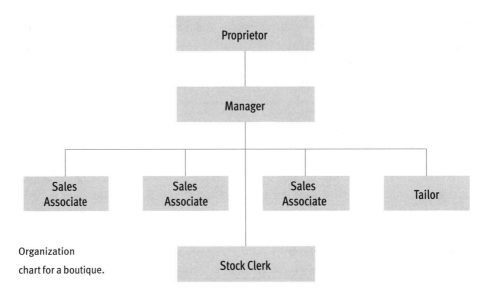

Organization
chart for a boutique.

responsibility of decision making. He or she merchandises the store, decides upon operating procedures, and generally sets the tone for the company. Next in command is the manager. This individual runs the day-to-day operation of the store. Directly under the owner, he or she is generally responsible for overseeing the sales staff, recording the arrival of merchandise, daily tallying of sales, inventory control, and selling. In the absence of the owner, who might be in the market to examine the new season's offerings, the manager is the one who makes any decisions that need to be addressed immediately.

At the next level are the sales and alteration positions. By virtue of the fact that they are depicted on the same line, it is a clear indication that they hold positions that are equal to each other. They report to the manager who supervises their activities.

At the bottom of the chart is a stock clerk whose responsibility it is to unpack incoming merchandise and set it on the selling floor according to the owner or manager's plan.

The general approach to this operation, and others like it, is to place all of the authority in one division, under the control of one individual. This arrangement works favorably for small companies, but as an organization becomes larger, separation into more than one division is necessary.

Mid-Sized Retail Organizations

Many mid-sized operations have several units in their company and need a more sophisticated table of organization than we have previously discussed. In such cases, it is not feasible for one individual to have his or her hands in every aspect of the business. Therefore, it is essential that the business be divided into major functions or divisions so that its goals may be better realized.

The term *mid-sized* is not one that has a standard definition. It merely suggests that it is not a small operation such as the previously mentioned boutique or a major retailing player

Organization chart for employees of a mid-sized chain.

such as many of today's department stores. In the following example, we will look at a small chain with 30 units that are all located within a 200-mile radius.

In the above example of the mid-sized operation, it has been assumed a **chief executive officer (CEO)** manages the company. He or she has the ultimate responsibility for policy development and managing the entire organization. The CEO supervises the directors of three separate divisions—merchandising, store management, and operations. These are all decision-making positions in which each director is responsible for managing the activities and personnel in his or her division. Directly under these executive positions are mid-managers, who have their own supervisory responsibilities.

It should be noted that this organization chart is not only a departure from the small store structure, but it also includes positions other than decision-making ones. It has been expanded into a line and staff table of organization. The line positions are depicted on the chart in a vertical hierarchy, and the staff positions are shown is a horizontal fashion, coming from the line executives for whom they work. For example, the fashion director position is adjacent to the merchandising and sales promotion director signifying that he or she provides advisory assistance to this line executive.

It should be stressed that this is merely a simplification of such a chart. There are many variations in operation according to the different needs of individual retailers.

Department Store Organizations

As retailing continued to expand in the twentieth century, it was the department store that was in the forefront of the expansion. Throughout the United States, companies like Macy's, Marshall Field's, Dillard's, Carson Pirie Scott, and Lord & Taylor grew into retailing empires. As the expansion continued, there was a need to alter organizational structures so that companies could better serve the needs of their customers and maximize profits. Although the plan that evolved is no longer used the way it once was, it is important to understand its history and how today's retailers continue to embrace some of its principles.

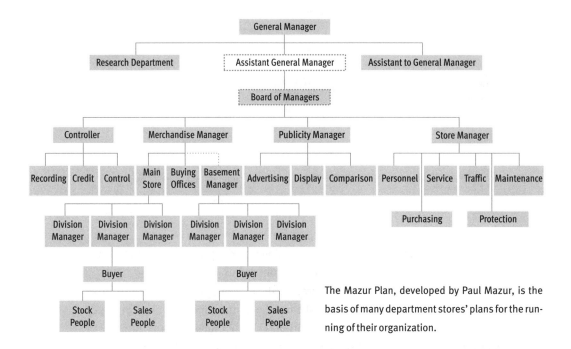

The Mazur Plan, developed by Paul Mazur, is the basis of many department stores' plans for the running of their organization.

Early in the 20th century, there was great confusion in organizational structuring. At the request of many merchants, retailing's largest trade association, then called the National Retail Dry Goods Association (NRDGA) (later it was the National Retail Merchant's Association (NRMA) and it is now known as the National Retail Federation or NRF), began to study organizational structuring. They hired Paul Mazur, an authority on the subject, to make recommendations for a more efficient organizational plan.

After 18 months of study, in which he interviewed department store executives and studied their operations, Mazur developed a **four-function plan** that is known as the **Mazur Plan**. Today, many department stores continue to use this plan, or a variation of it, to run their organizations.

Examination of the Mazur Plan indicates that it is based on four divisions, each one serving a specific function and overseen by an upper level manager. Although it is a line and staff structure, the chart that is depicted features only the major line functions. A total graphic presentation would be too cumbersome.

The Mazur Plan shows merchandising, publicity, store management, and control as the four divisions making up the plan. Each division, or function as it is also referred to, holds an equal level of importance in the organization. The success of a company that is organized this way is based on how closely the divisions interface with each other. The merchandising division, for example, must directly interact with the publicity division if the merchandise is to have the greatest sales potential. Similarly, without the control division overseeing the financial aspects of each division, it is unlikely that the operation will be profitable.

The Mazur Plan outlines the major tasks and goals for all the four divisions.

The Merchandising Function

This division is often referred to as the lifeblood of retail organizations. Without merchandise, it would be impossible for sales to be transacted. The overall responsibility of this division is to supply the best available merchandise at price points that will motivate the customers to buy.

Close inspection of the plan reveals a format that features the merchandise manager (today called the **general merchandise manager**) as the senior most player in the division. His or her responsibilities are as follows:

- To oversee the entire merchandising function and have the ultimate decision-making power for the goods that are brought into the main or flagship store, the buying offices of the company, and the basement operation. It should be noted that at the time the Mazur Plan was initiated by major department stores, the basement was unlike it is today in retailing. At that time, the lower level of a store was often run as a separate entity that featured bargain priced goods. Filene's, for example, ran its upper level in the traditional manner, while its basement store was one that featured goods that were generously marked down. Macy's used the basement as an arena for its lower priced offerings only. We will see later in the text that this principle has generally changed in most companies, with the basement being just another regular selling floor that simply features different departments. Filene's however, still utilizes its lower level as a clearance center because of its considerable success. A separate off-price retailer, Filene's Basement, grew out of the original basement.

- In the main store and basement departments, as depicted on the chart, divisional managers (or **divisional merchandise managers** as they are technically called) are next in command. They report directly to the general merchandise manager who distributes the budgets for merchandise procurement and sets the tone for the store's merchandising emphasis. The divisional merchandise managers are given the responsibility to oversee and manage specific merchandise segments. Although three managers are depicted in this chart, there are often many more. There might be one manager for women's wear, another for men's wear, another for home furnishings, and so forth. Among their tasks is setting the budgets for the various buyers in their divisions. They must also make certain that the offerings in their divisions complement each other. For example, in men's wear, if the tailored clothing styles and the shirts and ties are of the same direction, there may be larger individual sales. These managers also help establish the price points in their divisions and set the general tone for product merchandising.

- Just below the divisional merchandise managers in the structure are the buyers. Given a prescribed amount of money to spend on merchandise acquisition, the buyers are charged with planning their purchases for the next season, scouring the wholesale markets for the best vendors, making selections that will reflect the needs of their customer base, and negotiating the best terms for their companies. In each division there are numerous buyers to carry out these tasks. For example, in men's wear, there might be separate buyers for tailored clothing, trousers and shirts, sweaters, active sportswear, furnishings, and so forth. The actual number is determined by the different product classifications in the division and the projected sales volumes.

- At the lowest level of the merchandising division are stock and sales people who report directly to the buyers. The former are responsible for bringing the goods to the selling floor and placing them on the shelves and racks, while the latter are the ones who interface with the shoppers. At the time of the Mazur Plan, these employees were typically part of this division. Today, however, it should be noted that buying and selling has been separated in most department stores because of the buyers' increased roles.

The Publicity Function

Without adequate promotion of the store, it is unlikely that it would be able to compete favorably with other retailers. It had been deemed essential by Mazur that organizational structures that had the merchandising and publicity functions combined under one umbrella be separated into two separate divisions.

Specifically, advertising, display, and comparison were the major departments in the division. Today, the comparison department, which was charged with the responsibility of spying on the competition, has taken a lesser role in retailing. In fact, if a department store has such an area, it is generally a staff position in merchandising.

Some of the duties and responsibilities of the publicity division include:

- Developing an advertising philosophy that addresses the needs of the company and best promotes its offerings to the consumer. This department is headed by an advertising manager who oversees every aspect of publicity such as the various media—newspapers, magazines, direct mail, television and radio, as well as promotional endeavors such as special event campaigns. At the helm of the division is the publicity manager who plans the various publicity approaches.

- The display manager, today called the visual merchandising director, faces the challenge of presenting the merchandise in window and interior formats that sufficiently whet the consumer's appetite to more closely examine the merchandise. In addition, the overall appearance of the merchandise on the selling floor falls under this person's jurisdiction.

- As we have noted, the comparison department is no longer a separate entity as once established by Mazur. At the time, employees studied the merchandise in their competitor's environments, compared prices, and evaluated the advertisements of the competition.

The Store Management Function

In the Mazur Plan, this division dealt with the specific operations of the store. In fact, many department stores use the term store operations in place of store management. At the time of the Mazur edict, the division was headed by the store manager who handled personnel, service, traffic, maintenance, purchasing, and protection. Individual managers whose tasks were limited to those areas headed each of these subclassifications.

Some of the challenges that the store management division was responsible for were:

- Maintaining the company's physical plant, protecting the merchandise from theft, purchasing supplies, and overseeing customer service.
- This function also handled personnel, recruited, trained, prepared compensation packages, assisted in labor relations, and did everything possible to make the staff a professional and high-performing group.

The Control Function

This division is charged with the responsibility of safeguarding the company's assets and making certain that every purchase is carefully executed to gain the proper discounts and terms. It is under the supervision of a **chief financial officer** (**CFO**). In the past, the title was called controller.

In the Mazur Plan the three departments in this division were called recording, credit, and control. Some duties and responsibilities of these departments were:

- Establishing accounting procedures and carrying them out to make certain they conformed with the requirements of upper management and addressed the areas required by governmental agencies.
- Credit as a twofold task. First, this division had to make certain that the company's credit ratings were sound so that buyers could place their orders and receive the best possible credit terms from the vendors. This required the prompt payment of bills. Companies like Dun & Bradstreet regularly check with vendors to make certain that the retailers' credit status was up to date so that orders could be processed without delay. Without good credit, it would be impossible for a retailer to properly function.

  Second, this division managed customer credit which had become more important than ever at the time the Mazur Plan was being formulated. The divisions daily responsibilities were to determine the credit worthiness of potential customers, assign credit limits to new accounts, establish different types of credit plans, conduct interviews before offering credit, and to make certain that customers were billed in a timely manner. Today, of course, the credit operation has come a long way. Many of these tasks are performed more quickly and accurately via computer.
- The control area, which dealt with expenses and budgets. Regular sales audits were conducted to make certain merchandise plans were based on sound figures. Numerous

statistical reports were also prepared, giving the merchandise managers and buyers the information needed to make the right purchases. As in the case of most every other aspect of retailing, the use of the computer has enabled the offering of up-to-the-minute reports, thereby making the operation a more productive one.

Many department stores use a variation of the Mazur Plan. Most have enlarged their structures to include other divisions. Basically the functions are the same as in Mazur's concept. Perhaps the titles have changed, as have the roles played by the members of the company. Some positions have been eliminated, while others have been added to effectively bring the organization into the new millennium. Titles have also changed. Fashion coordinators have become fashion directors; display personnel have become visual merchandisers; and controllers have become CFOs.

It is essential that the department store organizational structure, and those of the other retail formats, be regularly updated to meet the company's ever changing needs.

 Focus on . . .
Federated Department Stores, Inc.

WHEN SHILLITO'S WAS FOUNDED IN 1830, Jordan Marsh in 1841, F & R Lazarus & Company in 1851, and R.H. Macy in 1859, there was no evidence that these would eventually be the forerunners of the now giant Federated Stores. Few could have imagined in the early days of retailing that such a major organization would become retailing's marquee department store group. Each store had been an independent operation without corporate affiliation before the formation of Federated Department Stores, Inc. in 1929. Corporate offices were established in Columbus, Ohio, where they still function today. Early on in the new partnership, there were several issues that needed addressing. Specifically, there were several family-owned department stores that made up this newly formed holding company. Each had its own table of organization that served its needs. Although a great amount of autonomy was evident in each store's operation, some changes in structure were necessitated by the formation of the new venture.

Division Principals

Department Stores	Burdines	Macy's West
	· Chairman	· Chairman
Bloomingdale's	· President	· President
· Chairman	· Vice Chairman & Director of Stores	· Vice Chairman & Director of Stores
The Bon Marché		
· Chairman	**Macy's East**	**Rich's/Lazarus/**
· President	· Chairman	**Goldsmith's**
	· President	· Chairman
Support Operations	· Vice Chairman & Director of Stores	· President
Federated Merchandising Group	**Federated Logistics & Operations**	**Federated Direct**
· Chairman	· Chairman	· Chairman
· President		
	Federated Systems Group	
Financial and Credit Services	· Chairman	
· Chairman	· President	

The divisions of Federated all have their own management staff.

As time went on, membership in the Federated family changed. Bloomingdale's came on board in 1930, Burdine's in 1956, Dayton's in 1959, Rich's in 1976, and Macy's in 1994. With its acquisition of Broadway Store's, Inc. and Macy's, Federated is the nation's largest department store retailer.

Making certain that their individuality played a key role in the running of the different companies that make up Federated, each is given a certain amount of freedom in its organizational structure. Of course, central headquarters oversees each operation to make certain that it is a viable player in the group. For example, consolidation was considered essential to the overall operation. Jordan Marsh became part of Burdine's; I. Magnin was converted to Macy's or Bullock's stores; Rich's/Goldsmith's and Lazarus became one division. With each move, a different organizational structure was put in place.

Corporate Management

Executive Officers	Senior Vice Presidents	Vice Presidents
· Chairman & CEO	· General Counsel & Secretary	· Controller
· President & CMO	· Chief Financial Officer	· Executive and Organizational Development, Diversity/Training/ Compensation
· Vice Chairman	· Design & Construction	· Tax
· Finance and Real Estate		· Real Estate
· Executive VP		· Corporate Communications & External Affairs
· Legal & Human Resources		· Deputy General Counsel
		· Employee Relations

Each division of Federated reports to corporate management.

Today, the original Federated organization chart and those of their component companies are a mere shadow of what they were in the beginning. It is a complex structure that gives overall responsibility at the corporate level.

Each division has a great degree of autonomy in the actual management and merchandising of its operation. Specifically, each is led by a chairman or a team that also includes a president and/or a vice chairman and director of stores.

Within each of the divisions of the corporation, there are the traditional upper level managers, mid-managers, other line personnel, and staff positions that perform such duties as merchandising, sales promotion, store operations, control, and human resource management. Each division or unit of the Federated family reports to corporate management where the ultimate decisions concerning its future are made.

It is a challenge for everyone on the team to make such a giant company a successful venture. Given their profit picture, it is safe to assume that Federated is perfectly structured to successfully operate in today's competitive business arena.

Chain Organizations

Key to the success of the chain organization is its organizational structure which involves central management of the company. Except for very small chains that have just a few units in the company and where management is carried out in one of the stores, the vast majority of these multiunit organizations operate from **central headquarters**. Control of most of the operating functions and management decisions are made at these centralized points. In the major companies that have as many as two or three thousand individual stores, there are regional offices that perform a variety of management functions. Specifically, they often act as merchandise distribution centers that serve the stores in their areas, and also perform such tasks as visual merchandising and making sure that the stores are carrying out their prescribed responsibilities as established by corporate headquarters.

As we learned earlier in the text, the term chain doesn't signify one type of retailer. It may be a clothing operation, a supermarket organization, a sporting goods company, a furniture specialist, or any company that operates two or more units.

Essential to the success of the chain is its ability to function away from the individual units. This is accomplished primarily through a multitude of computerized reports that are regularly analyzed by the members of the company's central management team. Most decisions, such as the ones that concern merchandising, are made using these reports. However,

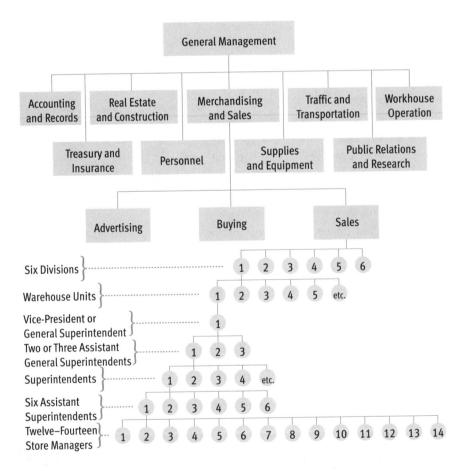

Organization chart for a grocery chain.

members of the central team or individuals from regional offices, do periodically visit problem stores or those that serve as testing areas for the company.

At the store level, the major emphasis is on sales. Managers are faced with the task of meeting their projected sales volumes and must make certain that they have the proper staffing to accomplish this goal. They rarely make merchandising decisions except, for example, which merchandise might be featured in displays and where they should be placed on the selling floors. In the larger chain organizations, however, these directions come from central headquarters. Companies like Gap and Williams Sonoma prepare visual presentations in the home office and develop books that tell each store manager exactly how the store is to be merchandised. The store manager merely executes these plans. This concept guarantees a uniform presentation in each store.

Of course, the hiring of sales associates, stock people, and cashiers is generally left to the discretion of the individual store managers. This must be done in accordance with the guidelines established by headquarters.

The complexity of a chain organization might be best appreciated by the organization of a giant supermarket chain. Close inspection of the chart reveals that it has many of the same functions of the department store except that the individual store units are further from the management team. Notice the number of different layers that make up this company's organization, and where the individual store managers fit into the plan.

CENTRALIZATION VERSUS DECENTRALIZATION

As retailers moved into the new millennium, the age-old problem concerning complete **centralization** still surfaces. Most retailers agree that the more centralized control is in a company, the more efficient and economically run its operation will be. On the other hand, many note that some decision making is better addressed at the individual store level.

J.C. Penney, a major department store chain that uses the central management philosophy, places some of the merchandise decision making in the hands of the individual store mangers. Central merchandising managers and buyers at the home office determine which vendors the company will use and which merchandise will be bought. They prepare a directives book that features the various vendors and the merchandise that they believe is best suited for the company. Then the individual store managers select those items from the book that best serves their individual store's needs. In other words, they determine their merchandise assortment from the predetermined selections of central management. In this way each store is able to better address the needs of its clientele.

At Home Depot, while the vast majority of merchandising is at the hands of the central team, some products are purchased in a decentralized manner. For example, locally grown plants are purchased by the individual stores or regional representatives. In this way, the company is able to access products that are suitable for the particular areas.

Those opposed to **decentralization** note that the buying power is greater if left to the centralized management team, and that there is less chance for improper management of the stores.

TRENDS FOR THE NEW MILLENNIUM

- In order to address multichannel efforts, retailers will continue to restructure their organizations. In addition, restructuring is necessary to accommodate retailers' overseas expansions.
- As retailers continue to expand into new trading areas, there will be a broadening of the regional concept— regional divisions will now have greater decision-making roles for their parts of the country.

CHAPTER HIGHLIGHTS

- Company activities and functions must be outlined before any organizational structure can be determined.
- Large retailers divide their organizations into the following divisions: merchandising, promotion, operations, human resources, and control.
- Store organizations use either line or line and staff structures to carry out the functions of the business. The former involves only decision makers or producers, while the latter utilizes advisory personnel to assist those in the decision-making positions.
- Most professionals agree that the merchandising function is the lifeblood of any retail organization.
- Once the company's structure has been established, it is important to graphically present it into an organization chart. The chart features all of the store's divisions and a hierarchy of the positions involved in carrying out the tasks of the operation.

- The basis of most department store structures comes from the theories of Paul Mazur. It is a four divisional plan commonly referred to as the Mazur Plan.
- A productive and profitable retail organization requires that the managers of each division regularly interface.
- Chain organizations rely heavily on centralization—all major decisions are made at a central headquarters by the management team.
- The rapid growth of many retail chains has facilitated a need for regional divisions to help management run more efficiently.

IMPORTANT RETAILING TERMS

table of organization

organization chart

organizational structure

functions

divisions

merchandising division

promotion division

operations division

human resources

control division

line organization

line and staff organization

decision makers

producers of revenue

advisory personnel

reporting structure

chief executive officer (CEO)

four-function plan

Mazur Plan

general merchandise manager

divisional merchandise manager

chief financial officer (CFO)

central headquarters

centralization

decentralization

FOR REVIEW

1. How has the multichannel retailing concept affected today's organizational structures?

2. How large must a retailer be before it develops an organizational structure with functional divisions?

3. Before any organizational structure is developed, what issues must the retailer address?

4. Which retail division is known as the lifeblood of the organization? Why?

5. What are the major tasks performed by the promotion division of a retail organization?

6. What other name is given to the operations division of a retail organization?

7. What activities is the control division responsible for?

8. In what way does a line structure differ from one that is line and staff?

9. What is meant by the term producer as it applies to line personnel?

10. What is an organization chart?

11. In an organization chart, how are tasks segmented?

12. Would a boutique be more likely to use a line structure or a line and staff format?

13. How was the early functioning of most major department store organizations determined?

14. Describe the Mazur Plan.

15. What is the major ingredient in a chain store's organizational plan?

16. Define the term decentralization.

17. What business condition has led many retailers to apply a certain degree of autonomy to their organizational structures?

AN INTERNET ACTIVITY

Using an Internet search engine, select a major retailer and determine the type of organizational structure it uses. The retailer could be a traditional or value-oriented chain, or a department store.

Some companies outline their structures on their Web site, for information on others you may need to contact the corporate headquarters directly.

Prepare an organization chart for the company you have selected. Indicate its major functions or divisions and two of the departments in each. The chart should be illustrated and mounted on foam board. Be ready to discuss the chart before the class.

EXERCISES AND PROJECTS

1. Pretend that you are planning to open a small retail operation. Prepare an organization chart to represent the company. In order to best develop a functional plan, the following areas should be addressed:

   - What are the operation's merchandise requirements?

   - What types of services will the operation provide (personal selling, gift wrap, credit, alterations, etc)?

   - How many and what types of employees will be hired?

   - Will any support services be needed?

2. Contact a major retail organization for the purpose of studying its merchandising division. Initial contact should be established through written correspondence and followed up with a phone call or via e-mail. You should try to interview a merchandise

manager, buyer, or human resources manager to obtain the following information:

- the title of the head of the division
- the titles of the major subordinates that report to the division head
- the duties and responsibilities of the managers in the division

Organize your findings in a written report.

THE CASE OF RESTRUCTURING THE MERCHANDISING DIVISION OF A MULTICHANNEL RETAILER

In the early 1900s, Hirsch & Company opened its doors in the northeastern part of the United States. Initially, it was a relatively small specialty store selling women's clothing and accessories. Its market was the upper middle class female whose tastes were simple, yet elegant. Because of the many social engagements frequented by its customers, the store stocked a large assortment of formal apparel. Daytime wear also had a presence in the store.

Not long after opening, the company began to realize sales far beyond expectations. Soon, the store needed to expand into an adjacent building. As the store continued to succeed, Hirsch & Company investigated the possibility of opening another store thirty miles away. The new unit was opened and merchandised in the same manner as the original. It too was an immediate success.

Today, the company has become one of the major specialized department stores in the East with 25 stores, carrying high-fashion merchandise ranging from bridge and designer lines to couture collections. The stores also feature numerous private label designs.

Wanting to stay current in today's retail arena, the management team is planning to expand its catalog operation and develop a Web site that will make it a multichannel retailer. While everyone in the company is excited about the company's new direction, many are not sure how the merchandising division should operate. Some believe that the division should be responsible for all of the merchandise purchases, while others believe that separate buyers should be hired for the catalog and Web site departments. (Currently the buyers purchase all of the merchandise for the stores as well as the catalog. Since the Web site is new, there is a question whether the same should be done for the off-site venture.)

Questions

1. What reasons might you offer for keeping the same merchandising format?
2. Would the separate buyers better serve the needs of the company? Defend your answer with sound reasoning.
3. Could a variation of these two plans be utilized? What format would it take?

CHAPTER 6
Human Resources Management

After you have completed this chapter, you should be able to discuss:

- ► The various functions of the human resources department.
- ► The concept of job analysis and how important it is in the recruitment of employees at all levels.
- ► Which specific routes human resources managers take to find the most competent employees for their companies.
- ► How the selection procedure is used to make certain that the most qualified candidate is hired.
- ► Why training of employees is so vital to the success of the company, and how that training is carried out.
- ► The manner in which employee evaluations are performed at all levels.
- ► Why different remuneration systems are employed in the industry.
- ► What types of benefits are being offered to today's retail workers.

Staffing a retail organization with the most qualified people is the responsibility of the human resources department. Today, the challenge to do so is greater than ever before. With multi-channel retailing being the direction in which most of the larger organizations are headed, proper staffing has become even more critical. Not only must personnel be recruited and trained for every division of the stores, but the same must be done for the company's off-site ventures, such as catalogs and Web sites. These relatively new approaches to retailing, coupled with the expansion undertaken by retailers, make the task a difficult one to accomplish.

The level of difficulty of store and off-site staffing varies according to the economy of the time. In the late 1980s for example, retailers had few problems finding an experienced **employee pool** to draw from because the country was in the midst of an economic recession. With unemployment at significant levels at the time, individuals who would have opted for other careers were now considering one in retailing. The number of college graduates were at all time highs, giving human resources managers a wealth of people from which to choose.

Staffing problems vary from year to year. As the retailers entered the new millennium, finding individuals with the most potential to fill positions was extremely difficult. Because the economy was booming unlike any other time in the past, other industries were offering more financial rewards and incentives than retailing. The difficulty hiring qualified people for retail positions reached critical levels. College graduates were being enticed to enter careers that paid more and often demanded less. It was a buyers' market, and retailers had to use their bags of tricks to entice people to consider retail careers. Whether it was in the recruitment of management level employees or those who might be needed as part-time sales associates, the task of staffing was a formidable one.

Toward the end of 2001, with a recession in place, it became easier to recruit people in all levels. Many employed by the dot.coms were out of work and turned to retailing for employment. Thus, we see, the tasks of hiring are not a constant. In reality the problem is one of supply and demand. If the job applicant pool is significant, the responsibility of finding suitable employees is relatively simple. If, on the other hand, the pool has shrunk to very low numbers, the challenge of staffing is extremely complex. In the very early days of the 21st century, human resources managers were much less stringent in their evaluation of potential employees than were their counterparts who made these decisions in other times. It wasn't a matter of carefully screening applicants for the positions, but it was more a matter of using all of their expertise to find workers and motivate them to come on board. Often times, managers settled for those who were willing to take the job.

As we will learn in this chapter, retailers, and more specifically those entrusted with staffing, follow a set of principles in searching for individuals with the most potential to meet the needs of their companies. It is a road map or plan that addresses all of the aspects of staffing such as recruitment, training, employee evaluation, compensation planning, and benefits and services.

EQUAL OPPORTUNITY EMPLOYMENT

Throughout the years, there has been considerable discussion regarding the rosters that make up the many different industries in the United States. Many believe that unfair advantages have been given to male Caucasians, especially in the upper reaches of management. Minorities and women have habitually complained that while the jobs at the bottom of the ladder have been relatively easy to come by, there was little room at the top for them. In most fields, women rarely break through the **glass ceiling**. Even if a woman reaches a mid-management level position, the top of the ladder is often unreachable. Some women who have achieved a level of success in upper management positions find that rewards and compensation are not the same as those of their male counterparts.

The federal government, even with the passage of legislation such as The Equal Pay Act, hasn't been able to guarantee the same monetary rewards for men and women. The Civil Rights Act protects people from discriminatory practices, but it still hasn't completely removed the biases in some industries.

While the employment opportunities continue to increase for minorities and women in most industries, few have offered unbiased opportunity for advancement, as retailing has. An examination of the retailing arena shows that women and minorities are engaged in every level of employment, including the highest positions in the company. General merchandise managers, buyers, promotion executives, store managers, and fashion directors are just a few of the senior level and mid-management positions that these groups have obtained. Retailing continues to set an example for other fields of employment as the leader for advancement based on ability.

THE HUMAN RESOURCES DEPARTMENT

Except for the smaller retailers, the industry utilizes human resources departments to manage all aspects of recruiting and maintaining a staff. The tasks are ones that involve every level of employment. In some instances, human resources focuses on the actual hiring of people for specific positions. In the area of selling, for example, employee selection is usually at the human resources department's discretion. Armed with a **job specifications** profile that that has been developed by merchandise department managers, employment managers simply hire those individuals who meet the preestablished criteria.

In positions that are above the selling and stock levels, human resources is often the initiator of the recruitment process, but doesn't usually make the hiring decision. Once the department has found the prospects and screened them, the actual hiring decision is left up to the discretion of the supervisor for the vacant position. Divisional merchandise managers make the final decision for new buyers, and buyers have the ultimate say as to who their assistants will be.

RECRUITING AND HIRING EMPLOYEES

As we learned earlier in the chapter, recruitment problems change according to the economics of the time. In any case, it is up to the human resources department's recruitment specialists to set up a plan that provides the best results. By understanding exactly what duties each position requires, they can select the most qualified candidates for company employment.

The Stein Mart Story
Developing a Sound Human Resources Program

ONE OF THE KEY INGREDIENTS TO THE SUCCESS of any retail operation is its employees. From the top of the organization, where the company is managed, to the bottom, where the daily interfacing with shoppers is essential to profitability, having the most qualified individuals is paramount to success. At Stein Mart, the importance of the human resources role is best exemplified by its placement in the organizational structure. It is one of the four divisions of the company, along with merchandising, finance, and store management.

One of the most important parts of the division's operation is recruitment. Although Stein Mart still utilizes the classified ad approach, this recruitment practice has given way to recruiting online and relying on in-house recommendations for staffing. The latter has been so successful that it has become an integral part of company staffing. Promotion from within is regarded as the primary method for bringing people into management positions. Employees who have performed admirably at the lower levels are quickly considered for promotion. Many a Stein Mart employee has risen from the selling floor to upper management and merchandising positions. The company is involved with many college programs in which students are assessed and brought into the Stein Mart family.

Regular employee evaluation is a practice at Stein Mart. The company believes this is the only way in which performance can improve and upward mobility can be achieved. Training is done in-house at all levels, beginning with the sales associates and culminating at the management levels. Buyers are specifically trained by merchandise managers to help them learn the unique merchandising techniques of the store.

Stein Mart rewards its employees with a sound benefits package which helps to reduce turnover.

It all begins with **job analysis**, an investigative research procedure that involves cooperation from the various managers in the stores' numerous divisions. Once the specifications of each position, such as its title, level of technical knowledge, and duties have been determined, the information is condensed into a format known as a **job description**. This simplifies the first stages of the recruitment process. Instead of having to make personal contact with those supervisors who have a vacancy to fill, the employment manager refers to the specific description of the job that is to be filled. Each job description is kept in a computer file that may be quickly retrieved, making the process one that is fast and accurate.

Typically, a job description looks like this:

Massey & Lowell, Inc.

Division: Merchandising

Title: Buyer

Department: Men's Active Sportswear

Immediate Supervisor: Men's Wear Divisional Merchandise Manager

Professional Experience: Five years as an assistant buyer

Duties and Responsibilities:

- Purchase of new merchandise

- Six month plan development

- Visits to domestic and foreign markets

- Analysis of computerized reports

- Adherence to open-to-buy parameters

A job description, like this one for a buyer, gives specific information and requirements for the position.

Recruitment

There are numerous sources from which potential employees may be drawn. It is the professional human resources specialist who, from experience, knows which ones will have the greatest potential for bringing the right prospect to the company. The sources are made up of two areas, one that is internal and the other external.

Internal Sources

Since the turnover rate is particularly high at the lower levels of retail employment, it is appropriate to elicit leads from current employees, or to conduct **internal sourcing**. If someone on the company's staff is a satisfied employee, it is relatively safe to assume that his or her recommendations will result in capable new candidates. Those currently employed by the company understand the plusses of working for the organization and could pass such information on to friends and relatives. Those who are satisfied employees often act as good will ambassadors for the operation. In order to motivate those on the retailer's team to make recommendations, many companies offer bonuses for their cooperation.

Upward mobility is the goal of many who have careers in retailing. Most retailers use the incentive of **promotion-from-within** to attract better people to fill their positions. With employees already on board who know the workings of the operation, this is a pool that is often tapped to fill positions that are higher on the ladder. An assistant buyer might be promoted to buyer, a department manager to a group manager, or a division merchandise manager to general merchandise manager. While this track might serve the needs of the company, it isn't always used to fill upper-level positions in the company. Reliance on in-house workers only may overlook the potential for people outside of the company to bring in new ideas that they have learned elsewhere. It is therefore essential that a combination of inside and outside sourcing be considered.

Classified ads in local newspapers and trade publications are one way employers recruit potential employees.

External Sources

There are many different external recruitment sources. **Outside sourcing** includes the more traditional formats such as **classified ads** and the relatively new ones such as the Internet. Each serves the retailer to find appropriate candidates seeking employment.

CLASSIFIED NEWSPAPER ADVERTISEMENTS

Classified advertisements have been regularly used ever since the early newspapers were published. It is generally considered the most effective method used to fill vacancies. Want ads, as they are often referred to, offer many advantages to the retailer. First, it is a relatively inexpensive tool to use. Second, the ad can be placed about 24 to 48 hours before newspaper publication, making it a fast technique to announce job openings. Third, if the ad is carefully developed, it can help to eliminate less desirable candidates. Fourth, the wealth of newspapers ranging in size from the local publications to the nationally recognized ones is significant. Every city, no matter what its size, publishes a paper that can be used for recruitment. Finally, newspapers such as the *New York Times* are read all around the country making the retailer's employee search widespread. Of course, the disadvantage of using classified advertising is that it doesn't provide for any pre-screening apparatus, as employment agencies do.

TRADE PUBLICATION WANT ADS

These ads are often used by retailers when they need to fill a management level position. *Women's*

Wear Daily, *DNR*, and *VM+SD* are just some of the trade papers that feature these ads. Since they are generally read by retailing professionals, it is the perfect place to seek employees. *VM+SD* is a monthly periodical that specializes in visual merchandising. Individuals in that aspect of the industry regularly read it and are aware of the career opportunities section.

WEB SITES

The Internet has become important in reaching potential job applicants. With the computer playing a part in the everyday lives of most everyone in the United States, it has become a tool for employers to reach future employees. Recruiting sites such as Monster.com, Careerpath.com, and Gottajob.com, are regularly used by such retail giants as Sears, JC Penney, and Best Buy.

The following table lists the most popular career Web sites based upon the number of visitors they had during August 2000.

More and more retailers are also using their own Web sites to attract the attention of potential employees. Looking at any number of the major retailers in the country, you will find sections of their Web sites that invite users to investigate job opportunities with the company. The Target Corporation offers one of the more detailed of these Web sites.

Web sites like www.monster.com bring together huge numbers of employers and job candidates.

TABLE 6.1
MOST FREQUENTLY VISITED CAREER WEB SITES

WEB SITE	VISITORS
jobsonline.com	8,747,000
monster.com	4,434,000
hotjobs.com	1,858,000
headhunter.net	1,449,000
careerpath.com	1,065,000
salary.com	1,012,000
careerbuilder.com	953,000
jobs.com	526,000
careermosaic.com	493,000
flipdog.com	423,000

Focus on . . .
Target Corporation

ONE OF THE FASTEST GROWING RETAIL ORGANIZATIONS in the United States is the Target Corporation. Comprised of Marshall Field's, Mervyn's, and its value-oriented discount chain, Target, along with its direct marketing divisions, it has become a major retailing institution.

In order for all its divisions to continue on a path of success, the company is always in a recruitment mode. Whether it is looking to fill a vacancy at the top of the organizational structure, at the mid-management level, or on a low-level position, the Target Corporation must find ways to attract competent workers to join its team. One of the methods that Target uses is through the Internet. While many retailers use Web sites to promote their businesses and sell specific products, few use them to carefully spell out job opportunities for every division of the organization.

The home page of the Web site, (www.targetcorp.com) makes a general statement to prospective customers. At the top of the page, a display banner features, among other areas of interest to consumers, a section on careers. Interested parties can then access this section to learn more about opportunities in the company. Within this section, prospective applicants can find out more specifics about the company, including "employer of choice," which briefly spells out the status of Target in relation to the overall retail industry, "benefits, diversity policy, awards, and technology services," and separate sections for each of its store divisions.

Those who might be interested in the company's benefits package, for example, might select that area before any other. It outlines programs such as 401(k) plans, pharmacy discounts, insurance, alternative work arrangements, and vacations. The next screen lists information on a wealth of careers, including advertising, assets protection, merchandising, finance, and store leadership. If someone is interested in merchandising, for example, a click on that page outlines the company's merchandising career path. If a potential candidate is interested in a career at a particular store, say Marshall Field's, for example, a full description of the company, its locations, and job opportunities can be also accessed with a mere click of the mouse. Additional screens outline how to apply and where résumés may be sent for further consideration.

All of the written information on the site is surrounded by photographs of smiling faces, company logos, charts, and a map featuring the locations of the company's major markets.

By focusing its recruitment efforts on the Internet, the Target Corporation attracts potential employees who might otherwise never have pursued a career with the company.

EMPLOYMENT AGENCIES

An **employment agency** is a company that specializes in matching job candidates to specific positions. There are both private and governmental agencies. In the private sector, some specialize in specific areas of employment such as retailing. Many of these companies focus on the lower to mid-management levels of employment, while others, the **executive search firms** or **headhunters** as they are often called, deal exclusively with the recruitment of upper-level management. These agencies advertise in consumer and trade papers, and also make significant contacts through the use of the Internet. For entry level and mid-management personnel, the site, www.careersinretailing.com, serves a host of the biggest merchants such as Best Buy, Toys "R" Us; Dillard's; JCPenney; Bed, Bath & Beyond; and Sears. By scrolling through the Web site, viewers can find the answers to questions concerning career paths, the manner in which to get started in retailing, retailing opportunities, and the potential for employment in every segment of the industry.

There are also Web sites offering executive search services that alert potential executive candidates to specific recruiters. When individuals log on to these Web sites, they are presented with a host of different executive recruitment organizations. For retailers, the biggest advantage to using employment agencies is that these agencies prescreen applicants for them. Applicant credentials, such as previous employment histories, are carefully scrutinized before a recommendation is made to the retailer. This saves the retailer a great deal of time and effort when seeking qualified candidates. Companies need only to interview those who have been recommended by the agencies. In most cases, retailers pay the fees required by the employment agencies only if they actually hire the recommended individuals.

EDUCATIONAL INSTITUTIONS

These are excellent resources for employee recruitment. High schools, technical schools, colleges, and universities all play an important role in the placement of their graduates. Retailers use a variety of methods to attract graduates. One of the most popular ways of attracting future graduates is through **internship** programs that allow for the assessment of individuals who are still in school and will be seeking full-time employment upon graduation. One such company that utilizes the internship route is Kmart. By logging onto www.kmartcorp.com/corp/careers2/general/college.stm, soon-to-be graduates can learn about opportunities that await them at Kmart. By clicking on "Send Us Your Resume," an interested candidate can fill out a form, like the one below, and send their credentials to the company for consideration.

By using this standardized form, the human resources department can quickly determine if the applicant has the proper credentials to be considered for the program. Those who meet the company's criteria are invited in for an interview.

Regular meetings with key faculty who serve as prescreeners for career candidates, participation in career days and job seminars, and the development of posters and brochures that can be delivered to the campus outlining the benefits of joining a specific company are other ways that retailers recruit at educational institutions. Continuous communication with the educational institutions also helps fill part-time positions for key selling periods such as Christmas. These temporary employees are often given full-time opportunities with the company.

WALK-INS

Going from store to store seeking employment is known as a **walk-in**. The invitation for such pursuits often comes from a sign in a store window. In times when employment is at very high levels, the signs might indicate **signing bonuses** to motivate potential employees to find out more about available jobs. Many retailers agree that those who are self-motivated enough to seek employment via a walk-in often make very capable employees. On the other hand, many of these prospects do not fit the company's hiring profiles because of a lack of experience, and end up taking up the recruiter's valuable time. It is, however, a good method for attracting part-time help and seasonal workers. Marshall Field's, the Chicago-based department store, has installed employment kiosks on its selling floors to inform shoppers of available jobs. The kiosks are replete with computer terminals that enable the user to complete an application form. Once the form has been completed, the respondents are directed to the human resources department in the store. These kiosks not only attract attention but also give the employment manager time to quickly assess candidates and make a preliminary determination before he or she arrives at the human resources department. Best Buy, one of the largest electronics retailers in the United States, uses attractive tear-away cards in its stores to motivate people to apply for jobs. The information on these cards instructs candidates on how to apply by phone 24 hours a day, and promises that the call will only take between three and six minutes of their time. In order to motivate the would-be employees, the card spells out some of the reasons why Best Buy is a wise career choice.

"Now hiring" signs outside stores attract walk-ins.

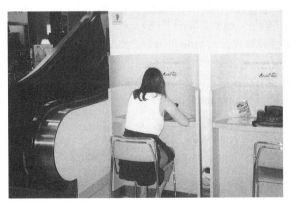

In-store employment kiosks are useful because they promote job openings and allow the manager to screen candidates before meeting with them.

TELEVISION PROGRAMMING

This has become an excellent tool to quickly announce job openings in a variety of industries. Local television stations, such as WTWN in Jacksonville, Florida, dedicate a specified amount of time during their regular schedule to inform viewers about the opportunities in the general area. Specifics such as the company's pay structure, hours of employment, and job specifications are clearly noted for each available position. Instructions on how to contact the company and apply for the job are provided.

INDUSTRY CONTACTS

This is an excellent, informal approach to use when a specific type of employee is needed to fill a vacancy. When a store buyer is looking for an assistant, one resource might be to contact a resident buying office merchandiser who generally interfaces with assistant buyers. Similarly, a manufacturer might give this same buyer information about people who might be right for the position. Since both of these industry contacts regularly meet with assistant buyers during their daily routines, they are able to assess their capabilities and make recommendations concerning their potential worth to a company.

Best Buy is one example of a company that uses a tear-away card as an in-store recruitment tool.

While each of these sources merits consideration from the company's employment managers, not every one brings equal results. That is, a particular retailer might find that classified advertising is most suitable for his or her needs, while another might get better results from an employment agency. The use of all of these resources to fill one position might not be a sound approach to use. The costs are considerable, and therefore more attention should focus on just one or two ways to fill the vacancy.

The seasoned human resources director keeps records of the successes and failures of the various sources of recruitment. Then, when a hiring need arises, the route that has brought the most favorable results in the past can again be utilized. Of course, different job titles might require different search techniques. The records might indicate that sales associates have been best secured through classified ads, whereas the recruitment of buyers has been more successful through industry contacts. Good record keeping will save the retailer both time and money in the recruitment process.

The Selection Process

When the employment sources have produced job applicants, the retailer is ready to begin the **selection process**. It is a procedure that attempts to match the candidate to the requirements of the position. Typically, the route used to ultimately select the individual with the most potential is a six step screening process. Not every company follows the same plan, but tailors one to fit the needs of their company. It should also be noted, that the best planning procedure might necessitate curtailment in times of low unemployment. When an employee pool is low, it is often necessary to circumvent some of the steps in the established procedure and make less scrutinized selections.

The following are the usual stages that most retailers use in the selection process:

1. Reviewing a résumé is generally the first step. Except for the typical lower-level jobs such as sales associates and stock personnel, a résumé that includes all of the applicant's educational, professional, and personal information is required. This document enables an employment expert to evaluate the candidate's background and to determine whether there is a potential fit. It is at this point in time that those worthy of consideration will be invited to go on to the next step.

2. Application forms are then generally completed by those who have passed the first stage. For lower level positions, this often serves as the first step in the procedure. In any case, the forms address such areas as personal information, educational achievements, professional accomplishments, and so forth. Once completed, the applications are carefully examined to see whether or not further screening is appropriate. It should be noted that today's application forms are quite different from those that were used in previous years. Questions regarding age and marital status, for example, are forbidden by the law. After the applications are reviewed a decision is made in terms of the applicant's match with the company's requirements.

3. Most companies schedule **preliminary interviews**. This is actually the first time in which a face-to-face meeting is held between the potential new employee and a representative of the human resources department. It is often a brief meeting that merely serves the purpose of further screening the applicant. For sales associates positions, this is often the first and last interview. Since the job specifications are listed on the job description, it is only necessary to determine whether the candidate possesses such attributes as good communication skills and dresses appropriately to meet company standards. This type of interview is sometimes referred to as a *rail interview* in a reference to a barrier separating the interviewer from the candidate. For more challenging positions, this interview serves only to determine whether a more intensive one is in order. The résumé and job application are both used as a basis for some of the questions that will be asked. By conducting

A typical job application form from a retailer.

these preliminary discussions, the interviewers will save time for the busy upper level executives who are engaged in a host of other activities. Of course, the preliminary review must be carefully executed to make certain that only those who do not meet minimum standards are not asked to move along any further in the selection process.

4. An extremely important part of the procedure is **reference checking**. It is often done at this point so that only those whose backgrounds have been cleared move onto the next stage. The résumé and application are used to conduct the reference search. Educational institutions are contacted to make certain that the prospect attended during the indicated dates, and that the level of education declared is accurate. Many secondary and postsecondary schools do not provide such information to third parties, therefore, the candidate must get official documents that verify his or her educational record. Former supervisors are also contacted to verify the employment information listed on the résumé and application. Technically, the only information that may be obtained is the validity of the candidate's past employment and the dates he or she worked for the company. Anything else might be considered an invasion of privacy. One way in which more and more retailers and other businesses are learning about an applicant's past is through the use of public record information. The leader in such investigative research is US Search.com. Employers wishing to check a candidate's past record may do so by logging onto the company's Web site, www.1800ussearch.com. Through customized searches, the user can quickly learn what he or she needs to know before considering a particular individual for employment. If the information checks out, the candidate moves on to the next stage.

5. Some form of testing is used by most retailers. The interview process can give the human resources representative only a feeling about the applicant. It cannot measure such competencies as mathematics skills, logical reasoning, or problem solving. Specific abilities are needed for each job, and through testing, these skills can be assessed. The testing may be conducted by the retailer's in-house experts or by outside agencies that specialize in the field. In addition to ability testing in areas such as computer literacy, personality, intelligence, and aptitude testing may be used to determine an individual's capacity to perform a certain type of job. Today a great deal of emphasis is also placed on drug testing. Drug problems have become so rampant, that most retailers use drug testing as a standard procedure in employee screening. Companies like Home Depot, for example, make applicants aware of their drug testing requirement as a condition of employment by posting large signs throughout the store. Any trace of drug usage immediately rules out the candidate's chance for employment. If drug tests are negative and the other standardized tests are completed satisfactorily, then the candidate is ready for the next stage in the process.

6. Final interviews are conducted for managerial level positions by the supervisor of the specific department. Sometimes, in cases where the position is one of great importance, a group or team interview might be conducted. In some instances, a series

of interviews are used to assess the candidate. In either case, the final interview is a lengthy one. If the screening process was carefully structured, there should be just a few candidates who will be considered for the job. The time involved in this process usually ranges from a few hours in a day to two or three days. The actual interview sessions generally take place in formal environments such as the supervisor's office or in a conference room if several company executives are involved. Sometimes off-premises locations, such as restaurants, are used to evaluate the candidate's demeanor in social situations.

7. Choosing the successful applicant is the task of the supervisor to whom the new employee will report. The actual decision may be spontaneous, but more than likely will take a great deal longer. Test results might need to be reevaluated, opinions of others might be warranted, or a closer look at references might be in order. Once a candidate is selected, he or she may be required to take a physical examination as a condition of employment. If everything checks out, the prospect is invited to join the retailer's team.

EMPLOYEE TRAINING

The purpose of employee training is usually twofold. It is used to introduce new employees to the company, and also to retrain those on staff who have been promoted or need to learn new systems or procedures. Those who are already on board may participate in individual instruction or group seminars, depending upon the scope of the new activities. The amount of training necessary before the new employee can assume his or her role in the company varies from job to job and retailer to retailer. Some merchants utilize formal training sessions to familiarize the worker with his or her expected duties and responsibilities. Others may subscribe to on-the-job training where those who have just joined the business are immediately put on the firing line. Most retailers use a combination of both approaches in their training programs.

New Sales Associates

Those on the firing line are the retailer's sales associates. They are primarily found on the selling floors, but many also work in catalog divisions, or on Web sites, where live interaction with a company representative may be necessary. In any case, the better trained the associate is, the more likely it is that a sale will be made. All too often, merchants short change sales associates in terms of training. Some only use a two- or three-hour session to offer the basic knowledge necessary to sell, while more progressive companies may develop sales training programs that last a full week.

The training at this level of employment may take a number of forms. The program might utilize professional videos that initially introduce the newcomer to the business and then concentrate on selling practices. The value of such visual presentations is not only that they teach selling techniques, but that they may be used over and over again. Guess, Inc. uses a combination of video and CD-ROM instruction in the training of its sales staff. Impressive sales improvements have been made since the program's inception. Presented in an MTV format, because the sales associates generally range in age from 18 to 25, the presentations are slick, fun, and brief.

One of the methods that best simulates an actual selling demonstration is **role-playing**. The concept involves two participants; the sales associate and the shopper. The two engage in a presentation that involves a particular product or service. Trainers evaluate every step of the way, beginning with greeting the customer and ending with a sale. In this way, the evaluator may reinforce the positive aspects of the sale, while the negatives can be pointed out and corrected. The arena for such role-playing is in a setting that simulates the actual selling environment. If the new sales associate tried his or her approach in a department with a real shopper, there might be some risk involved, thereby turning the potential customer into one whose needs were not satisfied. It is very important in this type of training to make certain that the consumer role-player conducts him or herself in a manner that approximates a realistic presentation.

Executive Trainees

Most major retailers utilize formal training programs for the people whom they expect to become managers in their companies. Whether it is a large department store group such as the Federated Stores or food franchises like McDonald's, the programs are vital to the future success of the companies.

Executive or management training programs use a variety of techniques to train the future leaders of retailing. Typically, the programs offer a combination of formalized classroom work coupled with on-the-job training. Specifically, lectures, videos, case problem solving, programmed instruction, demonstrations, and role-playing make up the training techniques used. Macy's Executive Development program is considered to be one of the bet-

ter programs in the country. It utilizes on-the-job training involving placement in a sales supervision environment; conferences with key executives that cover every aspect of the company's endeavors such as merchandising, sales promotion, and store management; counseling to provide answers to questions about the company; performance reviews; and a rotational plan that moves **executive trainees** from area to area.

Support Personnel

Throughout the retail organization there are many who operate in support positions such as cashiers, stock people, unit control, and customer service. Their responsibility, while neither management nor sales, is extremely important to the overall

Sales support personnel are a retailer's representatives to the public. Their training must include human relations skills to ensure customer satisfaction, which is an essential ingredient of profitability.

functioning of the company. Cashiers, for example, must be trained to make certain that the right prices are being charged, especially when markdowns have not been noted on price tags.

Many of the support staff are trained using real machinery, equipment, and other tools in simulations. A computer-driven cash register is used to train the new users, for example, and forklift is used to train personnel in placing stock on hard-to-reach warehouse shelves.

Retrainees

It should be understood that the initial training that a new employee receives is sometimes not sufficient for his or her tenure at a company. New computer systems might be installed thereby requiring the retraining of those who will use the system. Transfers and promotions also necessitate retraining. When a sales associate is promoted to a junior merchandising position, there is generally a need for training. Often this is on-the-job training where all the fundamentals and tasks of the new challenge can be learned.

No matter which employees are being trained, there are numerous advantages of these efforts including:

- Improving competency levels of the individuals makes them more productive in their assigned duties and responsibilities.
- Well-trained employees need less supervision, allowing managers to focus on their own activities.
- Sound training, particularly for those on the selling floor, helps present a better image of the store to the shopper.

Focus on . . .
McDonald's

IT WOULD BE HARD TO FIND ANYONE IN THE UNITED STATES who hasn't eaten at or at least heard of McDonald's. For that matter, with its worldwide expansion to a vast number of cities all over the globe, the recognition has become even greater. Ray Kroc, its founder, mortgaged his home and invested his entire life savings to open the initial restaurant in Des Plaines, Illinois, in 1955. Who would have believed that the company would become one of the most amazing entrepreneurial stories in business history.

In order to bring the company to this enviable position, emphasis has always been placed on having the best possible management team. To be sure the team was trained properly, McDonald's opened Hamburger University. Located in Oak Brook, Illinois, the university has grown to become a worldwide training center that exclusively instructs personnel employed by McDonald's Corporation or by McDonald's independent franchisees. Founded in 1961, it has come a long way since the company's first training facility which was located in the basement of a McDonald's restaurant in Elk Grove Village, Illinois. Since then, the university has moved twice, and the average size of a class has grown from 10 to more than 200!

Today, more than 65,000 managers in McDonald's restaurants have graduated from Hamburger University, now located in a 130,000-square-foot, state-of-the-art facility that employs 30 resident professors. Because of the organization's international scope, translators and electronic equipment help the professors to teach and communicate in 22 languages at one time. In addition to its international headquarters, the company manages ten international training centers, including Hamburger Universities in England, Japan, Germany, and Australia.

It is such attention to training that has enabled the company to remain a leader in this highly competitive business arena.

EMPLOYEE EVALUATION PROGRAMS

The breadth and depth of evaluation procedures vary from retailer to retailer. Small companies, such as boutiques where the number of employees is low, usually forgo the formalized methods of evaluation. Supervisors generally talk to their employees about their positive and negative traits in an informal manner, if they discuss them at all. In larger operations, the procedure is a formal one. Evaluation forms are central to evaluating employee progress. These forms are generally filled out by the individual's supervisor in conjunction with a human resources specialist. The reasons for such programs, whether formal or informal, are numerous. They include:

- Determining whether or not the employee has performed satisfactorily and should be rewarded with a salary increase.
- Deciding if the present position is appropriate for the worker or if he or she might better serve the company in a different capacity.
- Evaluating the employee for a promotion and monetary rewards.
- Determining if the individual has mastered the job for which he or she has been hired or if further training is needed.
- Eliminating those individuals who have not performed according to the specifications outlined in the job description.

Sound programs provide for regular and continuous evaluations of employees. These evaluations should be positive experiences, correcting shortcomings and underscoring the challenges that have been effectively met. By implementing a sound system that addresses all of the standard elements of evaluation, employees are apt to perform at their highest potential.

An Ethical Consideration

WHILE HIRING DISCRIMINATION HAS DIMINISHED in many businesses, minority groups still find upward mobility difficult. Companies such as Denny's have made news regarding charges of discrimination. In fact, Denny's has paid significant fines to settle the cases and has made efforts not only to correct the situation, but also to change the public's impression of the company.

Denny's is not the only major company that has paid the price for discriminatory practices. Not only are such tactics illegal, immoral, and unethical, but they attract such bad press that it eventually cuts into the profits of the businesses in questions. The NAACP has called for people to boycott such companies. This attention is not welcomed by retailers and other business enterprises, and can be avoided only when genuinely unbiased hiring and promotion practices are carried out.

COMPENSATION

The method of compensation used by retailers should reflect the needs of both the employer and the employee. The employee must be satisfactorily compensated to be properly stimulated to do his or her best for the company. If the remuneration system is carefully determined, it should provide the following benefits to the employer:

- Maximize the output of the individuals on the payroll.
- Reduce employee turnover, which can reduce training costs.
- Motivate an individual's performance, which can lead to in-house promotions and eliminate the need to look outside of the company for new personnel.

For the employee, a sound compensation plan should offer the following:

- An incentive to provide an honest on-the-job performance.
- An elimination of the temptation for internal theft because the salary is sufficient to meet the employee's needs.
- A desire to remain with the company instead of regularly seeking higher salaries elsewhere.
- The heightening of morale.
- The maintenance of a good standard of living.

Keeping these requirements in mind, management must establish a system that best suits the different jobs that are found within the company. Different levels of work necessitate different levels of compensation. Sales associates, department managers, buyers, merchandise managers, and sales promotion directors, for example, are each paid differently. Some are monetarily rewarded according to the number of hours worked in a week, some with salary and commission plans, and others by set salaries and bonus incentives. In each of these methods, it is essential that management assess the standards established by the industry so that they can meet or beat the competition to make certain that the best people are employed.

Of course, employers must obey the laws governing employee compensation. The federal government, as well as many state governments, has established a minimum wage. At the present time, the federal minimum is $5.15 per hour. In Santa Cruz, California, however, with the cost of living so high and a labor shortage, the minimum is $11.00 per hour. At times of greater prosperity, the minimums never really come into play because starting salaries are generally higher. On the other hand, if unemployment figures escalate, the minimum wage is often paid to new personnel.

Straight Salary

Many merchants use this arrangement to pay their staffs. It is particularly common with sales associates and some levels of management. This system of compensation has advantages for the employer and employee. For the employer, it establishes regular expenses. For the employee, it provides a steady income. On the other hand, it also has disadvantages. It doesn't motivate employees, thus guaranteeing minimal commitment from the staff. And, by reason of its fixed expenditure, it sometimes costs more than the value of the actual job performance. Because the salary is a fixed, steady one, employees find this arrangement favorable. Since the costs are easy to compute, this type of payroll works best for management.

Straight Commission

Unlike the straight salary plan, which affords safety and security to the employee, straight commission employees must perform in order to earn their salaries. There is no guarantee at the end of the week that the sales associate who sells on commission will receive a paycheck. This does, however, provide the employee with the incentive to perform to his or her highest potential in return for a greater salary than if he or she were being paid a predetermined amount.

More and more retailers have introduced straight commission to their sales associates. This is particularly true for the sale of high-ticket items such as designer clothing, major appliances, and computers. Those being paid in this manner must be well trained and ready to spend every available moment trying to make the sale. It provides the experienced, professional seller with the opportunity to earn more than the standard salary common to retailing, bringing the company the potential for more business.

Nordstrom's, the leading upscale retailer of fashion merchandise, was one of industry's first to introduce the system. Not only has it resulted it better monetary rewards for its employees, but it has also helped to establish the highest levels of customer service in retailing. Employees quickly learn that when you provide excellent customer service, a customer is likely to buy more. Following Nordstrom's lead, companies like Saks Fifth Avenue, and Bergdorf Goodman, have opted for the straight commission plan in many of their departments.

Salary Plus Commission

The best of both worlds for many employers and employees is the system that offers a guaranteed wage along with an incentive for better performance. A great number of retailers who have experienced lackluster commitments from their employees have turned to this method. By paying the minimum wage, and adding the opportunity for more money, merchants find that sales associates are ready to meet and greet more customers.

Commission rate varies from store to store and department to department. It might be as little as 1 percent or as much as 5 percent, with small ticket item commissions at the bottom of the scale.

Salary Plus Bonus

Department managers, store managers, buyers, and merchandise managers are sometimes rewarded with bonuses in addition to their established salaries. When their departments, divisions, or individual stores surpass the revenues that have been predetermined for them, they are sometimes awarded extra compensation. This plan not only motivates them to work harder, but it also stimulates them to encourage better performances from their subordinates.

The system usually sets a specific minimum goal for each manager to achieve. Once that amount is met, a bonus based upon the excess business is given to the supervisor. Often the

TABLE 6.2
BENEFITS OF COMPENSATION PLANS

PLAN	EMPLOYER BENEFIT	EMPLOYEE BENEFIT
Straight Salary	Easy to formulate, regular costs, simple bookkeeping	Guaranteed wages, easy to understand
Straight Commission	Motivates better performance, improved customer service, salaries in line with performance	Easy to understand, better pay for better performance
Salary Plus Commission	Provides some incentive so productivity increases, better customer service	Offers better salary opportunity, fairly stable wages
Salary Plus Bonus	Increases productivity	Opportunity for greater monetary rewards

bonus amount is based upon an escalating scale. For example, if the measured time period is a month, and the expected sales are $300,000, the manager whose department sells $330,000, would be rewarded, perhaps at extra 1% of the additional $30,000. If sales of an additional $75,000 are realized, then the incentive might result in 2%. There is no specific plan used by all retailers, just the one that best addresses the needs of each company. Stores like Dayton-Hudson and JCPenney use a quota bonus system.

Table 6.2 summarizes and compares the benefits of the four major compensations plans for both the employer and employee.

Other Monetary Rewards

In an effort to maximize the performance of their staffs, retailers offer some other types of incentives. These include **profit sharing**, which enables employees to share in the success of the company. By providing this type of monetary gain, each individual is encouraged to maximize his or her work effort since the rewards will be beneficial to him or herself. At the other extreme is the extra money that comes for selling slow moving merchandise. Small stores often reward **P.M.s**, or prize money, for items that the company is eager to sell. Typically, most sales associates try to sell the hot items first because they are easier to move. When given the extra incentive of prize money, many place their efforts on the less desirable merchandise. Contests and other promotional endeavors also bring extra pay to employees. The person who sells the most swimsuits in a week, for example, might be the recipient of a dollar prize.

More and more retailers, whether they are small entrepreneurs or the retail giants, have come to recognize that with the proper incentives sales will increase and customers will be treated to better service.

EMPLOYEE BENEFITS

While most people are motivated to work for one company rather than another because of the salaries offered, there is a growing trend to consider benefits as part of the package. The extremely high cost of health insurance, for example, has made it an important requirement for families. Those companies that offer sound medical plans have often been able to use this benefit to attract capable workers even though actual salaries might not be better than anywhere else.

Most retailers are also offering pension plans as another incentive. Not only do today's workers want benefits while they are employed, but also want the security of being able to have a quality life upon retirement. In the not too distant past, many retailers didn't offer pensions, except perhaps to their management teams. Today, most retailers provide some sort of retirement package. People looking at a retailing career generally compare one pension program to another before making a final choice.

One of the most important duties of the human resources benefits manager is to develop programs that help attract qualified candidates. At one time, classified ads merely focused on the wages being offered. Today, there is considerable emphasis on the benefits packages to entice people to apply for jobs.

At the Target Corporation, human resources has developed a program that is one of the most complete in the industry.

The features of the plan are as follows:

- Pretax salary set-asides to help pay for dependent care.
- Childcare resource and referral information.
- Alternative work arrangements such as telecommuting, **job sharing**, work at home, and flextime.
- Time off to care for a sick child or seriously ill family member.
- Maternity leaves.
- 401(k) plan and employee **stock options**/stock ownership plan that includes a dollar for dollar match for the first 5 percent of salary.
- A pharmacy discount program, including mail-order access for maintenance prescriptions.
- Vacation values programs that feature discounts on airfare, car rental, and hotel stays.
- Automobile and homeowner's insurance through payroll deduction at group discount rates.

Without programs of this nature it is unlikely that retailers will be able to attract qualified employees to fill their needs and remain competitive in the field.

LABOR RELATIONS

Satisfying employees is key to their performance. Those who are pleased with their working conditions are more likely to perform better on the job; those with issues are more than likely not to. The human resources department is assigned the responsibility of making certain that there is a comfort level in the business environment that is beneficial to both management and labor. They must be sufficiently competent to resolve employee problems and relieve any tensions that might hinder performance.

The problem solving is an ongoing challenge in major companies. It might be a relatively simple task between a manager and a subordinate or one that involves **collective bargaining**. Most major retailers have labor unions that spend a great deal of time trying to improve working conditions, salaries, and benefit plans. Human resources managers are called upon to participate in the drawing up of employee contracts and to settle disputes when these contracts are violated. The role is a sensitive one requiring sympathetic handling in order to prevent slowdowns or, at the extreme level, employee strikes.

SUPERVISION TRAINING

Human resources leadership is often called upon to establish guidelines in order to foster a better understanding between management and their subordinates. All too often those inexperienced in dealing with the people in their charge create problems that deter satisfactory working conditions. Many of the confrontations may be easily solved if there is an understanding of human relations and the manner in which unpleasantries can be avoided. To achieve an environment that maximizes the highest level of excellent behavior on the part of both the supervisors and their subordinates, human resources experts, with the benefit of sound psychological and behavioral training, often provide a set of principles and provisions to be addressed.

These include:

- Developing an orientation package that outlines, among other things, the importance of each employee to the success of the company.
- Setting up an appointment between the new worker and his or her supervisor to make certain that responsibilities are carefully discussed.
- Preparing a set of goals expected of each new employee.
- Informing the employee of the procedures to be followed in case of a dispute.
- Recognizing the need to be a team player.
- Developing a recognition program that singles out employees who have performed above and beyond expectations.

TRENDS FOR THE NEW MILLENNIUM

- There is a definite need for retirees to return to the workforce and fill part-time positions. This potential personnel pool is one that is dedicated and able to perform at very high levels. The government's decision to pay retirees social security at age 65 even if they work will bring more qualified people back to businesses.
- More disabled people will be utilized in retail positions. Company records indicate that these individuals' performances often surpass those who are not physically or emotionally challenged.
- Job sharing will become more prevalent. Employees who cannot work full time due to family commitments will share responsibilities with other staff members on a part-time basis. The Target Corporation has led the way in this area and others are starting to follow suit.
- Multimedia training for new employees will reach new levels through the use of CD-ROMS that can be used over and over again. This relieves the strain on human resource managers and allows them to perform other duties.
- There will be greater emphasis on motivational compensation plans.
- The addition of childcare programs to many retail organizations will attract a new group of workers.

- Online job searches will reduce the amount of time traditionally needed to find employment.

CHAPTER HIGHLIGHTS

- Even with the passage of key legislation by the federal government, there is still a disparity in pay between men and women who perform the same job.

- The tasks of the human resources department includes recruitment, training, evaluation, compensation, benefits, and labor relations.

- The recruitment problem is greatly affected by the economics of the country. In times of significant employment, many retailers lessen their standards so that they can have the staff necessary to carry out the company's tasks.

- In order to hire the right person for the job, the human resources specialists undergo investigative research known as job analysis.

- Retailers either recruit by means of looking internally for people to fill higher positions, or use outside sources to fill vacancies.

- While classified ads help to alert individuals of a company's available positions, more and more major retailers are turning to the Internet for recruitment purposes.

- Employment agencies are excellent for merchants to use for recruitment purposes because they carefully screen applicants, saving the employment managers a great deal of time and effort.

- Typically, the selection process involves a series of screening devices that helps lower the number or candidates being considered for the available position.

- Much time is saved by using online companies that check the credibility of job applicants. In this way, those who fail the test can be quickly eliminated from consideration.

- Training at the retail level is a two-part project; it trains new employees and retrains those on the staff when the need arises.

- In addition to the traditional methods of using trainers, many retailers are utilizing CD-ROM and video packages to instruct new employees and current employees who have been promoted to other positions.

- The evaluation of employees should be an ongoing process so that individuals can learn and correct their weaknesses and be rewarded for jobs well done.

- Compensation plans range from straight salaries to those that motivate employees through incentives such as commissions and bonuses.

- Because of the competitive nature of retailing salaries, more and more companies are offering extensive benefits packages to encourage employee longevity.

- The human resources department plays an important role in labor relations by resolving conflicts and making the working environment one that encourages better job performance.

IMPORTANT RETAILING TERMS

employee pool

glass ceiling

job specifications

job analysis

job description

internal sourcing

promotion-from-within

outside sourcing

classified ads

employment agency

executive search firm

headhunters

internship

walk-ins

signing bonuses

selection process

preliminary interview

reference checking

role-playing

executive trainee

profit sharing

P.M.s

job sharing

stock options

collective bargaining

FOR REVIEW

1. Why is the problem of staffing greater today than it was in the past?

2. How does the concept of supply and demand affect the human resources department in its hiring practices?

3. What is meant by the glass ceiling as it relates to promotions?

4. Why is it necessary for the human resources department to undertake the task of job analysis?

5. What is the difference between the terms job specifications and job descriptions?

6. Describe the concept of promotion from within. Why do most retailers utilize this method.

7. How have Internet Web sites assisted employment managers in their search for new employees?

8. Why are many retail organizations willing to use employment agencies to fill positions even though it is costly?

9. How can educational institutions assist in the recruitment process?

10. List each of the stages that most of the retailers use in the selection process.

11. How does the preliminary interview differ from the final interview?

12. Why are many retailers using Internet search firms as part of the screening process?

13. In addition to training new employees, why is it necessary to sometimes train employees who are already working for the company?

14. Explain the importance of employee evaluations to the employer as well as the employee.

15. Why are more and more retailers adding commissions to the compensation plans used to pay sales associates?

16. When does it sometimes become necessary for municipalities to exceed the minimum wage set by the federal government?

17. Define the term, P.M.s and why some retailers use this system.

18. What role have benefits packages played in the hiring and retention of employees?

19. Why are human resources managers involved in labor relations?

AN INTERNET ACTIVITY

Pretend that you are ready to graduate and have chosen retailing as your career goal. After some consideration, you have decided to pursue opportunities with two major retailers.

Go to their official Web sites and access the career opportunities area. Carefully scroll down each page in the career sections to compare their recruitment procedures.

Prepare a chart with the following headings, indicating the tools used by each.

Recruitment Procedures	
Name of Retailer	Name of Retailer

When the chart is completed, select the retailer that you think offers the better package for recruitment procedures. Note the reasons why you think it is the better choice.

EXERCISES AND PROJECTS

1. Examine the classified advertisements of the major newspaper in your area. Select three ads for the same type of position and analyze the contents of each. The ads should be attached to an 8 1/2 x 11 sheet of paper with the job title at the top of the page.

    For each one, note whether or not the following have been indicated:

    • Salary

    • Benefits

    • Working hours

    • Experience required

    • Academic requirements

Select the ad that you think best describes the employment opportunity and note your reasons for the choice.

2. Pretend that you are seeking part-time employment in a store while you are still attending school. Using the walk-in approach, choose three stores that you think would suit your preference. Go to the employment office and tell the representative of your desire to work part-time. Using the information gathered at the meeting, evaluate each retailer in terms of its approach to you.

    Each evaluation should address such aspects as courtesy, length of interview, if any, and application availability.

    Once the task has been completed, select the retailer you think was best organized, and indicate your reasons for choosing it.

THE CASE OF REFOCUSING TRAINING PROCEDURES

Hewlett's started out as a small chain operation in the West in 1950. It began as a single unit company that featured a limited number of sporting goods items such as golf equipment and tennis rackets. Year after year, the company continuously grew not only in size but also in terms of its product mix. Three years ago Hewlett's was operating 462 stores from coast to coast, which, in addition to its golf and tennis equipment, sold a wealth of exercise products, camping equipment, and apparel appropriate for these activities.

Two years ago, the company expanded its operation into a multichannel organization, adding catalog and Web site divisions. While the latter two are still in their infancies, the outlook has been excellent for their success.

The running of such a huge operation has had its problems, many of which are presently being resolved. The only one that still needs refinement is the training program. Until now, Hewlett's left the training of employees to the human resources management team at the company's headquarters. There the team developed guidelines for store managers to follow when orienting new employees to the company. Although this plan had some degree of success, it took time away from the managers.

Elaine Salter, the human resources director for the company, suggested to Hewlett's CEO that a plan might be considered to change its training program from one that used managers to one that centered exclusively on using CD-ROMs and video presentations. She was asked to study the availability of existing programs but none were available that specifically fit the company's needs. Further investigation revealed that customized packages would cost approximately $200,000.

Her presentation to the management team received mixed reactions. Jack Slaughter, the CEO, thought the costs were too high and that they should leave well enough alone. Sam Jacobson, the chief trainer was of the opinion that individual instruction is better, but perhaps a general video used by many businesses could also be employed. Ms. Salter, recognizing the need for more training based on the multichannel expansion, believed that the new methodology was a must if the company was to maintain a profitable base.

At this point in time the problem has yet to be resolved.

Questions

1. With which executive do you agree? Why?
2. Is there another plan that could be utilized? What would that plan be?

CHAPTER 7

Loss Prevention

After you have completed this chapter, you should be able to discuss:

- ► How inventory shortages have affected the retailer's profitability.
- ► The numerous deterrents to shoplifting that are being used by merchants all over the globe.
- ► Techniques human resources managers use to reduce internal theft.
- ► How employees are being trained and motivated to cut shoplifting losses.
- ► The different types of electronic surveillance systems that retailers are using in their stores.
- ► The technologies used to cut losses from fraudulent Internet purchasing.

As merchants all over the world entered the twenty-first century, most were plagued with the enormous losses due to shoplifting and theft by unscrupulous employees. More than $30 billion per year is still being lost, with the largest portion of that being attributed to internal theft. It is reported that the public is perpetrating 92 percent of the thefts. However, the 7 percent stolen by employees is valued at more than 9 times what is lost through shoplifting. The final 1 percent of losses comes at the hands of vendors who are also involved in cheating their customers through short shipments. These alarming statistics also reveal that losses due to theft run from between 1 and 8 percent of sales. When these numbers are actually calculated with a company's sales figures, the actual dollar losses may run into millions for a retailing giant.

Most honest shoppers don't realize that they are actually paying for these crimes. In order for retailers to turn a profit, it is necessary for them to calculate their expenses and use them, along with the cost of the merchandise, as the basis for determining how much they must charge for their goods. One of these expenses is dollar loss due to theft. Thus, if a merchant determines that theft is 5 percent of sales, he or she must adjust prices to reflect that 5 percent loss.

With the realization that these staggering figures have reached overwhelming proportions in every retailing classification, such as department stores, specialty chains, and supermarkets, the industry has started using more deterrents than ever before. A combination of educational approaches to loss prevention and new technology shows promise that the future will be brighter for merchants. Whether the focus is on a retailer's brick-and-mortar operation, Web site, or catalog division, closer control of the losses is taking center stage.

This chapter will concentrate on the two major groups that cause the losses—company employees and shoplifters. In addition, shortages due to dishonest vendors and Internet fraud will also be addressed.

SHOPLIFTING

Those people who enter stores posing as customers but steal the merchandise rather than pay for it, are called **shoplifters**. While many might think the individuals that comprise the group are suspicious, scruffy-looking characters, this is not the case. There is no stereotypical shoplifter. He or she is often well-dressed, and looks exactly like a typical shopper making a legitimate purchase. The shoplifter needs to be able to move through the store without attracting undue attention. Those with less than proper grooming are often suspect and are carefully scrutinized by store employees. Shoplifters come from all walks of life. They include professional business people, members of the clergy, educators, celebrities, students, and a host of others. Some commit the crimes because of drugs and other problems associated with economic pressures, while others perform the act because of **kleptomania**—a psychological problem that causes an irresistible urge to steal. Some act alone in their endeavors, satisfying personal needs without making payments, while others are parts of professional teams that set out to steal just about anything that can bring them a profit when resold. Many professional shoplifting gangs steal to order. Accomplices place their orders and pay these shoplifters for the delivered merchandise.

One of the causes for the escalating shoplifting problem is that today's retail environments almost encourage theft with their many open counters and airy merchandise displays. Another is the shortage of sales associates found in many stores. With easy access to the merchandise, and not many eyes in place to deter the thefts, shoplifting is relatively simple.

Recognizing the seriousness of the situation, merchants are arming themselves with many different deterrents to control the problem.

The Stein Mart Story
Reducing Shrinkage

AS IS THE CASE WITH EVERY RETAILER IN THE UNITED STATES, Stein Mart has its share of problems concerning merchandise losses. To address the problem, Stein Mart uses a variety of techniques. The company realizes that both shoplifting and internal theft can seriously hamper profits.

Its loss prevention program includes a number of different approaches. One is the education of every employee in its organization. Employees learn how to spot would-be shoplifters and the manner in which to handle them. In this training, they also are made aware of the dangers of employee theft, and how it could jeopardize their positions in the company.

Other techniques include the placement of plainclothes officers on the selling floor. These officers constantly roam the aisles looking for a shoplifter in action. Cameras are strategically placed so that those inclined to steal can be watched, and their actions recorded for legal uses. A security code is also in place to notify plainclothes officers of a potential shoplifting attempt.

As in most other retail businesses, the use of no-gos is important to merchandise security. These tags, which are attached to the merchandise, are part of an alarm system that is activated if merchandise leaves the store without being paid for. The tags are reserved primarily for high-ticket items.

- -

Major Shoplifting Deterrents

Retailers have three major options available to them in the prevention of shoplifting. Security guards and video surveillance systems, anchoring merchandise in place, and tag and alarm systems.

Security Guards and Video Surveillance Systems

The strategic placement of security guards at stores' entrances might deter some people from trying to leave with goods that they haven't purchased. The visibility of the guard is somewhat of a deterrent, but it also makes the honest shopper nervous. Because of this, many retailers have steered away from using guards, except, those that deal in high-volume, low-priced merchandise.

Instead, many use some type of **video surveillance system**. Typically, **closed circuit television (CCTV)** involves the installation of video cameras in prominent places in the store. The system observes shoppers and records their actions. Through observation by security

SpeedDome® ultra is a high-speed programmable dome camera system that clearly focuses on people, even in the dark.

guards, the offenders can be easily identified. This system is especially helpful when suspects are recorded in the act more than once. Repeat offenders are often apprehended in this way. By analyzing the tapes, retailers are able to learn the patterns of shoplifters and come up with solutions to the problem. The more sophisticated, state-of-the-art models that are in use today are hidden in places such as smoke detectors, sprinkler systems, thermostats and clocks. From these vantage points a security guard can use a camera that has the capability of panning and zooming to follow the suspect. Stores that do not have sufficient resources for security guards to man the camera, may use automatic panning devices to perform the task.

Anchoring Merchandise in Place

If you have ever shopped for an expensive item such as a leather jacket, you may noticed that the item is locked in place with security cables. While this technique secures the products, it also makes it difficult for customers to closely examine them and try them on. Accessibility to the merchandise is possible only when the keeper of the keys is available. Often times finding a sales associate who can assist the customer is impossible. Discouraged shoppers often leave the area frustrated. In this instance, the merchandise has been protected, but the sale has also been lost.

Tag and Alarm Systems

Better known as **electronic article surveillance (EAS)**, this system is considered to be the most effective method for protecting the retailer's inventory. When used in conjunction with closed circuit television, it is the best protection that the industry has developed to date. The technology identifies articles as they pass through a gated area in the store. If unpurchased merchandise leaves the store, an alarm system is triggered. Today, according to the Association of Automated Identification Manufacturers, there are more than 800,000 EAS systems installed throughout the world.

There are three major types of EAS systems used by retailers. Each involves the use of a label or tag that is attached to an item. Once the customer pays for the item, the tag is either deactivated or removed. A **detacher** is used to remove the **hard tags**, and a scanner is used to deactivate a disposable paper tag by swiping it over a pad or handheld scanner. If the tag is not removed or deactivated, an alarm will sound when the item is removed from the store.

One of the more productive types of tag devices is one that contains **ink reservoirs**. If these traps are not removed by a detacher, ink will spill onto the item and permanently damage it. Recognizing that the article will be destroyed, the perpetrator generally moves on to another area of the store.

The most widely used device is known as the **radio frequency (RF) system**. This system involves gates at the store's entrances and exits. When a shopper passes through the gates, an alarm will sound if the sensor tag hasn't been removed. Sometimes an automated message is sounded telling the

Ultra Max® anti-theft system, pictured here, is the world's most innovative electronic article surveillance system.

shopper to return to the department for tag removal. Of course, those who don't intend to pay for the items, attempt to quickly exit the premises. Sometimes invisible systems are used instead of entry gates. This technique involves using an antenna loop around the store's door, leaving it virtually undetectable by shoppers. While this might serve the needs of some upscale retailers who do not want a visible system to clutter their entrances, the system has not proven to be as effective as the visible type. In fact, there is proof that a visible system is more of a deterent to theft.

Another system that is widely used and is dominant throughout Europe, and in pharmacies and supermarkets in the United States, is the **electronic magnetic (EM) system**. In this technology, a magnetic, iron-containing strip with an adhesive layer is attached to the merchandise. The strip is not removed at checkout, but is deactivated by means of a scanner that uses a high magnetic field. Those who try to bypass the gates at the store's entrances without having the strip desensitized will trip an alarm. One feature of the system is that if goods are returned, the procedure can be reversed to restore the strip instead of applying a new one.

The newest system to be used is the **acousto-magnetic (AM) system**, which has the ability to protect very wide store exits and allows for high-speed label application. Stores like Home Depot are using acousto-magnetic tags from Sensormatic Electronics Corp., the largest surveillance system manufacturer in the United States.

Focus on . . .
Sensormatic Electronics Corp.

ONE OF THE LARGEST COMPANIES DEDICATED TO PROTECTING retailers' inventories is Sensormatic Electronics Corporation. Founded in 1966, it has grown to employ 5,700 people and has an annual revenue of more than $1 billion. The company designs, manufacturers, sells, services, and supports the world's most advanced lines of fully integrated electronic article surveillance (EAS), video surveillance, access control, **electronic asset protection (EAP)**, and security management systems. Sensormatic not only addresses the needs of the retailing industry, but it also services consumer goods manufacturers who apply the Sensormatic antitheft tags to their products before they leave for their customers' stores. More than 113 countries throughout the world have been users of Sensormatic products, with 93 of the top 100 retailers around the globe counted as clients.

When a shopper walks through a store he or she is likely to come upon one of the company's more widely used products, hard tags. These tags are affixed to the items and must be removed upon purchase. Some of the tags are equipped with ink reservoirs that if not properly removed will spill ink on the garment and permanently damage it. The alarm-equipped gates through which shoppers pass are most often part of a system that has been installed by Sensormatic.

The company's latest innovation is the smartEAS system, which comprises **radio frequency identification device (RFID)** and EAS systems, offering retailers the ability to implement customer self-checkout, enhanced inventory management, and stock cycle counts, as well as new antidiversion, return-fraud, and merchandising programs. At a time when many retailers are actively exploring customer self-checkout, the system will be widely used.

Retailers are always able to explore new product offerings of Sensormatic and obtain customer service at its Web site, www.sensormatic.com.

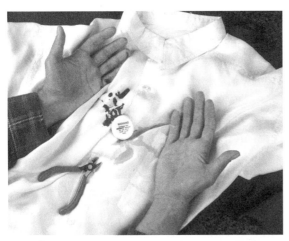

Inktag® releases permanent ink onto the merchandise if customers illegally remove the tags.

The Radio Frequency Identification, or RFID, system is the newest technology used by retailers.

Some of the components of the EAS systems include:

- Disposable paper tags that can be imprinted with a bar code containing a host of information including price.
- Reusable, hard plastic tags referred to as **alligators**.
- Benefit denial tags which feature ink reservoirs that damage the garment if the tag is improperly removed.
- Scanners that deactivate the merchandise tag.
- Detachers that easily remove the hard tag from a garment.

Supertag® is the world's most widely used hard tag.

Other Shoplifting Deterrents

While the aforementioned systems are becoming commonplace in most major retail enterprises, others have also been used by giants in the industry as well as the smaller companies that have neither the need for such elaborate methods nor the capital available to install such systems.

Two-Way Mirrors

Although **two-way mirrors** have raised invasion of privacy issues in the retailing industry, they are still being used in some stores. In order to prevent any lawsuits, management usually posts signs alerting the shoppers that they are being used in fitting room areas.

On one side, these mirrors are used by customers in an ordinary manner, while the other side allows employees to watch the customers. When they are used, most retailers report a decrease in shoplifting.

Magnifying Mirrors

It is mostly the smaller retailers who use **magnifying mirrors** in their attempt to spot shoplifters. The mirrors are strategically placed in areas that are generally concealed by merchandise racks. Store personnel are able to check these concealed areas for potential shoplifters by watching the mirrors. Even if the perpetrators are hard to spot, the mirrors often act as psychological deterrents. They serve a purpose for the merchant who cannot afford the costs of more sophisticated surveillance systems.

Control Access

One of the ways in which shoplifters remove merchandise from the store involves the fitting room. After they have selected a number of garments to try on, they head for the changing area and begin their scheme to steal merchandise. Some have been known to put several outfits on, one on top of the other, and leave the store without paying for them. Others have left their own clothing and replaced it with the store's merchandise. Still others merely enter these rooms wearing baggy, oversized apparel and stuff the new items into them.

Through **control access**, as it is known to these areas, retailers have significantly reduced theft. One method is to lock the fitting rooms and to open them only when a sales associate has counted the garments that a shopper will try on. He or she gives the customer a plastic number that is equal to the number of items taken into the room. When the customer leaves the room, the associate must reconcile the number of pieces taken out with the plastic marker. If employees carefully check the shoppers in and out of the fitting rooms, this system will reduce shoplifting. Gap and Old Navy use this method, as do many department stores.

Special Coded Signals

Some of the major department stores use a **coded signal** that alerts their store detectives to potential thefts. It is a method that involves the use of a signal that is sounded over the store's loudspeaker system. The code is one that is understood only by the employees in the store. A sales associate or manager might initiate the action by dialing a number that is directly linked to the store's security office. Another technique involves the witness of the potential crime using the store's speaker system to alert the in-house security team. In either case, using a code alerts the proper authorities of a problem without causing undue alarm to the customers.

Warning Signs

Some merchants post **warning signs** that help to deter shoplifting. These retailers usually sell value or discount merchandise and attract large numbers of shoppers to their stores. At the store's entrance or other strategic locations, signs are posted that state, "Free ride to the police station if you take merchandise without paying for it." Another might warn that "Those people committing in-store theft will be fully prosecuted." Each of these signs is usually an excellent method for deterring the theft of small items. It is usually the youthful offender who, given such a warning, refrains from committing the crime.

Another type of warning sign is found in the area of the fitting rooms. These signs alert shoppers to the fact that store security officers regularly patrol the area. In this way, some might think twice before stealing.

Warning signs are one way stores deter shoplifters.

Price Awareness

One very common practice that costs the retailer significant losses is **ticket-switching**. Instead of stealing the merchandise outright, some thieves replace one store ticket with a lower priced one. Professionals often have the same tools that the merchant uses to tag goods and merely remove the original tag and replace it with their own. Sometimes they take tags from other goods on the selling floor and use them on the merchandise they want.

In order to stop such practices, the retailer must make certain that the staff is familiar with merchandise prices. It is sometimes a difficult problem to correct, especially when numerous part-timers are employed. Additionally, with the use of scanners, many cashiers rarely look at the prices and simply charge the amount printed on the receipt.

Only through regular training sessions for cashiers can ticket switching be eliminated.

Incentive Award Programs

There is virtually nothing as effective as awarding someone with something meaningful for special performance. An **incentive award program** can be an effective tool to deter theft. When an employee has alerted the security team to a potential crime, recovers merchandise that has been earmarked for theft, provides information about a person suspected of shoplifting, or provides good prevention information, an award system might be the answer. Some retailers use a method that gives points to employees who have assisted in deterring shoplifting. The points may be used to redeem store merchandise.

Employee Workshops

Many retailers use workshops to educate new employees about shoplifting and how they might assist the company in combatting the problem. Through lectures given by managers and security personnel and through the use of video programs, a greater awareness emerges. Sometimes the sessions are followed up with quizzes to make certain that the staff understands all the issues that were covered. For example, the rights and wrongs of apprehension are generally discussed, such as how to never falsely accuse the suspicious-looking shopper, and to leave the actual detainment of the criminal to the security team. In most states, if the shopper is apprehended in the store, he or she can bring a lawsuit against the retailer.

Awareness Bulletin Boards

The placement of bulletin boards in areas where employees congregate has helped to control shoplifting. The bulletins on these boards highlight theft prevention techniques, as well as congratulatory notes to those employees who have assisted in apprehensions.

While training sessions are quite helpful, their impact is quite short lived. On the other hand, the bulletin boards are always there to remind employees of how they can help the store. These boards can also be regularly updated to feature new methods being instituted to prevent shoplifting. They can also be used as reminders of the incentive award programs offered by the company and how employees might personally benefit from the point system program.

Used either in combination or alone, all of these techniques drastically reduce shoplifting and help to reduce costs that are passed on to the company's honest clientele.

INTERNAL THEFT

As previously emphasized in the chapter, store employees account for significantly greater merchandise shortages than do the shoplifters. There are many reasons why the problem of **internal theft** continues to exist.

- An employee feels stealing is justified because his or her wages are lower than expected.
- An employee is dissatisfied with his or her immediate supervisor or the company itself.
- Because an employee knows the company's systems, he or she take advantage of that knowledge for personal gain.
- Security officers are so preoccupied with would-be shoplifters that they spend little time watching employees.
- Unsupervised workers are often the only ones working in the stockrooms.
- Knowledge of the company's lax nature in the prosecution of offenders.

There are many types of internal theft that continue to plague retailers. It is not only the stealing of merchandise, but also ringing up sales for lower amounts, aiding and abetting friends by charging for only some of the items being purchased, applying higher than appropriate discounts to merchandise, and knowingly allowing ticket-switching to take place.

While the total elimination of internal theft is impossible, there are several approaches that merchants use to significantly reduce the problem. When each of the deterrents and controls become part of an overall plan, curtailing internal theft can be a reality.

⋰ An Ethical Consideration

WHILE MOST RETAIL EMPLOYEES SHOW CONCERN for the losses that come about through shoplifting, many are also culprits who commit in-house crimes that cause a decrease in the company's bottom line. Even with all of the justification offered by these employees as their reasons for stealing, none justify the actions.

If prospective employees were educated about the safeguards that their employers have in place to deter internal theft, as well as the immorality of these crimes and how their personal success in the company can be affected by these losses, it might help to prevent some of these crimes.

It should be understood, that these unethical practices are not only taking place at the entry level positions, but also at every level of employment. In fact, management personnel, with easier access to merchandise and money, are often more guilty of such crimes than the lower level employees. They know the systems and can find the ways to cause shortages.

The problem must be presented as an unethical practice, not only at the time of employment, but through periodically held seminars.

Applicant Screening

A sound approach to the reduction of internal theft is to begin by screening those people who are being considered for positions in the company. Whether it is someone who is applying for a part-time sales associate's job or a top-level management role, careful assessment of the candidate's past is essential. When applications for employment are examined, often they are quickly skimmed and not really thoroughly studied. It is at this point that management can actually prevent suspicious candidates from joining the staff. For example, if a résumé indicates brief stays of employment with numerous companies, there might be reason for concern.

Online searches help retailers with applicant screening, usually a time-consuming process.

Since screening is often a time-consuming task, many retailers are making use of outside sources to check the backgrounds of potential employees. In Chapter 6, Human Resources Management, www.1800USSearch.com, was featured as a leader in this type of investigation. This company, and others, will, for a nominal fee, provide different levels of research that range from typical formats to more customized approaches.

By using the employment application to give the investigators basic information such as name and address, the external source can make the necessary background checks. Once these inquiries have proven positive, it is then appropriate for the human resources staff to move the applicant to the next level in the selection process.

Reference Checking

Most merchants require that those seeking employment supply references. In most states, the inquiries may be used only to verify the dates of employment and nothing more. In others, a more thorough questioning may take place to determine the reasons former employee left the company. In the latter situation, the candidate's honesty can be assessed. In the former situations, this must be left to the use of the previously mentioned outside search sources. If any doubt about the individual's trustworthiness is uncovered, it is at this point that consideration of the application should be terminated.

Closed Circuit TV

As we learned earlier in the chapter, most large retailers use cameras on the selling floor to record potential theft by shoplifters. The use of these cameras doesn't stop there. More and more merchants are investing in such installations to also check the honesty of their employees.

Focus on . . .
Foley's Department Stores

FOLEY'S FIRST OPENED ITS DOORS TO CUSTOMERS IN 1857. The Texas-based retailer built its reputation on providing the best quality merchandise, friendly service, and beautiful décor. As Foley's entered the new century, by staying true to its original concept, the retail organization, a division of The May Company Department Stores, sold more than $3 billion worth of apparel, jewelry, cosmetics, shoes, and other accessories in its 59 stores.

Its detail-oriented philosophy carries over into the company's loss prevention and security program. While merchandise protection on the selling floor has been an ongoing effort by Foley's, loss prevention methodology also plays a crucial role behind the scenes. At its main distribution center in Houston, which measures 1.5 million square feet, keen observation and state-of-the-art technology have reduced the amount of losses due to internal theft.

The center is regularly patrolled by a trained staff and overseen by more than 100 fixed cameras providing complete coverage 24 hours a day. The CCTV system used by Foley's is a technology introduced by Sensormatic Electronics Corporation, called Intellex. Intellex, a digital recorder, has the ability to simultaneously playback, record, and archive images from up to 16 cameras. It is more efficient that the use of VCR tapes, which may take hours of scrutiny to research a suspicious occurrence. The value of the installation is best understood by Foley's single recovery of more than $25,000 in stolen merchandise.

In this one example, the loss protection team was able to isolate the day the merchandise was taken. Then, by the use of Intellex, the staff programmed the parameters they were searching for and within seconds had the necessary documentation to proceed. The parties involved were quickly apprehended.

With its commitment to the new technology in the distribution center, the first three months of usage helped solve 40 percent of the cases. One year later, 70 percent of the cases were solved.

Not only has Foley's response to the problems of loss prevention resulted in the recapture of stolen goods, but also it has helped to increase employee safety by identifying the personnel who were improperly using equipment in the facility. This revelation helped the company provide better safety training for the individuals using the equipment.

Through the use of the latest in technology, Foley's has addressed both the seriousness of internal theft and the safeguarding of their staff through better training.

Mystery Shopping Services

Many major retailers use the old-fashioned method of checking on their employees' honesty with the use of **mystery shoppers**. For a fee, a company sends people to the store to pose as customers. This is often the standard procedure when a newly added staff member has been with the company for a few weeks. When the shopper makes a purchase, the individual being evaluated is observed as the sale is taking place. Any irregularity such as ringing up the wrong amount or failing to put cash in the register is immediately reported to a manager who is standing by.

Shoppers are also used in cases where suspicion surrounds a particular staff member. Whatever the uncertainties might be about this employee, careful scrutiny is used to determine whether or not an impropriety has occurred.

Drug Testing

As discussed in Chapter 6, as part of the selection procedure, more and more companies are resorting to drug testing for new employees, as well as random drug tests for those already on the staff. There seems to be a correlation between drug abusers and internal theft. Many users are in need of funds to support their habits, and increase their incomes by stealing merchandise and selling it for cash.

In order to ascertain the drug status of a potential employee, retailers often use outside companies to conduct the tests. For those already on staff required to undergo unannounced testing, many retailers make use of drug screening kits to conduct tests on their premises. One of the largest suppliers of drug testing materials is Noble Medical. Merchants can merely log on to its Web site, www.noblemedical.com, to learn about its entire product line.

The sign on the door of this Home Depot store informs potential employees that the retailer tests applicants for drug use.

Honesty and Psychological Testing

Another tool that retailers use to evaluate a candidate's potential for theft is testing. In particular, many rely upon the results of honesty and personality testing to make certain that those being considered for employment meet the ethical and moral requisites of the company. One source that companies such as Tandy Corporation and KFC use is Personnel Profiles, Inc. It administers a variety of tests such as Wonderlic, Thurston, Stanford Binet, Strong Campbell, and its own creation, The Achiever. The latter measures six mental aptitudes and ten personality dimensions, each of which is essential in employee screening to make certain that the candidates are unlikely to commit crimes within the company.

Smuggling Controls

One of the ways in which a great deal of merchandise has been stolen by employees is to place it in a refuse container ready for disposal, only to retrieve it once it is outside of the store. Stock personnel have the responsibility for bringing the goods to the selling floor and have total control of the items from the time they leave the receiving centers. By reserving an item or two in trash containers, they are able to collect them at the close of the day. Maintenance people, whose responsibility it is to clean the retailer's premises, also have considerable opportunity to participate in internal theft. Many of them perform their duties while the store is closed and are in close proximity to the merchandise that is stocked on racks and shelves. Left alone in an area, they are sometimes tempted to make their own selections without paying for them.

In order to reduce the internal theft attributed to this method of stealing, some merchants have installed systems for locking up the trash receptacles, and other merchants are going even a step further by installing **through-the-wall security systems**. Those responsible for trash removal must place the items to be discarded through an opening in the wall that is connected to a compactor. Any attempt to smuggle stolen items from the premises in this manner will be eliminated.

Control of Employee Purchases

Most retailers offer attractive discounts to their employees for purchases made from the company. While this is certainly a benefit that sometimes motivates an individual to take a job with specific retailer, it also has resulted in the loss of merchandise that hasn't been paid for. If the employee transaction takes place on the selling floor, and the items are packed and brought to the individual's locker, along the way, some other items may be placed in the package.

To stop this from happening, most retailers require that all employee purchases be retrieved at a behind the scenes location that is carefully controlled. Often, a security person who oversees the claiming of such merchandise mans the station. These counters are close to the employee entrances, making them inaccessible to the store's selling areas.

Rewards Programs

One of the most difficult problems that often confronts retailers is how to encourage honest employees to report criminal actions of their associates. While it is less troublesome for many to alert the security staff to potential shoplifters, revealing the names of fellow workers who are engaged in theft is another matter. They are either unwilling to participate in these circumstances because of friendly relationships that have been established, or they are fearful of any reprisals from the culprits.

To motivate individuals who have witnessed internal theft, many retailers have established programs that offer them monetary rewards for their assistance. Essential to the success of such methods is the assurance that the person reporting the crime will remain anonymous and not be later called to testify against the perpetrator. This guarantee often convinces the honest staff member to help.

Prosecution of Dishonest Employees

It is essential for any merchant to quickly take action against anyone found guilty of internal theft. The offenders must be swiftly terminated not only to make them pay for their misdeeds, but to also put others on notice that dishonesty will not be tolerated by the organization. Slaps on the wrist or second chances do not work. A reputation for laxity on the part of management relays a poor message to other employees.

A company's position and procedures on internal theft should be spelled out during an orientation program for new employees. In this way the immediate warning will serve to deter possible moral and ethical violations. Of course, the information should be tastefully offered in manner that doesn't sound threatening. Trained human resources personnel are best suited for such disclosure to make certain that the employer-employee relationship that is about to start will be beneficial to both parties.

According to statistical studies by such companies as Sensormatic Electronics Corporation, addressing internal theft by some or all of these techniques can help lower criminal activity.

INTERNET THEFT

The phenomenon of the Internet as a viable outlet for consumer goods has not only given merchants a new way to reach targeted markets, but has also created an arena for fraud. Numerous scams have been utilized to defraud merchants of payment for goods. So significant has **Internet fraud** been that its curtailment has become one of the major challenges of retailers who sell online. While no actual figures reveal the amounts lost due to these practices, the most recent opinion of experts estimates the losses to be about 10 percent of sales. This is a figure that is greater than internal theft and shoplifting combined. At the present time, MasterCard is in the process of setting up a procedure that will help combat these crimes.

To make matters even worse for Internet merchants, they are 100 percent responsible for fraudulent Internet credit card transactions, even when the credit card company has authorized the sales. Martaus and Associates, a payments research and consulting firm, predicts that with the problems now spiraling upwardly, card companies will rewrite the rules for Internet payments. With a prediction by Forrester Research, a Cambridge, Massachusetts-based company, that by 2003, 40 million American households will be shopping online, producing $108 billion in revenues and accounting for 6 percent of all consumer retail spending, the problem needs immediate attention.

The main reason criminals attempt online fraud is the anonymity factor. The Internet makes it easy for them to ply their trade. Tom Arnold, chief technology officer for San Jose, California-based CyberSource observes, "Nobody knows who you are."

To soften the blows of this fraud to retailers, a new Web site and Security Program (WiSP) offers insurance policies for companies selling online. It covers many types of losses at costs that range from $4,000 to $50,000 a year.

Fraud Prevention

One of the challenges of Internet businesses is to sharply reduce this problem. At this point in time, new techniques are surfacing to do just that.

Equifax Check Solutions has introduced PayNet Secure, a complete payment processing service for Internet sales. The key to the service is its customer authentication and certification components. The first time a consumer makes an online purchase from a PayNet Source client, he or she is asked a series of routine questions such as name, address, age, and so forth. Using the responses, Equifax checks the customer against the consumer credit base it maintains, as well as additional internal and external databases, such as lists of bad check writers. It then proceeds to ask other questions such as the identity of his or her mortgage lender. Once the company validates a consumer, he or she is given a password that bypasses similar security scrutiny in future online transactions involving any PayNet Secure merchants. The system is intended to help "ferret out fraudsters."

Although the overwhelming number of transactions are made with the use of credit cards, some purchasers want the option of paying by check, just as they do at the brick-and-mortar operations. A joint venture between TeleCheck Services and Payment NET offers guarantees to Internet merchants to safeguard against fraud by check.

San Diego-based HNC Software has developed another technique that is being used by the industry. The company, a pioneer in the use of neural network technology to predict consumer credit behavior, introduced eFalcon, a fraud detection system that can be installed by online merchants. Online transactions are run through eFalcon, which provides a statistical score reflecting the possibility that the transaction is fraudulent. The scoring process is based upon detailed transaction information and behavior profiling, and takes less than a second to complete during the normal card authorization process. If the probability of fraud is high, the system offers further verification suggestions. It asks the consumer to provide the CVV2 number, which is the three digits after the account number on the back of the credit card. Fraudulent users most likely will not have these numbers, indicating that the purchase is being illegally made.

NETrageous, a Maryland-based firm, has developed a list of scam prevention tips for online merchants that is available on a public service Web site, www.ScamBusters.com. Among some of the tips offered to merchants are the following:

- Be wary of orders with different bill to and ship to addresses.
- Be especially cautious about orders that are larger than typical order amounts, and orders requesting next-day delivery.
- Don't accept orders from customers using free e-mail services without first requesting additional information, such as the name of the card-issuing bank, which can provide further assurance that the transaction is legitimate.
- Pay close attention to international orders, and take extra steps to validate orders before shipping products to foreign addresses.
- If in doubt, telephone the customer to confirm the order.

At the time of this writing more approaches to the prevention of Internet fraud are surfacing. Just as there is the unlikelihood that instore fraud can be totally prevented, it is unlikely that the Internet fraud problem can be 100 percent eliminated.

VENDOR THEFT

A problematic area in which losses may be prevented is one that involves vendor transactions. The troubles attributed to this type of loss are not always due to intentional misdeeds but may come as a result of poor handling by manufacturer and wholesaler personnel. Specifically, the two major areas are improper billing and merchandise shortages in shipments. Of course, vendors, like retailers, have staff members who are dishonest and who sometimes intentionally omit the shipping of a few pieces for which the account has been billed.

The problem will continue at its present annual level of $2 billion if merchants are lax in making corrections. Before the methods that may be used to control the losses are examined, the following specific causes should be addressed:

- Improper billing—The vast amount of invoicing that takes place often results in charging the retailer more than the actual shipment requires. It might be keying in the wrong price for the merchandise or billing for more pieces than were actually shipped. The invoice is then in error. This may be an honest mistake or one that was intentional. Whatever the reason, the retailer is charged more than he or she should be.

Sometimes shipping clerks miscount the goods during packing, leading to shortages for the retailer.

Theft of merchandise in transit is a cause of shortages.

- Merchandise shortages at vendor premises—When shipping clerks are packing orders it is possible that they will not fill the order exactly as the invoice reads. They might, either by unintentional or intentional reasons, pack fewer items into the carton than what have actually been ordered. Sometimes quick handling of the orders results in a miscount, with the retailer bearing the burden of being overcharged. Other times the causes are due to the dishonesty of vendor employees. Just as retailers are confronted with unscrupulous employees, so are the vendors.

- Shipping point theft—Occasionally the packages that are shipped by the vendors are not carefully sealed. When such conditions are evident, the shipping company's handlers sometimes find ways in which to remove merchandise from the cartons, leaving a shortage. More and more theft is being attributed to the time between when the goods leave the vendors, and when they reach the merchant's premises. Only with careful packing, can this theft be reduced.

Retailers may substantially reduce losses that come as a result of vendor improprieties by establishing a careful system that checks every aspect of incoming merchandise and invoices.

- Careful checking of invoices—The staff whose responsibility it is to post the amounts due to the vendor must not rely upon the totals that have been determined by the vendor's billing department. Each invoice must first be compared to the original order to make certain that the prices correspond. In some cases, the price charged might differ from what the buyer had previously negotiated. Once this step has been addressed, computations should be made to make certain that there are no errors. If there are any discrepancies, the matter must be resolved with the vendor before the invoice can be made ready for payment.

Invoice checking with the original order is imperative in making certain vendor's figures are correct.

- Merchandise counts—Those in the receiving areas must make certain that the merchandise indicated on the packing slip is exactly what has been shipped. Too often, receiving clerks merely unpack the goods without actually making certain of the contents. Some retailers use a method that is known as a blind count. This system only provides the clerk with the numbers of the items that have been ordered, but not the expected amounts. The clerk is then required to indicate the exact amount of each item that has been received. This amount is then compared to the invoice that has been received by the accounts payable department. At this time, if there are differences, the matter can be resolved by notifying the vendor.
- Package examination—When the merchant receives merchandise, it is imperative that each package is carefully scrutinized to make certain that it has not been tampered with. Any package that shows some sign of a tear or opening should be called to the attention of the vendor. The receiving clerk should then either note the situation when he or she signs for the shipment, or return the questionable package to the vendor.

When retailers carefully address all of the circumstances and conditions that involve losses due to shoplifting, internal theft, Internet fraud, and vendor misrepresentation, their losses are likely to be reduced. The end result will be better prices for shoppers and better profits for the company.

TRENDS FOR THE NEW MILLENNIUM

- More and more companies are addressing the problems associated with Internet scams that rob merchants of millions of dollars each year.
- The use of outside agencies to screen employees will continue to increase. Through the investigative powers of these companies, retailers will be made aware of employees who are potential risks to commit internal theft.
- Companies who specialize in loss prevention will continue to develop newer devices to combat merchandise theft.

- Retailers will continue to provide honest employees with incentives to reveal the names of those involved in internal theft.
- Retailers will continue to use in-house videos and CD-ROMS to make employees aware of the problems associated with shoplifting and how to handle suspicious occurrences.

CHAPTER HIGHLIGHTS

- Internal theft, shoplifting, Internet scams, and vendor misrepresentation in invoicing account for more than $30 billion in losses to retailers each year.
- Video surveillance systems that involve closed circuit television are being used by most major retailers to watch and record the actions of shoplifters and dishonest employees.
- Most merchants who deal in high-ticket soft goods agree that the best method of curtailing shoplifting is to use electronic article surveillance (EAS) systems.
- Many EAS systems bring excellent results, especially the specialized ones that use inktags to deter theft.
- Incentive programs are being used by retailers to motivate their employees to report suspected shoplifters.
- Internal theft accounts for greater retailer shortages than shoplifting does.
- One of the ways in which employers are reducing internal theft is by using outside agencies, such as www.1800USSearch.com, to prescreen job applicants.
- Many retail operations use rewards programs to encourage staff members to report suspicious employees to the security division.
- In order to reduce Internet fraud, more and more companies are developing plans to more carefully assess Web site transactions.
- Industrywide, shortages that come at the hands of inappropriate vendor billing and inventory shortages account for $2 billion each year.

IMPORTANT RETAILING TERMS

shoplifters
kleptomania
video surveillance system
closed circuit television (CCTV)
electronic article surveillance (EAS)
detacher
hard tags
ink reservoirs
radio frequency (RF) system
electronic magnet (EM) system
acousto-magnetic (AM) system
electronic asset protection (EAP)
radio frequency identification device (RFID)
bar code
alligators
two-way mirrors
magnifying mirrors
control access
coded signals
warning signs
ticket-switching
incentive award programs
internal theft
mystery shoppers
through-the-wall security systems
internet fraud

FOR REVIEW

1. How much has the retail industry lost due to shoplifting and internal theft in the past year?
2. Who is typically the cause of greater theft, the shoplifter or the company employee?
3. Define the term kleptomania.
4. Describe how a video surveillance system works, and how it helps to reduce shoplifting and internal theft.
5. Briefly describe electronic surveillance systems and how they help retailers deter shoplifting.

6. In what way has the ink reservoir system made EAS systems even better?

7. What does the term *alligator* mean when referring to antitheft systems?

8. How does a retailer prevent theft of merchandise that is taken into a fitting room?

9. How are specially coded systems used to alert store security of potential shoplifters?

10. In what ways have retailers motivated employees to help control shoplifting?

11. Describe how the latest techniques in applicant screening hope to reduce internal theft.

12. Define the term *mystery shopper* and tell how it helps to reduce internal theft.

13. Why has drug testing become such an important part of the recruitment process in the retail industry?

14. Other than drug screening, what kinds of tests help to evaluate the honesty of job candidates?

15. How does the through-the-wall security system reduce internal theft?

16. Why has the advent of Internet shopping resulted in so many losses for the merchant?

17. Name two companies that have developed techniques to reduce Internet fraud. Describe their techniques.

18. How can a vendor contribute to a retailer's losses?

AN INTERNET ACTIVITY

Pretend you are a recently hired human resources specialist whose expertise is in recruitment. Your main role is to develop resources that will carefully screen job applicants before any face-to-face interviews take place.

Using any Internet search engine find five Web sites that run background checks on people. For each site that you find, note the following: Web site, services offered, and cost.

EXERCISES AND PROJECTS

1. Using either the Internet or Yellow Pages, research three companies that specialize in surveillance sys-

tems. Through direct contact with the companies or by examining its Web sites, gather information about particular products they produce that may help retailers. Request brochures or catalogs from these companies to share with the other students in the class.

Using the information obtained, write a brief report telling about each company's approach to surveillance systems.

THE CASE OF THE MISSING MERCHANDISE

Cannon & Abbott started a small mail-order company in the Southwest in 1972. Initially, Cannon & Abbott specialized in a very small model stock that exclusively sold women's wear through quarterly catalogs. The company operated out of a central warehouse that housed and shipped all of the merchandise.

The product line concentrated on women's apparel for both missy and junior sizes and accessories that included hosiery, handbags, gloves, scarves, and jewelry. In 1990, Cannon & Abbott expanded its offerings to include men's clothing and children's wear. The success of these lines helped make the company one of the more profitable of its kind in the industry. The company's success demanded considerable physical expansion. It moved from a small, three-story warehouse to several buildings. Its growth, while providing considerable profits for the company, also caused a number of problems.

The first problem was finding capable employees who could carefully carry out the responsibilities required of them. The second, and more serious, involved internal theft. Unlike retailers who operate out of brick-and-mortar locations, and deal with shoplifters every day, Cannon & Abbott needs to secure their merchandise only to prevent employee theft. When the company was small, the problem was almost nonexistent. Now, however, the problem has become extremely widespread.

The management team has just held a meeting to determine how the problem should be addressed. Some of the suggestions include:

- Calling the entire staff together to see if anyone could give information about the culprits.
- Pretagging the merchandise with alligators and requiring that employees must pass through surveillance portals when leaving the premises.
- Conducting a security check on everyone employed by the company.

At the conclusion of the meeting, there wasn't a consensus about how the situation should be remedied.

Questions

1. Do any of the suggestions merit further consideration? Defend your answer.
2. What other approaches should the company take to eliminate internal theft?

CHAPTER 8
Logistical Merchandise Distribution

After you have completed this chapter, you should be able to discuss:

- ▶ The concept of interenterprise collaboration.
- ▶ The manner in which electronic data interchange benefits both the supplier and the retailer.
- ▶ How information is gathered through the use of a vendor managed inventory system.
- ▶ The extent to which nonprofit organizations have been involved in improving the efficiency of the entire merchandise supply chain.
- ▶ Why many major retail organizations use outside marking.
- ▶ What role a centralized receiving department plays in retailing.
- ▶ Why some companies use regional receiving facilities to distribute the goods to their stores.
- ▶ How the concept of intermodal transportation facilitates the shipping of merchandise from the vendor to the retailer.
- ▶ The concept of barcoding and how it plays a role in merchandise distribution.

One of the vital components of any retailing venture is merchandise distribution. Before any purchasing is done, or any merchandising plans are considered, a company must address the problems of getting merchandise to the selling floors in the brick-and-mortar operations or to the stockrooms of catalogers and e-tailers in a timely fashion. If merchandise is not available for sale when the consumers' needs arise, it is likely that sales will be lost.

Inventory management decision making has become the focus of the retailing industry, and by addressing the problems associated with this part of the business before they occur, the potential for greater profitability is a reality. Unlike the retailers who preceded them, today's merchants have the benefit of numerous sophisticated technological advances to make the transition from the vendors to their own warehouses a smoother and simpler one.

Not only has the physical movement of the goods become easier, but so has the relationship between the supplier and merchant in terms of order processing and fulfillment. By dovetailing the retailer's and manufacturer's efforts in these areas, the former is able to reduce the amount of merchandise on the selling floor, resulting in a more profitable turnover rate, and the latter is able to respond to retailer merchandising needs as they arise. Through such programs as **electronic data interchange (EDI)** and **Quick Response (QR) inventory planning**, retailers and vendors regularly exchange information via their computers. Other routes available to both of these channel partners are accessed via the Internet.

In addition to the retailer interfacing with his or her vendors, in terms of merchandise planning practices, the merchant must also address the in-house problems associated with merchandise distribution. These include the physical receipt and handling of the incoming goods, the manner in which the shipments are scrutinized, and the marking of the individual items. For brick-and-mortar operations, there are also problems associated with the movement of the goods onto the selling floors, and their transfer to various units of the company if the receiving facility is a centralized one. For catalog and Web site retailers, the problem is a little different since the merchandise doesn't move to a selling floor but remains in the warehouse awaiting a customer order.

Today, retailers are investing many millions to upgrade the systems that concern merchandise distribution. By doing so, they are reaping the benefits afforded by these programs in terms of greater profitability for their companies.

INTERENTERPRISE COLLABORATION

By developing and maintaining close business relationships, vendors and retailers are better able to service each other's needs, making their companies more profitable and creating an **interenterprise collaboration**. Whether it is the brick-and-mortar operations, for example, who want to help their businesses with better turnaround times in regard to merchandise acquisition, or the Internet Web sites that want to reduce the time it takes for delivery of goods that go directly from the manufacturer to the consumer, a closer relationship is the key.

High-Tech Innovation

Merchants and manufacturers are involved in numerous technical innovations that make merchandise analysis and delivery more beneficial to both parties. Electronic data interchange (EDI), as it is commonly referred to in the industry, is an excellent tool to improve the retailer's purchasing plans. The process provides for the electronic exchange of machine readable data in standardized formats between one organization's computer and another's. It eliminates the need for a lot of paper pushing by retailers to get their goods shipped from vendors. Whenever ordering, invoicing, and shipping take place, the task can be accomplished more quickly, saving time, energy, and ultimately cost. With the use of laser scanners, satellite linkups, and wireless systems, retailers and suppliers can communicate as never before. One e-tailer that uses an EDI system is eBags.com. The company uses a system supplied by RnetEC, of Sacramento, California, that has given it greater control of its integration with sup-

This clerical worker for a vendor is checking a merchandising request from a retailer.

pliers and has significantly reduced the time it takes to get customers' orders filled. With customer purchase orders filled directly from suppliers, the delivery time has been reduced from a week or longer to 24 to 72 hours. The eBags system consists of a virtual area network that features a standard interface through which the e-tailer can communicate with vendors, sending machine orders and shipping information as electronic documents. Every major retailer, whether it is a brick-and-mortar merchant, cataloger, e-tailer, or participant in multichannel retailing, participates in one of the many available EDI systems.

Another technology that is affecting retailer-vendor relationships is **vendor managed inventory (VMI)**. Through the use of scanners at the retail level, manufacturers are able to gather information about the sales of their products through stores, catalogs, and Web sites, and replenish inventories on a continuing basis. Thus, the vendor is actively involved in making replenishment decisions for the retailers. Among the major companies who are significant users of VMI are JCPenney, Kmart, and Wal-mart.

Through the use Quick Response (QR) inventory systems, order processing and delivery can be greatly improved. In these systems, the manufacturer keeps close watch on the retailer's inventory levels and makes production decisions that will result in the delivery of the goods at the times that it anticipates the merchant will need them. By participating in this methodology, the retailer is able to reduce the amount of merchandise it has on hand, knowing that the manufacturer will be able to quickly restock the store's inventory.

This enables the retailer to capitalize on a better stock turnover rate which can translate into higher profits. With the proper use of an EDI system, and mutual trust between the retailer and the vendors that supply his or her company, Quick Response planning is easily achieved and is evident at most every major type of retailing classification in operation today.

Focus on . . .
Federated Department Stores

FEDERATED LOGISTICS AND OPERATIONS WAS CREATED IN 1994 to coordinate merchandise distribution, logistics functions, and vendor technology across all of the company's department store divisions, which include Macy's, Bloomingdale's, Burdines, Rich's, and The Bon Marché. Its primary goal is to reduce expenses and costs throughout the organization.

Order discrepancy, for example, is something that every retailer, including Federated, has experienced. When a carton is opened and red dresses instead of the blue ones that the purchase order specifies are packed inside, the problems begin. At Federated Department Stores' logistic division, a solution has been designed to avert such surprises. The application that the company uses feeds timely information about merchandise into the pipeline at several intermediate points, not typically covered as part of traditional electronic data interchange. It provides ongoing, up-to-date status reports on shipments so that any deviations can be dealt with proactively. The key is to keep buyers in the supply chain abreast of the status of orders. Potential problems or discrepancies are flagged in reports, enabling buyers to respond. They can determine whether the goods are exactly as ordered or whether there will be style, color, or size substitutions.

The system first notifies the stores of which purchase orders are booked into the manufacturer's order process. Next, the system tells Federated when the order goes into the various vendors' shipping systems and when it will be filled. The buyer is able to track the order at every stage, giving him or her an exact time that it will be delivered and what will be received. Vendors such as Carole Hochman Designs, Jockey International, and Oxford Industries are participants in the Federated supply chain program.

The system benefits the manufacturers as well as the stores in the Federated family. For the supplier, it eliminates the continuous nagging from buyers and their assistants regarding when orders will be shipped. The buyers and their assistants, in turn, are able to perform other duties and responsibilities while being kept abreast of their orders.

The application that is used is XML, which was developed jointly with Manhattan Associates in Atlanta. It has been designed in a manner that makes it compatible with various warehouse management systems on the market.

The Stein Mart Story
Managing the Supply Chain

EFFICIENCY OF THE MERCHANDISE SUPPLY CHAIN is of the utmost importance for Stein Mart to maintain its targeted profit margins. To that end, the company is involved in a number of techniques that assures that the merchandise that is purchased will reach the selling floors in the least possible amount of time.

Stein Mart makes significant use of the EDI method with all its trading partners. To assure that the relationships between the company and the vendors are completely understood before any transactions begins, Stein Mart makes its requirements known through personal contact with the buying team or via online instructions. The latter system is regularly used by those vendors wishing to sell to the company. When a vendor logs onto the Stein Mart Web site, www.steinmart.com, mapping and word documents spell out the entire story.

In order to maximize quick floor entry, Stein Mart requires that all hanging merchandise must be shipped floor-ready. That is, each item must be on a specified hanger, with the company's price ticket affixed to the item. Stein Mart alerts its trading partners to its vendor of choice for apparel hangers or provide details for hangers that are purchased elsewhere. By strict adherence to this policy, there is uniformity throughout the chain. This rack-ready program results in quicker sell-throughs with more reorders coming earlier in the season. The entire system, replete with price tag positioning for every single item that the company carries is available online, making it a foolproof system.

Finally, also available online, are routing instructions from the traffic department. Every single detail such as transportation costs, chargebacks, bills of lading, and packing guidelines are carefully spelled out on the Web site.

The systems are regularly updated to include the latest in merchandise distribution technology.

● ●

Nonprofit Industry Groups

Several groups have formed in order to improve the efficiency of the entire merchandise supply chain. Two of the principal organizations, both of which are nonprofit organizations are the **Voluntary Interindustry Commerce Standards Association (VICS)** and the **Collaborative Planning, Forecasting, and Replenishment Committee (CPFR)**. Each has initiated specific guidelines and recommendations that hope to foster closer supplier-retailer relationships.

CPFR is a trade organization that has a wealth of participating suppliers and retailers on its roster. Some of the merchants represented are Best Buy, Federated Department Stores, Kmart Corporation, JCPenney, Safeway, Sam's Club, Staples, Wal-Mart, and Walgreen's. The vendors include Gillette, Kraft Foods, Inc., Levi Strauss & Co., Nestle, Ralston-Purina, and Ocean Spray Cranberries.

Its mission is to take a global leadership role in the ongoing improvement of products and information throughout the general merchandise retail industry supply chain. It hopes to provide an environment for dynamic information sharing, integrating both the demand and supply side processes (linking manufacturers, retailers, and carriers), and effectively plan, forecast, and replenish customer needs through the total supply chain.

Early participants such as Wal-Mart and the Sara Lee Corporation have found considerable success through CPFR participation.

VICS, organized in 1986, has also worked continuously to improve the efficiency of the entire supply chain. It has established cross-country standards that simplify the flow of product and information in the general merchandise classification for retailers and suppliers alike.

The organization is made up of senior executives who have proven that a timely and accurate flow of product and information between companies significantly improves their competitive positions. They believe that by implementing VICS technologies and QR partnerships, along with a commitment by the participants to implement change, that bottom lines will improve.

Its goal is to create solutions, with input from its many member companies, such as Best Buy, Kmart, and Wal-Mart, which will improve processes throughout the supply chain. Members believe that businesses that do not know how to adapt to the technology available to them will be moving backward.

Through regularly produced newsletters, participants learn about the current issues that confront supply chain management.

Outside Marking

While many retailers have their own in-house marking facilities in their receiving areas, more and more of them opt for goods to be ticketed by either the vendors or freight carriers. By using **outside marking**, they are able to get the goods onto the selling floor more quickly. Either the retailer or the company that is doing the actual ticketing, may supply the price tickets.

Those who prepare their own tickets send them on to the manufacturers when the goods come off the production line. In this way, no time is lost and they can be immediately affixed and sent to the stores. The manufacturers also save the retailers time by placing the garments on hangers, putting them into individual plastics bags or boxes, or utilizing other merchant preferred formats. If it is the carrier who pretickets the

Many vendors pre-ticket the merchandise for their retail accounts to save time.

items, the supplier sends the goods to the shipping point for processing. Traditionally, staple goods are ticketed in this manner. With the replenishment of standard goods such as hosiery and basic men's dress shirts being typical for many retailers, and with price fluctuation relatively uncommon for long periods of time, price tickets may be prepared in anticipation of the goods ultimate production. This too is a time saver.

It should be understood that whenever marking outsourcing is the procedure, the information such as price, sizes, colors, or merchandise classification is provided by the retailer. The outside sources merely follow instructions.

 Focus on . . .
Gymboree

GYMBOREE, AN APPAREL RETAILER THAT SPECIALIZES in children's clothing, uses an allocation system that tailors merchandise distribution to its more than 600 stores in the chain. The objective of the company is to improve margins on inventory by sending the most appropriate goods to the units in the chain where they will be best utilized. The premise is based upon the company's belief that unless a store-by-store allocation is undertaken, much of the merchandise will find itself in places where it won't sell in quantities necessary to produce a profit.

Unlike most companies that allocate goods on a store cluster basis—where groups of stores receive identical inventories—this system addresses individual needs. Gymboree believes the cookie cutter distribution approach is far too imprecise to maximize profits. By clustering its units, the company feels that some will perform above average and some below average. The technology employed is from JDA Software Group, Scottsdale, Arizona, and focuses on the exact needs of the individual units.

Since the implementation of its new system, task time has been reduced by 25 percent. Distribution plans, based upon the reports that are generated by the methodology, are done one week in advance of the shipping. Not only has time been saved in the allocation process, but also the needs of each store are being more accurately addressed.

Gymboree management stresses that its intention is not necessarily to reduce inventory levels, as many big box retailers are apt to do, but to send the goods where they will be needed most.

VENDOR–RETAILER PHYSICAL DISTRIBUTION

Moving the goods from the supplier to the retailer is a major concern for both vendors and retailers in the channel of distribution. Time is generally of the essence, making it

Federal Express is a major carrier that guarantees overnight delivery.

imperative that the products get into the hands of retailer, and onto the selling floor—or the warehouse for catalogs or Web sites—as soon as possible for consumer ordering.

Merchants and suppliers alike have a number of different transportation modes from which they may choose. Their selection depends upon the origination of shipping point, the amount of merchandise to be delivered, how urgently the goods are needed, and the available shipping facilities where the goods have been purchased.

Overall, the choices are trucks, railroads, air, and water carriers. The retailer must analyze factors such as cost, speed of service, dependability, location, availability, and frequency of shipments before any decisions are made. Within each transportation systems there is generally a choice of shippers with whom transportation arrangements can be made.

TABLE 8.1
COMPARISON OF MODES OF TRANSPORTATION

	TRUCKS	RAILROADS	AIR	WATER CARRIERS
Transportation costs	High	Average	Very high	Very low
Door-to-door service	High	Average	Average	Low
Speed of delivery	High	Average	Very high	Very low
Schedule maintenance	High	Average	Very high	Average
Location availability	Very high	High	Average	Low
Shipment frequency	Very high	Low	Average	Very low

- **United Parcel Service**—A company that offers regular or express service in most parts of the globe.
- **Federal Express**—A major transporter of goods that need overnight delivery.
- **United States Postal Service**—The post office has numerous options including parcel post, an inexpensive delivery method, priority mail, a service that guarantees 2- or 3-day delivery, and express mail, the fastest of the methods.

In many situations there is a need for **intermodal transportation**. This refers to the need for two or more modes of transportation in order to move the goods more efficiently. For example, a trucking company might be needed to bring the order from the vendor to the air carrier and then to another trucker once the merchandise has arrived at it's destination. Thus, orders placed in France might take the route of a local trucker picking up the packages and delivering them to Air France who in turn, upon receipt in the United States, for example, would then have the goods picked up and delivered to the retailer by a company like American Freightways.

Table 8.1 offers a comparison of the different modes of transportations in terms of the features of their services.

IN-HOUSE DISTRIBUTION

Although the trend for supplier-retailer supply chain cooperation continues to upwardly spiral, there are many companies who still utilize in-house staffing to handle some of the distribution details. Needless to say, the major retailers interface with their suppliers via EDI, QR, and VMI to help manage order processing and its fulfillment. However, many still maintain departments that address some of their needs such as inventory checking and marking. Of course, small retailers generally rely upon less technically oriented systems for the entire process of getting the goods from the suppliers to their selling floors.

The major retail organizations that have in-house installations use either a **centralized receiving** department to process the goods before shipping them on to all of the individual units in the company or **regional receiving** departments that receive and mark the goods for the stores in their districts.

⚖ An Ethical Consideration

WITH ALL OF THE ADVANCEMENTS IN TECHNOLOGY, retailers are able to move their goods from the vendors to the selling floor faster than ever before. It is, however, during the physical movement of the goods that a percentage of this merchandise will never reach the selling floor. Of course, some items may be legitimately lost en route, but the vast majority of the misplaced items are deliberately taken by the handlers. There is no system in the world that can, in totality, safeguard every single piece of merchandise.

Just as was noted in the discussion of loss prevention in Chapter 7, similar ethical standards must be addressed. While those caught will undoubtedly be charged with the crime, they should also be taught that actions such as stealing goods that are headed for the selling floors would cause profits to fall and that the incomes of all employees will be affected.

The lessen taught should not be of a preachy nature, but one that is spoken in practical terms.

Centralized Receiving Departments

In many major department stores and chain organizations, receiving and marking the goods from the vendors is accomplished at a centralized location which is convenient to the movement of the goods to their stores. There are numerous reasons for this type of merchandise distribution.

- *Better physical control of merchandise.* Retailers go to great expense establishing facilities that handle all of the company's incoming merchandise. With the use of a wide variety of technological tools that interface with such programs as EDI and VMI, merchandise management is more likely to be better controlled. Receiving managers spend all of their time concerned with merchandise distribution, making certain that the goods are being properly accounted for, processed for entry into the company's inventory system, and made ready for quick movement onto the selling floors. By contrast, store or department managers who have other responsibilities often handle merchandise that is sent directly to the stores in the chain or department store organization. This makes the system less efficient and might result in improper handling that could lead to losses.
- *Better financial control of merchandise.* Receiving departments of this nature work very closely with the company's control division and make certain that the goods are accounted for in the various merchandising systems. If there are any discrepancies, the regular interfacing of these two important areas of the business can quickly address them. This reduces the risk of shortages, damages, and other concerns that might be overlooked in less sophisticated conditions.
- *Sophisticated equipment and supplies.* When companies subscribe to centralized receiving plans, they invest in machinery and supplies that are generally state-of-the-art and continuously upgrade them as new systems come on the market. This assures the prompt movement of goods from their locations to the selling floors.

Regional Receiving Departments

Some retailers who have enormous numbers of units segment their receiving operations into regions or districts. These facilities are responsible for supplying goods to a number of stores that might cover one section of the country or perhaps, a few states. In either case, the buyer prepares separate purchase orders for each of the regions. The suppliers then ship the goods to the respective receiving departments.

Retailers who use the regional approach often do so because of the time saved in getting the goods from receiving to the selling floors. If a large company with coast-to-coast stores, utilizes a totally centralized concept, the merchandise movement may take longer than if the receiving warehouses were in closer proximity to stores in a specific region. With time being of the essence, especially in fashion merchandise that has a built-in perishable factor, the faster the items get onto the selling floor, the more time it will have to be sold.

Single-Store Receiving

In some organizations, the receipt of goods is undertaken by the individual stores in the group. Of course, small, independent entrepreneurs have no other choice but to receive the merchandise that has been ordered directly from the suppliers.

Supermarkets are among the retailers who subscribe to direct receiving for some of their items. They might purchase produce from local farmers for each of their units making centralized receiving impractical. Even if some of the products, such as canned goods, are first sent to centralized warehouses for redistribution to the units in the chain, the actual marking of the items generally takes place in the individual stores. Stock personnel can be regularly seen marking the goods in the aisles. Marking at the centralized warehouse would require unpacking and repacking, both costing a great deal of time. The store manager, or an assistant, merely checks the delivery—to make certain that it is exactly what has been ordered—records the delivery, and makes it ready for marking.

OshKosh B'Gosh, an apparel chain retailer with 130 units, subscribes to the concept of individual store receiving departments. The company uses a software receiving package from Datavantage that involves the receipt of goods from the suppliers. Each store is able to determine the contents of the carton by scanning the barcode on the outside. The system links up with corporate inventory management system, which was developed by STS Systems, Pointe-Claire, Quebec.

RECEIVING AND MARKING OPERATIONS

Once the merchant puts a system in place, it is necessary to install a plan that will physically address the tasks involved in getting the goods properly recorded, marked, and transferred to the selling departments.

The plans involve the actual receiving of the goods, checking the contents to determine if they are exactly as indicated on the purchase orders, making certain that the invoices agree with the amounts that have been received, marking the items with the prices that have been established by the buyers, and getting them to where they will be featured in the store.

Receiving Records

When the merchandise that has been ordered is ready for shipping to the retailer, the manufacturer or the shipper might tag it, or it may come to the merchant without any ticketing. In any situation, the goods are delivered to the company's centralized, regional, or individual receiving facilities.

The receipt of the goods might be informal as is the case of small stores. Since the merchant is often the buyer, or at least has total familiarity with the goods that have been purchased by an associate, a formal **receiving record** is generally not necessary. In cases where the company has many units, a more formal recording device is used.

This record lists all pertinent information regarding the shipment including the name of the shipping company, date and hour of arrival, the number of pieces in the shipment, delivery charges, the amount of the invoice, the name of the department that has ordered the merchandise, and the condition of the packages. Each of the pieces of information is vital so that in cases of disagreement between the retailer and supplier, there is sufficient evidence to make a settlement.

Cartons that are damaged, for example, must be noted since there is the potential for losses. A slight opening could be sufficient for an item or two to be stolen. An order might be comprised of several dozen or more pieces, and only physical counting will reveal if all have been received. Here too any discrepancies must be noted. If delivery charges seem out of line with typical shipping costs, it too should be addressed in writing so that adjustments to the invoice can be made. It is at this stage of the game, when the delivery receipt has been signed, that the shipment becomes the property of the retailer and must be paid for according to the terms set force by the buyer. If suspicious circumstances haven't been resolved at this time, the merchant is responsible for payment even if shortages are discovered later.

Receiving Equipment

Once the handlers at the **receiving dock** okay the receipt of the goods, they are then moved along to an area that is housed with a variety of equipment that will be used in the checking process. Moving the goods is accomplished via means of hand trucks, movable racks, or as in the case of many major companies, on **conveyor systems**. By using the latest automated technology, efficiency is maximized. In small stores it should be noted that the packages are either hand carried to multipurpose back rooms, or right onto the selling floor where sales clerks undertake the receiving process.

The destination for goods in the aforementioned larger retail operations is replete with **stationary tables**, on which the goods are sorted and processed for delivery to the warehouse or selling floors, **portable tables** that have wheels to make the procedure simple, or conveyor systems which quickly and easily handle the movement of the goods.

Saks Fifth Avenue uses a national distribution center that houses state-of-the-art receiving equipment. After the goods have been received and the numbers have been entered into the computer, the way the merchandise moves is determined by the nature of how the goods were packed by the supplier. Those that are **flat packed** in cartons are placed on roller conveyors to a processing center where paperwork is completed to generate the appropriate tags that will be used to mark the items. In the next area the cartons are opened, tags are affixed, and the cartons are repacked for shipment to the stores. Once the packages have been coded for identification purposes, an automated system moves the goods to chutes that take them to the loading dock and ultimately to the stores. Hanging garments are placed on a **trolley conveyor** that moves the goods through the same stages as the flat-packed merchandise. After processing, the garments are placed in metal cages for shipping to the stores.

Integration with a sophisticated computer system enables the company to know exactly what has been received, where it is in the system, and when each store has received the goods.

It is this type of system that enables retailers to achieve a savings in both processing and transportation costs.

Quantity Checking

Once the goods pass the receiving stage, one or more pieces of equipment are used to check the quantities. This stage is of the utmost importance to verify that the contents of packages are in agreement with the packing slips or invoices. Only the physical inspection of the flat package's contents will reveal if the vendor has faithfully filled the order. In the case where the shipment comes on hangers that have been placed on merchandise racks, the same inspection step is necessary. There are three basic techniques that are used in quantity checking.

- **Direct quantity check.** In this system the checker uses the vendor's invoice to make certain that the amounts indicated are actually present, and that the colors, sizes, and prices are accurate. While this is the most widely used checking technique because it is quick, it also has a distinct disadvantage. Careless checking might result because the checker might merely give the contents a quick once over and not really count everything that has arrived. He or she might sign-off on the delivery noting that everything in the containers is in agreement with the invoice.
- **Blind quantity check.** This is a method that is designed to minimize checking errors. The checker must prepare a list of the items in the package that has been received without the benefit of the invoice. While it somewhat slows down the process, it makes the checker perform his or her job. Most retailers who use this system prepare forms that have such headings as style number, merchandise description, color, sizes, and total number of items in the package.
- **Semiblind quantity check.** This technique utilizes the best features of the two aforementioned plans. The person responsible to check quantities is given a packing slip that lists the styles that are in the delivery, but doesn't list the quantities. In this way the checker is obligated to make the physical count that will later be compared with the actual invoice.

Quality Checking

While it is relatively easy to have trained people in the receiving department make certain that the shipments comply with the purchase orders in terms of quantities and prices, **quality checking** is another matter. In small stores, verifying that the merchandise received is exactly the same as the samples from which they were ordered is a relatively simple matter. The buyer is often the store's proprietor and is generally on the selling floor, readily available to examine the shipments.

In the larger companies, the buyers are generally far from the receiving areas and are unable to examine shipments. In fact, where central receiving is utilized, the buyer might be hundreds of miles from the warehouse. Many retailers are now utilizing quality control experts to examine shipments and assess their conformity to the original purchase order requirements. These people are trained to evaluate the merchandise and determine if they meet company standards. While the receipt of nationally known brands rarely turns up inferior goods, it is the products from lesser-known vendors that are sometimes of poor quality. It is especially prevalent in goods that come from overseas resources.

If a system isn't in place to determine quality, unsuspecting shoppers could purchase them only to return them because of poor wear. This could lead to the loss of customers.

Once the receiving task has been completed, the information, either in the form of the invoice or packing slip, is sent to the control department for processing. The merchandise is then sent on to be ticketed. Of course, if the supplier has made the goods floor-ready they are moved to the selling floors or to in-house storage areas. Some retailers divide the merchandise into two parts. One portion is sent to the selling department and the other to a behind the scenes stockroom were it is placed in bins or on racks until it is needed on the selling floor. The trend in retailing has been to eliminate backroom stocking wherever possible. Goods that are ordered are generally readied for floor placement. If more merchandise of the same type is needed, then reorders are placed. This generally results in a better stock turnover rate, a concept which will be discussed in Chapter 13, The Concepts and Mathematics of Merchandise Pricing.

Marking Merchandise

Assuming that the merchant undertakes the ticketing procedures, an in-house procedure must be developed. In small stores, many proprietors still use the handwritten method. For their minimum merchandising requirements, and their close customer contacts, the method is sufficient.

The remainder of the retailers choose from a variety of automated systems that are on the market, with the computer as their centerpieces. Sometimes the tags are computer-generated, but other times they are printed by handheld equipment. In any case, the computer is essential in that, with the use of scanners, the tag's information is transferred and stored and eventually used for merchandise printouts.

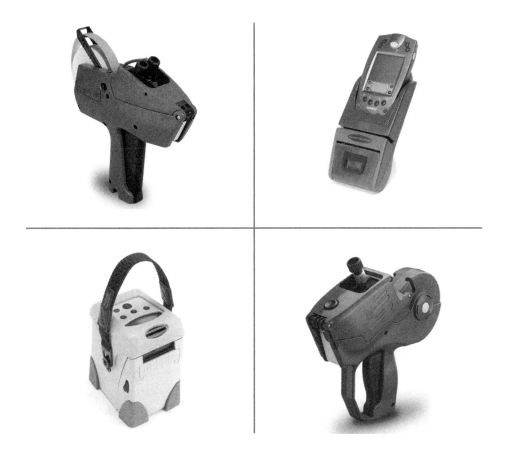

The latest in marking equipment for retailers in the new millennium includes the devices shown here.

The tickets not only list the prices, but a host of other essential inventory control items that assist the buyers and merchandisers in refining their purchasing decisions. The more complete the information, the more likely the merchant will be able to address the customer's needs.

Typically, the labels or tags include the department number, the classification of goods, its style or subclassification, vendor name, size, and of course, the price. Stores that are value-oriented, such as the discounters and off-pricers, often list the "regular price" on the ticket, along with the price at which it sells for elsewhere.

If you examine the merchandise tags at many of the large retailers, it is obvious that much of the information is coded. In this way the merchant doesn't give away any of the merchandise secrets to the competition that might be comparison-shopping. The only items on the tags that are easily recognized are the prices and sizes. Also present in many tagging systems is the use of barcodes. Recognized as a series of thick and thin black vertical lines, these are printed codes that store merchandise information that is recorded once the sale is made.

MONARCH MARKING SYSTEMS, HEADQUARTERED IN Miamisburg, Ohio, is a wholly owned subsidiary of Paxar Corporation, which has been in business since 1890. It counts more than 300,000 customers in the retail supply chain in over 100 countries as its customers. Manufacturing plants have been established in 9 countries, making it the largest international marking brand in the world. They offer an unmatched reservoir of expertise and are always on the cutting edge of producing products that make the retailer's merchandising operation more reliable.

Monarch provides marking systems for leading retailers such as Brooks Brothers, Federated, Kmart, Nordstrom, Office Max, Saks, Sears, Talbots, Wal-Mart, and Gap. Their combination of offerings include barcode products that are both stationary and portable. The products feature printers, markers, tags and labels, software and support services, as well as identification and pricemarking products such as portable, handheld marking systems that are ideal for price/date marking and promotional labeling.

Through continuous innovative research, Monarch has been able to solve the problems of individual major retailers. American Eagle, for example, reports how Monarch's DOS-based, Pathfinder Ultra handheld marking unit has revolutionized their price change process. Once relying upon a time-intensive, manual price changing process that involved a good deal of guesswork on the part of the store's sales associates, Pathfinder Ultra has significantly improved the efficiency of the procedure.

One of the problems that most major retailers who utilize barcode applications for their products encounter is that the vendors apply inaccurate labels and tags on boxes. Through another Monarch innovation, ComplyLine was born. The system allows suppliers to download the requirements of every major retailer, determining exactly what barcode information each requires. With every merchant having their own requirements that are designed to increase their own efficiency and improve customer service, marking is made simple with Monarch ComplyLine service. In this way, vendors will be able to reduce operating costs and improve profits by complying with retailer demands. For the retailer it captures more accurate point-of-sale data to track inventory flow, provides inventory counts, and improves accuracy of automated stock replenishment. With the apparent benefits of the ComplyLine service, Monarch has attracted such clients as JCPenney, Federated, and Wal-Mart.

The company has made the acquisition of their products and services easier than ever to obtain. Its Web site, www.monarch.com, features most of their products and online assistance for questions.

Re-Marking Merchandise

No matter how carefully buyers plan their purchases and select what they believe will be the most desirable merchandise, mistakes are often made. A walk through any store immediately reveals racks and shelves that feature markdowns.

Retailers must re-mark every single price tag that has been earmarked for clearance. There are two methods used by merchants. One is simply done by hand by a sales associate. The clerk generally draws a line through the original price and marks the new price with a different color ink. Some stores use a handheld machine that quickly adjusts the prices.

It is only when complete and competent handling of goods are undertaken that the retailer will be certain to avoid the pitfalls of sloppy merchandise distribution, and will be the beneficiary of greater profits.

TRENDS FOR THE NEW MILLENNIUM

- More and more companies will continue to integrate their merchandising efforts with vendors so that each might benefit from the relationship.

- The advent of electronic data interchange, vendor managed inventory, Quick Response, and other technological advances in logistical merchandise distribution promises to become more sophisticated than any of the systems that have been used in the past.

- The importance of VICS and CPFR, both nonprofit industry participants, will continue to soar. It is organizations like these that continue to underscore the necessity for better retailer-supplier relationships.

- Outside merchandise marking will likely increase to rid the retailer of some of the chores that may be more economically handled elsewhere. In the end this will free up employees to concentrate their efforts on other parts of the operation.

- The use of intermodal transportation continues to gain popularity. This allows retailers to use two or more carriers to assure efficient delivery of merchandise.

CHAPTER HIGHLIGHTS

- Interenterprise collaboration has enabled retailers and vendors to work together to better determine merchandise needs.

- High-tech innovation such as EDI makes merchandise analysis and delivery more beneficial to both retailers and suppliers.

- Through VMI vendors are able to gather information about their products once they have been shipped to the retailer. It also allows them to process reorders more quickly.

- Quick Response technology allows the manufacturer to monitor the merchant's inventory and anticipate future merchandise needs. This benefits the retailer, who is able to reduce the amount of merchandise on hand knowing that the vendor will react quickly to replenish the store's merchandise.

- Nonprofit industry participation to improve the efficiency of the supply chain continues to broaden with such groups as VICS and CPFR, playing key roles.

- Outside marking is becoming more prevalent in the industry since it enables the retailer to move the merchandise more quickly on to the selling floor.
- Most chains use centralized receiving facilities to check and mark their goods.
- Receiving records are kept to assure that the right merchandise was delivered and that the prices invoiced are the same as on the purchase order.
- The blind method of checking incoming merchandise is designed to minimize errors.
- Quality control personnel are often assigned to receiving areas to make certain that the quality of the goods is identical to the samples from which they were ordered.

IMPORTANT RETAILING TERMS

electronic data interchange (EDI)

Quick Response (QR) inventory planning

interenterprise collaboration

vendor managed inventory (VMI)

Voluntary Interindustry Commerce Standards Association (VICS)

Collaborative Planning, Forecasting, and Replenishment Committee (CPFR)

outside marking

intermodal transportation

centralized receiving

regional receiving

receiving record

receiving dock

conveyor systems

stationary tables

portable tables

flat packed

trolley conveyors

direct quantity check

blind quantity check

semiblind quantity checking

quality checking

FOR REVIEW

1. Why do suppliers and retailers get involved in interenterprise collaboration for merchandise distribution?

2. What does the term EDI mean and how does it affect the retailer's purchasing plans?

3. In what way can vendors gather information from the retailer using a VMI system?

4. How does a QR system help the vendor in terms of satisfying the merchant's merchandise needs?

5. What role have nonprofit industry groups played in improving efficiency between retailers and vendors?

6. Why have many retailers opted to use outside marking services instead of relying upon their in-house resources?

7. Why do most major chain organizations utilize central receiving departments in their operations?

8. What is the advantage of using of regional receiving locations to distribute goods to stores?

9. Why do most supermarket chains rely on direct receiving and marking of products from vendors instead of using a centralized distribution system?

10. Why are receiving records important?

11. Discuss the different types of receiving equipment that retailers use in marking and moving their merchandise.

12. Distinguish between the direct and blind methods of quantity checking.

13. How do retailers make certain that the quality of the merchandise received is the same as what was shown in the sample line?

14. What are the advantages and disadvantages of using air express for merchandise delivery?

15. How do merchants change the prices on tags of items that have been reduced?

16. Why do some merchants utilize intermodal shipping arrangements?

AN INTERNET ACTIVITY

One division of a retail operation that is constantly looking to upgrade its equipment is the department that is responsible for merchandise handling and distribution. Many manufacturers of products that help make merchandise handling and distribution more efficient are making significant use of the Internet to tell regular and prospective clients about the availability of new products. One such company is Monarch at www.monarch.com.

Using this Web site, or any other that deals specifically with distribution and marking products, research the company's products and complete the table below. Be prepared to deliver an oral report about your findings.

Company name _____

Web site _____

Products	Description	Uses

EXERCISES AND PROJECTS

1. Contact a major retailer that has a unit in your city and ask for permission to observe its merchandise receiving and tagging operations. Be sure to tell the company representative that this is an assignment for a college course.

   Take notes during your visit and ask if you can photograph the operation. When you have gathered all the information, it should be organized into a typewritten paper approximately three pages in length. Be sure to include the following in the report:
   - the exact names and uses of each piece of equipment
   - the costs of each
   - training necessary to operate the equipment
   - output that is tied into the computer for merchandise reports.
   - photographs that you have taken.

2. Visit a retailer and observe the various types of price tickets that are used on the company's merchandise. Carefully examine each type and record the exact information that is printed or written on it. If there have been markdowns taken on some goods, record the manner in which it has been changed on the tag.

   After the observation has been completed, write a two-page paper about the information you gathered.

   Note: Be sure to bring identification with you and explain that you are participating in a school research project.

THE CASE OF THE MERCHANDISE DISTRIBUTION DILEMMA

When the Archers first opened their retail business in 1973 they never expected it to become one of the fastest growing sporting goods companies in southern California. After initial success with the first Outdoorsman store, they began to open many more units. In addition to expanding into other parts of the state, they crossed into Nevada, New Mexico, Arizona, Oregon, and Washington. At the present time the Outdoorsman has 150 units.

When they began the operation, merchandise receiving was a simple matter. All packages were delivered to the back room of the store where, cartons were opened, and merchandise was counted, checked against purchase orders, tagged, and then put onto the selling floor. The operation consisted primarily of hand recording and was overseen by Tom Archer, the company founder. As the organization began to grow, Mr. Archer found it necessary to embrace a new merchandise distribution concept. It was no longer feasible for each store to receive shipments; a centralized system would better serve the company.

After considerable research a location, in the middle of the company's trading area, was chosen for the new distribution center. At the time, the chain was still primarily located in southern California and had 60 stores. An automated system was installed, replete with the latest in receiving and marking equipment. Every item was tagged in a way that allowed the information to be fed into a the computer so that merchandising reports could be produced.

Now that the company has 150 stores and its geographic coverage has extended to several states, it seems that there might be yet a better method of merchandise distribution. The management team, still headed by Tom Archer, has undertaken the task of determining whether or not the distribution requirements could be better addressed. Some of the proposals that have been made are:

- Using a regional approach. Stores could be divided into districts or regions with each location serving a specific number of stores.
- The centralized arrangement, now in use, could be enlarged to handle the merchandise.
- A system where each store would receive goods directly from the vendors could be arranged.

At this point in time discussions continue, but no solution has been found that satisfies each member of the management team. The company has employed the services of a research organization in the hope that it could make a meaningful determination in regard to merchandise distribution.

Questions

1. If you were the lead researcher in the study, how would you begin to evaluate the problem?

2. Which approach would you suggest and why?

PART THREE

Retail Environments

In addition to establishing an organizational structure determining the depth and breadth of the store's staffing, management must select an appropriate location in which to operate and plan a design for the premises that will best serve the needs of the targeted shoppers. These decisions must be implemented before opening the store. Unlike offsite operations that need only a viable center from which executives and rank-and-file personnel will operate, the brick-and-mortar organizations must make certain that their environments will be perfectly located and designed to attract customers and thereby earn a fair share of the consumers' disposable income.

In Chapter 9, the emphasis is on location analysis, and, more specifically, the trading areas that must be assessed before any location decision can be made, the types of retail arenas that are available for merchants to choose from, and the specific sites within these arenas that best serve their needs.

Contemporary retailing demands that an individualistic approach be taken to facilities design so that each merchant will operate from an environment that is different from the others. In Chapter 10, a wealth of design principles are explored. If these principles are carefully followed, the creative team will deliver a facility that significantly enhances the company's merchandise offerings. While some of the traditionalists still rely upon the conventional methods of store design, others have embraced newer concepts such as themed environments. Each of these, along with a host of others, will be explored to show how retailers are able to distinguish their premises from those of the competition.

A

B

C

Today's food retail outlets range from the most traditional forms that have existed for centuries to dazzling emporiums that utilize up-to-the-minute technology. All have the goal of bringing fresh merchandise to consumers at a fair price. At the farmer's roadside stand (a), the producer sells directly to the consumer. The country store (b) simulates its predecessors of the nineteenth and early twentieth centuries, appealing to modern shoppers' nostalgia for the personal relationship between merchant and customer of earlier times. However, contemporary products and services are available to satisfy customers' needs. The modern supermarket chain (c) offers a broad array of food and nonfood items from around the world.

A

B

C

Off-site retailing has a major presence in the marketplace of the twenty-first century. Traditional catalog retailers such as Lillian Vernon (a) operate customer service centers to process orders received online and by mail, fax, and phone. Scholastic Book Clubs (b) sell children's books through schools, catering to readers grades pre-k through middle school. Catalogs, sent monthly to teachers, feature appropriate reading level books and include order forms for teachers and pupils. Book and record clubs' mailings to members often include ads with order forms for other products along with the lists of their own available selections (c).

A

B

D

C

Central to the success of any brick-and-mortar operation is the place from which it operates. The Rouse Company, a major developer of shopping centers, operates many types of locations. Shopping districts in downtown urban areas have been revitalized by vertical malls with retailers at the street level and on lower floors and office space above. Westlake Center in Seattle (a) exemplifies this type of property. One of Rouse's festival marketplaces, Baltimore's Harborplace (b) serves as an entertainment and dining center as well as a shopping destination. CenterPointe Plaza in Las Vegas (c) is a planned village retail center. Beachwood Place in Beachwood, Ohio (d) is a super-regional mall serving the suburbs of Cleveland.

A

B

C

D

Brick-and-mortar retailers are often related to other public sites. The Art Institute of Chicago, like most museums, stocks its gift shop and bookstore (a) with merchandise related to its own collections, to traveling exhibitions, and to the fine arts in general. Bank One Ballpark, home of the Arizona Diamondbacks (b), has food concession stands and shops selling baseball souvenirs, as sports stadiums typically do. Gift shops in hospitals, such as the one in The Kingston Hospital in Kingston, New York (c and d), are conveniently located for visitors who want to buy get-well presents for patients.

A

B

The giant ferris wheel at the Toys "R" Us store in Times Square (a) helps to make shopping a form of recreation for both children and grown-ups. Adults also find the interior of the Prada store in the trendy Soho neighborhood of New York City (b) an invitation to view shopping as an entertaining experience. Designed by the world-renowned architect Rem Koolhaas, the space can be easily manipulated so that shoppers will have a new environment to explore on different visits.

A

B

C

D

Filling the store with salable merchandise is key to the success of the retailer. Buyers attend trade shows such as MAGIC in Las Vegas (a and b) and the international Istanbul Fashion Fair (c and d) to examine the latest offerings from producers and designers. Retailers who are searching for offshore sources for their private labels find the Istanbul fair a good place to meet Turkish manufacturers.

A

B

C

S pecial events may promote the store as an exciting place to shop or may feature particular brands or items. Some examples are designer Vera Wang's in-store launch of her new fragrance (a); a joint promotion of Macy's New York and *Seventeen* magazine, featuring the popular singing group, Hanson (b); and H & M's Valentine's Day promotion, in which customers entered a contest to appear in the store window (c).

The visual merchandising staff at Barneys sets up the Co-op department with eye-catching signage and attractive fixtures and mannequins to show the merchandise to its best advantage.

CHAPTER 9

Location Analysis and Selection

After you have completed this chapter, you should be able to discuss:

- ► The importance of demographics in the selection of a trading area.
- ► The concept of geodemographics and how it is used by merchants to assure that they have targeted the best markets for their company.
- ► The role that area characteristics play in determining the potential of a retailer's trading area.
- ► Why downtown or central shopping districts have remained important as retail locations.
- ► How outlet malls have grown to become one of the more important venues for value shopping.
- ► The concept of the festival marketplace and how it differs from standard shopping malls.
- ► Some of the factors that must be addressed before a specific site is chosen to open a brick-and-mortar operation.

Whenever retailing experts are asked what the three most important considerations for success in the industry are, many reply, "location, location, location." This response should apply to anyone with the intention of opening a brick-and-mortar operation. Before anything else is considered, the exact location must be determined. Too many inexperienced entrepreneurs, have found that by being in the wrong place, their businesses never got off the ground.

Planners at the major companies fully understand the necessity of being in the right place. The giants in the industry generally maintain their own in-house real estate departments that investigate location opportunities and assess them for new units. Others turn to marketing research experts who, for a fee, conduct studies before they make recommendations to their clients. In either case, the approach must be a scientific one where a host of different criteria are addressed, with the final decisions resting with top management.

The choices today are numerous. Merchants have the option to choose malls of every size and configuration both in cities and suburban areas; downtown shopping districts in the major and smaller cities; **mixed-use centers** that incorporate stores, entertainment offerings, residences, and commercial offices; **festival marketplaces** that are composed of shops and eateries in revitalized, unique areas; power centers where high-profile merchants dominate the scene; neighborhood clusters that generally feature small operations; or freestanding stores.

With so much opportunity, the retailer is able to find the sites that are best suited for his or her type of organization. Before a specific site can be selected, research initially focuses on selecting the general trading area in which the company chooses to operate, then moves on to the type of shopping district that will best serve the company's needs, and ultimately concludes with selecting the exact site in which the organization can open its doors to the consumer.

If the study is carefully conducted, then the location will serve the merchant well when his or her merchandising concepts are applied.

TRADING AREA ANALYSIS AND SELECTION

The United States, and for that matter, the entire world is comprised of general trading areas in which retailers may choose to establish business outlets. A trading area might be an entire country, a region of a country, a city, or a community within a city. Many major retailers such as Wal-Mart are expanding their businesses into overseas arenas and therefore must consider the entire globe as their potential trading area. On the other hand, smaller merchants generally narrow their markets to more restricted locales such as a particular city. Whether it is the establishment of a new retailing venture, or the expansion of one that already exists, the task of selecting a trading area is a formidable one for any size retailer.

Demographic Analysis

The actual procedure usually begins with **demographic analysis**, a study of the trading area's demographics (see Chapter 4). Some of the specifics of the population investigation must center on the following:

- *The size of the population and its potential for expansion.* Actual, present day figures are insufficient by themselves. Statistical models must be used to determine whether the number of people in the area will remain constant, or whether it will increase or decrease. The southern tier of the United States, for example, continues to serve as a place where retirees flock for their later years. Projections indicate that states like Florida will maintain its population growth due to the number of senior citizens who move to warm climates during their retirement years. Because of this reality, this trading area is a must for merchants who count the seniors as their customers. Geographic projections are easily obtainable from the Census Bureau, which studies the United States population every 10 years. Trade associations also conduct population analysis so that they can provide statistics to their members who are considering expansion programs. Of course, major retailers might address the problem by conducting their own investigations in which they can more specifically concentrate on their own needs.

- *The dominant ages of the population in a specific region.* This is extremely important to the success of most retail businesses. The needs of the young contrast considerably with those of the elderly. While most general trading areas are comprised of across-the-board age classifications, some have heavier concentrations in one age group than in another. Southern New Jersey and Southern California, for example, are experiencing significant growth as retirement communities. With the wealth of planned communities for the elderly on the rise in these regions, it is an obvious place for merchants who count on this group as a major part of their customer base to expand there. On the other hand, major cities such as New York, Boston, and Chicago are experiencing enormous population growth with younger consumers. This fact has encouraged companies like Banana Republic, Gap, Abercrombie & Fitch, and Ann Taylor to undergo considerable expansion in these trading areas.

- *The size and makeup of the family.* This is also an important factor to consider. It cannot be assumed that every region of the country is made up of typical households. Where one city might have at its population core a family that consists of two parents and two children, others might be quite different. In major cities, there are large numbers of families that are by no means traditional. A family might consist of two unrelated people, a married couple without children, or a single parent home with children. Researchers are finding that typical is no longer the standard in American culture. Thus, careful research must be undertaken to discover the different types of families that comprise the trading area under consideration, and whether or not the retailer who is considering expansion there will have the appropriate goods to satisfy their needs.

- *The stability of a trading area in terms of seasonality.* While the vast majority of general trading areas are traditionally comprised of consumers who reside there year round, some are primarily made up of part-timers, who call these places home for a short part of the year. Palm Springs, California, and Southampton, New York, for example are areas where the population isn't constant throughout the year. Each caters to a clientele that frequents these resort towns for just a few months of the year. In such cases, only those merchants who can profit in such short seasons can consider expanding into these regions.

- *Income.* This is a vital concern for any retailer to address before a trading area can be considered. Data on per capita and family earnings is available from the Census Bureau. Consumer spending is directly related to their incomes. If a particular trading area is at the upper level of the income ladder, such as is the case in Beverly Hills, California, or Palm Beach, Florida, then high-profile boutiques and designer shops can consider these areas excellent locations. On the other hand, if the median income in a geographic area is at the lower levels of the earnings scale, then value-oriented stores such as Kmart and Wal-Mart will be best suited to these locations.

- *The type of residences in which consumers reside.* If the majority of dwellings are apartment buildings, retailers of outdoor furniture wouldn't find a market for their goods there. By contrast, if the region were dominated by single family homes that are situated on large lots, then outdoor specialists would likely succeed in their ventures.

An Ethical Consideration

IT IS GOOD PRACTICE TO USE ALL OF THE ABOVE DEMOGRAPHIC CRITERIA in analyzing and selecting a trading area before making a commitment. This is, of course, essential to the success of the company. However, when all of the scientific approaches have been completed, often times, communities are rejected because there isn't a guarantee of success. It might be that the average income doesn't warrant an addition to the company, or that some of the other established criteria haven't been met. While this is sound business, it leaves something to be desired in terms of ethics.

In the supermarket industry, for example, the major chains tend to shy away from trading areas that are replete with the lower-lower class segment of the population. While these citizens might not be able to afford the frills that are enjoyed by their more affluent counterparts, they too must eat. Many in these communities are hard workers who need conveniently located stores to satisfy their needs. It is incumbent upon the giants in the industry, whose profits could support less than high volume units, to ensure that the needs of all consumers are met.

One concept that retailers often use in their demographic studies is a segmentation system that involves clustering descriptions. One of the major sellers of this information is Claritas, Inc., based in San Diego, California. This company and other researchers of this nature believe that most variations between neighborhood types can be explained by social rank, household composition, mobility, ethnicity, population density, and housing information. The Claritas segmentation system, called PRIZM (Potential Rating Index Zip Code

Market), defines neighborhoods in terms of 62 different codes assigned to 15 social groups. These codes are used to describe consumer behavior and categorize individuals with similar characteristics. Five digit zip code descriptions form the basis of the predictions and are available free on the Claritas Web site (www.claritas.com). Another major player in this type of **community segmentation** is ESRI Business Information Solutions, which features the ACORN® (A Classification Of Residential Neighborhoods) product. A view of its offerings is available on the Internet at http://www.infods.com.

From either of these services, a retailer, who is seeking to open a new business or expand an existing one, may discern where it has the most potential for success based upon the characteristics of the consumers that reside in a particular location.

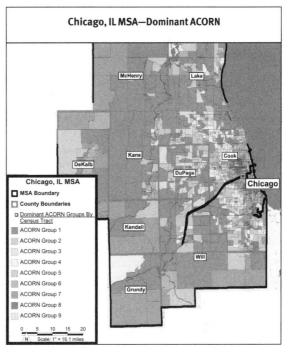

A map showing ESRI Business Information Solutions' ACORN® lifestyle classification segments.

Area Characteristic Assessment

Once the demographics have been thoroughly analyzed, it is important for the retail research team to investigate the trading area under consideration in terms of its characteristics. The characteristics that must be assessed include the following:

- *The amount of competition that already exists there.* The lack of any competition might be an indicator that the area doesn't warrant stores of this nature. Of course, if there is a great deal of competition it might be a signal that another store, similar to what is already in place, is one too many to achieve success. If there are existing stores, their operations should be evaluated in terms of how the new merchant's operation will be similar or different. **Me-too stores** run the risk of being unable to distinguish themselves from what is already there, and might not be able to successfully compete.
- *Area accessibility.* This is extremely important. The type of roadways that are in place must provide easy access to the stores so that a sufficient amount of customer traffic will be generated. Major malls are always located in areas that are adjacent to highway networks and convenient for vehicular traffic to reach the stores. Public transportation is also essential if the proposed trading area is in the city. Unlike suburbanites who generally rely upon their automobiles to bring them to shopping areas, residents of the cities

usually depend upon buses and trains. The retailer who is considering a particular trading area must assess each of the available modes of transportation and whether they are sufficient to bring in the numbers of people necessary to be successful.

- *Area attractions.* The availability of area attractions should be evaluated in terms of attracting potential shoppers. Other than the residents who call certain cities their home, visitors often provide another segment of the population that accounts for a great deal of purchasing. Tourists generally spend more on their vacations than they would at home. New York City, with its abundance of museums, theaters and other attractions provides its retailers with a constant flow of out-of-town consumer traffic; Orlando, Florida, home to Disney World and other theme parks, is a mecca for a host of different types of retailers; and Paris, with it's legendary historical attractions, is a natural environment for the tourist to purchase a wealth of mementos.

- *Area growth.* This is another signal that helps retailers consider expansion. Throughout the United States there are numerous cities that continue to awaken and have population explosions. Las Vegas, Nevada, for example, once a place exclusively frequented by gambling enthusiasts, has not only expanded its environment to become a place where entire families

New York City, with its abundance of exciting attractions, is the home to many world famous retailers.

can be entertained, but has also become a city where permanent residence is significantly increasing. Many southern cities such as Charlotte, North Carolina and Jacksonville, Florida are realizing enormous population increases making them excellent locations for retail expansion. Very often, these areas have been underserved by the retailing community. They make for excellent choices for retailers because of the lack of competition.

- *The availability of educational institutions that offer business programs is essential to training retailing managers.* If a retailer is to succeed, then it must be able to recruit skilled personnel to run the business. If colleges and universities do not offer curricula that could provide the number of trained specialists needed to run a business, then it must look elsewhere to fill its management ranks. This is sometimes problematic, especially when the economy is at full employment levels and relocating isn't a benefit to employees. Colleges and universities are also excellent providers of specialized training courses that fit the specific needs of retailers. If, for example, there is a need for better understanding of computer operations, the educational institution could provide such training. The success of any company is dependent upon its employees' performances.

- *Local laws that could improve or hinder sales.* These should be assessed. Sometimes local legislation limits store hours or imposes certain restrictions that prevent the retailer from maximizing sales. Occasionally, the laws actually benefit merchants. Delaware, for example, has no sales tax. The sales tax advantage serves as an inducement to draw consumers from neighboring states in the mid-Atlantic region, giving the retailer an extra customer base from which to draw.

Once the demographics have been evaluated, along with the area's characteristics, a decision can be made as to the viability of the region as another company outlet. Of course, some areas do not score perfectly in each of the assessment criteria. In those cases, management must determine whether or not the shortcomings will negatively impact on the retailer's potential success.

The Stein Mart Story
Expanding into New Locations

WITH OFF-SITE RETAILING HELD TO A MINIMUM AT STEIN MART, the company actively seeks new locations for its brick-and-mortar operations. Expansion is a constant issue for the company, with markets both east and west of the Mississippi being targeted. The two areas are separately researched. The western tenant company that researches locations and makes recommendations to the company is The Place Commercial Real Estate. To date, the majority of its efforts are in California and Texas. Its eastern counterpart is Regency Realty Corporation, whose efforts have focused mainly in Florida and Michigan, with Illinois and Pennsylvania not far behind.

The primary locations being sought are strip centers, the majority of which feature supermarkets. Stein Mart believes that its customer regularly frequents these grocers and places them in close proximity to the stores. Some Stein Mart's are also located in power centers, where co-tenants include bookstores, sporting goods retailers, and stores like Target, Kmart, Blockbuster, and a variety of restaurants.

In spite of the store's value-orientation, it prefers to locate in very affluent markets. More than ever, the stores are located in the highest average household income areas with at least 150,000 inhabitants.

Once a new location has passed the test by the two realtors, the recommendations go to the board where the final decisions are made.

SHOPPING DISTRICT CHOICES

A close inspection of the places where retailers open their outlets immediately reveals that there is an abundance of shopping district choices available. A century ago, this was not the case. The choices were either the downtown, central district which was the dominant location, or the main street of the town or village where merchants set up shop. This radically changed in the middle of the twentieth century when families began to make the trek from the inner cities to the suburbs. As the population began to move from its urban environments to outlying areas, retailers began to follow in record numbers. Recognizing that shopping convenience was the factor that motivated many consumers, it was necessary for the retailers to head wherever their customers moved.

Department store branches abounded everywhere, with the downtown flagships not only to continuing to serve the needs of those who remained in the cities, but also to serve as company headquarters where buyers, merchandisers, and other key executives continued to make decisions for the main store as well as the newly opened branches. Chain organizations also headed into the new towns that consumers called home. They too opened stores in record numbers to serve these newly formed communities.

It would not be long before a host of different shopping districts would emerge as viable places for retailers to open new companies or expand their existing operations. Today, we see a variety of different types of retailing formats that serve every segment of the population.

Central Shopping Districts

Often referred to as downtown, **central shopping districts** are the main places in a city where people shop. They house the flagships of many department stores as well as a host of

Chicago's "Magnificent Mile" is a renowned central shopping district, housing such retail giants as Neiman Marcus and Saks Fifth Avenue.

other retailers. Macy's, for example, has the centerpiece of its vast empire located in New York City's midtown area, while Marshall Field's is located in the heart of Chicago. With the stores located within the center of the business community, the stores are able to serve the needs of those who commute to work from outlying areas, along with people who call the city their home. In addition to the region's regulars, the tourists and business visitors who frequent these locales add significant numbers of people to the shopping population.

There are other reasons why these areas have remained important retailing centers, including:

- A significant amount of public transportation, which provides a steady stream of shoppers.
- A vast number of stores that generally feature a variety of merchandise at all price points.
- A wealth of pedestrians who pass by the stores while they are going to and coming from work. During lunch breaks, in particular, the streets of these avenues are filled with these potential customers.
- A large number of restaurants and entertainment venues draw people to the area.

While these are advantageous conditions, the central districts also have disadvantages:

- For those who prefer to come to these locations with their own automobiles, parking facilities are often minimal.
- Those living distances from the downtown areas are often greeted with considerable traffic on the roads, making the trips very time consuming.
- Some inner cities, while still serving as viable business communities, are experiencing high crime rates that often make the shoppers feel insecure.

Even with these negatives, the United States is experiencing a renaissance in their cities making them excellent outlets for retail enterprises. Chicago, for example, has recently witnessed an enormous investment by retailers in their downtown area. Nordstrom has opened; Lord & Taylor underwent a renovation in its central district location; and Marshall Field's spent millions of dollars to return its flagship to the elegant setting that it enjoyed in the past. In New York City, Saks Fifth Avenue undertook an extensive renovation in midtown, and numerous designer shops have opened flagships there. Even in the smaller cities, the downtown revitalizations have made these areas locations that shoppers are returning to in record numbers.

Shopping Malls

The history of the **shopping mall** is attributed by most industry professionals to the Highland Park shopping Village in Dallas, Texas, which opened its doors to the public in 1931. It was by no means as extravagant as today's malls, but it had the requisites of the **controlled shopping center**, as do all of the malls now in operation around the country. It had a unified image, was under the management of a single owner, and occupied a site that was not bisected by public streets.

Through the years, as different malls were introduced to the public, innovative concepts were introduced to make these shopping arenas superior to those that preceded them. Some of these included:

- The introduction of nighttime shopping, which took place at the Town & Country Shopping Center in Columbus, Ohio, in the 1940s.
- The building of the first two-level center in Shoppers World in Framingham, Massachusetts, in 1950.
- The first fully enclosed mall, Southdale Center in Edina, Minnesota, opened in 1956. The advantage of climate control enabled consumers to shop in comfort year round.
- Regional malls like The Galleria in Houston, which opened in 1972, became the forerunner of the many large malls that now operate in the United States.
- Faneuil Hall Marketplace, developed by the Rouse Company in Boston in 1976, was the first festival marketplace in the country.
- The country's first urban **vertical mall**, Water Tower Place, debuted in Chicago on Michigan Avenue, the hub of the downtown shopping district, in 1976.

- Potomac Mills opened in northern Virginia in 1985. It was the first of many enclosed factory and retail **outlet centers** to open in the United States.
- **Power Centers**, arenas that house about six category killers, came into prominence in the mid 1980s.
- Following on the success of the West Edmonton Mall in Canada, America witnessed the opening of its own **mega-mall** in Bloomington, Minnesota.

The number that continue to open all across the United States is evidence of the strength of these shopping malls. Most every format, as will be discussed, is still in existence, with more and more of those already operating undergoing extensive renovations and expansions.

The mall phenomenon that is sweeping the country is due in some part to the involvement of the Simon Property Group, the nation's largest developer of shopping centers.

 Focus on . . .
Simon Property Group

FOUNDED IN 1960, SIMON CONTINUES TO EXPAND on its history of innovation and creativity in developing the highest quality retail properties in North America. At the present time, the company manages a retail network that drives more than $30 billion in annual sales. The group owns more than 275 properties comprising regional malls, community shopping centers, and specialty and mixed-use properties. In these vast shopping arenas, the group holds more than 20,000 retail leases. Adding to these staggering numbers is the fact that one-half of all Americans shop in Simon malls, accounting for approximately 2.5 billion mall visits each year. One million employees work for retailers at Simon malls.

The types of retail operations that are either owned or managed cut across the industry's entire spectrum. These include high fashion boutiques, specialty stores, designer shops, department stores, mass merchants, category killers, discounters, and manufacturer's outlets.

In the Simon portfolio are some of the country's most productive and recognizable properties. Included are The Forum Shops at Caesars Palace in Las Vegas, a high fashion shopping arena, The Mall of Georgia, a 1.7-million-square-foot super regional mall, Mall of America, America's largest mall, which incorporates shopping with unique entertainment venues, and Town Center in Boca Raton, Florida, an upscale shopping environment.

One of the innovative techniques that Simon Properties uses involves branding. Much like the retailers who have established their own merchandise brands, Simon has adapted the concept to publicize its malls. While each of the shopping arenas maintains its own identity, they are all tied together by specific elements. It all begins with the Simon name that is emblazoned on mall entry doors, parking lot banners, and signs. Also visible in every one of their properties is a pledge signed by each member of the mall staff to provide superior shopping with special incentives and amenities. One such incentive that rewards shoppers for their patronage is the Mallperks Program. Participants in the plan enjoy points for their purchases that may be later redeemed for rewards.

With its unrivaled success as a retail developer, the organization believes that "giving back" is also one of its obligations. Through the Simon Youth Foundation, it fosters economic and career development in youth through the implementation of focused and appropriate educational initiatives and programs. Specifically, it provides students with the opportunity to learn and receive a high school diploma in a nontraditional setting, the shopping mall, as well as enabling students to participate in internships at mall retail stores. They also award scholarships for continuing education.

The company's expansion continues to soar with many more mall openings and the acquisition of other properties that are already in existence.

Traditional Shopping Malls

Every major region of the United States has at least one traditional shopping center that serves the needs of its residents. A consumer generally needs to travel no more than twenty miles from his or her home to arrive at a shopping arena that is anchored by two or more department stores, has a host of stores that are units of nationally prominent specialty chains, and features single store operations that are unique to its locale. Included in these arenas is the obligatory food court, restaurants, and some entertainment facilities.

Initially, these retail environments began as outdoor, single-story operations. Although most of today's major malls are housed in enclosed structures, there are many throughout the country that still successfully operates outdoors. Two extremely successful ventures are Old Orchard in suburban Chicago, and The Falls in Miami. Some of the outdoor malls occupy two stories such as The Esplanade in Palm Beach and the Bal Harbor Shops in Bal Harbor, Florida.

Old Orchard in suburban Chicago is a traditional mall that features many well-known anchors.

Today, with the benefit of climate control, the vast majority of the traditional malls are enclosed. They provide the shopper the convenience of being able to comfortably shop no matter what the weather is like outside. Many malls that began as outdoor centers have enclosed their premises. Roosevelt Field, in Garden City, New York, was one of the major malls to enclose its premises after it was in business many years.

Many malls are also undergoing significant expansions to their regular configurations so that they may better serve the communities in which they are located. Roosevelt Field, for example, first added a second floor and then further expanded to include new anchors such as Nordstrom. Beginning as a modest shopping center it now is one of the largest in the United States.

Vertical Malls

Amid the clamor of both vehicular and pedestrian traffic in some downtown areas of major cities, vertical malls are rising because of the lack of traditional street level space. Chicago led the way with the first high rise called Water Tower Place. It is anchored by Marshall Field's and Lord & Taylor, and features a mix of many specialty stores such as The Limited and Gap. It is also unique in that its eight retail floors are topped by the Ritz Carlton Hotel.

Its success spawned other vertical configurations in Chicago, including Chicago Place, anchored by Saks Fifth Avenue and a host of other merchants including Room & Board, a contemporary home furnishings center, and small shops; and 900 Michigan Avenue, which is anchored by Bloomingdale's and is home to a small unit of an upscale supermarket, Bockwinkles.

Except for the anchors which occupy a portion of these malls' main floors, the rest are on upper levels resulting in lower rents than if these stores occupied street level space.

Water Tower Place in Chicago was one of America's first vertical malls, with eight floors topped by a hotel.

Mixed-Use Centers

Building on the traditional mall concept, developers began to expand their environments with centers that along with shopping facilities featured commercial districts and housing. The idea was based upon the fact that a captive audience was on the premises and that it would more than likely patronize the surrounding stores.

Copley Place in Boston was one of the earliest of these centers. It is not only anchored by large department store branches, but by two hotels, four office buildings, and private residences. By virtue of the two hotels, it has the advantage of reaching visiting tourists, and with the businesses and apartments located in the facility it has a built-in customer base.

Outlet Malls

Joining the traditional shopping centers where regular pricing is expected and customer service is the forte, manufacturer's outlets and off-pricers have joined forces to open value-oriented malls. In locations all across the United States a multitude of indoor and outdoor shopping venues continue to account for enormous success.

The earliest of these entries were in Reading, Pennsylvania, and Secaucus, New Jersey, where many manufacturers opened warehouses to sell off slow selling inventories. The concept was quickly embraced by consumers who learned of them by word of mouth. There was no formality in these arenas; each vendor acted independently, establishing their own days and hours of operation.

Today, the outlet phenomenon is an ever-expanding concept. Retailers wishing to dispose of slow sellers that weren't sold in regular stores, along with manufacturers who must make room for the new season's arrivals have each opened units in the outlet malls.

The largest of the indoor environments is part of the Mills organization. Beginning with its first entry, Potomac Mills in Northern Virginia, the group has expanded into arenas that feature as much as 2 million square feet under one roof. The largest and most successful of these malls is Sawgrass Mills in a suburb of Ft. Lauderdale, Florida. Occupying enormous spaces are Off-Fifth, Saks Fifth Avenue's clearance facility, and Last Call, the Neiman Marcus closeout center. Also in residence are manufacturers of marquee labels, such as DKNY, Ralph Lauren, and Calvin Klein, and upscale specialty retailers that include Barney's New York. Also prominent are enormous food courts and well-known eateries such as the Cheesecake Factory, along with entertainment facilities that feature multiplex theaters.

The distances from which shoppers that are served by the various Mills properties travel, its population size and growth, average household income, and other information such as the stores that the properties feature are shown in the Opry Mills example. It should be noted that it is typical of all the Mills' ventures.

Potomac Mills was the first of the Mills organization's outlet malls; this commercial real estate developer now owns malls across North America.

Outdoor value-oriented malls continue to open all over the country. There, too, consumers are treated to the closeout offerings of retailers and manufacturers. Names like Coach, Ann Taylor, Gap, Calvin Klein, Mikasa, Liz Claiborne, Nautica, and Brooks Brothers dominate.

Akin to these planned shopping meccas are locations that evolved because of a **popular area destination**. Initially, these sites served the purposes of unique retail operations that

Opry Mills is a major enclosed outlet mall.

were not value-oriented. One such place that has become a major shopping stop on the East Coast is in Freeport, Maine, where LLBean is headquartered. With this enormous brick-and-mortar operation, open 24 hours a day all year round, except for Christmas Day, the crowds that come to patronize it are tremendous. No matter the time of day or night, the parking lots are filled with campers, mobile homes, and cars. With LLBean as its centerpiece, Freeport, Maine, soon became a haven where outlets of well-known companies set up shop. Dooney Bourke, Patagonia, Banana Republic, Cole-Haan Shoes, Dansk, Ralph Lauren, and Calvin Klein all operate closeout or factory stores that are in close proximity to the landmark retailer's facility.

The presence of these outlet arenas now includes more than 14,000 factory stores and 350 shopping centers. The names and locations of each are readily available to shoppers at www.outletbound.com, where with a click of the mouse store names, location, brand or product category, phone numbers, hours of operation, and basic directions can be accessed.

Mega-malls

With the opening of the West Edmonton Mall in Canada, and Mall of America in Bloomington, Minnesota, North Americans were introduced to the concept of the mega-mall. Occupying about 4 million square feet of space, they offer a wealth of shopping and entertainment to the families that frequent them. Aside from the Nordstrom's, Bloomingdale's, and Sears' anchors and more than 500 specialty stores, Mall of America features a tremendous mix of restaurants, movie theaters, and attractions such as Camp Snoopy, a pool replete with waves, a miniature golf facility, and many night clubs.

While these two massive retail arenas initiated the mega-mall concept, they are not alone. Others have joined the fray, albeit on a smaller scale. The Mall of Georgia opened to great fanfare in 1999, with a 1.7-million-square-foot site. It is a planned development that occupies 500 acres and includes apartments, a power box retail center, a village concept, an open air concert venue, an Imax 3D theater, and a 90-acre nature park. Anchors include Nordstrom, JCPenney, Rich's, and Dillard's. With Georgia-inspired architecture, store facades draw upon the state's small town retail history. Broken down into five mall zones are Atlanta, the North Georgia mountains, the Piedmont area's manufacturing heritage, the plains made famous by Jimmy Carter, and the coastal areas. Each features its own design such as the Atlanta zone that is a replica of Union Station, the city's main post-Civil War train terminal. Also unique to the mall concept is the clustering of stores according to price points. This plan enables shoppers with limited time to quickly head for their area of interest.

Festival Marketplaces

It was the redevelopment of the waterfront area in Boston that gave us the first festival marketplace. Specifically, the Rouse Company totally refurbished historic Faneuil Hall, at the waterfront, into Quincy Market, the center of this new shopping arena. The term festival marketplace was coined to describe centers that offered festive settings along with places to shop and innovative eateries.

With the immediate success of the Faneuil Hall venture, other unique centers began to spring up. In old railroad terminals and downtrodden or underutilized waterfront warehouses, other festival marketplaces were born. South Street Seaport in New York City soon became a destination where tourists would flock to make purchases and enjoy the sights. Once home to the Fulton Fish Market that served the

The entrance to Bayside Marketplace, a Rouse Company festival marketplace in Miami, welcomes shoppers with its attractive local architecture and greenery.

cities seafood restaurants, it now features Pier 17, a shopping facility, cobblestone streets reminiscent of earlier times and numerous restaurants whose themes replicate the old fish market that was once there. St. Louis' Union Station was refurbished into another of these marketplaces. HarborPlace in Baltimore was yet another festival marketplace that was built on another eyesore, the city's seedy waterfront area.

The success of these enterprises has gained popularity all over the country. Many cities have erected festive settings that provide a renaissance in otherwise forgotten places.

 Focus on . . .
International Council of Shopping Centers

FOUNDED IN 1957, THE INTERNATIONAL COUNCIL OF SHOPPING CENTERS (ICSC) has thousands of members in more than 75 countries. ICSC's members include shopping center owners, developers, managers, marketing specialists, investors, lenders, academics, public officials, and of course, retailers.

Its principal aim is to assist members in the development of their businesses through professional education, conferences and conventions, publications, research, and legislative action. Specifically, the council:

- Collects and disseminates information pertaining to the techniques of profitable operations which serves to improve the individual shopping center and the industry.
- Studies economic, marketing, and promotional conditions that affect the shopping center industry.
- Promotes the prestige and standing of members as reputable specialists in the field of shopping center development and management.
- Encourages research for the architecture and design of shopping centers, and the development of improved management and maintenance methods.
- Promotes the role of shopping centers in the marketing of consumer goods and services.

In carrying out its vital role in the shopping center industry, the ICSC organizes more than 250 conferences a year where as many as 75,000 individuals participate. The council also offers more than 70 books, reports, audio books, and computer disks to its members on a variety of topics ranging from retailing and architectural design to marketing and management issues. On one of its Web sites (www.retailernews.com), ICSC connects subscribers to the latest in industry developments. In order to keep the professionals in the group up to date about industry happenings, ICSC offers an educational component—the University of Shopping Centers. It is specifically designed as a continuing educational forum in which the curriculum covers asset management, retailing, finance, lease administration, development, design, architecture, construction, law, technology, and a host of other areas of specialization. Through distance learning, ICSC is able to reach the far corners of the globe.

Among the many high profile members of this organization are Mall of America, Sawgrass Mills, The Forum Shops, Desert Hills Premium Outlets, and Pier 39.

Power Centers

These are small shopping venues that are tenanted by about six high profile category killers. Typically they feature retailers such as Borders Books, Bed Bath & Beyond, Best Buy, CompUSA, Office Depot, Sports Authority, Toys "R" Us, and PetsMart. Each of these merchants advertises heavily and draws large crowds of shoppers to the premises. The centers usually occupy from 225,000 to 500,000 square feet. The key to the success of these centers is that they offer a wealth of merchandise at value-oriented pricing structures, guaranteeing that there will be something to satisfy each shopper's needs.

Power centers generally house about six high volume retailers such as Office Max, PetsMart, and Bed, Bath and Beyond.

Fashion Avenues

In many of America's most affluent communities there are **fashion avenues** that feature a host of upscale shops. The marquee names on the storefronts include internationally renowned designers such as Hermes, Louis Vuitton, Giorgio Armani, Chanel, Yves St. Laurent, Calvin Klein, and Ralph Lauren.

Rodeo Drive in Beverly Hills, California, is one such fashion avenue. With the film and television industry located close by, it has remained a destination for the rich and famous. Worth Avenue in Palm Beach, Florida, is also a thriving street of fashion. Its inhabitants are social elites like the Kennedys. Lining the streets waiting to cater to the wishes and whims of the "upper-upper class" are many of the same stores that are found in Beverly Hills.

Also prime fashion avenues are New York City's Madison and Fifth Avenues. The former is housed primarily by designers who feature the latest in fashion-forward merchandise, upscale boutiques, and art galleries. The latter features the flagships of Saks Fifth Avenue and Lord & Taylor and a host of designer emporiums. Since New York City is home to some of the wealthiest families in America, a place where many international businesses are headquartered, and a spot where tourists visit each day in record numbers, these avenues are a natural place for fashion devotees to satisfy their desires.

Flea Markets

The antithesis of the fashion avenue are the bargain arenas that house the flea markets and swap shops. In the vast parking fields of racetracks and drive-in movies, vendors line the aisles with stalls that feature everything form electronics to apparel and accessories. The atmosphere is very often carnival-like making it a fun place for the entire family to shop for value merchandise.

The smaller of these markets tend to operate limited hours such as weekends. The major flea markets, such as the Swap Shop in a suburb of Fort Lauderdale, Florida, operate daily and feature more than 1,000 vendors. The Swap Shop has booths that are surrounded by a circus and a stage that spotlights a variety of entertainers.

Many of the vendors who own these businesses may actually be considered chain operators in that they have branches in several of the markets. The vast number, however, are individual entrepreneurs who use this type of selling as a means to supplement their incomes.

Airports are becoming major shopping venues for travelers, who often have endless time to spend shopping because of flight delays. Shops at London's Heathrow Airport are shown here.

Airport Terminals

Today's travelers are finding that many of the flights they have booked require airport stopovers. Often, these plane changes require stays that last a few hours. Add to this the ever increasing delays due to security checks and inclement weather, and the terminal is now filled with people with nothing to do but wait for their departures.

Enter the age of airport shopping. Once housing only newsstands, bars, restaurants, and duty-free shops, these locales are now home to retailers like Gap, Victoria's Secret, The Museum Shop, Wilson's Leather, and many others. While the phenomenon is relatively new in the United States, European airports have long catered to the traveler. In London's Heathrow Airport, numerous small stores surround an outpost of the world-famous Harrods. At France's Nice Airport designer boutiques of Hermes and Gianni Versace are bordered with numerous upscale jewelers and perfumeries.

Pittsburgh International Airport was one of the first in America to get on the airport shopping mall track. Apparel and accessories stores, gift shops, bookstores, golf shops, and restaurants are in abundance, catering to those waiting for their connections. Its more than 10 merchants have access to about 60,000 passengers daily and are averaging per passenger sales of approximately $10. Jumping on this bandwagon are LaGuardia Airport in New York City, and Ronald Reagan National Airport in Washington, D.C., where annual sales average $950 per square foot. That is more than three times the business of an average mall store where the figures tend to be closer to $250 to $300 per square foot. Chicago's O'Hare Airport, a hub for United Airlines, is another that is moving forward with significant expansion.

As is the case of conventional locations, those in airport retailing benefit if they are in key locations. Being in hubs where plane changing is a given, the passengers are forced to linger longer and have the time to peruse the shopping facilities. Heavy international traffic is also a plus. The best locations are in spots beyond the security checkpoints.

Neighborhood Clusters

Neighborhood clusters are unplanned locations that are either replete with stores that provide services to their clienteles or shops that offer a broad selection of apparel and home furnishings. Unlike the malls that are set up in a controlled fashion, where the developer determines the number of each merchandise classification that will make the center profitable for retailers, these venues are anything but controlled. Generally comprised of buildings that have no central ownership, each landlord has the freedom to rent to anyone he or she desires.

In some small cities and towns, these clusters typically feature a grocer, bake shop, dry cleaner, beauty salon, and pharmacy. They are the places that the locals frequent on a daily basis. Other clusters might be more apparel or accessories oriented and feature small specialty shops, haberdasheries, boutiques or jewelry shops. Most of the stores are independently owned and operated, but occasionally there is a chain present.

Strip Centers

In communities all over the country, the main shopping outlets are located in **strip centers**. The types of stores that are found in these configurations are similar to those that are situated in neighborhood clusters. There are, however, some differences between them. Unlike the unplanned situations that were addressed above, a single developer who maintains control regarding the tenancy owns the strip centers. This refers to the fact that he or she determines the tenant mix that will make the center profitable for those who have leased the premises.

Another feature of this type of location is the availability of parking. Unlike the neighborhood clusters that rely upon street parking for the shoppers, this arrangement makes store access simpler.

Freestanding Stores

The concept of a single retail entity being situated all by itself is not dominant in the retail scene. Most merchants want to locate their stores in places where others operate so that each can bring its own customer traffic there. Thus, the consumer is more likely to visit places where there are a great deal of shopping options.

The only type of retailer that still subscribes to the **freestanding store** concept is the one that, by virtue of its reputation, draws vast crowds of shoppers to its location. These stores can be located just about anywhere they choose as long as the public will be able to access the premises. The major warehouse clubs such as Sam's, Costco, and BJ's are proponents of such venues. Their merchandising philosophies and reputations, which are based upon value, bring the crowds in masses. They need not rely upon other retailers to attract the crowds.

SITE SELECTION

Within every shopping district there are particular locations that are better than others. The difference between one place and another may contribute to the success or failure of a company. Each merchant's needs are unique and are generally based upon his or her retailing format. Supermarkets, for example, need convenient parking facilities, while boutiques might prefer the quiet, secondary streets where there is less hustle and bustle. In order to make certain that the best possible site has been selected, competent research is needed before any final decision is made.

Several of the factors addressed in site selection include pedestrian traffic, neighboring stores, accessibility to public transportation, and parking facilities.

Pedestrian traffic is vital to the success of retailers, because of the number of people who see stores as they pass by.

Pedestrian Traffic

Stores that thrive upon passersby for their success must first consider the amount of pedestrian traffic at the site. Not only are the numbers important, but so is the composition of the people in terms of age and income. Tower Records, for example, with a large portion of its revenue coming from sales of rock music CDs, would benefit from a downtown site that is regularly seen by passing teenagers. Even in the malls, there are some sites that get more pedestrian traffic than others. Each mall has main arteries and secondary spurs. The former is seen by the vast majority of the shoppers and is, of course, more productive in terms of providing potential shoppers. The latter is seen by a lesser number, but might serve the purposes of a retailer with little competition in the area, making it a destination that people will seek out.

Optimally, a store that is situated on a corner can be assured of greater pedestrian traffic and visibility because of the converging traffic produced by the two streets that cross.

Neighboring Stores

Ideally, a retailer who is rewarded with a site that is adjacent to a department store is guaranteed a steady stream of potential customers. Since department stores rely heavily on advertising to attract potential customers, the surrounding merchants are the beneficiaries of the traffic they generate from such promotional endeavors.

Another plus would be a site that is bordered on both sides by stores that sell complementary merchandise. The ladies' accessories boutique that is located between an apparel shop and a shoe store will have a regular flow of customer traffic.

It is also better if the stores that lie next to each other feature merchandise of the same price points. An upscale men's clothing store would not benefit from a next-door neighbor who sells low-priced shoes; nor would a high-end children's boutique gain traffic generated by a value-oriented merchant.

While these are all sound considerations in site selection, it should be understood that the ideal situation isn't always available. Often times vacancies in existing shopping centers do not provide the optimum neighboring stores. In newly built arenas, such as malls, the chances of leasing optimal space are more likely since the developers are aware of the benefits of complimentary neighboring stores.

Competition

The number of competitors carrying similar merchandise is an important factor. If there are too many, the competition might be too keen to make the new entry a viable one. Breaking into an area that has established businesses of the same nature requires some amount of uniqueness to lure customers away from the established companies. Unless the new store has something unique to offer, it is unlikely that a success can be made in that locale.

Public Transportation

Stores that are located at bus stops or subway exits are treated to a steady stream of potential shoppers. It is especially favorable if the mass transit system is one that brings shoppers from outlying areas. This broadens the merchants trading area.

In downtown areas, where private transportation is limited because of increased driving time due to heavy traffic, public transportation is more likely to bring a more relaxed consumer population to the store. These customers will have time to spare for some shopping either before or after work.

Vehicular Transportation

Many shopping sites are visited by consumers who drive their own automobiles. If the location under consideration is one of these, it is important to count the number of vehicles that visit the area, as well as the types of vehicles. In this way, an assessment can be made as to the incomes and lifestyles of the automobile owners, and from there, the type of merchandise that they would more than likely want to purchase.

Parking Facilities

One of the keys to the success of the suburban shopping center is the availability of parking. Shoppers are generally guaranteed places to park their cars to gain easy access to the stores of their choice. Similarly, strip centers and power centers provide ample parking for customers.

In major downtown shopping arenas, on the other hand, shoppers who prefer to use their automobiles to visit their favorite stores, often find parking problematic. On-street parking is hard to come by and, where available, private parking garages are often expensive. In some major cities like Chicago, the vertical mall developers addressed the problem by building parking facilities that are adjacent to the malls themselves. At 900 Michigan Avenue, where Bloomingdale's is the anchor store, Water Tower Place, home to Marshall Field's and Lord & Taylor, and Chicago Place where Saks Fifth Avenue is the main store, on-premises parking is available. Not only are the costs of parking relatively modest, but it is also convenient for the shopper.

Convenient and abundant parking is essential where supermarkets are located. Shoppers must be able to move shopping carts to their cars when they have finished making their purchases. Stores such as Home Depot and Lowe's also only consider locations that provide ample parking to accommodate the often cumbersome purchases made on their premises. Without such facilities it would be impossible for them to sell in large quantities.

The manner in which the specific site is evaluated is through a rating system and the use of a checklist that addresses each of the factors that are to be considered. The following form is typical of those used in these evaluations.

OCCUPANCY CONSIDERATIONS

There are two choices available to merchants when it comes to making arrangements for the occupancy of a retailing outlet. They may either own their own premises or lease it. While ownership generally provides fewer restrictions, the opportunity is not always available.

Leasing

Retailers whose primary locations are in shopping malls, for example, must lease space from the developer. These are primary locations for large department stores and chain organizations, and are generally chosen in place of their own structures. While there are numerous restrictions by which the tenants must abide, the major department stores that anchor these malls are in positions to dictate their own terms. Since they are the venues that bring shoppers to the malls, they are often in the driver's seat. The benefit of a having a Macy's, Bloomingdale's, Marshall Field's, Lord & Taylor, or Nordstrom's, for example, is so important to the developer that they are

SITE SELECTION EVALUATION FORM	
Factors	*Rating*
Pedestrian Traffic	People per hour _____
	Ethnic composition _____
	_____
Neighboring Stores	Types _____
	_____
	_____
Competing Stores	Number _____
Public Transportation	Types _____
Vehicular Transportation	Types of Cars _____
	_____
	Number of Vehicles per Hour _____
Parking Facilities	Number of Parking Spots, Total _____
	Covered _____
	Outdoor _____
General Impression of Site	_____
	_____
	_____

This site selection evaluation form helps retailers make informed decisions on the benefits of a given site.

generally awarded concessions that make occupancy worthwhile. Others who wish to take advantage of the traffic that is generated in these malls are less likely to obtain the same considerations afforded the anchors. They must be willing to adhere to the rules and regulations established by the mall operators in exchange for the advantages that such locations provide.

In the strip and power centers, leasing is also the order of the day. Developers often accommodate merchants by offering them the amount of space they need to properly function before the structures are built. In this way they can have their facility tailored to fit their specific needs.

Leasing costs in any of the aforementioned shopping centers vary from one to another. The rental is usually based upon a cost per square foot basis. The merchant pays the agreed upon set price each month. Other arrangements might involve a set rental rate plus an additional amount based upon the retailer's sales. Sometimes a percentage of profits is the established method. **Graduated leases** are also commonplace in the industry with escalating rent clauses built into the agreement. Maintenance costs that cover expenses of the structure and care for it are sometimes part of these agreements and are over and above the amounts called for in the leases.

Whatever the arrangement is for a property that is leased, the retailer must carefully assess all of the costs and determine if the outlay is worth the investment.

One of the considerations that must be addressed in the leasing of retail space is the **rule of occupancy** that has been established by the lessor. Regular hours and days of operation as well as uniformity of exterior signage are just some of the rules that must be followed. Retailers are often forbidden to follow their own instincts under certain leasing agreements.

If the established conditions are inappropriate for the merchant, he or she will either have to look at another leasing possibility or resort to property ownership.

Ownership

Some retailers opt to own their own premises. This frees them to proceed with the property as they please and not be restricted by the real estate developers. The practice includes ownership by small retailers as well as the giants in the industry.

From the downtown central districts to neighborhood clusters and large tracts of land in suburban areas, stand individual buildings in which retailers operate their businesses. On fashionable streets such as New York City's Madison Avenue, and on main and secondary streets that are found in cities and towns all across America, merchants open their doors for business.

The occupants range from the small independent entrepreneurships to the giants in the industry and include every size business in between. It might be a boutique, a supermarket, a specialty store, department store, or a big box retailer. Major retailers such as Home Depot, Lowe's, and Best Buy often purchase tracts of lands on which they set up shop. Downtown flagships, such as Macy's Herald Square in New York City and Marshall Field's on State Street in Chicago, own the buildings in which they are housed. Sam's Club and Costco purchase acreage to open their value-oriented retail warehouses.

Each of these companies finds this form of occupancy more favorable to its bottom line. These retailers also benefit by being able to establish their own hours of operation and any other guidelines that they deem imperative to the success of their business.

TRENDS FOR THE NEW MILLENNIUM

- Malls will continue to become advertising alleys for developers. Structures in the center and around the mall will feature advertisements of the tenants and the malls themselves.
- The proliferation of malls will continue through the next decade. Many will be smaller, open-air environments, while several giant, traditional, and outlet centers are in the pipeline. Between the years 2000 and 2002, about 32 regional and super regional malls have opened.
- In many new shopping arenas the clustering concept will be a dominant feature. Stores with like product mixes such as GapKids, Abercrombie Kids, and Gymboree will be clustered to make shopping more convenient for those with less time to shop.
- More and more entertainment features will be evident in the newer shopping centers. This will enable each member of the family to find a place in the mall that makes shopping more pleasurable. It will also extend the amount of time families will spend in these arenas.
- The success of the retailers located near airports will motivate others across the world to expand their shopping facilities.

CHAPTER HIGHLIGHTS

- Most industry professionals agree location is the single most important factor in a brick-and-mortar operation's success.
- In assessing the viability of a location, the retailer must initially address the problem by conducting demographic research.
- Many merchants in their quest for sound retail locations are emphasizing geodemographics, the study that involves the clustering of the population according to zip codes.
- Area characteristic assessment is vital to the success of any potential retailing location.
- Shopping districts come in all sizes and shapes, with the downtown central district being the main one for city dwellers.
- Regional malls are found all across the country and feature a wealth of shopping opportunities, as well as entertainment and dining facilities for their patrons.
- Mega-malls, such as the Mall of America, are super retail environments that provide unique shopping and entertainment centers.
- Festival marketplaces, which feature fun shopping and dining have opened in many abandoned areas and facilities.
- In many cities' downtown shopping areas, vertical malls have risen to accommodate the retailers who cannot find sufficient space in street level locations.
- Freestanding stores are extremely popular for companies like Costco and Sam's Club, which have great customer appeal.
- Site selection is based upon the amount of pedestrian traffic that passes the location, neighboring stores

which feature complementary goods, and the proximity of the site to public transportation.

- Retailers must carefully assess the advantages of leasing a store versus owing the property.

IMPORTANT RETAILING TERMS

mixed-use centers

festival marketplaces

demographic analysis

community segmentation

me-too stores

central shopping districts

shopping mall

controlled shopping center

vertical Mall

outlet center

power center

mega-mall

popular area destination

fashion avenues

neighborhood cluster

strip center

freestanding store

graduated leases

rule of occupancy

FOR REVIEW

1. When retailers assess a general trading area, what is the first type of research that they should undertake?

2. Why is it necessary to determine the dominant ages of an area's population before any location decision is made?

3. Is the stability of a trading area necessary to assess in trading area research?

4. How does the geodemographics concept work?

5. What information can a reailer gain from zip code analysis?

6. How do area attractions benefit a retail operation?

7. What role does local legislation play in trading area assessment?

8. Why has the central shopping district remained as one of retailing's more important centers?

9. How have developers of downtown shopping districts solved the shortage of space there?

10. How can the Internet be used to learn the names and locations of the majority of the outlet centers in the United States?

11. What is a mega-mall, and how does it differ from the traditional regional mall?

12. In what way does the festival marketplace differ from a traditional shopping center?

13. Why have airport terminals become important centers for shopping?

14. How does a neighborhood cluster differ from a strip center?

15. What type of retailer will probably have the most success as a freestanding store?

16. Are neighboring stores an important consideration when choosing a specific retail site?

17. How have many downtown vertical malls addressed the problem of parking facilities?

18. What is a graduated lease?

AN INTERNET ACTIVITY

One of the most important factors in the assessment of a trading area by brick-and-mortar operations is demographics. Before they can even consider a particular location for their stores, they must determine whether the people who inhabit the locale fit the customer profile necessary for success. The Internet has provided a wealth of information in this area, and is regularly used in demographic research. Some of it comes from governmental agencies, some from research firms such as Claritas (www.claritas.com), and some from industry periodicals such as *Stores* magazine, which may be viewed online at www.nrf.com.

Pretend that you are a small retailer who wishes to open another unit in an area that is different from the one in which your store is now located. Using any of the above Internet resources, or any others that can be found online, prepare a report that outlines how you would go about properly researching the area under consideration. The paper should be typed and include a bibliography of your sources.

EXERCISES AND PROJECTS

1. By accessing Clarita's Web site (www.claritas.com) or by writing to the company, obtain information about the consumers in the zip code in which you live. Once you have completed the information on a chart with headings as shown below, determine what type of retail operation would have a chance for success in that area and the reasons you believe it will be profitable.

Clarita's "labels"	Households	Description	Interests

2. From the following shopping districts, select four and prepare a chart that addresses distinguishing characterisics, primary tenants, location and accessibility.

   - downtown central district
   - traditional mall
   - outlet center
   - mega-mall
   - mixed-use center
   - power center
   - festival marketplace
   - neighborhood cluster
   - strip center
   - vertical mall

   After completing the chart, write a one-page paper about the district that you thought best served the needs of the shoppers and note the reasons for your selection.

THE CASE OF EXPANSION INTO A DIFFERENT SHOPPING ARENA

Tiny Elves, a fashion boutique for children, first opened its doors in one of Baltimore's main shopping streets. The location was typical of many such areas in that it featured a men's shop, women's clothing store, shoe store, bookstore, party favors shop, video rental outlet, stationery merchant, home furnishings center, gift shop, and two restaurants. Since none of the merchants competed with each other, they acted together to promote the area, and, the shops became popular with customers.

With the immediate success of Tiny Elves in this location, the owner, Judy Franklin decided it was time to open another unit. She surveyed areas similar to the one in which the first store was located and decided another main street 50 miles away would be perfect. After checking the shopper demographics, she found that her instincts were right, and the second Tiny Elves store was opened. It was also a successful venture.

Based on the success acceptance of these two stores, she thought it might be time to expand once again. This time, one of the city's major malls was her goal. Given the popularity of these shopping centers and the throngs of people they attract daily, the location seemed to be a natural. With major department stores anchoring the mall, she believed she could spend less on advertising to generate interest in her store since the anchors' advertising expenditures brought a great deal of traffic to every merchant in the mall. The promotional dollars she saved could be used to pay the rental fee that was somewhat higher than she was accustomed to paying.

A store, similar in size to the other units, has become available and she is seriously considering leasing it.

Questions

1. Should she study the demographics of the area's from which the mall draws it customers or should she assume they are the same as for her other stores?

2. What factors should she assess in terms of the specific site that is available to her?

3. What types of leasing possibilities for the new location might be different from the other two locations?

CHAPTER 10
Designing the Facility

After you have completed this chapter, you should be able to discuss:

- ▶ The various elements that are part of a store's physical design.
- ▶ The different types of window structures that retailers use in their brick-and-mortar operations.
- ▶ Why open windows are used extensively by today's merchants.
- ▶ The reasons why many retailers are using individualistic approaches to interior design rather than the traditional formats.
- ▶ The basis for determining department locations.
- ▶ The new fixturing concepts that are used in today's retail environment.
- ▶ The various types of surfacing that merchants use in their stores.
- ▶ Why nonselling departments play a secondary role in terms of location.

Once a merchant has decided on a location for a new brick-and-mortar operation, he or she is ready to tackle the problems associated with facility design. With the enormity of the competition that retailers continue to face, it is imperative that a plan be in place to distinguish its concept and premises from the others. Relying upon old ideas and formats may not give the new retail entry a uniqueness or difference; using a **me-too design** no longer works.

First and foremost, merchants must, of course, differentiate themselves from their competitors by offering a merchandise plan that projects a specific image, and has the potential to motivate customers to buy their goods. Once the plan is in place, attention must now focus on a store's design where attractiveness and function interrelate. It is essential that the design and layout create a specific image that best shows the store's personality and addresses the potential productivity of the sales space.

As we travel from shopping center to shopping center, we are treated with a host of individual facility designs that provide a combination of qualities that makes an impression on the shopper. It might be a **theme environment** like the Disney Stores use, a sophisticated, sleek look as seen in the Banana Republic stores, or a grand salon-like environment such as the American Girl Place in Chicago. Even supermarkets are transforming newer units into more visually appealing premises. Harris Teeter, the North Carolina-based food chain, has designed its newest markets to feature such elements as a circular island with meal solutions for the shopper who wants quick meals.

Looking back at the initial Banana Republic interior and exterior designs, consumers walked into safari-like environments, jeeps appeared as though they were coming through the display windows, and rattan and reed dominated the concept. This look served the organization until it decided upon a new merchandising format. That design was replaced with a sleek, contemporary look that would enhance the new product line. Management decided that designing a new facility was as important as the merchandise itself. The power of store design was deemed important to the success of the new road the company was to take. The total revamping of Banana Republic's stores was a great success in that it helped make the stores a destination that would motivate shoppers' to satisfy their clothing and accessories needs there. This is but one example of how store design plays a role in retailing. Sometimes a new focus must be initiated to underscore a change in company direction.

Throughout the United States, merchants of every size are making significant investments to provide their customers with new, exciting environments. Saks Fifth Avenue, for example, has invested millions of dollars in the refurbishment of their flagship in New York City and in many of the branches throughout the country. Belk continues to do the same so that its clientele will find shopping more pleasurable. Updating store designs is a way that retailers are bringing excitement to their businesses in the twenty-first century.

It is important for retailers to not only carefully design the new units in their organizations, but also regularly evaluate the premises of existing outlets to determine if a facelift would prove beneficial to their images.

An examination of *Visual Merchandising and Store Design* (VM+SD) magazine and visits to trade expos such as **GlobalShop** proves that facilities design is reaching new heights. In each issue of the trade journal, everything from fixturing to lighting is presented, expressing the ways in which retailers can set off their brick-and-mortar units with unique designs that are both functional and eye-appealing.

EXTERIOR DESIGN CONCEPTS

The exterior design of a store is very important because it is this first impression that motivates a shopper to enter. Retailers who have taken this concept to an extreme include the Steuben Glass flagship on New York City's Madison Avenue, which has 25-foot-high windows that dramatically showcase the store's interior, Lord & Taylor on Fifth Avenue, which has display windows that are equipped with elevators to showcase a bi-level presentation in the animated Christmas displays, and the American Girl Place in Chicago, which has a museum-like façade. Each immediately conveys the message that there will be more dazzling treats to see inside the store.

Some of the major franchises have used their exteriors to attract consumers' attention. McDonald's golden arches is such an example. Drivers or pedestrians all over the world immediately recognize the sign and know exactly what to expect once inside.

TABLE 10.1		
THE TOP 12 RETAIL DESIGN FIRMS		
COMPANY	WEB SITE	MAJOR CLIENTS
Callison Architecture Inc.	www.callison.com	Nordstrom, Saks Fifth Avenue, Seibu Department Stores (Japan)
Pavlik Design Team	www.pavlikdesign.com	Properties, ShopKo
RPA	www.rpaworldwide.com	Adidas, Starbucks
Gensler	www.gensler.com	Aveda, Gucci
FRCH Design Worldwide	www.frch.com	Lazarus, Velvet Pixies, Discovery Channel
Carter & Burgess	www.c-b.com	AutoNation USA, Tower Square Food Court, Big Y World Class Markets
Little & Associates	www.littlearch.com	Harris Teeter Supermarkets, Fore The Links
Fitch	www.fitch.com	Timberland, Burger King
Entolo	www.entolo.com	Gateway, Duck Head
Design Forum	www.designforum.com	Lindt Chocolate, Grodman's 1/2 Stores, West Marine
MCG Architecture	www.mcgarchitecture.com	Sephora, Los Angeles Sporting Club
Walkergroup/CNI	www.wgcni.com	Iwataya Passage (Japan), Barnes & Noble, Neiman Marcus, Hawaii

Even movie theaters, considered by many to be a specialized segment of retailing, have added unique designs. They, like their merchandise-oriented counterparts, are faced with significant competition and need more than films to get their fair shares of the market. One grand movie complex exterior is found at the Muvico Paradise 24 in Davie, Florida. At the grand entry, visitors see massive Egyptian columns, and a pair of sphinxes. The fiber-reinforced, faux-painted concrete calls to mind the ancient temple at Karnak, setting the complex apart from any other movie theater.

The NBA storefront utilizes giant windows to give passers-by an impression of the exciting merchandise inside.

Of course, the impact made by these and other imaginative designs must deliver a sound merchandising concept once the consumer crosses the threshold. The interior should be an extension of what has been witnessed outside, making the whole environment a pleasurable shopping experience. Numerous design firms throughout the United States are building new environments and are busily engaged in transforming established retail facilities into more exciting ones. The leaders in the retail design field are featured in Table 10.1.

STORE ENTRANCES

Before doing any actual shopping, a customer must pass through a store entrance. There are many types of entrances. Each is based on the shopping district it is in and the retail classification under which it falls.

Merchants whose operations face onto the street, as in the case in downtown central districts, neighborhood clusters, power and strip centers, and many festival marketplaces, must, by necessity, feature doorways that open and close. Since the stores are confronted with different weather conditions throughout the year, these passageways are necessary. Stores that are sheltered from the street, as in the case of the enclosed malls, need not utilize the traditional entrances, but merely provide open spaces that allow access to the selling floors.

Depending on the retailing concept, entrances are either functionally designed to enable store entry or are embellished with window structures that tell the shopper what he or she will find inside the store. Retailers such as Target, Kmart, Wal-Mart, and the warehouse clubs, for example, forgo display windows. Through extensive advertising, shoppers know exactly what to expect in these stores. On the other hand, department store flagships and other merchants of fashion and seasonal merchandise make extensive use of their windows to attract shoppers. The exterior display stations are the **silent sellers** that help to presell the merchandise. They are designed in many different ways, with the final configurations based upon space availability and the merchant's needs.

Window Structures

Each window structure serves a different purpose to the retailer. Some are constructed so that they serve as separations between the store's exterior and interior. Others are dividers that feature merchandise displays and also allow the shopper to look into the store.

Parallel-to-Sidewalk Windows

Department store flagships are generally the primary users of **parallel-to-sidewalk windows**. They are the stages where these retailing giants put their best feet forward. These windows are usually 10 to 15 feet wide and up to 10 feet deep. They flank the store's main entrances. Flagships such as Chicago's Marshall Field's and Carson Pirie Scott, New York City's Lord & Taylor, Saks Fifth Avenue, and Macy's, Atlanta's Rich's and Dallas' Neiman Marcus have several of these showcases built into their structures.

Rich's in Atlanta utilizes the parallel-to-sidewalk window configuration to show potential shoppers the best the store has to offer.

Open Windows

The antitheses of these display configurations are those typically found in the malls. With space at a premium in these locations, merchants generally resort to the use of glass walls that enable shoppers to see inside the store. The store itself is the display. In place of the formal visual presentations that are found in the traditional display windows, merchants concentrate on making interiors as attractive as possible to call attention to the store's offerings. One retailer who embraced **open window** was Brooks Brothers in its New York City Fifth Avenue flagship. Instead of the typical Brooks Brothers windows, this store's façade is a three-level sheet of glass. Its designer calls it "a vitrine for the architectural interior, enticing customers to come in and participate in a sophisticated, urban shopping environment." Its open, 35-foot atrium entrance glows with outside light that is filtered through a metal scrim lit from the outside.

Another retailer that has taken to the glass wall concept is Levi's in its San Francisco flagship. Its expansive windows allow customers to see the entire store at a glance. At night, the huge upper glass panels are transformed into a 27 by 48 foot screen on which young,

Williams-Sonoma places its seasonal merchandise at the front of the store so that shoppers will see it immediately upon entering.

independent digital artists find an audience for their work. With the use of three projection screens, the stage is set to attract shoppers.

Also part of these structures is the use of open doorways that allow potential customers to enter without the need to open the door. This easy access often helps to generate customer traffic.

Miscellaneous Store Windows

Other type of windows include **arcade fronts**, **angled windows**, and **corner windows**. In the arcade front design, the store's entrance is set back about 10 or more feet from the building line so that two window showcases can be constructed to feature the merchandise. The angled window concept features glass panels that extend from the store's building line and end at the entrance way, which is set back about 5 feet. The corner window design benefits from traffic that converges from two streets and island cases which are situated in a retailer's vestibule.

INTERIOR DESIGN AND LAYOUT

Today's seasoned merchants have taken design to a level that is more exciting than ever before. Relying on professional design teams has afforded retailers the opportunity to showcase their goods in environments that are both visually appealing and functional. Not only has the space been designed more creatively than in the past, but it has been developed to maximize customer comfort and shopping convenience. Whether it is the upscale fashion retailer, the value-oriented merchant, or some business in between, the aim for most retailers is to offer appointments that will motivate shoppers to buy and return again and again.

The creative forces must address aspects of design such as the location of the sales and sales-support areas, department layouts, and shopper traffic flow. Decisions must also be made as to the types of flooring, wall and ceiling materials, and lighting and fixtures that will be used.

By selecting a professional design team to create the environment, the retailer will more than likely meet the challenge to successfully compete in the marketplace. It is not always easy to select a design team since there are scores of creative forces available. A good way to start the search is to contact the Institute of Store Planners by logging on to www.ispo.org.

THE **INSTITUTE OF STORE PLANNERS** WAS FOUNDED IN 1961 as a professional association for retail planning, design, and visual merchandising specialists. The organization includes more than 1,300 professional members and has 14 international chapters. Members include store planners, designers, visual merchandisers, associate planners, educators, industry contractors, product suppliers, and students preparing to enter the design field.

Retailers of all sizes and specialties utilize the Institute so that they can improve their status in the highly competitive global market. The design specialists in the group are not only creators of interiors; they also have a keen understanding of the retailers' merchandise needs and requirements. The design members understand what the merchants want their customers to experience and are able to advise retailers how to save time, money, and effort in developing a new or remodeled store.

Carrying out the Institute's mission involved establishing and maintaining high standards and professional ethics, excellence in store planning and design, and the nurturing of the profession as a distinct discipline within the design community.

The Institute helps both design companies and retailers meet their goals. This is accomplished through a number of different means. First, its Web site features the latest news and developments pertaining to store planning. The site features an online version of the Directory of Store Planners and Consultants, which assists merchants in finding design firms in specific geographic areas with experience in particular types of projects.

Next, by holding monthly chapter meetings that include presentations by design professionals and contractors, members learn about design innovation and trends that can be passed on to their clients.

Other Institute programs include sponsoring competitions for store planners and employee referral services, which enable retailers to find competent store planners for their in-house teams.

Finally, through its cooperation with universities and technical colleges, the Institute provides lecturers, critics, and judges for the international student design competitions it sponsors.

Interior Design Concepts

Deciding upon the design that the store will choose to make it both functional and attractive is no easy mater. It is as difficult as the decisions the merchandising team must make in the selection of the particular styles they will add to their merchandise mixes. Many merchants take the traditional path of store design and join the parade of the me-too companies, repeating what has been constructed in the past. While it is a safe approach to store design, it doesn't offer the individuality that is the key to success in today's competitive retailing environment. Others have chosen a new route where a theme is the centerpiece of the design concept. This makes it a more exciting place for customers to shop.

An Ethical Consideration

WHILE ESTHETIC AND PRACTICAL APPLICATIONS MUST BE CONSIDERED in the planning of a store, it is also essential that consumers be considered before the plan is finalized. Often, while the majority of the shopper's needs are discussed in the planning stages, too often, one area is overlooked. The concern centers upon refund counters and service departments. The placement of these locations shouldn't be out of the way, as they are in so many stores, but within easy reach of the shoppers. Obviously, retailers must utilize their prime space for selling, but it is inconvenient and unethical to make the shopper travel through the entire store in search of a place to obtain refunds or make complaints. It seems that many merchants locate these areas in places where the customers will have to pass through many merchandise departments. The retailers' purpose seems to be to divert customers' attention so that they will see something else to purchase. Although this might be an effective merchandising policy, it is really a disservice to customers. A truly customer-oriented policy makes the shopper more comfortable with returns and complaints by locating this service department in an easily accessible spot. The company will benefit from customer loyalty when it demonstrates real concern for its customers' needs.

The Traditional Approach

When shoppers enter many of today's retail operations, they are greeted with interiors that, while tried and true, are reproductions of many others in the field. Whether it is the department store with its traditional grid-like layout, or the supermarket where each of the product classifications are found in aisles that are identical to their competitors, standardization is the key. Of course, different materials subtly differentiate one from the other, but the sameness in each store is obvious.

Those who stay with the conventional approach generally do so because their selling arenas serve the purpose of satisfactorily housing all of the merchandise categories in the store.

During his address at Fairchild's CEO Summit in Carefree, Arizona, in 1999, Ralph Lauren summed up the state of department store design best by accusing retailers of cheating shoppers of an exciting experience because they are afraid to take risks. "They're not in the business of passion," he charged. Instead, he said, they have become "boring and depressing."

Whether it was his comments that initiated change in the department store design concept, or whether the industry came to the realization that change was needed as the new millennium approached, is not certain. The same old homogenized stores are still there, however, many are beginning to break the mold. The cookie cutter approach is giving way to new ideas. One case in point is Saks Fifth Avenue's Boca Raton branch which debuted as the new millennium was ushered in. Replete with the elegance of fixturing that rivals the finest in furniture and grand lighting, that not only effectively illuminates the store but gives the impression that one is in a fine home, the new Saks store is indicative of what some department stores are doing to break the me-too mold.

Uniqueness of store design is especially important since there is an abundance of merchandising sameness in many of the stores. What might motivate the shopper to choose one store over another are the environments in which they shop.

The Individualistic Approach

It is in the specialty store arena that individuality is best being served. Merchants, in large numbers, are relinquishing the tired looks of their stores and are embracing new concepts in record numbers. Early entries into this approach include the first wave of Banana Republic stores and Ralph Lauren who enhanced his signature styles with antique-laden selling floors.

Today, companies like Old Navy, Abercrombie & Fitch, OshKosh B'Gosh, and Sephora have redefined store design. Each has left the realm of sameness to provide its customers with new shopping arenas.

Individualism can sometimes be carried to the extreme as in the case of REI's Denver flagship. The Seattle-based retailer, which appeals to sporting goods and outdoor enthusiasts, has completed the most exciting environment for its operation. Using a brick power plant in downtown Denver, which previously housed the Denver Ramway Power Company that provided electricity for the city's streetcar system during the first half of the 1900s, has made the company one that stands head and shoulders above the crowd. A local and state historic landmark replete with pipes, ductwork, and brickwork that were part of the original building was preserved and serves as the setting for the nation's most exciting sporting goods concept. A mountain bike trail and a mammoth climbing pinnacle give customers the opportunity to test and compare products. It is this type of ingenuity that separates the stores of the future from the rest of the pack.

OshKosh B'Gosh uses a thematic approach in store design to enhance the company's distinctive image.

Themes are also prominent in today's specialty retail operations. The NBA store on New York City's Fifth Avenue and the many Niketowns that are found across the country are examples of the thematic approach in retailing. Both of these organizations have designed their facilities to replicate the playing arenas in which their products are used. At the NBA store, for example, basketball hoops are available for use by would-be superstars before they buy a basketball. By providing these types of environments, the companies have taken their stores and the products they feature away from the mainstream of retailing.

The uniqueness of the OshKosh B'Gosh store design took months of planning by people like this man, who works for the FRCH design team.

Upon entering the new OshKosh B'Gosh stores, shoppers find themselves inside a mini train station with boxcar fixtures, a ticket booth, and train track graphics. These are all used to enhance the company's origins as the makers of overalls for railroad workers. A caboose playhouse where children may play while their parents shop is an exciting albeit functional addition to the design. The merchandise itself is featured on a host of counters and racks that bear the same thematic design.

Retailers like these understand the need for individualization to make their stores unique within their product classifications.

Locating the Selling Departments

Every store has a limited amount of space in which to locate all of its departments. Most important to the success of the company is the amount of business it generates. Bearing this in mind, the most important areas are the selling floors. Aside from determining the amount of space that will be designated for selling, a plan must be established to place each department in an area that best serves its merchandise classification.

A series of meetings between management and the design team that will execute the plan is essential in deciding where the particular selling departments should be located. Designers, although experts in their field, do not necessarily understand the specific needs of each retailer. In single-story operations, the placement is less complicated than if it were a multi-story unit. Retail organizations that feature just one classification of merchandise as does a shoe store, will not be as difficult to apportion as will the department store with its multitude of product lines.

Single-Storied Operations

The amount of space found in these brick-and-mortar companies vary from relatively small spaces to cavernous ones. In the former category are the boutiques and specialty stores, where 4,000 square feet of space is commonplace. Somewhere in the middle are the units of chains such as Gap, Banana Republic, Casual Corner, Abercrombie & Fitch, Williams-Sonoma, and The Limited where 6,000 square feet plus is typical. At the other end of the spectrum are big box stores like Best Buy and Circuit City, category killers such as Toys "R" Us, supermarkets and warehouse retailers such as Costco and Sam's Club. Each has its own needs in terms of where the placement of the different merchandise classifications will best serve the store's customers.

Gap, for example, generally uses the same department configuration in its stores. The newest merchandise is arranged on islands close to the store's entranceway. After a few weeks in the store's spotlight the remainder of the merchandise is moved back to make place for newer arrivals. One side of the store features menswear and the other, ladies apparel.

Williams-Sonoma uses the front of the store as a place where its seasonal offerings may be shown. As newer items come into the inventory, they take center stage.

Supermarkets, on the other hand, are most often traditionally comprised of a series of aisles with each featuring a specific product classification. Generally, around the store's perimeters the produce, meat and poultry, and deli departments are located. Some, such as Harris Teeter, which specializes in freshly prepared dinner entrees, locate that department near the store's entrance for the convenience of the shopper who has little time to spend in the store.

The key for any of the single-storied entries is to arrange their selling departments in a manner that addresses the most immediate needs first, and then motivates investigation of the remainder of the merchandise offerings.

Multistoried Operations

The major full line and specialized department stores occupy at least two or three levels with some utilizing as many as eight floors for selling. The downtown flagships, where the companies feature the largest selections, are the ones with several levels, while the branches are usually confined to two or three floors.

The Stein Mart Story
Designing an Environment to Satisfy the Shopper's Needs

UNLIKE MANY LARGE RETAILERS WHO USE OUTSIDE RESOURCES to design their facilities, Stein Mart maintains an in-house staff that creates its shopping environments. Typically, the stores are approximately 36,000 square feet, although some stores are as small as 30,000 and as large as 50,000 square feet. The prototype is a store that is 180 feet by 200 feet, with a 166-foot frontage.

The designs for all of the stores are basically the same. Stein Mart settled on a format that maximizes merchandise exposure and comfort for the customer. The checkout counters are up front so the shopper can pay for all items in one place. (The only exception is the shoe department which is a leased space that handles its own sales.) Adjacent to the checkout counters is a customer service desk where returns and other adjustments are quickly handled.

The Stein Mart store design was developed through the use of CAD systems, and was simple to accomplish since each entry was a clone of the others. Construction for new units is handled by outside contractors who follow existing designs.

Except for a few older stores, each Stein Mart is housed on a single level. Stein Mart believes that customer traffic flows better this way, and that it allows the customer to peruse the merchandise in a shorter period of time.

The locations of the selling departments are based upon the merchandise classifications that are featured. While there is no absolute standard arrangement, there are some considerations that must be addressed. In most multistoried brick-and-mortar organizations, the

Counters of cosmetics usually dominate the department stores main floor.

main floor selling area is generally utilized for those departments that by their mere presence, provide a motivational purchasing element. That is, when shoppers walk through the store, certain products are likely to be purchased on impulse. For example, the cosmetics department is generally located on the first floor and takes up the majority of the space that is closest to the entrance. Counter after counter of marquee fragrances and makeup often attract the customer who has just entered the store. Many are drawn to these areas because of the usually appealing displays. If these departments were located elsewhere, the spontaneity of the purchasing might be lost. Of course, the placement of the cosmetics department is not engraved in stone.

 Focus on . . .
Bergdorf Goodman

ALTHOUGH CONVENTIONAL WISDOM DICTATES that cosmetics counters be located adjacent to the store's main entrance, Bergdorf Goodman, one of New York City's premiere fashion emporiums, has taken a different approach. With insufficient space on the main level to properly merchandise its vast line of cosmetics and fragrances, management moved the department to the lower level. With a 15,000-square-foot space that is a 250 percent enlargement of the original space, the company opened its Level of Beauty.

The challenge to transform a basement into a viable selling floor was a formidable one for the Toronto design team, Yabu Pushelberg. Creating a venue that gives the impression of being in the home of a person with refined tastes required the use of elegant appointments such as custom-finished cabinetry, a 21-foot chandelier, and unique terrazzo flooring. The team used a neutral palette, which helped to exude an air of elegance, while also helping to brighten the space that was devoid of windows. Internally-illuminated glass display cabinets also helped to create a sense of light and space.

The selling floor was divided into key zones in a U-shaped path. Once the shopper arrives by escalator, he or she is greeted by a flower show leading to the first cosmetic section, which features new lines, and then on to the more traditional brands in a second room, and finally into a third space, featuring more avant-garde offerings. A fragrance room, replete with a nail spa and optical center, is another attraction.

At a cost of $10 million, Bergdorf Goodman is betting that this unconventional department location will not only pay off but will help to recapture some of the sales of its rival, Sephora.

• •

Also typically found on the main floor is the jewelry department. Other product groups that are located on the main floor and account for spontaneous buying include shoes and handbags. The menswear department is also located on the main floor and although it is not a merchandise classification that is bought on whim, the male shopper is one who often likes to reach his department as quickly as possible. Thus, this department is traditionally located within easy access to the store's entrance. In some stores, where space isn't always available to house the entire menswear collection, a **split department** is used as a problem solver.

The location of the remainder of the departments is generally based upon the company's belief about what will better serve the needs of the shoppers. Furniture, for example, is most often found on the highest floor. Since this is a classification that doesn't rely upon **impulse buying**, its shoppers will be more likely to seek it out no matter where it is located. Housewares is often found on either a high floor or on the store's basement level. Sometimes retailers will actually have two different selling venues for these items, separating them according to price points.

One plan that many department stores use in the location of their individual departments is to have those products with some degree of compatibility located adjacent to each other. The same customers, for example, often visit the ladies shoes and handbag departments, during a trip to the store. If a pair of shoes was selected first, it would then be easy to find a matching handbag. This increases the probability of a larger sale for the store. Sometimes stores even set up satellite cosmetics departments adjacent to women's clothing so that the shopper who has just made an apparel purchase can buy the right makeup to enhance her new clothing.

Focus on . . .
American Girl Place

THE 35,000-SQUARE-FOOT, THREE-STORY BUILDING that is home to a wealth of dolls and related products is American Girl Place in Chicago, Illinois. Primarily a catalog company that was founded in 1986, its brick-and-mortar operation is a blend of retailing and entertainment which capitalizes on the American Girl culture. The challenge to the design firm Donovan and Green was formidable and required the construction of a special home to unite the company's products with real American girls and their families. The idea was to design a space that presented the products in a memorable way.

Unlike the typical retail emporiums that dot the country, this environment includes a bookstore, café, 150-seat theater, and photo studio, each of which is used to augment the merchandise it offers for sale. Individualized spaces were created to showcase the company's distinct merchandise categories that include the dolls, their clothing and accessories, books and crafts. Each is housed in a boutique setting and is connected to the entertainment areas. The layout resembles a museum. Unlike most toy stores where it is difficult to find an empty patch of space, the American Girl Place is a quiet, peaceful environment in which shopping is meant to be a pleasurable experience.

Upon entering the store, little girls and their families are greeted by a concierge desk. Adjacent to this area is a display of the only complete collection of American Girl dolls in the United States. Preprinted tickets accompany each doll and when the ticket is presented to the cashier, the customer is given the selected doll. To the rear of the store is the theater where live hour-long musical productions based upon the American Girl dolls are presented. The next level houses the bookstore and photo studio. All of the items available for sale are attractively featured on this level.

On the top level, is the café. It is a 138-seat restaurant where girls and their families can dine. For a touch of fun, doll-sized high chairs are attached to the tables so that the dolls can dine with the family.

Now owned by Mattel, the long lines of patrons outside the store signal that this is not merely a typical toy store, but one in which continuous pleasure is being realized by little girls.

Departmentalization

Once the retailer has determined where the different merchandise areas will be located, the next step is to decide how the product offerings will be grouped. This is known as **departmentalization**. Should the merchandise in a particular classification such as sportswear be grouped all together, or should it be segmented according to brand or designer name? In single-story premises with limited floor space, little can be done to provide an individualism to the collections. In the multitiered operations, however, a different approach is sometimes the answer.

Standard Departments

By and large, once having chosen the general area for a merchandise classification, retailers use the **standard department** arrangement. Department stores will have areas that are called Juniors, for example. The department will be designed to feature all of the products in the classification as a mix. No particular space is allocated for each manufacturer or designer. The same is true for all of the other merchandise classes such as home furnishings, and housewares.

This plan enables the retailer to easily merchandise the department no matter which vendor is in favor at a particular time.

Stores Within the Store

A departure from the aforementioned traditional approach is the one in which small boutiques or specialty shops are found within the store. One of the early proponents of this arrangement was Ralph Lauren. Stores that carried his collection were required to set aside a separate portion of their selling floors to merchandise his offerings. Whether it was through the use of glass partitions or different types of fixturing, the Ralph Lauren collection became a distinct department in the store.

Today, the concept is being widely used by many retailers. In stores like Saks Fifth Avenue, Bloomingdale's, Macy's, Marshall Field's, and Neiman Marcus, designer boutiques are the order of the day. Each has its own small store in which the collections focus on individual designers. Separate shops that feature Christian LaCroix, Donna Karan, Ralph Lauren, Calvin Klein, Chanel and the like give the shoppers the feeling that they are inside couture settings, and not in large retail environments.

Of course, to qualify for such status department settings, the merchandise collections must have significant sales potential, or provide the store with an image that separates it from the competition.

Fixturing

Brick-and-mortar organizations, unlike their catalog and e-tailing counterparts whose customers never set foot into these premises, must create fixture designs that are functional as well as visually appealing. The standard, traditional fixtures that once were central to most retailers' facilities have, for the most part, been replaced with newer ones that are not only functional, but also help to better visually merchandise the store's products.

A case in point is the premises of Sephora, the French cosmetics purveyor that has taken the United States by storm. Instead of relying upon the typical vendor-supplied fixtures that are used to form cosmetic islands, Sephora's approach is quite different. Sephora relies on the **open-sell concept** in which shoppers are able to help themselves instead of having to wait for a salesperson to assist them. The walls are lined with **universal fixturing** in which all of the vendor's products are arranged alphabetically. Also present is a perfume organ that entices women to sample hundreds of scents. The success of this concept is evidenced by the rapid expansion of the company in America. It debuted in 1998, with one store and now has more than 50 in the United States and 140 worldwide. It should be noted that the brands are the same as those that have been featured by other retailers for years and years, except for the Sephora private brand. It is the design concept and fixtures that have given the cosmetics a boost. Fixtures are available from a wealth of different producers. Each focuses on different products and designs. Table 10.2 represents the top fixture manufacturers.

Some of the unique fixture choices of the new millennium include those that grace the Movado Rockefeller Center store in midtown Manhattan. A Bauhaus-inspired design was chosen to showcase Movado's watches, jewelry, and glass art accessories. Augmented by a palette of marble tile flooring with mother of pearl chips, taupe-stained bird's eye maple paneling, and satin-finished nickel along with museum-style niches, the modern classic

TABLE 10.2 THE TOP STORE FIXTURE MANUFACTURERS		
COMPANY	**WEB SITE**	**CLIENTS**
Leggett & Platt	www.leggett.com	Wal-Mart, Kmart, Sears, Best Buy, TJ Maxx, Barnes & Noble
Harbor Industries	www.harborind.com	Sears Brand Central, Wal-Mart
RHC/Spacemaster Corp.	www.rhcspacemaster.com	Retail Mix
IdX Corp.	www.idxcorporation.com	Reebok, Tourneau, J. Crew, Nordstrom, Gucci, H & M, Polo, May Co.
Madix Store Fixtures	www.madixinc.com	Toys "R" Us, Ace Hardware, Kmart, Staples, Walgreens, Safeway
Ontario Store Fixtures	www.osfinc.com	Tommy Hilfiger, The Limited, Canadian Tire, Perry Ellis
Entolo	www.entolo.com	Retail Mix
Oklahoma Fixture Co.	www.ofc-usa.com	Dillard's, Bass Pro Shops, Federated Department Stores
Unarco Material Handling Inc.	www.unarcorack.com	Home Depot, Lowe's, Nike, Kay Bee Toys
Cotempo Design/ Spacecraft	www.contempodesign.com	Nike, Real Goods, Adidas

design of Rockefeller Center is carried throughout the store. Overall, the shopper is treated to a jewel box look of a fashionable boutique.

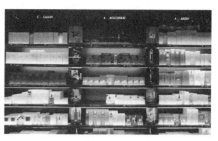

At the other end of the design spectrum is MacySport, a high-tech, high-energy, state-of-the-art shopping environment that imparts an exciting dimension for shopping. Instead of the lackluster fixtures that are traditionally used in this type of premise, the creative design team used stainless steel tubing to display the hanging items— all of which are visually enhanced by a wealth of high-tech video displays and lively graphics.

Sephora has departed from traditional vendor-supplied fixturing and instead uses the "open sell" concept, allowing customers to help themselves to the product. This design has been contributed to Sephora's quick success in America.

With minimal fixturing, DKNY opened a flagship store on New York City's Madison Avenue. Unlike the fixtures that grace the competitor's stores in this upscale fashion arena, the designers opted for simplicity that is enhanced with chartreuse beanbag chairs, lamps with orange nylon shades, and kitschy fixtures to hold the merchandise. Clothing is hung from tubular rods. Its shock value separates it from the competitors in the area.

Finally, Nordstrom has undertaken a reinventing process through the use of fixtures. Instead of the typical walnut wood furniture and cases, metal fixtures with splashes of white and color merge with flea-market finds. Nordstrom's designers believe that a fun environment is just what is needed to reverse its old, sometimes stodgy image.

While the aforementioned fixturing approaches might not satisfy the needs of most retailers, unique design is one way for a merchant to distinguish itself from the rest of the field in today's marketplace.

Whatever approaches retailers are utilizing, it is imperative that they follow certain guidelines to make sure that they are selecting the most effective store fixtures for their selling floors. In an interview conducted by *The Retail Challenge* publication with Madix Store Fixtures Assistant Marketing Manager, John Klotz, the following suggestions were offered for fixture selection:

- Identify what fixtures need to do.
- Review the space available for them.
- Select fixtures in styles and colors that will complement the merchandise and the store décor.
- Keep sight lines in mind.
- Allow for good light penetration.
- Use fixtures that are interchangeable so that you can configure them in many ways.

These rules are particularly valuable for smaller merchants, who often make their own fixture selections.

Surfacing

The walls and floors of retail establishments are dressed with the traditional coverings as well as a wide range of newer products. The purpose of this is to provide an aesthetic look to the premises along with a degree of functionality. Some of the materials are more permanent in nature, such as ceramic tiling, while others, such as paint, are more readily changed to fit the momentary needs of the environment. Designers painstakingly select the materials for both wall and floor use that help to further the concept that best highlights the retailer's image.

Floors

Walking through the wealth of brick-and-mortar operations in the United States and abroad, one comes upon numerous types of floors that have been chosen by the design teams. Each provides some degree of attractiveness and comfort for the shoppers and store employees. Carpet, rugs, wood, marble, and ceramic tile are popular materials.

There is nothing that treats the feet as nicely as carpet. It also conveys luxury. With a wealth of textures, grades, and colors available, it is generally the choice of interior design teams wishing to impart a feeling of warmth and comfort. Piles and flat weaves in a host of fibers and colors offer the merchant a diverse selection from which to choose. One of the benefits of using carpeting is that it may easily cover floors that are not in the best condition. With a layer of heavy padding, the blemishes are quickly concealed. Today's carpet is often color-sealed making it safe where the sun and artificial light might otherwise fade it.

Although considerably more expensive to install than carpet, wood is a material that is being used in greater numbers than ever before. Whether it is wooden planks that lie in a simple arrangement, or the intricate parquet designs, the result is not only one that assures a great degree of permanence, but one that provides aesthetic quality. While wood does scratch easily, especially in high traffic areas, prefinished treatments of polyurethane make them virtually scratchproof. It is the artistry of the installers that can make the wooden floor a masterpiece in design.

Many types of rugs are being used on top of wooden flooring. Choosing from kilims, dhurries, Persians, and contemporary styles, designers are able to enhance any retail setting. Each has its own personality and imparts a flavor that quickly adds to the image of the environment. Rugs are practical in that they are easily cleaned, and when constructed of durable fibers, can withstand the abuse of constant abrasion.

Marble is certainly a product that has enormous resistance to any type of customer traffic. It is extremely impressive and tends to impart an air of elegance. It is, of course, one of the more costly floor coverings, and is used primarily in upscale fashion emporiums. It is hard on the feet, and thus is often augmented with area rugs.

Ceramic tile is another product that provides permanency for the selling floor. While traditional styles and designs are readily available, a new breed of ceramics is being featured on a host of floors. The patterns are digitally imaged and can provide just about any feeling a designer wishes to impart. The Frey Boy cigar store in Grand Central Terminal in New York City, for example, uses smoke tiles that were produced through stock photography of smoke, and further enhanced to create the images for the 16-inch tiles. This photographic floor creates the illusion that the customer is walking through a cloud of smoke.

Linoleum, brick, stone and poured terrazzo, and concrete are just some of the other materials that are being used on retail selling floors. They, along with the others that have been discussed, offer the interior designer a host of options to choose from in creating environmental schemes.

Walls

Typically, walls are covered with paint, wallpaper, fabric, wood, or mirrors. Each imparts a different feeling and must be selected with the overall design concept in mind.

Paint is the most widely used product because of its comparative low cost, ease in application, and its ability to be quickly refreshed. A wealth of new formulas has given rise to paint that can take on many different textures and surfaces. Ralph Lauren, for example, has created a line of paint that can give the impression of denim, chambray, suede, linen, antiqued leather, or crackling.

It is extremely practical in stores that often change wall colors to complement the particular selling season. In a matter of hours, a department can be quickly transformed into one that signals something new is happening.

Wallpaper is another material that can almost immediately transform a mundane setting into one that provides interest. A wealth of patterns ranging from the traditional to the contemporary are available.

Fabrics are used on walls to create a warmth that is usually unachievable from paint or wallpaper. They come in a many different weaves, with each providing a particular look that will enhance the store's image. Jacquards, for example, might be used in areas to impart a feeling of luxury, while denim, with its rugged appearance, would best serve the surroundings of departments that feature outerwear.

A more permanent wall covering is wood. The natural beauty of the material immediately conveys richness. Whether it is the traditional paneling that can be quickly installed, or narrow planks of wood, the effect is an everlasting one. New wood products are being developed so that difficult curved surfaces can be easily covered. Color Wall Prefinished Wall Covering, by Ventee of Chicago, for example, is flexible wood sheeting that can be used on rounded walls. Its flexible fabric backing makes it easy to fit rounded contours. It is held in place with special adhesives instead of nails.

Mirrors are also used in areas as a means of visually enlarging the space. Entire walls are covered with mirrors that range from the clear variety to the more elegant, antiqued types. These too are rather permanent, maintenance-free materials that can add considerably to store interiors.

Lighting

Whether it is used for general illumination, or to dramatically enhance the store's visual presentations, lighting is the one element that can immediately add excitement to the retail premises. The range of products available to today's designers is enormous. Every retail establishment has a wealth of lighting fixtures and bulbs from which to choose. The requirements of each merchant necessitates a different type of lighting installation. Some, such as the vast barn-like warehouse clubs and the big box merchants are most often concerned with cost-efficient products. At the other end of the spectrum are the upscale, fashion merchants whose requirements include a wide array of light fixturing, ranging from elegant crystal chandeliers to **halogen pin spots**.

Crystal chandeliers impart elegance in store lighting.

Lighting is important not only for the purposes of general illumination, but also in the highlighting of visual presentations. Because of its significance in visual merchandising, a more detailed overview of its use is discussed in Chapter 15, Visual Merchandising.

Locating the Nonselling Areas

To make certain that the store is perfectly merchandised and managed, certain areas that are out of the shopper's sight must be carefully planned. These include the offices that house the management staff, the receiving rooms, and the storage facilities for merchandise that is waiting to be placed on the selling floor.

These spaces are found in a number of different places in the store. In the major department stores, for example, the buyers and merchandisers are more likely to occupy one or more separate stories in the flagships. Macy's flagship in New York City utilizes the first eight floors in the store for selling, with several above them used for various organizational managers and merchandisers. With retail space becoming extremely expensive to lease, some merchants have moved their management teams to other locations that are outside of the retailing forum. Belk, for example, in its southern region operation, maintains a separate facility for merchandisers, buyers, and advertising executives. This leaves in-store space primarily for selling and receiving. In cases where on-site availability is a must, such as with store managers and the human resources team, a portion of an upper floor is set aside to house these people. Sometimes, there are also very small offices adjacent to the selling floor in which staff members perform some of their daily tasks.

Receiving rooms are located adjacent to the store's loading docks. Depending upon the methodology used by the individual retailer in marking the goods and getting it onto the selling floors, the amount of space needed varies. Stores that use outside sources to mark their goods require less space, while those that perform all of the receiving tasks require more.

Merchandise warehousing is another matter for which space must be set aside inside the store. The trend today is for the vast majority of merchants to minimize the amount of inventory that is kept in reserve. By doing so, not only do they generally improve their turnover rates (a concept that will be discussed in Chapter 13, The Concepts and Mathematics of Merchandise Pricing), but also they are able to provide more space for the selling floors. In cases where some reserve items are stored, they are usually found behind each merchandise department. The key is that primary focus be placed on the location and size of the sales areas, with less important spaces set aside for nonselling purposes.

Once the designers and retailers have finalized their plans, the stage has been set for the buyers and merchandisers to fill the premises with the product assortments that will transform the shoppers into customers.

TRENDS FOR THE NEW MILLENNIUM

- Retailers will continue to use more individualistic store designs so that they can separate themselves from their competitors.
- There will be less space for store windows because of the ever increasing costs associated with premises leasing.
- In order to create a particular shopping mood, sound systems will begin to play an important part in store planning.
- Cosmetic departments will begin to make use of universal fixturing instead of the traditional types supplied by vendors.
- Open selling spaces in large stores will give way to the individual small shop concept to emphasize certain collections.

CHAPTER HIGHLIGHTS

- With the wealth of competition that retailers face today and the similarity of merchandise assortments

in the stores, one of the only ways retailers distinguish themselves is through individualistic premises design.

- Exterior designs are beginning to reflect the creativity of innovative teams that keep retailer brick-and-mortar operations from being mundane.
- More and more retailers are opting for the open back store entrance which enables shoppers to see the store interiors from the outside.
- With space limitations imposed on many merchants, there is a need to carefully assign selling departments to locations that will bring the most positive sales results.
- Some major department stores are making extensive use of separate small boutiques in their stores to give extra clout to marquee designers and to give the customers a more intimate shopping experience.
- The fixtures that a store uses not only must be attractive and carry out the desired image, but also must be functional.

- Floor and wall surfacing, while traditionally made of standard materials, has more recently been made from a variety of new and innovative products.
- Nonselling departments, while necessary to the success of any retail operation, must not utilize the primary spaces reserved for the store's selling departments.

IMPORTANT RETAILING TERMS

theme environment

GlobalShop

silent sellers

parallel-to-sidewalk windows

open windows

arcade fronts

angled windows

corner windows

Institute of Store Planners

split department

impulse buying

departmentalization

standard department

open-sell concept

universal fixturing

halogen pin spots

nonselling areas

FOR REVIEW

1. How does the theme design approach differ from the more traditional concepts that are utilized by most brick-and-mortar operations?

2. What was the first change that Banana Republic initiated to transform its image?

3. Why is the exterior design concept for a store so important?

4. How might a new retailer, or one that is considering a renovation, go about discovering the companies that specialize in retail design?

5. Define the term *silent seller.*

6. Why are so many merchants opting to use open windows rather than the more traditional parallel-to-sidewalk variety?

7. What purpose does the Institute of Store Planners serve?

8. Discuss the term, *me-too designs.* Why doesn't it serve the purposes of the retailing industry?

9. What are some of the companies that have created interest through the use of individuality of store design?

10. Which departments in a store should take preference in regards to location?

11. Why is it more difficult to determine and design department location in multistored operations?

12. What type of innovative designs have some cosmetic merchants utilized?

13. Why do some retailers make use of split departments rather than placing all the merchandise for that classification in one area of the store?

14. How does the store-within-the-store concept differ from the traditional approach of departmentization?

15. In addition to visual appeal what must the retailer consider in selecting store fixtures?

16. Why do nonselling departments take a back seat to selling departments when it comes to department location?

AN INTERNET ACTIVITY

Pretend that you are about to open a new brick-and-mortar operation or redesign one already in existence. In order to make certain that you have considered many of the new design approaches, you realize the importance of evaluating the various design team specialists in the field. With your attention focused on day-to-day management, your time is limited. To make a comparatively fast analysis of the retail design firms available to you, you turn to the Internet.

Explore the Web sites of The Top 12 Retail Design Firms listed in a table earlier in this chapter. After logging on to each site, select the firm that you believe should be considered to do the job.

Write a brief paper on your findings. Be sure to include the following:

1. The type of store you are opening or refurbishing.
2. The location of the store.
3. The design company you have selected to create the facility.
4. The different clients already served by the company.
5. Your reasons for the choice.

EXERCISES AND PROJECTS

1. Visit any malls, downtown central shopping districts, neighborhood clusters, or any other retail venues to observe the storefronts and window configurations used by the retailers. Once you have spent time looking at a host of these brick-and-mortar establishments and studying their structures, select the five that you find most interesting. Take a photograph of each of your selections and mount your photos on a foam board. Note the store name, window configuration, and outstanding features of each and be prepared to give an oral presentation that compares the different structures.

2. A visit should be made to any shopping arena in the city in which you live. The purpose of the trip is to observe the different types of flooring that are being used in the stores. While carpet, wood, and tile are typical flooring materials, you might find some newer types that are attractive as well as functional. Once you have selected five stores with different surfaces, complete a chart with the following headings:

Name of Store	Type of Flooring	Compatibility with Décor

Write a one- or two-page paper offering your analysis of each type of flooring and how it conveys the stores' image.

THE CASE OF REDESIGNING THE STORE'S INTERIOR

After being in business for more than 40 years, the Wagman Supermarkets have started to notice that sales in most of their stores have decreased. When the company opened its first unit, it was considered by industry professionals and consumers alike to be the most modern food chain in the areas it served. Its popularity helped it grow from a single unit organization to one that now included forty stores.

Although its interior design was traditional in nature, its fixturing, lighting, flooring, and other merchandising components were top of the line. Cash registers were placed at the front of the store, with a variety of aisles used to feature the different product classifications. Produce, meat and poultry, and dairy and deli sections were situated around the perimeter of the stores, making the store very shopper-friendly.

Management's concern about poor sales figures was expressed at the company's annual meeting. After the operation's figures were shared with those attending the meeting, including store and department managers, and buyers and merchandisers, a general discussion invited suggestions on how the problem could be corrected.

Some of the managers offered the following ideas:

• Current nonfood lines could be expanded to bring greater profitability to the company.

• Prepared food offerings could be increased to cater to those who have less time to make their own meals.

• A new design could be created, transforming the present environments into ones that provide better shopping surroundings.

After the daylong session, it was concluded that all three suggestions should be considered. The one that seemed to provide the greatest interest was the concept of a new store design. Everyone agreed that a more modern approach would transform the stodginess of the stores into more appealing environments.

Those in attendance offered the following suggestions:

• A few design teams should be contacted for ideas.

• A prototype should be constructed and tested before any large-scale renovations take place.

• More space should be given to new departments that feature pets and pet supplies, catering facilities, and gourmet products.

The company is still in the midst of considering these suggestions.

Questions

1. Do you think any of the ideas offered by the management team warrants further consideration? If so, which?

2. How would you go about assessing some design firms before calling them in to make formal presentations?

3. How might the Wagman supermarket chain earn more about trends in interior design before they proceed with the impending project?

PART FOUR

BUYING AND MERCHANDISING

No matter what principles and philosophies are established by today's merchants in running their operations, none are quite as important as the merchandise that is on hand to motivate the shopper to become a customer. Without the appropriate merchandise mix, there will simply not be an audience to patronize the company.

The ever-important roles of the buyers and merchandisers are carefully addressed throughout this section. In Chapter 11, Buying at Home and Abroad, the duties and responsibilities of the buying team are examined to show the importance of these positions in retailing. Not only will it be shown how carefully the buyers must involve themselves in forecasting, but also how diligently they must prepare before any purchasing can be accomplished. Also significant, as will be seen in this chapter, is the wealth of merchandise that is globally available. Where buyers once only shopped domestic markets, the far reaches of the world are now their marketplaces.

While purchasing merchandise that is available from vendor resources is often the main thrust of their merchandising needs, product development, which is explored in Chapter 12, Private Labeling and Product Development, is another area in which many buyers focus their attention. They are often responsible for helping in the creation of private label items. Although most are not professionally trained as designers, their buying trips familiarize them with everything that is out in the marketplace, and, by carefully observing these offerings, may bring ideas back to their companies that can be considered for new products.

Finally, if merchandise is not carefully priced, it will not bring the expected profits to the company and the purchase will not be considered successful. Chapter 13, The Concepts and Mathematics of Merchandise Pricing, explores the various concepts of merchandise pricing as well as the mathematics which are required to make certain that the right prices are charged.

CHAPTER 11

Buying at Home and Abroad

After you have completed this chapter, you should be able to discuss:

- ▶ The buyer's numerous tasks in acquiring the best merchandise assortment to satisfy the customer's needs.
- ▶ Which internal resources the buyer addresses in planning purchases.
- ▶ Why past sales play such an important role in future purchasing considerations.
- ▶ The need for the retail buyer to use external assistance when undertaking future purchasing plans.
- ▶ The way in which quantitative and qualitative elements are addressed in the planning of inventory acquisition.
- ▶ How open to buy calculations are accomplished and why they are so important to inventory replenishment.
- ▶ Market week visits and their importance to the buyer's assessment of industry offerings.
- ▶ How buyers who are unable to make trips to the market for their purchases learn about new offerings.
- ▶ The value of business-to-business Web sites in terms of product overview.
- ▶ Use of chargebacks to vendors by professional buyers.
- ▶ The manner in which purchases are negotiated with merchandise suppliers.

The merchandise that is available to today's retailers is by far greater than in any other time in history. No matter what the product classification, merchants have a significant number of resources from which to choose. Not only does the wealth of individual items give the buyers vast selection opportunities, but it also tends to complicate the selection process. Choosing from all that is available requires a great deal of expertise to recognize which products will have the potential for the greatest profits.

The global nature of the resources from which purchases may be made puts further strain on the buying process. In the recent past, retailers shopped wholesale markets that were close to their operations for the majority of their goods. Regional markets were in operation in many parts of the country, making regular buying trips routine. Just about anything was available in manufacturer's showrooms, wholesaler's sales offices, or trade expositions. When market trips were inconvenient for the buyers to make, "road" selling staffs visited the stores. Today, purchasing is anything but a routine task. With the vast competition in brick-and-mortar retailing, catalog, and Web site operations, merchandise selection has become more challenging than ever before. In their quest for merchandise that is unique or profitable, buyers must embark upon trips to the far corners of the globe. It is not unusual for fashion buyers and merchandisers to head to third world countries to locate items that will be exclusively theirs. Trips to the world's fashion capitals to purchase cutting edge items are also commonplace.

Overseas merchandise sourcing is not limited to fashion apparel entrepreneurs, but also to buyers of gourmet food items, electronics, and home furnishings. A look at the labels on many of these items reveals that the countries of origin are not limited to our shores. In fact, for many product classifications, it is more likely that offshore suppliers outnumber domestic suppliers.

It is generally conceded by industry professionals that proper merchandising is the lifeblood of the retail business. While such factors as location, staffing, promotion, and the like contribute considerably to the success of the retail operations, it is the merchandise that draws shoppers. Without the proper product assortment, brick-and-mortar operations, catalogs, and Web sites would not be able to satisfy the shoppers' needs.

BUYERS' DUTIES AND RESPONSIBILITIES

The task of bringing the best available merchandise to their companies is the job of the buyers and merchandisers. They are charged with difficult decision making, and must be able to carry out their roles to ensure that shoppers will be satisfied with the products they find.

The depth and breadth of the various functions of a buyer depend upon a number of different factors. These factors include the size of the organization, the merchandise classification, the nature of the company, the manner in which business is transacted, the goals that have been established, the number of available staff assistants and associates, and the out-side professional market specialists that are involved in product analysis.

Planning the purchases, making trips to the global marketplaces, vendor selection, com-munication with market specialists, price structuring, and interaction with in-house man-agement teams are just some of the day-to-day responsibilities that buyers are called upon to perform. Each duty presents a different challenge, and must be carefully addressed to guarantee that the end result will be the most profitable position for their company.

While most buyers are responsible for all of the aforementioned duties, it should be un-derstood that buyers for brick-and-mortar retailers often are held accountable for tasks that their catalog and Web site counterparts are not. Without selling floors, display win-dows, sales staffs, and "physical" departments to manage, the buyers employed off-site pri-marily concentrate on merchandise procurement. This is not to say that their roles are less challenging. On the contrary, the very nature of catalogs and Web sites makes the buyers' tasks formidable but different.

Keeping in mind the differences, the following overview offers a general account of the various roles played by professional buyers. Each of these areas are more fully examined in this and in other chapters.

An Ethical Consideration

THROUGHOUT THE RETAIL COMMUNITY there is a continuous flow of "counterfeit" merchan-dise. Fake Cartier watches, designer jeans, Polo knit shirts, and the like, for many years, have been marketed as the real thing. Even companies such as Sotheby's, dealers in fine art, have been known to sell the fakes as the real thing. That is not to say that the vast majority of busi-nesses intend to misrepresent the merchandise they sell. The counterfeits are very often so perfect that even the seasoned professional is unable to distinguish the real from the imposter.

There are, however, some retailers who knowingly try to pass off counterfeits as the real thing. By practicing this type of merchandising, ethics are ignored. This is not only illegal and unfair to the consumer, it is a practice that could eventually cost the retailer future sales. From time to time these scams are uncovered causing the merchant to lose the con-sumer's trust and the potential for future business.

While it may be that some buyers are actually duped by the purveyors of such bogus mer-chandise, the problem can be avoided by making certain that the vendors with whom they trade have integrity. By doing so, there will be little chance that counterfeit goods will find a place on the selling floor.

Assortment Planning

A key duty of a store buyer is the planning of assortments prior to any purchases. The buyer must know exactly what the store needs will be so that he or she can offer the "model stock" that will best serve the customers needs and bring a profit to the company. The manner in which assortments are determined is discussed later in this chapter

Purchasing

First and foremost for every buyer is the selection of merchandise that will ultimately be offered to the consumer. In order for the right items and assortments to be purchased, significant buying plans must be initiated. This not only involves careful scrutiny of the vendors in the field to make certain that the ones chosen provide the necessary cooperation to foster a good, professional relationship, but also the careful selection of items in the suppliers' lines that will generate the greatest sales. The ability to negotiate the best prices and terms is also essential to successful purchasing.

The buyer is responsible for choosing the best merchandise available in the marketplace.

Merchandise Pricing

Since they operate in a vastly competitive arena, buyers must be aware of their competitors' pricing on identical or similar merchandise. While specific markups are necessary to bring a profit to the company, prices that are not in line with what other retailers are charging, could be problematic. The expansion of the catalog industry and the nature of online selling have helped to better educate the public on merchandise availability and prices. The ease with which consumers can compare prices by these two methods makes it even more important for brick-and-mortar buyers to price their offerings appropriately. Of course such factors as image, product perishibility, and buyer judgment each contribute to pricing.

Product Promotion

The use of advertising is important to the sale of much of a store's merchandise. It is the store buyers who are often responsible for the selection of the items to be advertised, promoted through special events, and visually merchandised. The buyer, by virtue of the fact that he or she is the product expert, is called upon to complete advertising request forms so that the right information will be presented to the public. Buyers are generally provided with six-month advertising budgets that they must carefully manage in order for funds to be available to properly promote the goods in their departments.

In-house Department Management

Although fewer and fewer buyers are being held responsible for the management of store departments, some companies still make this a buyer responsibility. It is especially true in smaller stores where the buyers oversee the selling floor. When management centralization is part of the overall plan, and buyers function from locations that are outside of the store, the in-store department responsibility is in the hands of department and assistant department managers. In the supermarket arena, buyers are never part of the store operations, but instead utilize information from managers that is made available through faxes, e-mail, and other communicative devices.

Interaction between the buyers and the in-store managers is regularly maintained so that the purchasing can reflect the recommendations of those who interface with the customers.

Product Development

Major retailers of most merchandise classifications generally create private label items as part of their overall product mixes. Whether it is apparel, wearable accessories, home fashions, or food, carrying one's own exclusive brands serves the retailer with a degree of exclusivity. In many companies, the buyers are charged with the **product development** of items that are earmarked to become part of the overall inventory.

The Stein Mart Story
The Responsibilities of the Buying Team

THE COMPANY'S BUYERS NUMBER THIRTY, with the same number of planners, who determine which stores need specific items. Since the stores are located in many different parts of the country, they do not all need identical merchandise. Thus, careful planning is necessary to make certain that each unit's model stock is perfect for its clientele.

The buying takes place at a variety of venues. Each of the buyers attends the major trade shows throughout the United States. They also visit their vendors to make direct purchases at the showrooms. Except for gifts and linens, which sometimes take the buyers abroad, all of the purchasing is accomplished domestically.

Buyers visit the wholesale markets about once a month, with New York City being the major destination. Unique to a company of its size, is the fact that a buying office is maintained in New York, a luxury generally reserved for the retailing giants. There is a permanent buyer in that office who covers the market and reports to the store buyers about what's hot. This is used as an advisory tool to make certain that the buyers, although far from the wholesale market, are able to keep abreast of the news. Stein Mart also has an affiliation with the Doneger Group, which is a full-service market specialist organization, and Directives West, a Los Angeles-based resident buying office that covers the West Coast. Additionally, Stein Mart uses the services of the Tobé Report to keep current in the market.

Although Stein Mart is an off-price chain, its buying procedures parallel that of the traditional departments stores. Buying is done at the same time, except that buyers seek different pricing arrangements. For example, department store buyers expect advertising allowances, chargeback allowances, etc., all of which cost the producer additional money.

Stein Mart buys net, and is therefore given a better price that is passed on to the customer. Sixty percent of the buying is accomplished this way. The remainder of the purchasing dollars is devoted to manufacturers' closeouts and overruns at the end of the season.

Stein Mart takes pride in the fact that much of its merchandise is in stores at the same time as department stores, only at lower prices.

● ●

The nature of the concept has caught on with retailers all across the country. The fundamentals of such programs, and the role buyers play in their development, will be closely examined in Chapter 12, Private Labeling and Product Development.

PLANNING THE PURCHASE

Once a company has established its goals and parameters, those responsible for purchasing must follow them when buying decisions are being made. Unless the company is a very small business, such as a boutique, where the buyer and proprietor are one and the same, and purchasing decisions are made on the spot, there are guidelines that must be followed before any actual purchasing can be done.

Involved in this preplanning are studying past sales records, forecasting sales, focusing on staff support interaction—all of which are accomplished in-house—and outside assistance that includes interfacing with industry professionals, such as resident buyers, fashion forecasters, reporting service specialists, and the editorial staffs of retail trade and consumer periodicals.

Internal Planning Resources

While the professional sources outside of the retail operation are important to most company's functioning, none play a role as important as those available inside the business itself. Once these are addressed, it is then that the buyer generally focuses on the external group.

Past Sales Records

Nothing provides as much pertinent information in the area of buying as past sales records. The computer has made the study of past sales records much simpler than it was in the past. Prior to the advent of computer-generated reports, retailers used a host of hand-recorded inventory methods to produce reports that would assist the buyer in gaining an insight into merchandise ordering and stock replenishment. As the new technology continued to provide a wealth of information based upon past sales figures, the buyers were better able to assess their merchandising needs for the future. At any time of the day, store purchasers could immediately access up-to-the-minute data that reflected sales experiences and trends.

With these reports in hand, information concerning vendor performance, price-point analysis, colors and sizes, and a host of other pertinent areas serve as the basis of purchasing plans. Sales forecasts, either in whole or in part, are formed with the use of these reports.

While sophisticated reporting procedures have vastly improved computerized reporting documents, buyers are also prone to rely upon other, more personalized sources of information during the planning stages.

Merchandise Management Input

Often times, buyers call upon their supervisors to review their purchase plans. Since their superiors—namely the general and divisional merchandise managers, have come up from the buyer ranks—they are completely knowledgeable about the planning that their subordinates have undertaken. They can lend professional support concerning the addition of new vendors, the elimination of those suppliers who have served them in the past, the analysis of future product trends, the restructuring of price-points, and so forth. With their expertise, the buyer is more likely to proceed upon a buying path that will be beneficial to the company.

Staff Support

Many retail operations have management level personnel, outside of the senior merchandisers, who act as advisors to the buyers and merchandisers in the formulation of their purchasing plans. Fashion retailers, for example, often employ fashion directors whose responsibility it is to scout the market before the buyer enters it, to discover what trends will be at the forefront of the industry. Through visits to designers, vendor showrooms, textile mills, forecasting studios, and market specialists, helpful information can be obtained before any market visit is made.

Sometimes department managers serve as liaisons between buyers and customers. Through regular shopper contact, department managers and their sales teams are able to assess what's hot and what's not. While computer-driven reports are able to relate what has sold and in what quantities, they are not able to tell the buyer what items have been requested that weren't part of the inventory. The human factor plays an important part in preplanning, and when properly used, it satisfactorily augments written formats.

External Planning Assistance

Although the basis of the planning is internally oriented, sources outside of the company also play a vital role in terms of future merchandise acquisition plans. There are many different types of market specialists who are under contract with the retailers to keep them abreast of the climate in the industry and of any initiatives that will help them make better merchandising decisions. In addition, the editorial pages of consumer and trade publications, when examined religiously, also provide additional pertinent information.

Retail Consultants

In many retail classifications, and those primarily engaged in fashion merchandise, there are numerous organizations that supply a wealth of information to the retailer's buyers.

Most notable are the **retail consultants** formerly known as **resident buying offices**. Retail consultants collectively perform a host of activities that enable the retailer and its buying staff to make better decisions in the procurement of merchandise. Overall, the vast majority of these groups perform the following preplanning activities for their member merchants.

VENDOR ASSESSMENT

In retailing there are always new merchandise resources that come into the marketplace. Many just starting out are either too small to gain immediate recognition, or are located in places where there is no convenient buyer access. The retail consultants,

Retail consultants offer valuable advice to store buyers regarding the pulse of the market.

with their favorable locations inside the wholesale market, are able to scout these newcomers. By meeting with the vendors and examining their collections, they can then report to their clients about the vendors' potential to become a retailer's merchandise resource. Since buyers are often preoccupied with what seems to be an endless array of chores, this service can help them study the new vendor without having to make time-consuming trips to their premises.

PRESCREENING LINES

Trips to the wholesale arena are very challenging and time-consuming activities for most retail buyers. The time spent during the beginning of the purchasing period, known in many industries as **market week**, can be limited and insufficient to satisfactorily visit a host of vendor showrooms or trade expositions. In order to maximize the time spent in the market, the retail buyer often relies upon his or her **market consultant** or **resident buyer representative** to evaluate the lines and recommend those that seem worthy to fit into the merchant's merchandise plans. In this way, attention can be focused on the collections that seem to warrant the closest inspection.

EVALUATION OF MATERIAL'S PRODUCTION

Each new season, especially in the soft goods arena, new materials are being readied for introduction to the creative design teams and manufacturers. While retailers have little to say in terms of which materials will make their way into the actual products that will be designed, learning about them will help them to better plan their merchandise assortments. Visits to mill and textile companies, leather processing plants, and other places of raw material conversion, help consultants gain an overview of the coming season's offering. They can then alert the retail buyer to the what's hot and what's not. In this way, the buyer will be ready to evaluate the manufacturer's and designer's lines in a more educated manner.

INTERNATIONAL MARKET EVALUATION

With the ever expanding global merchandising opportunities available to today's merchants, no preplanning would be complete without a look at the vendors and merchandise being offered in these venues. Although buyers often visit overseas centers to make some of their purchases, often the preplanning phase doesn't include these on-site visits. The larger retail consultants maintain offices in many of the major international markets and call upon their representatives to provide market and merchandise overviews. With this information in hand, the brick-and-mortar, catalog, and e-tailer buyers are able to determine whether visits to such purchasing arenas are imperative to their merchandise plans.

DEMOGRAPHIC ANALYSIS

Every merchant, particularly those that conduct their business exclusively via the brick-and-mortar operations, or who use other means to enhance these sales, are vitally interested in learning about any consumer changes that might affect their purchasing decisions. Such factors as population shifts, changes in the makeup of the potential consumer markets they serve, consumer spending patterns, changes in lifestyles and tastes all contribute significantly to the buyer's ultimate purchasing decisions.

The Web site for Doneger, a major consulting firm, provides a description in Spanish of HDA International, its international office.

When such information provided by the retail consultants is carefully addressed, the buyer's merchandise plans will more likely bring favorable results to the company.

Focus on . . .
Barnard's Retail Consulting Group

KURT BARNARD, PRESIDENT OF THE CONSULTING ORGANIZATION that bears his name, has been an economist who specialized in the study of retailing and consumer behavior for more than 40 years. He launched his firm in 1984, after serving as the founding CEO of the Federation of Apparel Manufacturers and CEO of the International Mass Retail Association.

Considered by many professionals to be one of the most important "voices" of retailing in America, his company is actively engaged in forecasting retail industry trends and consumer spending patterns, developing retail marketing strategies, and consulting with advertising agencies on retail industry issues and companies.

Buyers and merchandisers are made aware of the company's research by means of its Retail Trend Report. The publication is read by the management teams of more than 1,200 leading U.S. retailing chains, department stores, discount and specialty retailers, and shopping center developers. It is particularly valuable to retail buyers who need to be aware of trends in the field. Through its interpretation and analysis of these trends, merchandisers and buyers are able to steer clear of the hurdles that lie ahead.

The knowledge offered enables better focusing on ways in which to address the competitive nature of the industry. Buyers are equipped to understand the changes that are taking place in the economy and how they will affect future purchasing. With too many stores carrying too much of the same merchandise and battling for the customer's attention and share of the pocketbook, a thorough understanding of the problem enables better merchandise planning.

Specifically the Barnard Consulting Group performs the following services for its client base:

- Economic analysis of consumer propensity to buy
- Development of marketing strategies
- Analysis and forecasts on consumer spending patterns
- Analysis and forecasts on changing consumer tastes and lifestyles
- Reports on what product lines will gain strength or weaken
- Competitive analysis of retail chains

The organization promises to answer the questions faced by management and merchandising teams in order to master the challenges in today's retail arena.

With its significant roster of clients, it is obvious that this is an invaluable resource for merchants to use in their problem solving.

Fashion Forecasters

Another important outside resource for fashion buyers to utilize are the **fashion forecasters**. These groups are located all over the world in the major fashion capitals where they regularly scout the industry and bring back pertinent news to their clients. Buyers of fashion merchandise, especially those who specialize in fashion-forward products, learn about trends as far as 18 months in advance of the selling season. By digesting this information, they are better able to assess which styles will be more than likely headed for customer acceptance, thus making their purchasing decisions more realistic.

Fashion forecasters provide buyers with trend information based on industry research.

Trade Publications

Numerous **trade publications** offer a wealth of information that helps to guide the buyer in his or her quest for up-to-the-minute news on products, vendors, and merchandise trends. They range from those that are published five days a week such as *Women's Wear Daily* to those that are published once a month such as *Stores* magazine. These formats are the simplest and least expensive means of keeping pace with industry news. For the price of a subscription, buyers and merchandisers are able to get the latest scoop from editorial press coverage and the numerous vendor ads.

Consumer Newspapers and Magazines

These are also invaluable sources of information for the buyer. In their pages, writers often address such issues as the economy, new products on the horizon, merchandise recommendations, and the like, each of which often helps the buyer to better understand what the consumer is likely to buy. The *New York Times*, and other leading newspapers, as well as a host of magazines are faithfully read by retailers so that they can learn what information is being fed to the consumer, and how their purchases may reflect their observations.

No source of information should be overlooked by the buyer. Every one presents a different angle and slant, and must be digested so that proper decision making will follow.

Development of Assortments

Once the internal and external sources needed to formulate the buying plan have been reviewed, the buyer is ready to embark upon the task of developing the necessary merchandise mix that will hopefully help to maximize the company's profits.

Trade publications such as *Women's Wear Daily*, *Children's Business*, and *DNR* provide buyers with up-to-the-minute news about segments of the apparel industry.

One of the initial undertakings is to produce an all-encompassing merchandise plan that will incorporate all the essential products to satisfy the customer's needs. The outline that is produced is known as the **model stock**. It includes the breadth and depth of the merchandise offerings for each of the product classifications for which the buyer is responsible. It is a complex blueprint that addresses the organization's goals and the merchandise that is needed to achieve them. The better the plan is formulated, the more likely it will lead to accomplishing projected sales.

In the model stock plan, the buyers must address elements that are both qualitative and quantitative in nature. That is, they must know *what to buy, how much to buy, from whom to buy,* and *when to buy.*

What to Buy

In companies that deal with **staple merchandise**, that is, products that are ordered over and over again without seasonal or fashion considerations, the decision is less problematic. Buyers of groceries such as canned goods, as well as those who purchase small appliances or some hosiery, are not terribly concerned with consumer buying patterns. On the other hand, the buyers and merchandisers who are charged with the responsibility of purchasing for fashion or seasonal oriented product classifications rely heavily on the information generated from past sales reports and other sources.

Printouts are routinely obtained by even the smallest entrepreneurs, who can study them and make future buying decisions. Brick-and-mortar operations, especially those that are medium-sized or larger, are privy to information that is fed into the computer every time a purchase is made. Through the use of scanners or other technological means, data regarding prices, styles, and colors are immediately recorded and ready to be called for in the numerous merchandise reports. Catalog companies and e-tailers also utilize the latest in technology to record their sales, and make the information available to the buying team that will make the new purchases.

In addition to giving the buyer information about specific products, the automated systems also reveal such information as the time it took for a product to sell once it became part of the inventory, the percentage of the assortment that sold at full price, the amount of merchandise marked down for disposal, and a profile of each vendor in terms of its product's performance.

With all of this information in hand, the buyer can begin to lay out the plans for new purchases. This, of course, is insufficient for complete decision-making plans.

376 Cutter and Buck
Belks Southern Division Thru 02/3/01
Fall 2000 Sales/Inventory

Stores	GM%		Aug-00	Sep-00	Oct-00	Nov-00	Dec-00	Jan-01	Fall 2000 Total/Feb BOM	YTD 2000 Total/ act% to plan sis Fall 00
74	26.7	Actual Sales	1.6	1.2	1.3	2.8	3.8	1.3	12.0	12.0
		Planned Sales	2.7	2.1	1.8	2.3	5.0	1.1	15.0	80.1%
		BOM INV	6.2	4.6	16.8	19.1	18.9	12.4	16.4	
		Planned BOM INV	12.9	15.2	14.5	15.7	17.2	15.4	14.7	
141	19.7	Actual Sales	1.2	1.7	1.7	3.9	6.7	3.1	18.3	18.3
		Planned Sales	2.9	3.5	1.7	3.4	6.8	1.0	19.3	94.6%
		BOM INV	10.3	15.2	25.9	33.1	30.7	20.2	20.9	
		Planned BOM INV	17.5	18.4	16.2	18.9	22.0	14.5	11.8	
142	2.1	Actual Sales	1.5	1.3	0.8	1.9	2.5	1.5	9.6	9.6
		Planned Sales	2.7	2.1	1.8	2.3	5.0	1.1	15.0	63.8%
		BOM INV	12.3	10.7	16.8	19.6	18.7	14.3	17.8	
		Planned BOM INV	12.9	15.2	14.5	15.7	17.2	15.4	11.8	
202	14.7	Actual Sales	2.6	2.6	1.9	3.6	4.6	1.2	16.5	16.5
		Planned Sales	3.2	2.5	2.1	2.7	5.9	1.5	17.9	92.4%
		BOM INV	10.8	8.4	24.8	32.2	26.4	18.1	20.2	
		Planned BOM INV	12.9	14.7	13.6	14.5	15.6	12.9	11.8	
239	4.8	Actual Sales	0.9	1.0	0.6	1.5	3.2	1.3	8.5	8.5
		Planned Sales	2.7	2.1	1.8	2.3	5.0	1.1	15.0	56.7%
		BOM INV	10.0	9.0	15.2	18.0	17.4	12.2	13.7	
		Planned BOM INV	12.9	15.2	14.5	15.7	17.2	15.4	11.8	
534	29.1	Actual Sales	1.2	1.8	1.5	3.2	5.0	1.1	13.8	13.8
		Planned Sales	3.2	2.5	2.1	2.7	5.9	1.5	17.9	77.0%
		BOM INV	8.8	7.8	21.0	26.3	23.2	15.1	14.1	
		Planned BOM INV	12.9	14.7	13.6	14.5	15.6	12.9	16.0	
		Tot Actual Sales	9.0	9.7	7.9	16.9	25.8	9.5	78.7	78.7
		Tot Planned Sales	17.4	14.8	11.3	15.7	33.6	7.3	100.1	78.6%
	july	Tot BOM INV	58.4	55.7	120.4	148.3	135.2	92.3	103.1	0.0
	eom margin	Planned BOM INV	82.0	93.4	86.9	95.0	104.8	86.5	77.9	0.0
	17.3	Margin%	21.3%	21.8%	23.2%	17.0%	18.2%			

Reports of past sales help buyers plan future purchases.

Many sources external to the company—some of which have been addressed—also provide additional pertinent information. The recommendations of the market specialists and editorial press, for example, provide economic forecasts, overviews of fashion forecaster predictions, and anything else that might help with the buyer's final decisions. Companies like the Doneger Group, for example, provide a wealth of information to their clients that concern hot items and new resources. Available either through mailings or online, the information is up-to-date and can quickly help the buyer alter purchasing plans. *Chain Store Age*, *Stores*, *Women's Wear Daily*, regional publications, such as the *California Apparel News*, and others, each contribute their take on the state of the industry and how buyers might approach the next purchasing season.

Other external sources of information include governmental reports that concern the state of the nation, such as the census, which is taken every ten years, and trade association findings that could impact the nature of future purchasing.

How Much to Buy

Once the data concerning qualitative considerations have been digested, and a merchandise concept for the next purchasing period has been put in place, quantitative considerations are the next factors to consider in the planning phase.

Buyers are appropriated specific dollar amounts to spend on the merchandise. The sum comes from the buyer's superior, the divisional merchandise manager, if the company has an extensive merchandising division, from an owner if the business is a small venture, or from some other intermediary depending on how the operation is organized. In any of these cases, the amount earmarked for purchasing must be translated into different product classifications, with attention focused on making certain that every product category is adequately covered to satisfy shopper needs. Retail sales forecasts, company plans for expansion or curtailment of the merchandise classifications in question, and economic indicators generally direct the amounts that will be given to the buyer to spend.

In times when unemployment is on the increase there might be a tendency to spend less on career apparel. Similarly, if times are prosperous more dollars might be expended for luxury items. There is no hard, fast rule in terms of what dollar amounts will be available to the buyer.

It should be understood that in every retail organization there is always merchandise available for sale. Companies do not completely sell off their entire inventory before they replenish the stock. Each and every day, companies sell goods to the consumer and replace them with newly arrived items. New merchandise is always being bought by the buying teams whether those purchases involve goods that warrant reordering, or entirely different products that will be added to the inventory.

Thus, buying is an ongoing process that requires constant attention by the retailer's purchasing staff. Although many retailing segments place the bulk of their orders during specific time periods, many days in the year will be used to add newer products. The most difficult problem for buying professionals is to maintain a merchandise level that doesn't cost more than the allocated funds. In order to best control their inventories, buyers utilize a concept known as **open to buy**.

Technically, open to buy is the difference between the merchandise needed for a particular selling period and the merchandise that is available. This concept considers not only the amount of **merchandise on hand**, but also the **merchandise commitments** that have already been made by the buyer. Thus, if a buyer is restricted to $100,000 for a particular time frame and has $60,000 on hand and $40,000 on order, there is no money left for that purchasing period. Keep in mind, however, that sales are made constantly in many large organizations, changing the dollar amounts in the inventory. Therefore, it is easy to see that the open to buy concept changes virtually every time a sale is made.

It should also be understood, that in most retail operations the merchandise needed for a particular period changes. Holiday seasons warrant greater inventories, while sales times require less. To achieve proper inventory levels, the buyer, in conjunction with his or her

Open to Buy

Updated 6/5/00

Month: May

Dept 370 Moderate Collections

								Plan Purchases							
							Net Reciepts	27.8	30.2	15.2	24.9	6.9	8.2	13.3	12.0
Vendor	P.O. Number	Ship Date	Cancel Date	MU %	Total Units	Total $	Description	141	142	202	239	149	151	463	490
IZOD	320448805	4/25	5/25	64.3	2284	95.9	Microfiber Short	3.5	3.5	3.5	3.5	2.2	2.2	2.2	2.2
								84	84	84	84	52	52	52	52
IZOD	622710903	4/25	5/25	62.1	720	20.9	Swim	3.5	3.5	3.5	3.5	2.3			
cancelled 4/7/00 re-approved 4/27/00								120	120	120	120	80			
IZOD	420448803	4/25	5/25	62.5	3432	164.7	Golf	7.3	7.3	7.3	7.3	4.6	3.5	3.5	3.5
JULIAN	668245802	4/25	5/15	69.8	2238	85.8	Fathers Day Promo	6.4	3.9	5.1	5.1	2.6		3.9	5.1
BUNGALOW	282827808	4/25	5/25	63.6	6300	216.1	May Fashion	7.4	7.4	7.4	7.4	6.0	4.4	7.4	6.0
								222	222	222	222	174	126	222	174
BUNGALOW	754091903	4/25	5/25	58.7	882	17.6	T-Shirt Reorders	0.7	0.7	0.7	0.7	0.6	0.4	0.7	0.6
								36	36	36	36	30	18	36	30
IZOD	811780907	4/25	5/25	64.3	1738	73.0	Merc. Knit	4.0	4.0	4.0	4.0	1.8	1.8	2.2	2.7
cancelled 4/7/00 re-approved 5/01/00								96	96	96	96	42	42	52	64
BUNGALOW	936578800	4/25	5/25	58.3	822	39.5	Bedford Cord MF Pant	1.2	1.2	0.9	1.2	1.2	0.9	1.2	1.2
								24	24	18	24	24	18	24	24
Total								32.8	30.3	31.5	31.5	20.1	12.3	19.9	20.1
OTB								-5.0	-0.1	-16.3	-6.6	-13.2	-4.1	-6.6	-8.1

Computerized open-to-buy records give buyers current information about inventory and funds available for further purchases. Part of an open-to-buy report is shown here.

supervisor, must plan accordingly to have the proper merchandise levels needed to meet consumer demand.

In each of these cases, planned inventories and sales figures are determined from which the buyer must calculate his or her open to buy. The following illustrates this concept:

On February 1, the ladies shoe buyer for Bentley's Emporium wanted to determine how much money was available for additional purchases for the time period that would end on February 28. Her figures revealed the following:

Merchandise on hand...$216,000
Merchandise on order (commitments) ....$ 54,000
Planned end of month inventory...$270,000
Planned sales..$108,000
Planned markdowns ....$ 9,000

What was the shoe buyer's open to buy on February 1?

Merchandise needed for February
    planned end-of-month inventory $270,000
    planned sales...$108,000
    planned markdowns ....$ 9,000
        Total merchandise needed.......................................$387,000

Merchandise available (June 1)
    merchandise on hand..$216,000
    merchandise on order (commitments) ....$ 54,000
        Merchandise available $270,000

Merchandise needed   —   Merchandise available   =   Open to buy
    $387,000   — $270,000   = $117,000 OTB

The open to buy calculation can be determined at any point in time, not only at the beginning of the month. It can also be quickly calculated by inputting the buyer's actual figures into a specialized computer program.

Buyers need to stay within their open to buy designations for a number of reasons, including supervisory merchandisers mandates and the need to avoid overbuying, which often leads to unplanned, high markdowns. Of course, even the best planning can not account for unforseen conditions. When plans call for specific purchasing levels, and something unpredictable occurs that affects the planning, such as the terrorist attacks on the United States on September 11, 2001, significant markdowns might be warranted. The 2000 Christmas selling season was expected, by most merchants, to exceed the previous year's sales figures. With attention focused on an upbeat economy, buyers' purchasing plans called for larger inventories. However, with a sudden economic downturn, and looming threats of a recession, higher sales never materialized for most retail companies. The vast majority of retailers had to take significant markdowns to move goods and make way for new products.

In a more perfect retail world, merchandise budgeting would be a given, and poor sales showings, as in the above example, wouldn't occur. This, however is a fact of retail life. In fact, disastrous sales results for holiday 2000 was the reason the Ward retailing empire posted "going out of business" signs.

While the major retail entries each have their own in-house staffs to examine purchasing and sales information that is pertinent to determining open to buy levels, their smaller counterparts generally do not have this level of resources. In such cases, outside companies are available to help. One such company is OTB Retail Systems which offers an online system for retailers of all sizes. By logging on to their Web site, www.otb-retail.com, a potential user could get a firsthand look at the system they employ.

After learning about the benefits of open to buy calculations, such as proper inventory levels, higher returns, reduced markdowns, and increased cash flow, the user is taken through a number of different screens that will help to produce a better profit picture. The first screens deal with eliminating buying confusion, the prevention of overbuying, and reduction in markdowns—each of which can help to move toward a better **bottom line**. Next, individual statements featuring a plan to set up departments, projected stock turn rates, ideal inventory levels, inventory comparisons between the actual and projected figures, and projected markdowns lead to the final open to buy calculation.

Offerings like this one and others have enabled the least experienced retailers to grasp the importance of open to buy in their quest to maximize profits.

From Whom to Buy

With the **qualitative** and **quantitative decisions** now made, the buyer must perform yet another task on the road to developing the perfect **buying plan**. There are numerous resources from whom to buy the merchandise, some being tried-and-true suppliers and others being newcomers to the playing field. Even those that have been the mainstays of the buyer's vendor list do not always continue to be used as a supply source if their track records have been negative in the past selling period. To make certain that those presently being used should remain as suppliers, an evaluation of each one's recent record must be undertaken.

Vendor's lines must be regularly assessed to make certain their goods fit into the buyer's plans.

The research involved to study regularly used vendors is relatively simple. Sales records for each vendor are examined to see whether sales numbers were achieved and the maintained markups were as expected. Those that pass the test are likely to remain part of the resource roster, while ones that haven't proved to be successful, will likely be eliminated from further purchasing consideration.

Before a purchasing strategy can be put in place, in terms of resource selection, it is necessary to review the different classifications of vendors from whom merchandise can be procured. Typically, product acquisition is made from one or more of many supplier groups. These include manufacturers, full-service and limited-function wholesalers, rack jobbers, retailer-owned production companies, market specialists and private label producers. The nature of the retail operation generally dictates from which of these classifications purchasing will be made. Appliance retailers most often buy from wholesalers, while fashion merchants generally use manufacturers for their merchandise. Retailers who sell greeting cards and stationery rely on rack jobbers. **Rack jobbers** are actually wholesalers who provide a host of services to retailers such as on-site inventory adjustments.

Table 11.1 lists **purchasing channels** and the merchandise that is typically obtained from these resources.

TABLE 11.1	
RETAILER SUPPLIERS AND PRODUCTS OFFERED	
SUPPLIERS	**PRODUCTS**
Manufacturer	Apparel, wearable accessories, home fashions
Full-service wholesaler	Appliances, food products
Limited-function wholesaler	Major and small appliances
Rack jobber	Greeting cards, paperback books, stationery supplies
Retailer-owned production company	Private brand merchandise
Market specialist	Private label fashion items for clients affiliated with resident buying offices
Private label producer	Products made for the exclusive use of individual retailers

It should be understood that the merchants are not restricted to just one supply group. Different circumstances could contribute to their buying from some that they wouldn't ordinarily purchase from. For example, manufacturers generally require minimum orders for their merchandise. If a particular item is needed in a smaller quantity, the purchase would be made from a wholesaler whose order requirements are less stringent.

Having decided which vendors should be used and which should be eliminated, the buyer must always be ready to bring new ones on board. It might just be a new supplier whose products are unique or whose prices are better than the rest of the field. Before any of these new relationships are made, it is essential to assess the companies and their ability to make deliveries as promised. Retailers who subscribe to market specialist organizations, such as resident buying offices and reporting agencies, or are members of trade associations are in the best position to promptly evaluate new resources. These groups are always interfacing with manufacturers and other suppliers and are therefore in a position to determine their potential as good vendors. Trade paper perusal is also a means of learning about new resources. Those that seem to have the likelihood for success are often written up in these publications.

Geographic location is another consideration when selecting a resource. If the manufacturer is domestically based, faster receipt of goods is more likely than if the production is done overseas. When time is of the essence, as is the case with most fashion merchandise, prompt delivery is a factor to consider. Of course, placing orders earlier than required will generally alleviate delivery problems.

While off-shore suppliers sometimes offer merchandise that is not only unique but is priced better than that which can be obtained in this country, it is important to consider that there will be a **landed cost**.

Unlike goods that are produced and bought in the United States and are sold at specific wholesale prices, those that are produced in overseas venues have a number of add-ons that actually increase the cost to a retailer. For example, most items are **dutiable**, that is, they have **tariffs** applied to the original price that are as much as 50 percent extra. Additional costs are added for commission fees, insurance, shipping, and so forth. Thus, an item that is initially priced at $50 can actually cost the retailer $100! Another factor that affects the wholesale price is the fluctuation of the dollar. Every day the value of the American dollar fluctuates against foreign currencies. During volatile periods there might be a great deal of change that can severely affect the price of goods. The dollar fluctuation coupled with the landed costs can place merchandise outside of the range the retailer is able to charge to bring a profit to the company. This is not to say that global purchasing should be abandoned. It is just that extreme caution must be exercised whenever these purchases are made.

When to Buy

Timing the purchase is a very important part of the planning stage. If goods are purchased too soon and are placed on the selling floor before they are actually needed, their early arrival will affect the buyer's **stock turnover rate**, a concept that will be discussed later in the chapter. If the merchandise arrives later than needed, it will most likely result in lost sales. It is thus the buyer's responsibility to time purchases carefully so that they will be available exactly when their customers expect them.

Silver Edition Spring 20XX 6 Month Flow Plan							
ASST A	Feb	Mar	Apr	May	June	July	TTL
BOM	25.0	28.3	31.1	33.5	35.7	27.7	181.2
SALES	2.5	3.3	2.8	4.3	10.0	2.3	25.0
	10.0%	13.0%	11.0%	17.0%	40.0%	9.0%	100.0%
PURCHASES	6.8	7.3	6.3	8.1	6.0	7.0	41.5
	16.4%	17.6%	15.2%	19.5%	14.5%	16.9%	100.0%
MARKDOWNS	1.0	1.3	1.1	1.7	4.0	0.9	10.0
EOM	28.3	31.1	33.5	35.7	27.7	31.5	31.3

Average Invty   30.4
Turnover   1.22
Markdown %   40%
Stores: 74, 109, 141, 534

The 6-month flow plan provides information about the value of inventory at the beginning and end of each month.

The actual decision for when purchases should be made are based upon several factors such as the amount of production time needed, the time it takes to physically deliver the goods, when the goods are needed on the selling floor, and what, if any, discounts are awarded for early delivery.

In some retail segments, such as those that sell fashion merchandise, orders are placed as much as six months in advance of their need on the selling floor. For foreign-produced items, the lead time might be from nine months to one year. The actual timing comes from the buyer's past experience and the standard industry practices.

VISITING THE MARKET TO MAKE THE PURCHASE

Armed with all of the preplanned information, the buyer is ready to embark upon the actual purchasing of the merchandise. Many buyers choose to visit the wholesale markets in their quest for the season's latest offerings, while others opt for alternative methods of merchandise procurement. In retail organizations like department stores and specialty chains, where fashion merchandise is their forte, trips to the marketplace are the order of the day, especially when a new season is dawning. In supermarkets, and operations where staple

Itenerary for: Donna Lombardo

Travel to: New York Holiday Market

Sun	04/09	Mon	04/10	Tues	04/11	Wed	04/12	Thurs	04/13	Fri	04/14
8:30		8:30		8:30		8:30		8:00		8:00	
								8:30	**Greg Norman** 609 5th Ave	8:30	Recap meeting
9:00		9:00	**IZOD** 200 Madison Ave b/w 35th & 6th	9:00	**Perry Ellis** 1114 Ave of Amer b/w 5th & 6th	9:00	**Claiborne** 1441 Broadway 212-777-3456	9:00	b/w 40th & 6th ave	9:00	
10:00		10:00	16th floor 212-777-3456	10:00	36th floor 212-777-3456	10:00		10:00		10:00	
11:00		11:00		11:00		11:00		11:00		11:00	
12:00		12:00	**Alexander Julian** 1350 6th Ave b/w 55th & 6th	12:00		12:00		12:00		12:00	
1:00		1:00	12th floor 212-777-3456	1:00		1:00		1:00	**Cutter & Buck** 80 w 40th Ave & 6th 212-777-3456	1:00	
2:00		2:00		2:00	**Bungalow Brand** 1071 Ave of Amer 11th floor 212-777-3456	2:00		2:00		2:00	
3:00		3:00 / 3:30	**Ashworth** Warwick Hotel 65 E. 54th Street 212-777-3456	3:00		3:00	**Chaps** 90 Park Ave b/w 39th & 40th 12th flr 212-777-3456	3:00		3:00	
4:00		4:00		4:00		4:00		4:00	**J Khaki N44** 140 57th Street b/w 6 & 7th 212-777-3456	4:00	
5:00		5:00		5:00		5:00		5:00		5:00	
		IZOD dinner		Perry dinner		Claiborne dinner		Cutter & Buck dinner			

Itineraries for market visits are preplanned to make sure the buyer will see all the important vendors and other resources.

goods such as packaged foods are the main products, ordering is usually done at the company's home offices through vendor visits. For other merchants, the goods may be bought in the store from **road sales staffs**. Still others may use online resources to fill their merchandise requirements.

A trip to the market often takes approximately one week, and involves numerous meetings with market specialists and vendors. In order to accomplish the desired goal, the buyer must make numerous arrangements before leaving the home base. The plans include arranging for travel, hotels, and appointment scheduling.

Market Week Visits

In many merchandise classifications, specific periods of time are set aside each year when new lines of merchandise are to be previewed to the retail buyers. In arenas all across the globe, vendors ready their collections and hold their collective breath awaiting the buyer's arrival. The pace during market week is hectic, with buyers converging from many parts of the world in the hope of finding just the right merchandise mixes to bring profits to their companies.

In order to maximize the effectiveness of these adventures, most buyers first arrange meetings with outside retail specialists who will help them attack the problems of merchandise selection that lie ahead of them. Most often, retailers of soft goods, and some who buy hard goods, enjoy affiliations with companies such as resident buying offices, or those in expanded roles from purchasing specialists to generalists advising on every aspect of retailing. The largest of these advisory groups is the Doneger group.

Focus on . . .
The Doneger Group

FOUNDED IN 1946 BY HENRY DONEGER, the company has gone on to become the largest of its type in the world. It originally served as a resident buying office for women's specialty retailers in the United States. Today the company counts as its members, department stores, family apparel stores, mass merchandisers, and discounters here in America and in many overseas nations.

In 1980, the company was one of 50 buying offices all offering similar types of service and information. Today, the Doneger Group is considered by most retailing professionals to be the most dynamic resident buying office and fashion consulting firm in the industry. The company advises hundreds of retailers on merchandising concepts and specific trends and offers sourcing capabilities and a breadth of other opportunities. With more than 7,000 retail locations served throughout the world, Doneger generates annual sales of more $25 billion.

Although they initially started their organization as one that was oriented to women's apparel and accessories, the company also now specializes in men's and children's apparel, accessories for the family, and home furnishings. In meeting its obligation of providing the best information to their retail clients, the company provides a great deal of services to help clients make the right merchandising decisions and meet the ever-changing challenges of the fashion and retail business. The ultimate Doneger goal is to help retailers generate greater sales, increase profits, and gain market share.

Located in the heart of the **garment center** in New York City, the company's ten divisions are supported by a staff of industry experts who have a wealth of experience in market research, merchandising, and trend forecasting.

When buyers come to their headquarters in preparation for market visits, they are greeted with a host of individual conference and presentation rooms in which they can meet with company executives and preview the merchandise highlights for the season. Individual client work areas are also available when the need arises for a quiet space in which to rework plans. Augmented by an art department that prepares advertising layouts for in-staff and client use, a digital photography studio that can quickly record images of merchandise, and in-house print production rooms that can generate a wealth of different direct-mail pieces, the company is one that provides a wealth of information needed for retailers to make their merchandising decisions.

A relatively new addition to the wealth of services already offered by the company is the Doneger online Web site. It was launched to provide clients with access to the company's market research and analysis efforts, product recommendations, and trend forecasting. In addition, the Web site offers manufacturers the opportunity to present products to retailers in a virtual showroom via the Internet. In addition, the Internet service provides newsletters, merchandising concepts, market overviews, new resources, key item identification, reorder activity, and special offerings.

Buying Venues

Buyers have a number of different places in which to preview collections and make their buying decisions. These include permanent vendor showrooms, trade expositions, and temporary selling facilities.

Permanent Vendor Showrooms

Designers and manufacturers maintain selling environments in many parts of the globe. They are housed within buildings that are located in the wholesale markets or in special marts. The Chicago Apparel Mart is one such merchandising tower in which buyers from the Midwest may shop the lines. In New York City, the major wholesale market for fashion merchandise in the world, the garment center—often referred to as Seventh Avenue—stretches for many streets and houses the collections of a wealth of producers. The buildings are usually tenanted according to merchandise classifications and price lines. This enables the visiting buyers to more quickly cover the lines in which they are interested. Often times these selling arenas are also home to the creative teams that design the lines.

Permanent vendor showrooms are found in all major markets, often occupying entire buildings.

Trade Expositions

Many product classifications are found in various **trade expositions**, or trade shows around the world. In places like Las Vegas, home to one of the largest of these expositions, MAGIC, and New York City, host to the International Boutique Show, buyers are able to screen many of the vendor's lines they are already using in their merchandise assortments

Trade expositions are held throughout the world. The show seen here took place in Paris.

and evaluate new manufacturers' collections. This format enables the purchasing agents to cover an entire market without going from one building to another.

Temporary Facilities

Some manufacturers operate relatively small businesses and cannot afford the costs of a permanent showroom. Instead, they opt to utilize temporary spaces during peak selling periods. Some of the merchandise marts and commercial hotels in a city offer space to these companies on a limited basis. At other times these vendors try to sell their lines through resident buying offices and by calling on the retailers in their places of operation.

The buyer then visits the companies, screens the lines, and makes notations before any ordering is completed. This approach is necessary so that every line may be considered before any decision may be reached.

ALTERNATE METHODS OF MERCHANDISE PROCUREMENT

While market visits are considered to be the most valid way in which to evaluate the state of the market and to screen the available lines, a host of buyer duties and responsibilities might prohibit such excursions except in the case of new season openings. The distance from these wholesale centers to the buyer's home bases also makes frequent visits difficult to work into the schedule.

In order to avail themselves of a continuous flow of new goods, retail buyers resort to on-premise meetings with road sales staffs, catalogs, and business-to-business Internet Web sites.

In-House Buying

Most manufacturers and wholesalers maintain either their own "road staffs" or contract with **manufacturer's representatives** to make regular visits to retail operations. The former group is a part of the producer's company while the latter is an independent seller who represents a few different manufacturers. In either case, the purpose is to get to those clients who have not visited the marketplace to make their purchases, or to **cold canvass** for new accounts.

In addition to not having sufficient time for firsthand market coverage, some buyers prefer purchasing from these road sellers because the lines that they represent have generally been edited, leaving only the best sellers in the collection. Those who travel from retailer to retailer usually do so after the new lines have been presented during the aforementioned market weeks. During these periods, the collections are first shown in their entirety, with gradual weeding out taking place. Only those items that have captured the attention of the buyers remain. Thus, when the sales reps take to the road, they only take with them the products that seem to have the best chance for success with the consuming public. In this way, the buyers who opt for purchasing in-house, are only shown the potential winners, and do not have to make judgments on the entire line that was first presented.

Of course, waiting to buy after the initial market showings often leads to later deliveries. Since the earlier purchasers have the opportunity to receive their goods first, the remainder must wait a little longer. When time is of the essence in terms of delivery, as is the case with many fashion-forward retailers, visits to the market at the very beginning of the selling season is the only way to guarantee early delivery.

Catalogs

Many lines that are sold to retailers are done so through catalogs. Products for the home, for example, are often marketed in this manner. Manufacturers and wholesalers publish catalogs that accurately describe their offerings.

Many buyers prefer this manner of ordering since it allows them to do so during their own time frames. As discussed, market visits are time-consuming and visits by reps may come at inopportune times. But, catalogs may be examined at any time that suits the buyer.

The disadvantages of catalog ordering include the potential for the actual product to seem somewhat different from what was ordered and that buyers do not have the opportunity to have their questions answered. Of course, contact with the sales reps is always possible via telephone, fax, or e-mail.

Business-to-Business Web sites

Today's technology makes purchasing easier than ever before. Just as a wave of consumers is making use of the Internet for their personal needs, professional buyers are also using online purchasing at **business-to-business Web sites** for merchandise acquisition. Many manufacturers, wholesalers, retail consultants, and surplus sellers have Web sites that retailers may log on to and buy the merchandise being offered.

In the closeout arena, www.tradeout.com, the world's leading online business surplus marketplace, offers a wealth of products to merchants that include apparel, computer products, food and beverage items, health and beauty products and housewares. Buyers simply log onto the Web site and access the product classification in which they are interested. A computer retailer might wish to view any one of a particular group of merchandise that TradeOut has available. After examining the availability list, which includes name of the seller, the quantity remaining, the regular price, and the end date for which the merchandise will be ultimately sold, the potential buyer clicks in a bid and finds out if he or she has been sold the merchandise. It is a system that is similar to the one used by consumers on the e-Bay Web site, except this one is restricted to professional merchants who have the ability to buy in large quantities.

TradeOut.com services its buyers with a number of different advantages. They include 24-hour-a-day, 7-day-a-week service, side-by-side price comparisons, and an enormous product offering, all without additional cost to the buyer.

One of the major clearinghouses, RetailExchange.com is a business-to-business Web site that helps buyers find off-price merchandise.

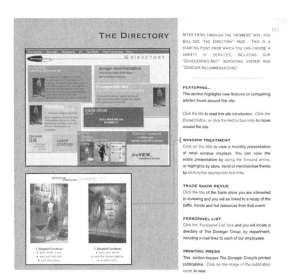

The Doneger online directory guides users to a variety of company services and allows buyers to view virtual images of products.

Another major **clearinghouse** is www. Retailexchange.com. Unlike the auction businesses, this company provides a managed negotiation format that lets the purchaser negotiate and control all of the terms of the deal. The Web site provides sales team assistants that take the purchasers through every step of the buying process. It is the fastest way for clients to access the world's largest selection of off-price consumer goods in 16 categories from the world's most prominent vendors.

Unlike RetailExchange.com and Trade-Out.com, a visit to www.doneger.com reveals a host of buyer online services, the newest of which allows buyers to screen the lines of numerous resources. By clicking onto the Marketplace Exhibition Center, retail buyers are able to view digital images of products through **virtual showrooms**. Users are able to select a particular manufacturer or product category to review for style, color, sizing, price, and delivery information. They can build and edit a line sheet as they shop the various manufacturers' collections, creating a merchandise assortment tailored to their specific company's needs.

Virtual showrooms act as extensions of the physical showrooms and are readily available for those who are too busy to make in-person trips to the market.

Doneger.com is used by clients who pay a fee for all of the services. Retailers who are not Doneger members can visit the showrooms, free of charge, as guests of a manufacturer who is a member. Each user is assigned a login number as well as a password that enables them to access the site.

NEGOTIATING THE PURCHASE

Once the buyer has shopped the market and narrowed the offerings to fit the allocated dollar amounts, it is time to consummate the deal. It is not merely a matter of selecting the items that seem to fit the buyer's needs; the process also includes possible price negotiation and a discussion of shipping terms, delivery dates, and chargebacks.

Price Negotiation

The price that is quoted by vendors is sometimes negotiable. But even in cases where suppliers are willing to give special price considerations to their clients, they are generally

Purchase Order Worksheet

Vendor	Greg Norman	Dept#	376	Start Ship	A/O	Terms	N30
Vendor #	3201501	PO #	TBD	Cancel	01/25	OTB Month	Jan
							5

STYLE #	DESCRIPTION	TTL PER STYLE	COLOR	UNIT COST	UNIT RETAIL	MKUP%	ASST 1 UNITS	COST	ASST 1 RETAIL
GNS9J004	Microfiber Crew Neck Windshirt	170	401—Navy	$23.40	$78.00	70.0%	12	$281	$936
GNS9J004	Microfiber Crew Neck Windshirt	170	604—Red	$23.40	$78.00	70.0%	12	$281	$936
GNS0J010	Microfiber Full Zip (Reversable Jacket)	170	614—Black	$32.40	$110.00	70.5%	12	$389	$1,320
GNS0J011	Nylon Full Zip Jacket	142	328—Hunter	$22.20	$75.00	70.4%	10	$222	$750
GNS0J011	Nylon Full Zip Jacket	142	401—Navy	$22.20	$75.00	70.4%	10	$222	$750
GNS0J011	Nylon Full Zip Jacket	80	423—Royal	$22.20	$75.00	70.4%	10	$222	$750
GNH0J060	Windshirt "Windstopper" 1/2 Zip	40	001—Black	$26.40	$88.00	70.0%	8	$211	$704
		914					74	$1,828	$6,146
						Extention	370	$9,138	$30,730

The purchase order worksheet summarizes the details of the purchase. A portion of a worksheet is shown here.

prohibited from doing so by the **Robinson-Patman Act**. This piece of federal legislation was enacted to limit price discrimination and protect small businesses from the industrial giants who otherwise would get lower prices. Under the law, all buyers must pay the same price except in certain instances where:

- The price reduction is made to meet competition.
- The price is reduced because savings result from sales to particular customers.
- The merchandise is damaged or is part of a **closeout**. A closeout is generally an assortment of end-of-season merchandise that the vendor sells at reduced prices.

Working within this framework, the seasoned buyer may be able to agree on a better price for the merchandise by taking discounts for prompt payment, quantities, early acceptance of merchandise, advertising, and promotion.

Prompt Payment Discounts

In order to encourage buyers to pay their bills quickly, vendors generally offer different types of discounts. **Cash discounts** are provided for merchants who pay their bills by the end of a particular time frame. Typically, it might be a 30-day period, but it may be longer. If the invoice is paid on or before that time, the buyer receives a discount that could run as high as 8 percent in some industries.

When suppliers are extremely anxious for payments they sometimes offer an extra discount known as **anticipation**. This discount might be an additional 1 or 2 percent. It helps the manufacturers get their money quickly so that they can use it to reduce operation costs, and also it enables the retailer to achieve a better profit margin.

Quantity Discounts

Many manufacturers and wholesalers offer pricing structures that are based upon quantities. As the size of the purchase increases for each item, the cost to the buyer goes down. Sometimes when goods are needed over a long period of time, the buyer purchases them in the quantities needed for the entire period, accepting shipments as required, thereby enabling them to get the lower price.

Seasonal Discounts

When merchandise such as swimsuits, for example, is purchased prior to the beginning of the retail selling season, vendors are likely to offer **seasonal discounts** for early delivery. There are several reasons why suppliers propose such discounts. Acceptance of early delivery allows the product to be tested prior to the main selling season, giving the retailer an opportunity to reorder the best sellers. It also enables the vendor to get paid sooner and helps to alleviate the problems associated with limited storage space.

Advertising and Promotional Allowances

One of the ways in which buyers can gain an important advantage is through the negotiation of dollars for advertising and promotion. Given in the form of **cooperative advertising**, the vendor usually pays for a percentage of an ad with the remaining expense coming from the buyer's budget. The percentage is determined as a result of buyer-vendor negotiation. With advertising costs continually spiraling upward, this is an important aspect of negotiation.

Slotting Allowances

One of the areas of negotiation getting a great deal of attention is **slotting allowances**. This is when the buyer is able to get money from the vendor for the privilege of having his or her merchandise featured in prime locations in stores or on Web sites. The practice is one that is found primarily in supermarkets and bookstores. In brick-and-mortar operations, items that are placed at the end of an aisle or featured in a prime display area generally sell better than if they were mixed in with other merchandise. Even on Web sites, vendors are often willing to pay extra sums to have their titles prominently displayed. Because the cost of slotting is often high, it is something that only major suppliers can afford.

Shipping Terms

Whenever an order is written, it is important for the buyer to specify the method of shipping that he or she requires, as well as who will be paying for the shipping.

There are numerous shipping arrangements from which the buyer may choose. Some, while less expensive than others, may take longer periods of time for the goods to arrive. By contrast, the faster the delivery is, the more costly it is. Not every shipment requires the same speed for delivery. Buyers must predetermine exactly how long they are willing to wait for delivery and how much they are willing to expend for this cost.

Shipping charges are generally borne by the retailer. However, some negotiators are able to persuade the vendor to absorb the shipping costs in turn for a larger merchandise commitment.

Specific terms such as **FOB shipping point** and **FOB destination** must be written on the order so that payment will be assigned to the proper party. Under the former designation, the buyer must pay all of the shipping costs from the place of origin. In the latter situation, all costs are the responsibility of the vendor.

Delivery Dates

When buyers finalize their purchasing plans, they earmark the delivery of merchandise for specific time periods. If merchandise arrives after the required time, it can create a problem. An advertising campaign might have been developed that requires the merchandise to be on hand for that time frame, or it might be a major selling season, such as Christmas, when the merchandise must be available to meet shoppers' needs.

If the merchandise is in stock, as is the case with many wholesale operations, delivery is not a serious problem. It's a matter of getting the goods packed and shipped according to the buyer's instructions. On the other hand, if the goods are to be manufactured for the retailer, then delivery terms must be carefully noted. Often times, there is a beginning and ending delivery period if the order involves a number of different items. If delivery isn't made by the promised date, then the buyer has the right of refusal. Of course, this results in a void in the inventory, with lost sales the most likely result.

Chargebacks

An area where the expert negotiator is able to gain an advantage on the vendor is the agreement about **chargebacks**. By convincing the supplier to offer allowances either for merchandise that had to be marked down because of lackluster sales or shipping problems, the buyer is able to defray some of the merchandise's costs. The practice has become a standard occurrence in the fashion arena with such retail giants as Lord & Taylor, Federated Stores, Neiman Marcus, and Nordstrom always looking to improve their chargeback positions.

The seasoned buyer prenegotiates the amounts and is covered for any merchandising mishaps. The more detailed the purchase order is, the better position the buyer is in to make certain that his or her buying plans will be accomplished.

It should be understood that many professional buyers do not finalize their purchases at the times the lines are being examined. They often just make notes about what they have seen, reserving final judgment until they have conferred with their divisional merchandise managers or supervisors, market representatives, or others who might provide assistance. **Note taking**, especially during market week, is a typical occurrence.

Once the orders have been reviewed, it is on to the vendor for processing.

EVALUATING THE BUYER'S PERFORMANCE

Buyers are evaluated in many ways, the most important being the actual markups that they achieve and the stock turnover rate for their departments. The former will be closely addressed in Chapter 13, The Concepts and Mathematics of Merchandise Pricing, and the latter in the following section.

The stock turnover rate indicates the number of times a store's average inventory is sold within a year. It is perhaps easiest to understand by these two completely different product classifications. Bread that is baked everyday is targeted to sell out completely every 24 hours. Thus, it is said that its turnover rate is 365. On the other hand, precious jewelry, because of its cost and infrequent purchasing, might only sell out once every six months, making its turnover rate 2.

In the following example, the women's shoe buyer produced the following figures for last year.

Opening inventory (Jan. 1) ....$
660,000
Closing inventory (Dec. 1) ....$
540,000
Sales for year ....
$2,400,000

The formula used to determine stock turnover is:

$$\frac{\text{net sales}}{\text{average inventory at retail}} = \text{stock turnover}$$

First the average inventory must be determined:

$$\frac{660,000\ +\ 540,000}{2} = 600,000$$

Then:

$$\frac{2,400,000}{600,000} = 4$$

The turnover rate is 4 times every year.

In order to determine if the rate is appropriate it should be compared with other depart-ments in the store, previous year's rates, and the rates that are considered to be average for that merchandise classification in the industry. If it is above the standard that is expected, the buyer is doing an excellent job. If it is below, then investigation is in order to determine the problem.

Some of the contributing circumstances to poor turnover rates include:

- retail prices that are too high
- merchandise selections that aren't in line with customer preferences
- poor quality merchandise
- inexperienced sales personnel
- poor promotional techniques
- lackluster visual merchandising
- competition

Once these problems have been addressed, a determination may be made as to the causes of the poor turnover showing. When corrected, the turnover rate should improve.

A DAY IN THE LIFE OF A BUYER

The buyer studies past sales to predict future sales and gauge how much merchandise to reorder.

Reordering hot items ensures their availability to meet consumer demand.

The buyer checks ads to make certain that they describe the merchandise accurately. Consumers expect to find the advertised items when they shop the store.

Regular communication with store personnel keeps the buyer abreast of merchandise needs.

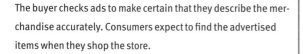

Pre-planning is the key to a successful market visit.

Store visits help the buyer determine whether displays are appropriate.

TRENDS FOR THE NEW MILLENNIUM

- Global purchasing is becoming more prevalent for today's retailers making the buyer's job one that requires a significant time away from the store.
- There is a trend to move away from purchasing large reserve inventories because this often adversely affects the company's stock turnover rate.
- More and more Web sites are being developed to enable buyers to screen and purchase merchandise without having to visit the wholesale markets.
- Chargebacks to vendors are on the increase and are causing major problems.
- Trade expositions will continue to gain importance in most product classifications because of the advantages they afford the buyers.

CHAPTER HIGHLIGHTS

- Purchasing by retailers, once a task that focused on domestic markets, now demands coverage of a vast, global marketplace.
- The role of the buyer is considered by many industry professionals to be one of the most important in the retailing industry.
- While professional buyers perform a host of different activities, the major one is purchasing the merchandise.
- When purchase plans are being formulated for the next buying period, major emphasis is placed on past sales records.
- Besides looking at internal sources of information when planning is undertaken, buyers seek assistance from numerous external sources.
- The most notable outside planning source for fashion merchandise are the resident buying offices, also known as retail consultants.
- Buyers develop model stocks that address both qualitative and quantitative needs.

- In order to make certain that the buyers stay within their allocated merchandise budgets, they regularly focus on the open to buy calculations.
- Retailers have a variety of suppliers from which to choose. They must evaluate each of them before any actual purchasing decisions are made.
- Stock turnover rates are important since they affect profitability.
- Most buyers generally place the bulk of the upcoming season's orders during a period called market week.
- Buying may take place at permanent vendor showrooms, trade expositions, temporary facilities, business-to-business Web sites, and the retailer's premises.
- Negotiating the purchase is the responsibility of the buyer. If handled effectively it can bring the retailer a better deal.

IMPORTANT RETAILING TERMS

product development

retail consultants

resident buying offices

market week

market consultant

resident buyer representative

fashion forecaster

trade publications

model stock

staple merchandise

open to buy

merchandise on hand

merchandise commitments

bottom line

qualitative decisions

quantitative decisions

buying plan

rack jobbers

purchasing channels

landed cost

dutiable

tariffs

stock turnover rate

road sales staff

garment center

trade expositions

manufacturer's representatives

cold canvass

business-to-business Web sites

clearinghouse

virtual showrooms

Robinson-Patman Act

closeouts

cash discounts

anticipation

seasonal discounts

cooperative advertising

slotting allowances

FOB shipping point

FOB destination

chargebacks

note taking

FOR REVIEW

1. Why is the time spent on purchasing in the market-place more involved than in past years?

2. In addition to purchasing, what are some of the other duties and responsibilities performed by buyers?

3. Why are buyers often called upon to select the products that will be promoted?

4. What is the first source of information that the buyer utilizes in purchase planning?

5. To what extent are merchandise managers involved in the planning stages of purchasing?

6. Why do professional buyers utilize the services of external resources in the planning of their purchases?

7. What preplanning activities are provided by resident buying offices to their clients?

8. Why do some buyers use the services of fashion forecasters in their search for new merchandise?

9. What advantage does the reading of consumer periodicals afford the retail buyer?

10. What is a model stock?

11. List and briefly describe the four elements of buying.

12. Define the term *open to buy*.

13. How is open to buy calculated?

14. Should a buyer always use the same merchandise resources or should he or she continually look for new suppliers?

15. Which products are typically purchased by the retailer through rack jobbers?

16. Define the term *landed cost*.

17. How important is the stock turnover rate in evaluating the buyer's performance?

18. What is market week?

19. What advantage does the visit to a trade exposition provide the buyer that individual showroom visits do not?

20. If a buyer cannot get to the market to make purchases, what other means can he or she use?

21. How do the business-to-business Web sites differ from the ones used by consumers?

22. What is a chargeback?

23. How does the Robinson-Patman Act affect buyer–seller negotiation?

24. On what two bases are buyers generally evaluated?

AN INTERNET ACTIVITY

The use of business-to-business Web sites by retail buyers is growing. Log on to any of those described in the chapter, such as www.tradeout.com and prepare a summary of your findings as follows:

• List the name of the site and describe its function.

• Discuss how long it has been in business.

• Describe the types of merchandise it offers.

- Discuss the various types of businesses it attempts to sell to.
- Describe how you become a member or user of the Web site.
- Discuss any fees or costs, other than those for merchandise, required of users.
- Describe the visuals used and how effective they are.
- Offer your comments about how effective a tool the site is.

EXERCISES AND PROJECTS

1. Visit or write to a retail buyer in your community to learn about how he or she plans purchases. If the retail operation is not headquartered in your city, find out from a local unit where its operation is located so that you may communicate with one of the buyers. It is not necessary to contact a major company. A small entrepreneurship would also be appropriate. The information that you have obtained should be organized in a form similar to the one that follows:

```
Company Name_____

Buyer's Name _____

Merchandise Classification _____

Internal Planning Sources



External Planning Sources




Purchase Locations (showrooms, trade expos, on-premises, etc.)


```

2. Through the use of the Internet or a trade journal such as *Stores*, develop a list of 20 trade expositions that are earmarked for retail buyers to purchase merchandise. The form should be organized with the following heads:

Trade Exposition	Types of Merchandise	Location(s)

THE CASE OF THE SEARCH FOR UNIQUE MERCHANDISE

With competition reaching an all time high for Bancroft Department Stores, a fashion-oriented company, the merchandising team has decided it must take a step in a new direction in terms of the lines it now features in its stores. Ever since the store first opened in 1960, Bancroft's philosophy has been that the best approach to merchandising, was to offer highly publicized national brands. Stores are stocked with labels that include Liz Claiborne, Calvin Klein, Ralph Lauren, DKNY, Jones New York, and Ellen Tracy. While each of these labels guarantee a high degree of consumer recognition and quality, they are the same products that are found at Bancroft's competitors. Other than the customer service that they offer, there really isn't another reason why shoppers should patronize Bancroft's over other stores.

To make matters worse, Bancroft's has witnessed an increase in these lines at the off-price stores in their trading areas. Each of these labels is prominently displayed and prices are considerably lower than what Bancroft charges. Although the merchandise arrives at these merchants much later in the season, their presence still makes them competitive in the shopper's eyes.

In order to distinguish themselves from other merchants who carry these lines, the company has decided to begin a program that features lesser-known names, but, at the same time, remain competitive in terms of fashion emphasis and quality. Understanding that locating these lesser-known collections would be a major chore, the merchandising team is not certain of the best approach to take.

John Gallop, general merchandise manager, is an advocate of firsthand research to discover these new merchandise offerings. He believes that visits to offshore venues would be the best place to start. He suggests that the buyers in the store should travel to global centers such as Hong Kong, Korea, London, and Milan to see what's available that hasn't yet made an impact in American stores. While this seemed to be a sound strategy by some of the buyers, top management, particularly the company's CEO, Marc Litt, thought the approach was too extravagant and costly to warrant consideration. He suggested that a better plan should be adopted before foreign visits are made.

With the next season only two months away, a meeting was called by John Gallop. The meeting included his eight divisional merchandise managers and eighty buyers. Each person involved in the meeting was asked to prepare some thoughts about the direction the team should go in solving the merchandise acquisition dilemma. Specific remedies were expected from each of them at the planning session.

Questions

1. Pretend that you are one of the buyers asked to attend the meeting. What initial approach would you suggest that the buyers and merchandisers take before any offshore visits are made?

2. Do you believe that trips to foreign shores are necessary to locate new vendors that do not have marquee appeal?

3. What portion of the merchandise should be of the new variety and why?

CHAPTER 12

Private Labeling and Product Development

After you have completed this chapter, you should be able to discuss:

- ► Some of the advantages of purchasing merchandise that bears a manufacturer's or designer's label or brand.
- ► The beginnings of private branding and the concepts used by those retailers who first introduced them to their customers.
- ► Why most retail organizations choose to use the proportional approach when stocking private brands and labels.
- ► The store-is-the-brand concept and how it differs from the proportional approach utilized by some retailers.
- ► The advantages for merchants who subscribe to some form of private branding and labeling.
- ► How merchants avail themselves of privately branded and labeled merchandise.
- ► The ways in which smaller retailers may participate in private labeling.
- ► Several of the promotional techniques used by retailers to publicize their own brands and labels.
- ► The importance of the name that is given to the company's private label collection.
- ► Why some merchants subscribe to licensed, private branding.

All over the United States, retailers are facing competitive challenges that have never before been witnessed in the industry. Not only is there a wealth of brick-and-mortar operations all across the country, but there is also a record breaking number of catalogs being marketed to consumers. To complicate matters even more, these two traditional forms of retailing are facing yet another competitive arena—retail Web sites.

In this age of multichannel retailing, when merchants are showcasing their offerings in their stores and catalogs and on their Web sites, the sameness of the merchandise that is available from a majority of retailers is troublesome. Shoppers, whether making visits to the stores, perusing the hundreds of catalogs that come into the home, or logging on to their favorite Web sites, are finding the same merchandise being offered over and over again. **Marquee labels** such as Liz Claiborne, Ralph Lauren, and Calvin Klein are in every major department store, making retail operations clones of each other. While a large percentage of shoppers prefer well-known labels to lesser-known brands, their presence often creates problems for retail outlets. Of paramount concern is the pricing factor. During slow selling periods there is nothing to prevent a merchant from taking markdowns on these products. This, of course, may cause anguish for the retailer who isn't prepared to lower the price. Since shoppers often go from store to store to comparison shop, the store with the lowest prices wins. The end result is the inability to maintain the initial markup that is necessary to maximize profits. In a competitive society, it is imperative that different offerings be available to avoid the complications associated with identical product assortments.

In order to make operations more profitable, many retailers have taken the route of private labeling. While most recognize the need to carry **signature brands**, many have opted for a portion of their inventories to be exclusively their own. Major companies like Macy's, Bloomingdale's, Marshall Field's, Belk, and Dillard's, for example, commingle nationally advertised brands along with their own products. Others, such as Gap, Banana Republic, Eddie Bauer, The Limited, and Abercrombie & Fitch have taken the private label concept to its extreme and have become store-is-the-brand operations. That is, the entire merchandise assortment is exclusive to their respective companies.

Each of these retailers recognizes the need to distinguish itself from the others if it is to sustain a positive profit picture. Whether it is in the brick-and-mortar operations, in catalogs, or on the Internet, product differentiation is a necessity to maintain customer loyalty. Of course, other factors, such as service, play an important role in the success of any business, but it is the merchandise mix, and its prices, that helps a consumer decide whether or not to patronize the retailer.

Private label merchandising is significantly more difficult to manage than merchandising that focuses on national branding. The former requires a retailer to develop his or her product line or to have some outside resource to provide the items. Buying merchandise from existing lines avoids the problems associated with product design and manufacturing.

In this chapter, attention will focus on the comparisons between manufacturer's and private brands, the trials and tribulations of private labeling, and rigorous demands placed on those in the company who develop the products.

MANUFACTURER'S BRANDS AND LABELS

In most retail operations, be they the brick-and-mortar, catalogs, or Web sites, the greatest proportion of the merchandise is based upon products that are produced by manufacturers. The products are not restricted to any one merchant, but sometimes their purchase comes with exclusivity terms for certain merchants. That is, the goods are restricted to specific retailers in a trading area.

Although the merchandising of these brands, many of which enjoy national and sometimes even global exposure, present potential problems such as **price cutting**, their prominence makes them desirable. Some of the specific reasons why most retailers continue to use **manufacturer's brands** in significant amounts include the following:

Manufacturers' brands such as Dockers enjoy global exposure and improve retailers' profitability.

- *Exposure to the public.* Retailers who carry national brands benefit from the wealth of advertising and promotional endeavors undertaken by the producers of these products. Companies such as Calvin Klein, which have large advertising budgets help presell their products through advertising and promotion and motivate the consumer to purchase them. Retailers then place these items on the selling floor, in their direct-mail pieces, or on their Web sites, and customers purchase them. This investment by the manufacturer helps retailers save their own advertising budgets to promote other lesser-known brands or their own private labels.
- *Reorder availability.* With the abundance of merchandise needed to satisfy the orders of merchants all over the country, and sometimes to those in foreign venues, many manufacturers keep an assortment of their best sellers on hand to quickly fill reorder requests. When time is of the essence, especially in the case of fashion items whose shelf life is relatively brief, the prompt receipt of these goods will assure quick sales. In most retail organizations, it is usually just a few items each season that capture the public's attention, and there in-stock availability helps to satisfy customer needs. Without this immediate

replenishment, sales could be lost and the company's bottom line could be adversely affected.

- *Quality assurance.* Manufacturers of branded merchandise are keenly aware that their products must be produced with the highest standards in order to protect their reputations and maintain interest in their offerings. Given this scrutiny, they can assure their clients that their customers will be the recipients of the goods that will meet their needs. With adherence to quality control, the retailer will benefit by having fewer complaints about the merchandise and will be able to build regular patronage.

- *Consumer preference.* Through marketing research studies, retailers have been made aware that a significant percentage of consumers prefer national brands. Whether it is for food products, appliances, clothing, home furnishings, or other items, 45 percent of men and 35 percent of women prefer these products, according to the National Advertising Bureau, in a study they conducted regarding manufacturer brands. Only when the retailers they patronize are looked upon as reliable do they begin to accept unbranded merchandise. Using questionnaires and focus groups, many retailers conduct similar studies of their own to determine manufacturer brand preference. It is these findings that lead the merchants to determine the proportion of branded goods to the non-branded variety.

Couture collections, such as Armani, offer clout to shoppers motivated by prestige.

- *Prestige.* Although value is in the forefront of the minds of many of today's consumers, and more and more are looking to discounters and off-pricers to satisfy their needs, a large number of consumers are motivated to buy certain marquee labels and brands. Price is not a factor with these consumers. They are motivated by the prestige and status of these products. A telling study, concerning the purchase of prestigious automobiles, such as Mercedes Benz, revealed the extent to which some consumers would pay more for identical products that bore the prestigious signature than those that didn't. Study respondents were asked, "If you were able to purchase a Mercedes for 30 percent off the list price with the condition that it wouldn't have the company logo or name on it, and if you revealed to anyone it was, in fact, a Mercedes, the car would be taken from you, would you make the purchase? The result was that 40 percent would rather pay the extra money to have the car emblazoned with its identifying trademarks. While this is but one study, it is safe to assume, that prestige is a factor that plays an important part in many purchases. Given this motivational aspect of buying, it is important for the retailer whose customer base is replete with prestige-motivated shoppers to merchandise such image products properly.

PRIVATE BRANDS AND LABELS

For many years, some retailers opted to introduce **private brands and labels** into their merchandise mixes. The idea was to provide quality products, which were essentially the same as the nationally recognized ones, but at lower prices with the store's own brands. Proponents of this concept included A & P, the largest supermarket chain at the time, and Sears, America's leading catalog merchant. The former lined its shelves with a vast array of food items that bore its own name, and the latter merchandised hard goods such as appliances and tools under the retailer's brand.

In both of cases, the items that were marketed as private brands were almost identical to those that bore manufacturers' brands. These very same producers manufactured goods for Sears and A & P. The differences between these and brand-name products was in the packaging or in some minor feature. Using this type of merchandising, the businesses weren't affected by price cutting or any of the other obstacles that came about through competition. After a great deal of promotional efforts brought favorable results, Sears made the Coldspot and Kenmore brands household names, and A & P did the same with its Ann Page labels.

Ironically, as the trend toward private branding and labeling caught fire in the 1970s, these two retail giants began to redirect their efforts toward regular brands. Sears, in particular, began to introduce nationally advertised manufacturers' products along side its own brands primarily because their customers showed an interest in them. A & P began to lose its dominant position as a major supermarket chain and closed countless stores.

In any event, the wealth of private label products that retailers began to feature in their assortments grew at significant rates. Macy's led the way with countless brands that were produced exclusively for its stores. Labels like Jennifer Moore, Alfani, Christopher Hayes, and Charter Club coexisted with the likes of well-known brands and soon began to play a major merchandising role for the company. Today, other Federated stores also carry these private labels. What many believe was imperative to their success was not only the quality and styling of the merchandise, but the choice of the names coined to enhance each collection. It was not accidental that these names were designated for the different merchandising collections.

I.N.C. is one of Federated Department Stores' numerous private labels.

At the time of their introduction, it was quite obvious that designer type names were the rage in the apparel market. In order to capitalize on this concept, Macy's cleverly chose names that seemed to denote a specific designer. Thus, more and more consumers were under the impression that Jennifer Moore and Christopher Hayes were nationally prominent designers. Little did they realize that the only place to purchase the items that bore these signatures was Macy's. At the time of the Alfani introduction, Italian clothing was the rage in America, particularly in men's fashion. A close inspection of the garments that were introduced with the Alfani signature revealed that the garments were actually produced in Korea. The clout of an Italian sounding name gave it greater appeal. Rounding out the keen merchandising of the company was the introduction of the Charter Club label. Not only was the clubby sound of Ralph Lauren's collections bringing vast numbers of shoppers to the stores, but the offerings were typically those of the polo set. Capitalizing on this merchandising phenomenon, Macy's developed its Charter Club label featuring styles that were quite similar to those of Ralph Lauren.

Private branding has become commonplace in most retailing classifications. In addition to department stores and apparel chains, discounters, off-pricers, and warehouse clubs, for examples, have embraced the concept. Kmart has made headlines with its own Martha Stewart home furnishings lines; Costco has introduced its own brands, such as Kirkland, as has Stein Mart.

It should be understood that the introduction of one's own brand or label requires a great deal of effort on the part of the retailer, beginning with the choice of a name that will motivate purchasing, a collection of products that can compete with the better-known manufacturer offerings, and prices that can compete with those products that have made their reputations.

The entry into this type of merchandising is a formidable one, and, in order to be successful, one must have the complete attention of the organization's staff. Aside from all that is required to make one's own private brand or label successful, there is also a need to determine to what extent these new offerings will be featured in the company's merchandise assortment.

An Ethical Consideration

A VAST NUMBER OF SHOPPERS REGULARLY PURCHASE private label merchandise from the major retailers in the United States. Most do not know that these are brands are developed exclusively by and for specific companies and buy them as if they were nationally branded items. This is by no means an unethical practice among retailers, but just a way to gain more exclusivity in their offerings. What is a question of ethics, however is the nature of the names that they use on their labels as discussed in the preceding paragraphs. Why do companies like Macy's, for example, use the Alfani label for merchandise that is actually produced in Asia? Is it that this label leads the consumer to believe the merchandise is designed and made in Italy, a place where fine menswear is produced? This may be considered unethical since Asian produced goods, which cost less than those produced in Italy, are named to gain the clout of an Italian label.

Again, this is not an illegal practice, but one that gives a false impression.

The Proportional Concept

By and large, most retailers feature a merchandise mix that incorporates their own brands along with others that have either gained national prominence or are new manufacturers' designs with the potential for significant consumer acceptance.

Recognizing that a large percentage of their clientele are easily satisfied with manufacturer brands and labels, most retailers understand that the presence of these brands in their model stocks is a given. They set aside separate departments that bear these instantly recognizable names and locate them in spots that are easily accessed by customers. Liz Claiborne and Ralph Lauren, for example, have their merchandise featured in self-contained areas that resemble small shops and bear signage that announces their existence. With the sales volumes and ultimate profits achieved through the offering of such goods, their inclusion in the store's product mix is a must.

While these recognized merchandise collections are essential to the success of most companies, the incorporation of the private brands and labels have also proven to be of paramount importance to retailers. The proportion of the overall inventory that should be devoted to these private brands is a matter of concern for retailers.

Most retailers gradually introduce their own labels into the mix, studying the results after each selling season. Stock of those that have achieved success is increased.

Table 12.1 lists some of the major retailers who subscribe to the **proportional inventory concept**.

COMPANY	MAJOR PRIVATE LABELS	MERCHANDISE CLASSIFICATION
Sears	Kenmore, Coldspot, Craftsmen	Tools, appliances
Kmart	Martha Stewart, Jaclyn Smith[1]	Housewares, linens
Costco	Kirkland	Food items
Macy's	Charter Club, Jennifer Moore, Alfani, Christopher Hayes	Apparel, bedding, jewelry
Dillard's	Preston & York, Daniel Creimeux	Apparel and accessories
Saks	St. John, SFA Folio	Apparel and accessories
Belk	J. Khaki	Apparel and accessories
Lord & Taylor	Kate Hill, Identity	Apparel and accessories
Bloomingdale's	Sutton, Aqua	Apparel and accessories
Marshall Field's	Frango, Field Gear	Chocolates, apparel
Nordstrom	Classiques Entier, BP, Caslon, Baby N, 81st and Park, Ewear	Handbags, apparel, shoes, juniors, men's clothing
Tiffany	Tiffany	Jewelry

TABLE 12.1
SELECTED RETAILERS WITH PROMINENT PRIVATE BRANDS

[1]These private labels are part of licensing agreements. The names on the brands are well known celebrities who, along with their designs, bring extra recognition to the products.

The Stein Mart Story
Product Development and Private Labels

UNLIKE THE STRATEGY OF MANY MAJOR RETAILERS, product development and private labeling is not a major factor in the merchandising practices at Stein Mart. It is able to satisfy most of its needs though merchandise acquisition from designers and well-known manufacturers. This is also important to the company since its customers generally prefer these marquee labels which are available for less than at department stores.

When these types of goods are not available from its vendor resources, it must resort to some private labels. This merchandise accounts for between 10 and 12 percent of the overall product mix. Women's hosiery and men's dress shirts, under its own "Charles Reed" label, are the most typical items found in its stores.

The product development that does take place in-house is done so to improve upon the products under consideration from its vendors. For example, a fit model is used to make certain that the product's specifications are appropriate for Stein Mart's customers. It might require a change in the hemlines or a different sleeve length. This information is then passed along to the manufacturer who then produces it. This generally causes no problems with vendors because of the enormity of Stein Mart's purchasing power.

Sometimes, trim or closures are also redeveloped to better suit customers' needs. The role of the product developer is a major one in the company since the changes are imperative for the specific product's success.

· ·

Sometimes, as in the case of Macy's, the proportion of private brands to the national entries is significant. Initially, they began with a smattering of their own labels so that their impact could be tested. Each year the company seems to add more and more private labels, with the different ones numbering more than twenty. There is no real formula for what the proportions between private and manufacturer brands should be. It is up to management to determine what makes the most sense in terms of profitability.

Merchants generally must invest enormous promotional sums to publicize these brands so that customers will be motivated to buy. The producers themselves, on the other hand, promote manufacturers' brands and labels, so that the public will be aware of them and seek out the retailers who sell them. The private label offerings require extensive investments in terms of advertisements, special events, and visual merchandising efforts since the products are sold only through their outlets. It is essential to convince the public that these private offerings have the same or better quality than their national brand counterparts.

When Dayton Hudson Corporation initially introduced its Boundary Waters Collection, a line that featured outdoor apparel for men, it used a unique approach to make customers aware of the line. Not yet having settled on the name for the collection, management developed a contest to select a name. After a great deal of promotion surrounding the contest, they eventually decided upon the entry, Boundary Waters. The attention derived from the consumer-based label research resulted in a significant amount of interest in the new line. It soon became a mainstay of menswear, quickly increasing its proportion of the department's overall merchandise.

The Store-Is-the-Brand Concept

All over the United States, and sometimes in other global venues, companies like the Gap are reaping the benefits of total private label merchandising. In these outlets, the need to determine proportionality between national brands and private labels is eliminated. The entire offering is the company's own. The concept is based upon the philosophy that the organization's name and the brands that it features are one and the same. Once the brand has been established, the public immediately comes to understand that only one brand is available.

The apparel and accessories segments of retailing dominate the store-is-the-brand concept. With companies such as Limited Brands, which feature a host of private brands in different stores and catalogs under its umbrella (including Express and Express Men's), Eddie Bauer, Abercrombie & Fitch, American Eagle, and Nine West making a

Companies that apply the store-is-the-brand concept use only their own label on the merchandise they sell.

significant presence in the retail arena, it is certain that the consumer has confidence in this format.

Focus on . . .
Gap Inc.

THE GAP WAS FOUNDED IN 1969 BY DON AND DORIS FISHER with a handful of employees in a single store in San Francisco. Today, it is an international company with three distinct brands, Gap, Banana Republic, and Old Navy. Still headquartered in the San Francisco Bay Area, the Gap has product development offices in New York City and distribution operations and offices coordinating sourcing activities around the globe. It has become a household name for every member of the family. The Gap's cumulative revenues topped $11 billion in 2001.

By 1976, just eight years after Gap opened its first unit, the company went public with an offering of 1.2 million shares of stock. Little by little, additional labels were added to the Gap roster. First came GapKids in 1986, to be followed by babyGap in 1990. In 1983, Gap bought Banana Republic, a small retail operation that sold safari and travel clothing. It wasn't long before this retail entry was transformed into a more sophisticated concept that emphasized modern, versatile, and relevant apparel and accessories for style conscious shoppers. In 1994, Gap's newest brand entered the retail arena with much fanfare and immediate success. Old Navy was born with an emphasis placed on "fun, fashion, family, and value." It quickly grew to more than 500 stores by 2001.

One of the keys to the company's success is its ability to recognize the needs of the consumer and to offer products that fill those needs. Product development at the Gap begins with a creative team of designers, product managers, and graphic artists who develop the look and feel of each season's merchandise. From color to concept, it all begins with inspiration. Whether it's people watching on the streets of Tokyo, a flash from a dream, or a visit to a local art gallery, the team translates its stimulations into salable designs.

Once the individual styles have been created, Gap provides them to third-party manufacturers for production. These producers are located in more than 50 countries around the globe, including the United States. They don't own any of these manufacturing facilities, but have developed a Code of Vendor Conduct to ensure that the factories are not only capable of producing high quality goods, but also feature safe and humane working conditions. More than 80 company employees assure quality control and inspect the production facilities to make certain that they are in compliance with established policies.

In 2001, there were more than 2,000 Gap stores in the United States, the United Kingdom, Canada, France, Germany, and Japan, 300 Banana Republic stores in the United States and Canada, and more than 500 Old Navy units in the United States, along with successful catalog and Web sites operations. With considerable growth earmarked for each of the divisions, it is certain that store-is-the-brand retailing is alive and well at Gap Inc.

● ●

The Private Label and Brand Advantage

Of course, exclusivity is the obvious reason why retailers subscribe to having their own brands and products available either as parts of their inventories or in the store-is-the-brand concept. Inherent in this exclusive approach to merchandising are specific advantages that make the approach profitable.

TABLE 12.2 SELECTED STORE-IS-THE-BRAND COMPANIES		
PARENT COMPANY	**PRIVATE BRAND**	**MERCHANDISE CLASSIFICATION**
Gap Inc.	The Gap	Men's and women's casual apparel
	Banana Republic	Men's and women's fashion apparel
	Old Navy	Value apparel for the family
Limited Brands	The Limited	Women's apparel
	Express	Women's apparel
	New York and Company	Popular price apparel
	Express Men's	Men's apparel
	Victoria's Secret	Intimate apparel
	Bath & Body Works	Body care products
The Spiegel Group	Eddie Bauer	Men's and women's apparel, Home furnishings
Sears, Roebuck and Co.	Lands' End	Casual wear
Ann Taylor Stores Corp.	Ann Taylor	Women's apparel
Abercrombie & Fitch Co.	Abercrombie & Fitch	Men's and women's apparel
American Eagle Outfitters	American Eagle	Apparel
J. Crew Group	J. Crew	Men's and women's apparel
Jones Apparel Group, Inc.	Nine West	Shoes
Brooks Brothers	Brooks Brothers	Men's and women's apparel

- There is no interference by vendors. Often times, manufacturers with well-known brands require that a certain amount be spent on advertising or that the products be visually merchandised in a particular manner. Since the retailer has the ultimate decision-making authority, there is no need to conform to anyone else's demands.
- Profitability is like to be higher since the costs of middlemen are avoided. Through the elimination of the vendor's markup on the goods, the prices offered by the retailer to the consumer could be lower, and the profits greater.
- Price cutting, which is often problematic for retailers, is avoided since the competition cannot obtain the same merchandise. In poor economic times, or in situations where inventories might not move at the desired pace, merchants are sometimes prone to cut prices, thus causing profit losses for competing merchants.
- Such factors as the timing of markdowns, as is sometimes dictated by suppliers, or the setting of retail prices are avoided since the retail operation is the only one that can make these decisions.
- Purchasing requirements, as dictated by many vendors, are not present in privately branded merchandise. Some suppliers, especially those with marquee brands and labels, often require that purchases be made in predetermined assortments. For example, **prepacks** might be based upon the manufacturer's concept of a particular size allocation to meet his or her own production requirements. Merchants, according to their past sales records, might prefer a size breakdown that is heavier in the large sizes, where as a vendor could demand the ordering of more smaller sizes. In such cases, the retailer is often left with the smaller sizes that ultimately turn up on the markdown racks, thus affecting profits.
- Customer **comparison shopping** is eliminated since the merchandise is of an exclusive nature. When national brands are inventoried, some consumers go from store to store in an effort to find the lowest price.
- Product specificity can be tailored to the company's individual needs. When buyers set out to purchase their inventories from the independent suppliers, they are obligated to make selections that are earmarked for broader audiences. In the case of one's own brands, the exact product requirements will become part of the design.
- Customer loyalty can come as a result of the consumer being satisfied with a particular label or brand. If the item belongs to a nationally known manufacturer, it is his or her product that attracts attention, and may be purchased at many venues. In the case of retailer exclusivity through private branding, if the customer is satisfied, then he or she is likely to patronize that store for those labels.

LICENSED PRIVATE BRANDS

The typical type of private branding comes as a result of the retailer's initiative to produce or obtain products for its exclusive use. Retailers also use another approach—one that benefits from the names of well-known celebrities. Through **licensing agreements**, products are offered that feature famous people's names, and are merchandised exclusively through one retailer's operation. The appeal of this personality's image often leads to the successful sales of the products provided.

Several major retailers have successfully entered into these agreements, capturing the attention of their customers. One of the leaders in this approach is Kmart. Merchandise bearing the Martha Stewart label continues to dominate the bedding and linens departments of their stores. With her unofficial title as guru of good taste, and the attention given to her by the media, her name has instant recognition with the public. Another licensed private label success story at Kmart is the Jaclyn Smith collection. As a former star of the television show *Charlie's Angels*, she continues to capture the attention of those who watched her fame rise. Her signature collection is made up of fashion apparel. Those who admire her appearance and demeanor seem quick to embrace her line of merchandise.

Home Depot is another retailer that has used a licensing agreement to gain exclusive rights to merchandise. Most notably, a large proportion of its paints bear the name of Ralph Lauren. As a top designer, his name quickly spells success for any merchandise with which he is associated.

The advantages of this type of private branding are numerous:

- The merchandise does not require direct design or planning by the retailer as it does in traditional private branding and labeling.
- The advantage of name recognition immediately gives the retailer a selling edge.
- The quality of the merchandise is generally excellent since the celebrity whose name appears on the label doesn't want to ruin his or her reputation.
- A wealth of promotional **point-of-purchase** materials is generally available to use in windows and other visual presentations.
- Personal appearances by the celebrities, if part of the promotional package, guarantee crowds of potential customers.

The only requirement of such exclusivity involves the guarantee by the retailer to use a predetermined amount of goods for the year. Thus, it is the organization that has a vast number of stores in the chain, and the use of other channels such as e-tailing to give broad exposure to the products, that typically benefits from this form of private branding. Companies like Kmart, Wal-Mart, Home Depot, and Target are all excellent candidates for such branding.

PRODUCT DEVELOPMENT

There are many different types of arrangements that retailers use in the acquisition of private labels and brands. In the vast majority of these endeavors, the retailer either produces the designs that ultimately are translated into products, or works with outside resources in their creation. In certain situations, these exclusive merchandise assortments come from intermediary groups such as resident buying offices and retail consulting specialists. Whether it is through **company owned production**, direct purchasing from national manufacturers who produce lines expressly for private label merchants, or acquisition from **private-label developers**, the result is the same. That is, the retailer is afforded the exclusivity of private branding.

Company Owned Production

The giants in the retail industry, especially those that subscribe to the store-is-the-brand philosophy, obtain their products from their own resources. Companies like Gap and Limited, in particular, with a wealth of different divisions requiring a continuous flow of their privately branded merchandise, own their own manufacturing facilities.

Focus on . . .
Mast Industries, Inc.

FOUNDED BY MARTIN AND DENA TRUST in their home in Canton, Massachusettes, in 1970, Mast Industries has gone on to become one of the world's largest contract manufacturer's of men's, women's, and children's apparel. As of 2001, its revenues totalled approximately $13 billion at wholesale, with $2.5 to $3.0 billion at retail.

In 1978, the company was acquired by The Limited, Inc. (now Limited Brands) and today produces the vast majority of the products featured in Limited's retail outlets including The Limited, Express, Express Men's, New York and Company, Henri Bendel, and Bath & Body Works.

Unlike other contractors of the same nature, which are based in only a few countries, Mast Industries has offices in the United States, Hong Kong, Taiwan, Korea, Italy, Portugal, China, Indonesia, Sri Lanka, Egypt, Mauritius, Mexico, and the Philippines. All of the areas of the company, from design to manufacturing to distribution are global. With this organizational structure, Limited is able to control all of the activities involved in the production of private label goods, and bring them to the consumer at the best possible prices. Through the ability to tap the resources in the numerous countries in which they are based, the market demand for quality, quantity, and price are achievable.

With the extent of the globalization of Mast Industries, Limited is assured that on-time delivery will be exactly as needed regardless of unfavorable global events, unanticipated increases in product demand, or material shortages. The depth and breadth of their manufacturing facilities enables them to shift from one venue to another if the need arises.

In order to assure that their company functions at the highest possible level, they have developed a wealth of joint ventures and strategic partnerships. By doing so, through these

Mast initiatives, Limited is able to avail themselves of products that are manufactured in plants that have local involvement. This arrangement is considered by most industry professionals to be the soundest approach to overseas production.

With the seasonal demands of fashion merchandise, and the intensely competitive needs of the retail community in terms of timely, high quality products, Limited's outlets are able to meet these challenges.

Purchasing from Private-Label Developers

Although in-house production affords the retailer many advantages, the route is not necessarily the one used by most retailers. First and foremost in the decision not to proceed in this manner is the size of the vast majority of retail operations. Most are either too small to warrant such privately held facilities, plus the amount of private brands or labels marketed by them are insufficient to maintain such facilities.

An alternative method to private brands and labels is to purchase from vendors who are strictly in the business of producing goods to the retailer's own specifications. Throughout the United States and many countries abroad, a significant number of manufacturers are in business to expressly satisfy the specific needs of retail clients. With input from stores, catalog companies, e-tailers, and the cable TV home shopping channels, these suppliers produce exactly what is required.

One such fashion merchandise company based in New York City is Lizden Industries, Inc. With the help of a well-known designer, Lizden is able to meet the challenges of most retail organizations.

Designers at companies like Lizden, design products for exclusive use by many clients including QVC.

They have access to the world's leading textile mills and production plants, and are able to produce goods that are priced appropriately for their clients. One of their major customers is QVC, for whom they design a variety of products.

Purchasing from National Manufacturers

Throughout the world are numerous manufacturers of a variety of merchandise classifications that primarily produce goods under their own labels. Their primary focus is to promote their own brands and make them household names. While this is their major challenge, some manufacturers also choose to accommodate clients by producing products that do not bear their own labels.

Many manufacturers produce private brands, such as these sports logo products, along with their own lines.

Supermarkets were among the first retail outlets to utilize the services of manufacturers of nationally branded products for their own private brands. They began by purchasing the **overruns** of well-known products, affixing their own labels to give the appearance that they were produced by the retailer itself. Today, many of the supermarket's private brands come not only from these overruns, but as a result of contractual arrangements that have been made with these producers.

More and more retailers of every merchandising classification are opting for well-known manufacturers to produce their goods. Some buy a proportion of their products under the marquee labels, with the remainder produced by these very same companies, except that these items bear the retailer's very own label.

Alternative Private Label and Brand Acquisition

When any of the aforementioned practices are inappropriate for the retailer, there are some other approaches that might be taken to the acquisition of private label merchandise. Specifically, these are through the services of resident buying offices or by way **group purchasing**.

Resident Buying Offices

The largest of these buying offices, the Doneger Group, not only advises clients on manufacturer sourcing and other pertinent information that assists their companies with the right decision making, but also produces collections for clients.

Through their own product developers, the Doneger Group creates styles and silhouettes, complete with the latest in fabrication and color, and contracts with manufacturers to produce them. Using a variety of its own labels such as Lauren Matthews, Complements, and Greg Adams, the company presents the lines to its clients via in-house presentations, brochures, individual meetings, and the Internet. The purchase of these products assures exclusivity within a specific geographic area. That is, each retailer is guaranteed that the line will be his or her's alone, without the fear of any competition.

It should be understood that this acquisition practice doesn't afford the retailer absolute private label merchandise, as in the case when merchants develop their own lines. Instead, it might be considered a semiprivate label, since distribution is limited to only those who maintain noncompeting outlets.

Smaller retailers who are unable to tailor their own private label collections either because of their limited financial resources or their inability to market large quantities often find this alternative plan satisfactory to their needs.

Group Purchasing

In many retail classifications, independent merchants join in **group purchasing** to gain the advantages enjoyed by their large retailer counterparts. That is they pool their orders so that they can gain price advantages as well as other purchasing benefits. An additional practice that some of these buying groups have become involved with is in the private label arena.

With the expenses of developing their own collections shared, smaller retailers are able to get into the business of private label merchandise. They initially meet to discuss the nature of the merchandise that should be produced

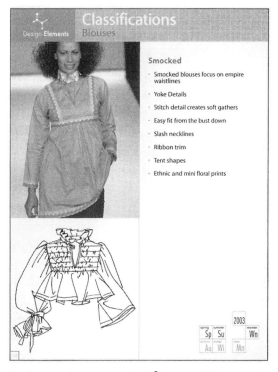

The Doneger Group, through its D3 designs division, develops its own products for retail clients.

exclusively for their use, and then, with this information in hand, employ the services of a designer or product developer to create the products. When the individual items have been evaluated, the line is then edited to include only those that have appeal to the group. The identifying private label is chosen that best reflects the companies that have joined forces in the group venture.

The ultimate step is the selection of contractors who will carry out the production stage. It might be a local manufacturer or one that is based off-shore. As in the case of private label acquisition from resident buying offices, this arrangement assures the participants a degree of exclusivity in their own trading areas.

PROMOTION OF PRIVATE BRANDS AND LABELS

In order to ensure that the consumer is aware of their latest merchandise collections, designers and manufacturers take it upon themselves to make the necessary promotional commitments. Major companies often have their own in-house publicity divisions to undertake these chores, while others opt for the use of public relations firms to do the job. Whatever the situation, the end result, if the campaign is professionally carried out, will be that the public is aware of the product's existence. Labels and brands like Liz Claiborne, Nike, Ralph Lauren, Zenith, Del Monte, and Levi Straus have become household names, and need little attention from retailers to make them known to their customers.

On the other hand, although the advent of private branding and labeling has given the retailer specific merchandising advantages, it doesn't guarantee that the line will achieve consumer recognition. Retailers must be willing to spend significant sums to promote their private labels and brands so that sufficient exposure will be achieved. They use a variety of techniques to publicize their own privately produced merchandise, beginning with its initial introduction and continued awareness by the public. Some of these endeavors include:

- *Advertising campaigns.* There is virtually no better way in which retailers can inform their regular customers and potential purchasers about a private label line of merchandise than through advertising. Generally, a multimedia campaign is developed that encompasses the use of the print and broadcast media. Through newspapers, magazines, television, and radio, a general audience is likely to be reached. For more focused campaigns, direct marketing is often the answer. With their own mailing lists comprised of charge customers, and others purchased from marketing research firms, the retailer is able to get the message across to a specific audience. The key to the effectiveness of these promotional endeavors is continuity. By regular blitzes, a percentage of those exposed to the different media approaches will ultimately be curious enough to find out more about the product line. Potential customers might do this through direct store visits, or perhaps, inquiries on the company's Web site.

Nike has opened giant retail facilities called Niketown to promote its own lines.

- *Stores within the store.* When the goal of the retailer is to maximize exposure to its private collections, it sometimes creates an area called a **store within a store** that seem to be separate and apart from the other departments. These self-contained selling areas are much like those that merchants set aside for their couture collections. Not only do these areas showcase the private brand, but they also give greater importance to the line by moving it from the mainstream of the typical merchandise offerings. Macy's, for example, generated a great deal of interest in one of its private labels, Charter Club, by giving it an appearance of a specialty store within the store.

- *Promotional tools.* The ingenuity of the retailer's in-house staff, and those that come from outside sources, bring forth a variety of giveaways that often leave an indelible impression in the consumer's mind. One of these promotional tools are shopping bags with the name of the new private label conspicuously emblazoned on them. If the bag is especially attractive, and sufficiently sturdy for future use, many people are apt to keep them for long periods of time. Each time they use them, they are actually publicizing the company's name. Other promotional items that continue to serve as reminders to the users are small items such as pens. Every time the writing implement is taken in hand, it serves as a reminder of the new private label.

- *Special events.* A host of different activities, or **special events**, are usually mounted to serve as part of the new label's introduction process. The presentation of a fashion show featuring the new collection may presents a vivid impression of the line. It might be a runway show that will introduce the collection with significant fanfare, or informal modeling for a specific number of days that serves to introduce the products throughout the store. The use of celebrities during the introduction phase could help to generate considerable in-store traffic, and motivate purchasing. One of the ways in which the shopping channels have created consumer interest is by utilizing the services of a personality to motivate buying. QVC and the others have used this promotional tool with great success. The vast majority of the products introduced via this format are new to the public and actually are the end result of the work of designers who create them especially for these programs. They are, in fact, private labels that are not found in any other venues. With a large segment of the population captivated by celebrities, their use could be invaluable in promoting the new private label.

- *Staff training.* While it is desirable to have those responsible for selling the merchandise completely knowledgeable about all of the company's merchandise offerings, it is especially important to make certain that they know the ways in which to help discuss the merits of a new private label. Customers often have questions about the new products, and only if they are satisfied with the answers might they opt to try them. The consumer is fully aware of the benefits of nationally advertised brands, and must be convinced that the company's own brand will satisfactorily meet his or her needs.

- *Visual merchandising.* One of the ways in which brick-and-mortar retailers catch the shopper's attention is through the use of window and interior displays. If carefully conceived, there is no better way in which to silently sell the new in-house brand. Professional visual installations are the motivating tools that can stop passersby, and perhaps sufficiently stimulate them to enter the store for a closer look at the goods. If the department's visual presentation is also carefully developed, it will bring the shopper one step closer to making the purchase.

The promotion of the new private collection is almost as important as the specific products themselves. It is the only way in which retailers can bring these offerings to their clients. They must be able to peak consumer interest, and stimulate them to take a chance on the new items.

WHAT'S IN A NAME?

The name selected for a retailer's own private label is the result of countless hours of brainstorming by the company's top management team, often in conjunction with experts who deal with such matters. For those merchants who subscribe to the store-is-the-brand philosophy, the matter is quite simple. The name of the store and the brand itself are one and the same. For retailers who are introducing a new label into their merchandise mix, the matter is quite different. The new entry must be able to attract enough attention to make it an alternative to what has come from nationally known producers.

Many years ago, when the giants in the retail industry began using privately developed merchandise, they generally identified these items with labels that merely stated it was the store's own brand. While this was an accurate representation of what was being offered, it generally didn't arouse enough curiosity to turn shoppers into buyers. In fact, the impression was that this was actually lesser-quality merchandise, with the only benefit being lower prices.

Merchants were still convinced that the route of private label merchandising was sound, and took another approach to its label identification. They ultimately came to the decision that the new label should have a catchy sound that would exude quality and timeliness. The names used would eventually mirror some of those that were in favor with the consumer.

One of the approaches was to coin names that could be promoted alongside of those that were often internationally recognized. Ralph Lauren, for example, enjoyed a great deal attention from the public with his creative design efforts, as did Calvin Klein and others. Before the era of the name on the label, it was the company signature that was dominant. McGregor, for example, was a well-known label that gave no credit to the designer. Soon the company name was joined by the designer's name on the label, and ultimately it gave way to the listing only of the designer for many collections.

With this in mind, many retailers began to develop their own "names." Macy's, as already discussed, created Christopher Hayes and Jennifer Moore. They quickly created consumer interest and stood on their own as quality lines alongside of those that featured marquee names. In fact, to this vary day, a large percentage of the consuming public is unaware that much of the merchandise they buy is private label.

Another approach in the naming process is to use labels that are reminiscent of the products they represent. Marshall Field's successfully markets some of its own products under the labels Field Gear and Field Sport. The former has been long associated with rugged merchandise while the latter is used for active sportswear.

No matter what labeling decision is made, it must serve the retailer by ultimately establishing itself as a brand among other brands. Except for those consumers bent on purchasing widely acknowledged brands, the key is to offer privately produced products that stand on their own and are identified by labels that the consumer will remember and continue to seek out.

TRENDS FOR THE NEW MILLENNIUM

- The store-is-the-brand concept will continue to expand. Companies like Gap, Limited Brands, Intimate Brands, and others are not only opening brick-and-mortar operations at a record pace, but they are also expanding their online operations.
- A vast majority of department stores are paying closer attention to private labels and will continue to increase the percentages of these items in their merchandise assortments.
- With the success of such names as Martha Stewart on private label collections, more retailers will begin to embrace the licensing concept so that they can use these celebrities' names on their labels.
- The need for the elimination of competition will give rise to the introduction of private brands and labels in every segment of the retail arena.

CHAPTER HIGHLIGHTS

- The vast competition among retailers has caused more and more of them to enter the arena of private brands and labels, thus providing them with more distinctive merchandise.
- Most retailers, especially department stores, have approached private labeling by using these brands as a proportion of their overall inventories.

- Merchandising private label goods is more difficult than merchandising nationally branded goods because the former requires a great deal of development which is not the case for regularly manufactured goods.
- Manufacturer brands afford the retailer immediate exposure to the public, reorder availability, quality assurance, and in some cases, prestige.
- Sears, although one of the earliest entries in private branding, has gone against the tide and is now touting manufacturer brands along with their own store brands.
- The store-is-the-brand concept is used by merchants who exclusively sell their own brands and label them with the company's name. Leaders in this area include Gap, Inc. and Limited Brands.
- The private brand and label approach promotes greater profitability for the retailer, avoids unfair price competition, eliminates purchasing requirements as is typical with manufacturer brands, reduces customer comparison shopping, and ensures product specificity.
- The giants in the private brand arena maintain their own production facilities so that they can control every aspect of the operation and avoid middleman markups.
- Private label goods, when not produced at the company's own plants, come from national manufacturers

who also produce goods to order under the retailer's own labels. Goods also come from producers who are solely in the business of making products for private label clients.

- One way in which smaller retailers may avail themselves of private brands is by purchasing the lines of resident buying offices. These lines are produced expressly for their customers.
- In order to make customers aware of private labels and brands, retailers undertake advertising campaigns, create separate shops within their stores, use a variety of promotional tools, plan special events to draw shoppers, and train their sales associates on the benefits of such products.
- One of the biggest factors in the success of a private label is the name that is given to it. More and more of those who are involved in the concept use names that sound like designers or celebrities as their signatures.
- Some retailers who have the potential to sell enormous quantities of merchandise, such as major value chains, enter into exclusive licensing agreements with celebrities who have merchandise collections bearing their names.

IMPORTANT RETAILING TERMS

marquee labels
signature brands
store-is-the-brand operations
price cutting
manufacturer's brands
private brands and labels
proportional inventory concept
prepacks
comparative shopping
licensing agreements
point-of-purchase
company owned production
private-label developers
overruns

group purchasing
store within a store
special events

FOR REVIEW

1. Why do most retailers primarily stock their inventories with manufacturers' brands?
2. Why can retailers be certain that manufacturers' brands will have the quality assurance expected by consumers?
3. Why is prestige an important motivational factor for some consumer purchases?
4. Which was the first major retailer to use private brand merchandising for appliances?
5. What is meant by proportional use of private labels?
6. How does the store-is-the-brand concept differ from the proportional use of private branding?
7. What are some of the most famous proponents of store-is-the-brand merchandising?
8. Is profitability generally higher or lower for private brands than it is for manufacturers' national brands?
9. Why do merchants who use their own brands avoid price cutting?
10. What is meant by the term prepack assortments?
11. Is customer loyalty more likely to come from private or manufacturer brands?
12. How do licensed private brands differ from those typical of traditional private branding?
13. Which methodology of private brand and label development is the most difficult for the retailer to undertake?
14. What role does a resident buying office play in private labeling and branding?
15. How might group purchasing help small retailers avail themselves of private label goods?
16. Why do some merchants utilize stores within the store for private label offerings?
17. What are some of the typical promotions that retailers use to publicize their own labels?

18. Why is it necessary to train the sales staff in terms of private label benefits?

19. How important is the name that is given to a private label collection?

20. What approach have some major retailers used to give their private brands a designer impression?

AN INTERNET ACTIVITY

Log onto the Web sites of ten major U.S. department stores. Utilizing your favorite search engine, do a search on department stores to locate these web addresses.

Once you have logged on to these sites, research each one to learn whether it identifies merchandise that is its own brands.

Prepare a table to summarize the information you collect. Use the following column heads:

Retailer name	Are private brands identified?	Private brand name

EXERCISES AND PROJECTS

1. Visit five discount or value-oriented retailers in your city for the purpose of determining if they have collections that bear the signatures of celebrities. If you are uncertain about a particular line, ask to speak to a manger to learn if the collection is exclusive to the company. Stores like Wal-Mart, Target, Kmart, Home Depot, and Sears are typically participants in these licensing agreements. Complete a chart with the following headings using the information you have gathered.

Retailer	Signature private label(s)	Merchandise type

2. Contact a major store-is-the-brand retailer for the purpose of determining how they come by their products. (The table in the chapter that lists many of these companies may be used as a guide for finding the one you would like to research.) You may obtain product information either by writing to the corporate headquarters or by logging onto their Web sites. A two-page, typed, double spaced report should be written containing the information you have gathered.

THE CASE OF DETERMINING THE APPROPRIATENESS OF PRIVATE LABELS

Caldwell and Fine is a specialized department store in the northeast that has been in business since 1968. They operate a flagship store and twelve branch stores—all of which are located within a five hundred mile radius of each other. Their forte is high fashion designer apparel for women and men, with a merchandise assortment that includes couture, designer, and bridge collections. Featured among the numerous lines that they carry are internationally known labels as Armani, La Croix, Lauren, DKNY, Versace, and a host of others. Their reputation is flawless, and the store enjoys continued loyalty by their customers.

With the opening of a few off-price merchants near some of their units, and Internet Web sites that feature some of their lines at discounted prices, Caldwell and Fine has begun to hear some complaints from their regular customers in the past two years. In addition, some of the lines they feature, the bridge collections, in particular, were becoming more visible at many of their competitors. The now high visibility of these lines makes them less desirable for Caldwell and Fine customers since they prefer a greater level of exclusivity.

At their last general merchandising meeting, the question of the inclusion of private labels in their assortments came under discussion. With the problems surfacing regarding the proliferation of well-known brands in their trading areas, Janet Rogers, the divisional merchandise manager for women's bridge apparel, suggested that the time was ripe to develop some of their own collections. Philip Rivers, a buyer in that division stressed that their reputation was built on fashion labels that offered prestige to their customers, and perhaps the unbranded offerings would be inappropriate for the company.

After a great deal of discussion, the members of the merchandising team were asked to present their opinions on the possible inclusion of private labels, and how they believed their inclusion would affect overall sales.

Questions

1. If you were a member of the team, would you be in favor of private labels for the store? Defend your answer with sound reasoning.

2. Supposing the decision was for private labels, what proportion of the inventory would you suggest be devoted to this exclusive merchandise? Why?

3. What methodology would you use in the development and acquisition of the private brand?

CHAPTER 13

The Concepts and Mathematics of Merchandise Pricing

After you have completed this chapter, you should be able to discuss:

- ► The way each merchant selects the pricing policy that best addresses his or her business.
- ► How retailers calculate their markups.
- ► The numerous factors that affect the retailer's pricing structure, with special emphasis on competition in the marketplace.
- ► How competition can be eliminated through the use of private label brands and exclusivity arrangements with vendors.
- ► The importance of a retailer's image to pricing decisions.
- ► How pricing strategies run the gamut from keystone pricing to the concept that allows for judgment on every item before it heads for the selling arena.
- ► How merchants select price points or price ranges for their companies so that they better serve the needs of a narrower market segment.
- ► The relationship between markdowns and the original selling price, and why markdowns must be taken to dispose of less desirable merchandise.

After the buyers and merchandisers have completed their purchases, and decided upon the percentage, if any, of private label products, they must properly price the goods to maximize profit. The pricing philosophy is established by the company's management team, and is adhered to by the buyers and merchandisers who must stay within mandated guidelines.

Retail operations utilize pricing procedures that best serve their company's format. For example, the traditional merchant who uses brick-and-mortar outlets for the vast majority of its business generally subscribes to larger markups than its discount or off-price counterpart. No matter what pricing structure is being utilized, it must remain constant so that the consuming public will be able to determine if it is in line with its expectations. Those individuals who frequent the value shopping arenas, for example, want to be assured that the prices charged are rock-bottom. Those who patronize the more traditional venues or luxury stores will be less inclined to care about price, but will more than likely want a wealth of services offered along with the merchandise.

In addition to the overall pricing concept of a company, there are numerous factors that eventually help management determine the actual prices that it will charge their customers. These factors include the competition in the retailer's trading area, the exclusivity of the merchandise, how quickly the merchandise sells (or its turnover rate), the specific characteristics of the merchandise, the promotional endeavors of the organization, its image, the services that are rendered to the clientele, and **inventory shrinkage** due to internal theft and shoplifting.

Once these factors are analyzed, the organization is ready to decide upon the **markup** that will be needed to bring the company the profit it expects to achieve. Of course, as we will learn later in the chapter, not every item that is marked to retail for a particular price actually sells at that price. Often, **markdowns** are needed to dispose of some items because they can't attract customer attention. When these reductions are taken, the retailer is not able to achieve the initial markup that was applied to these goods, but in reality is actually left with a **maintained markup**—the actual markup that has been achieved based upon retail selling prices that were adjusted because of markdowns.

Markup and markdown mathematical computations are easily achieved through the use of computer programs. However, in order to give the reader a better understanding of the concepts, mathematical illustrations are presented here.

MARKUP

Once the merchandise has been purchased, it is necessary for each item to be priced at an amount that will hopefully bring a profit to the company. It begins with the concept of markup, which is the difference between the amount that is paid for the goods by the merchant and the price for which they will be sold to the consumer. It is essential that all of the company's expenses be carefully considered so that the markup will be sufficient to render a profit.

The following illustrates the mathematics of markup:

$$\text{Retail (selling price)} \;-\; \text{Cost} \;=\; \text{Markup}$$

For example, a dress that is purchased by the buyer for $100 and retails for $200 would have a markup of $100.

$$\$200 \,(\text{retail}) \;-\; \$100 \,(\text{cost}) \;=\; \$100 \,\text{markup.}$$

The above illustration addresses the **dollar markup**. In actual practice, retailers utilize a system that focuses on **markup percents** rather than dollar markups. These markup percents may be expressed on either retail or cost.

▓▓▓▓ Markup Percent on Retail

By far, the most widely used markup percent computations are based upon retail. Through the efforts of the National Retail Federation (NRF), the world's largest retail trade association, and numerous research organizations and universities, the markup percent on retail approach has become commonplace.

Markup percent on retail affords these advantages to the retailing community:

- Since sales information is much more easily determined than cost, a markup based on retail greatly facilitates the calculation of the estimated profits.
- Inventory taking requires the calculation of the cost of merchandise on hand. The **retail method of inventory** used by most merchants is based upon markup at retail and provides a shortcut for determining inventory at cost.
- Sales associates' commissions are based on retail as are management's bonuses and other operating data. It is therefore practical to base markup on retail as well.
- When consumers speak of markup, the smaller the markup percent they believe they are paying the better. In pure mathematics, the percent rendered by the retail approach is significantly lower than if it were based on cost. Although this is a psychological matter, it alludes to the fact that the company is working on a lower markup.

To find the markup percent based on retail, the dollar markup, as we saw in the previous illustration, is divided by the retail price.

For example, a pair of athletic shoes costs the retailer $50 and is marked to retail for $100. What is the markup percent based on retail?

For the solution, the dollar markup must first be determined:

$$Markup = Retail - Cost$$
$$Markup = \$100 - \$50$$
$$Markup = \$50$$

To find the markup percent based on retail:

$$\frac{Markup}{Retail} = Markup\ \%\ based\ on\ retail$$

Substituting the numbers:

$$\frac{\$50}{\$100} = 50\%\ based\ on\ retail$$

By using the same dollar markup in the preceding example and the following one, we will be better able to understand the necessity of using the percent method and showing how identical dollar markups bring different returns to the retailer.

In the following illustration, a merchant purchases a set of luggage for $150 and sells it for $200. What is the dollar markup and markup percent based on retail?

To find the dollar markup:

$$Markup = Retail - Cost$$
$$Markup = \$200 - \$150$$
$$Markup = \$50$$

To find the markup percent on retail:

$$\frac{Markup}{Retail} = Markup\ \%\ based\ on\ retail$$

$$\frac{\$50}{\$200} = 25\%\ based\ on\ retail$$

When we compare the two examples, we note that both reward the retailer with $50 markups. However, in the first example, the merchant had to invest only $50 to get the $50 markup, while in the latter, he or she had to invest $150 for the same dollar return. In the former he achieved a markup of 50 percent on retail, while in the latter it was only 25 percent. It is simple to see that the first was far better than the second, further explaining the need to calculate markup percents rather than dollar markups.

Markup Percent on Cost

Although retailers most often use markup on retail, some in the industry rely upon the markup percent on cost computation. Typical of those who use this concept are the purveyors of produce where fruits and vegetable prices vary from day to day, according to the supply and demand of the wholesale market. Under such conditions, where the cost of inventories is relatively unimportant, since they sell out every few days, and the profit and loss figures can be easily determined, the use of markup on cost is preferable. Others merely use the system because they have done so for may years, and find change difficult to address.

For instance, a camera cost the retailer $66 and retails for $88. What is the markup percent based on cost?

To find the solution, first determine the dollar markup.

$$\text{Markup} = \text{Retail} - \text{Cost}$$
$$\text{Markup} = \$88 - \$66$$
$$\text{Markup} = \$22$$

To find the markup based on cost:

$$\frac{\text{Markup}}{\text{Cost}} = \text{Markup \% based on cost}$$

$$\frac{\$22}{\$66} = 33\ 1/3\% \text{ markup on cost}$$

FACTORS THAT AFFECT PRICING

As we have just learned, the retail price of an item is based upon its actual cost from the vendor plus a sufficient markup that will yield a profit after covering the operating expenses of the business. With management's prime responsibility being the maximization of profits to the company, or its principals or shareholders if it is a corporation, appropriate pricing is essential. Care must be exercised by those who have been given the responsibility to run the company, to make certain that they chose the right pricing policy to assure the highest profit margins. This does not by any means warrant unusually high prices, since competition is always a key factor to any retailer's operation. If the prices are too high, consumers will certainly look elsewhere to have their needs satisfied. Understanding this, retailers must choose from a variety of pricing plans that will maximize profits. These plans range from the traditional retailers' approach where relatively high markups are the order of the day since a host of services are offered to the clientele, to the value merchants approach where lower markups are utilized in the hope that larger sales volumes will make up for the lower prices. Of course, there are different alternatives such as those used by prestige retailers where the prices are high because often times their customers are willing to pay for the image that company offers, to the merchants who operate the **wholesale clubs**, and charge less because they obtain a great deal of income from their membership fees.

The Stein Mart Story
Pricing Strategies

THE KEY TO SUCCESS AT STEIN MART is offering customers value for their dollars. While Stein Mart is technically considered to be an off-price retail operation, the store does not merchandise the way most of its counterparts do. About 60 percent of Stein Mart's goods are purchased early in the season.

Stein Mart buyers get a price advantage because they are willing to forgo some of the extras that go into the vendor's regular prices. For example, most suppliers provide advertising and promotional dollars for their accounts, and build in additional markup to allow for retailer chargebacks. By eliminating the need for such costly extras, Stein Mart buyers are able to obtain lower wholesale prices and, in turn, price their merchandise lower than the traditional retail outlets. This pricing strategy allows them to offer better value.

The pricing strategy for the remaining 40 percent of their purchases is the closeout route. Vendors, including marquee types that make up a considerable portion of the Stein Mart inventory, are often left with merchandise at the end of the season that didn't sell. Stein Mart is always ready to purchase these goods as long as they are deeply discounted. The goods can then be retailed at very low prices, bringing excellent markups to the company.

By using these two pricing strategies, Stein Mart is able to deliver quality merchandise at prices that shoppers are willing to pay.

The Buyer's Judgment of the Merchandise's Appeal

If you have ever entered a brick-and-mortar operation, shopped the pages of a catalog, or surfed the Web to make a purchase, occasionally a specific item seemed to reveal it was worth more than its retail price. While this is not a typical occurrence, it does happen. Although the buyer who was given the responsibility to price the goods stayed within the company's overall pricing strategy, he or she missed an opportunity to charge more for the particular item. By having a feel for creative pricing, the buyer might be able to add a few more dollars to the price, giving it the potential for greater profitability. Of course, pricing every piece of merchandise with added markup is not wise since the goods don't always warrant extra dollars.

Prices are often set within specific minimums and maximums. These are in place to help the buyer use his or her own judgment. Being able to charge more for one item leaves room for the buyer to charge less for others that might be used for promotional endeavors. It is really a juggling act, and not one that is based upon automatic markups. It should be understood that a buyer is generally given an **average markup** to achieve. That average markup is based upon his or her entire inventory instead of just one item. If automation were the key to pricing merchandise, then it wouldn't be necessary for retailers to employ individuals who have the instincts necessary to maximize profits. The buyer who has the skills to evaluate each piece of merchandise affords the merchant its greatest potential for profit. It must be remembered that every product that sells for a little more than the traditional markup, helps make the company's maintained markup greater.

The buyer's ability to judge each item's appeal can result in higher markups—and increased profitability—for some items.

Competition

Having established that merchandise judgment is a factor to consider each time a product is being priced, it is also essential to understand that competition in one form or another can always take business away from the merchant. As we are discovering in this new millennium, competition is at an all-time high. Many brick-and-mortar operations within the same classifications, such as the department stores, are often clones of each other. A walk through any of the major department stores quickly reveals Liz Claiborne, Ralph Lauren, and DKNY departments. The offerings are so familiar to the shoppers that they not only come to expect certain styles from them, but they are also aware of the exact prices to expect. Thus, the merchant who is foolish enough to price these collections at higher than traditional markups will certainly be met with customer resistance. A departure from the pricing norm for lines that are available almost everywhere would spell failure.

In order to make certain that the prices being charged for these widely distributed collections are in line with the prices being charged elsewhere requires a careful watch on the competition. It might come by way of a formalized approach that utilizes **comparison shoppers** who go from store to store to check out the competition, or to examine the catalogs and Web sites that feature the same goods. They make notes on the competitor's prices and bring them back to the buyers for further scrutiny.

Allowing their customers to discover identical merchandise at lower price points can cause irreparable harm to the merchant. Although many retailers advertise that they will meet or beat competitors' prices, this practice might encourage customers to shop around, and the retailers might have to reduce the price of some items to make good on their promise.

In an attempt to minimize the effects of widespread competition, more and more retailers are developing their own private brands and labels. With the **exclusivity** factor now a part of the overall merchandising scheme, the merchant may make up for less than expected markups necessitated by the nationally prominent brands. Private label goods are not found anywhere but in the merchant's own premises, catalogs, and Web sites. Companies such as Macy's, Bloomingdale's, Marshall Field's, Dillard's, Belk, and Lord & Taylor continue to increase the proportion of their own brands in the overall merchandise mix. By doing so, they need not fear competitor price cutting.

Exclusivity

One of the ways in which exclusivity is achieved is through the aforementioned private label collections. This, however, is not the only means of stocking an assortment that is solely for a particular company. Often times, relatively unknown manufacturers with limited production capability are eager to sign exclusive agreements for specific geographic trading areas. In this way, the vendor gets the advantage of having his or her lines on the selling floor in quantities and assortments that are generally greater than if the lines were widely distributed. Retailers are often prone to expend significant promotional dollars to sell collections that are theirs alone. Bloomingdale's, and other major department store organizations, are always waiting to discover new designers whose collections can be exclusively theirs.

While it is possible for these lesser-known entities to offer exclusivity, this is not the case for marquee labels. Companies such as Ralph Lauren and Liz Claiborne, for example, will rarely ever grant the rights to a single merchant to solely represent their companies in a particular trading area. They do, however, satisfy some of their better accounts by confining specific groupings within the collections to them. Thus, although the Lauren or Claiborne label is seen in every fashion-oriented department store, certain groups may be seen in just one area. This gives the vendor's most important clients the privilege of a certain degree of exclusivity.

With the knowledge that no other competing merchant may take advantage of competitive pricing, sole rights to particular products sometimes enable the beneficiaries to gain better markups.

Membership Clubs

A growing, value-oriented retail operation is the one that warrants membership before any consumer purchasing may take place. Companies such as Sam's Club, Costco, and B.J.'s are examples of **membership clubs**: Prices at these retailers are affected by the breadth and depth of their membership.

Focus on . . .
Costco

SINCE IT FIRST OPENED IN 1976, in a converted airplane hangar in San Diego, under the Price Club name, Costco has gone on to become the premier wholesale club in many parts of the globe. Its concept is to bring members the lowest possible prices on quality, brand-name products. It provides a wealth of different types of merchandise that includes, but is not restricted to packaged and fresh foods, electronics, giftware, jewelry, accessories, automotive supplies, and wines.

It began as a company that only served small businesses, but soon recognized that by expanding its customer base to nonbusiness members, it could achieve significantly better buying clout. In 1993, Price Club and Costco merged and generated $16 billion in annual sales. At the present time, Costco operates more than 350 warehouses around the world.

It is interesting to note that the prices charged at Costco are considerably less for identical merchandise found in other operations. While the enormous volume it enjoys certainly contributes to its ability to sell for less, that is not the only key to its pricing strategy. The cost of each membership, $45 annually at the time of this writing, allows Costco to minimally markup the goods offered for sale. If there wasn't any profit reaped from the sale of these items, the membership dollars alone would bring in sufficient revenue to turn a handsome profit for the company. By simply multiplying the $45 by the many millions of members it serves around the world, one can easily understand the nature of Costco's pricing structure. The single most important factor that affects its pricing is the membership fee.

Of course, the retail price charged for each item is above Costco's wholesale cost. The fee simply allows for a lower markup making it highly competitive with other merchants.

While price is certainly the single most important factor to the success of the company, Costco also provides other services to maintain a satisfactory relationship with its customers. The company provides real estate services, mortgage services, long-distance phone programs, check printing, auto sales, travel arrangements for all members, and special services to its executive members, including 2 percent savings on purchases up to $500, business payroll processing, business equipment leasing, small business loans, business credit card processing, and health care programs.

But above all, it is the pricing of its offerings that brings the consuming public and business enterprises to Costco.

The Nature of the Goods

Different types of merchandise require different pricing considerations based upon their characteristics. Some, for example, plague the retailer with a certain degree of perishability, as is the case of fashion merchandise, while others require a great deal of security to safeguard them from shoplifters, as is the case with precious jewelry. Due to the nature of these classes of goods, they typically require higher markups.

Fashion Merchandise

The typical culprit in this product classification is women's apparel and accessories. Rarely does a specific item successfully transcend the seasons. While some styles gain immediate success and account for significant sales, others are not as readily accepted by the consumer. Even in the cases where early acceptance has taken place, there always seems to

Markups on short-lived fashion products are normally high to compensate for end-of-season markdowns.

be end-of-season leftovers that need to be marked down to make way for the newer fashions.

In order to make certain that these short-lived styles help the retailer to maximize profits, it is essential that the initial retail price be sufficiently marked up. That is, a larger amount must be added to the wholesale price to make sure that when the markdowns are taken at season's end, a certain degree of profitability will be maintained.

When merchandise of this nature is contrasted with the staples that many retailers stock in their inventories, it is apparent that the latter classifications are more likely to bring steady sales at the initially marked prices.

The business of fashion merchandise is a risky one. Retailers must always be prepared for the choices that their buyers have made to fail to attract customers. It might be the right silhouette but the wrong color, or the right color but the wrong fabric. In terms of pricing, these fashion-oriented goods must be marked up as high as the competition will allow. When the figures are in, the winner's revenues should make up for the purchasing errors.

Seasonal Merchandise

Products that last for only a short selling period due to their seasonal nature, must, as in the case of fashion items, be sufficiently priced to make up for the inevitable markdowns at the end of the selling season. It might be swimsuits, raincoats, snow boots, or any other items that fall into the short-lived categories. Like their fashion product counterparts, they must be disposed of at season's end to make room for the newly expected merchandise. One might assume that the unsold seasonal, as well as fashion items, could be stored and carried over to the next year, but with the numerous design changes that regularly take place, this is risky business. Also negating the carry-over concept is the cost of warehousing. Retailers do not have the storage space necessary to stock merchandise for long periods of time.

The raincoat buyer may be plagued with a limited amount of rainfall in the spring, a time when rainwear sales generally peak; the swimwear buyer may be confronted with cool and rainy summer months; and the skiwear merchants may be deluged with large inventories due to lower than expected precipitation. It is only then when higher markups can be appreciated. Adding additional dollars on to the initial selling price allows for markdowns that will hopefully move the slow sellers and still bring something of a profit to the company. If lower retail prices were affixed to these items, the end results would be disastrous.

Perishable Merchandise

While the aforementioned seasonal products do bear a degree of perishability, others pose even greater risks to the merchants who sell them. One of the prime examples of **perishable merchandise** is fresh cut flowers. Florists must deal with time frames that are as brief as a few days in this type of retailing. Once the rose has faded, it is no longer salable. Thus, products of this nature must be priced to take into consideration that not everything will sell. A high markup will offset the losses.

Whether it is farm produce, or fresh baked breads and pastries, their appeal is extremely short lived. Unlike the leftover fashions that may be marked down to encourage purchasing, these goods are often tossed into refuse containers. Their sellers must make certain that the items are sufficiently priced to offset the inevitable markdowns.

Bulky Merchandise

Of particular importance in this category is furniture, carpeting, and rugs. Because of their size and the space they warrant either in warehouses or on the selling floor, their merchandising necessitates higher markups. They must be priced so that this additional expense can be offset by higher markups.

Precious Jewelry

One of the cost factors that must be considered in the pricing of gemstones and precious metals is security. Since these items must be carefully secured and safeguarded from would-be shoplifters, state-of-the-art alarm systems are put in place. Not only is this a necessity as understood by the retailer, but it is also a condition of most companies that insure this precious merchandise.

In addition to the security systems that protect the showcases in which the items are displayed, large tamper-proof vaults are maintained for storage at the end of the selling day. Merchants regularly remove their goods from the selling floor and place them in these vaults for safekeeping.

These protection costs are significant and must be considered when the merchandise is being priced. Hence, precious jewelry requires markups that are higher than most other goods.

Stock Turnover

As we learned in Chapter 11, Buying at Home and Abroad, the number of times an inventory totally sells out during the year is a major factor for the retailer. The standard rule that is addressed by the buyers who determine retail prices is as follows:

The higher the turnover rate, the lower the markup; the lower the turnover rate, the higher the markup.

Thus, fresh baked rolls, which generally sell out every day, require a low markup to be considered profitable. On the other hand, diamonds, because of their high prices, turn over at a low rate, requiring a larger markup.

Retailer Promotional Endeavors

Today's competitive environment necessitates a considerable amount of promotion whether it is at the brick-and-mortar operations, in catalogs, or on the Internet. Merchants must set aside large sums for advertising campaigns, as well as special events that bring attention to their businesses. Whether it is the use of the print or broadcast media, or the development of special promotions such as fashion shows, the costs of such involvement are spiraling upward. While these expenses must be taken into account by the retailer when selling prices are being established, it should be understood that successful promotion also helps to generate more business, often enabling the retailer to be more profitable.

In any case, the promotional budgets must be carefully considered when merchandise is being priced. The cost of the advertising and special events must be included in determining what prices must be charged in order to maximize profits.

Company Image

Although there is a major trend for the new millennium that focuses on value shopping, not every segment of the population patronizes a merchant because of the lowest selling price. In fact, there is also a trend in which more and more **prestige retailers** are cropping up throughout the country.

Designer shops like Louis Vuitton mark up their merchandise at higher percentages than value retailers do because they know their customers are willing to pay high prices for prestige items.

As we look to places like New York City's Fifth Avenue and Palm Beach, Florida's Worth Avenue, we notice a wealth of new retailers whose business centers on high-profile merchandise. Designer shops, along with companies like Nordstrom and Neiman Marcus, are undergoing extensive expansions to capture the market motivated by labels that at once bring image to the forefront. That is not to say this group of retailers do not bring quality along with their prestigious labels. They do indeed, but at the same time, they add yet another dimension that stimulates purchasing.

Just as the designer logos became commonplace on the outside of apparel and accessories in the 1970s and '80, so have the image-building retailers. This phenomenon has enabled many merchants to use higher markups for their products. A few extra dollars might not bring the shopper a different item from what is available elsewhere for less, but it affords them the opportunity to bring prestige to their dress.

It is the retailer who early on must establish this prestige image if it is to successfully merchandise its inventories with higher markups, just as its value-oriented counterparts must promote their discount and off-price images from the outset.

Services

The more services afforded the consumer, the more likely it will be reflected in the price. As we note by shopping in the stores, through catalogs, or online, multichannel retailers offer about the same services in each of their selling formats. For example, brick-and-mortar operations might offer free alterations and companies such as Levi's feature "made to measure" jeans to their customers.

Whether it is alterations, concierge services, personal shoppers gift registries, or any other service, they all come at additional expense to the merchant. While these services do attract customers, the expenses attributed to these offerings must be considered when selling prices are established. Customers who frequent the service-oriented merchants are often willing to pay the little extra that is being charged to make their shopping experience more pleasurable.

The extra services offered to customers in stores like this fashionable Hong Kong shop often necessitate higher markups.

Pilferage

Shoplifting and internal theft, also known as **pilferage**, are among the most troubling factors to plague retailers. Naturally, brick-and-mortar merchants bear the brunt of the problem since they are the only retailers who have on-premises customers. This is not to say that catalog and e-tail divisions do not have problems with internal theft or losses due to unscrupulous online purchasers. In any case, the pilferage figures continue to climb. As we learned in Chapter 7, Loss Prevention, more and more state-of-the-art systems are being installed to help reduce the problems. Nonetheless, the losses must in some way be made up. To this end, merchants find that they must consider their pilferage rates in their markups, and ultimately in the prices they charge. The result is that honest consumers pay more in order to make up for these losses.

PRICING STRATEGIES

Before any retail operation gets off the ground, attention must be focused on the company's pricing strategy. Each merchant must consider all of the available approaches and decide upon the best one to satisfy the company's needs. Some of the strategies include keystone pricing, keystone plus pricing, overall uniform pricing, department pricing, individual merchandise pricing, negotiable pricing, and average pricing. Each can stand on its own merits and can be utilized to maximize the company's profits.

Keystone Pricing

Perhaps the simplest method for determining the selling price is through the use of **keystone pricing**. Retailers who subscribe to this strategy merely double the wholesale cost to determine the retail. Thus, if a product costs $25 it will be automatically marked $50. In many retail operations this approach covers the organization's expenses and brings the expected profit.

Keystone Plus Pricing

Similar to keystone pricing, **keystone plus pricing** takes the concept one step further. In cases where doubling the cost doesn't provide for sufficient expense coverage and shortfalls in profit, an additional amount is added to arrive at the selling price. For example, a merchant might double the cost and add an additional 10 percent. In this situation, a product that costs $25 would carry a retail price of $55. First, the cost ($25) is doubled ($50). Then an additional 10 percent ($50 $\times$ .10 $=$ $5) is added for a selling price of $55.

Overall Uniform Pricing

Overall uniform pricing is the strategy used most often by off-price retailers. They do not necessarily look at specific merchandise classifications to make their pricing decisions, but treat all of the purchases as one. Thus, if it is determined that a 48 percent markup will bring the best results to the company, every individual item is marked up exactly that amount. It is a simple, straightforward method that doesn't require any decision making.

Department Pricing

In most retail organizations, merchandise assortments are segmented according to the departments in which they will be displayed and sold. Full-line department stores, for example, feature a wealth of hard goods and soft goods, with each department called upon to utilize a specific markup formula. The reason why **department pricing** is prevalent in this type of retailing is that some departments, because of competition from the **big box operations**, must price their products to stay competitive. In the selling of appliances, department stores, for example, must be able to compete with the prices being charged by the likes of Best Buy. Other departments within the same organization need not worry about this value pricing and are able to achieve higher markups on those items. Thus, when departments have their own pricing goals, they are able to bring the highest possible profit to their company.

Individual Merchandise Pricing

The ingenuity of pricing is often left to the discretion of the buyer. This is known as **individual merchandise pricing**. He or she is given a markup goal to maintain, but is left to decide which merchandise should be marked up lower than usual, which should take advantage of higher markups, and which should be priced according to traditional practices.

Bearing in mind the optimal markup, the buyer considers such factors as the appearance of the goods, the competition for such products, and the exclusivity factor in creative pricing. When merchandise comes to the selling floor premarked by the vendor, few adjustments can be made. Hence, by working on lower than the typical prices, the buyer might increase sales volume, or by gaining the additional markup, more dollars may be used to offset markdowns. It should be remembered that individual pricing is only successful if the buyer has a complete understanding of the marketplace and the competition.

Negotiable Pricing

Negotiable pricing, the practice of the consumer being able to negotiate a price that is different from the asking price, is not commonplace in the United States except at automobile dealerships and jewelry stores.

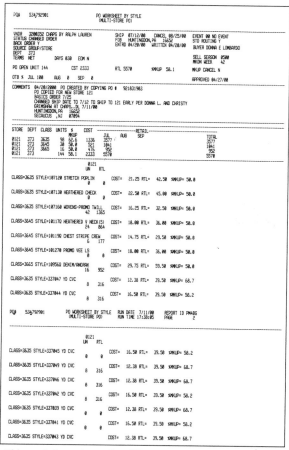

This worksheet shows that different styles command different markups.

While in many countries throughout the world such as China haggling is expected, Americans have come to understand that the price on the item is the price that must be paid.

An Ethical Consideration

A CUSTOMER ENTERING AN AUTOMOBILE SHOWROOM is often able to negotiate a price that is lower than the asking price. The better the negotiator, the better the price! Although this has become standard practice, the ethics of the technique are questionable. Why should an individual who hasn't mastered the art of negotiation pay more than someone who has?

Often, dealers have legitimate reasons for negotiating—a trade-in of the customer's old car, a large down payment, or the purchase of a car at the end of the season. However, retailers who abuse this pricing technique are doing a disservice to their customers. Not only is it unethical, but it can cause a lack of trust by the public. If after paying a certain price for an automobile, one was to learn that someone else paid less at the same dealership for the identical car under identical circumstances, his or her business can be lost to the company forever. It is bad business and could hamper profits in the future.

Average Pricing

It is the goal of the retailer to make certain that an optimum markup is achieved when the entire inventory is considered. No system is better than any other. Its imperative, however, that **average pricing** goal is met. By averaging all of the markups that have been applied, the result must be the one that produces the greatest revenue for the company. It involves careful planning, teamwork, and experience to bring this pricing to fruition.

PRICE POINTS

Just about every retail organization restricts its offerings to specific **price points** or **price lines**. That is, the range of prices charged by a company must not be at every level, but at some established level that has been determined by management. Few brick-and-mortar operations, or for that matter catalogs and Web sites, attempt to make their merchandising appeal at every price point.

The reasons for this restrictive measure are many, including the following:

- The size of the store generally limits the depth and breadth of price points within the merchandise classification.
- Goods in the same overall classification that are at opposite ends of the pricing spectrum generally require different visual merchandising approaches.
- Upper and lower price points require different types of merchandising strategies.
- By remaining with a particular price range, the customers are more likely to know what the company is offering before entering the store, examining its catalogs, or logging on to Web sites. In the brick-and-mortar operations, in particular, the overcrowding of a selling floor with shoppers who, because of the prices, will not buy, makes the environment one that is less desirable for those who are apt to be the purchasers.
- Easier purchase planning for the buyer. Since wholesale markets and merchandise collections are segmented according to price points, the necessity to cover many becomes time consuming and might warrant additional buyers for each range. Thus, the expenses of the company will be adversely affected.

Bearing all of this in mind, it is necessary to carefully determine the outside merchandise parameters in terms of pricing. That is not to say that a single price is the only one to consider, but a range that addresses the needs of the company. In cases where the same merchandise classification has a wide span, the company must separate the goods according to prices. In women's apparel, for example, a major department store might feature separate departments with each concentrating on its own price points. Typically, the costliest items would be in the couture area. The designer department would follow, with bridge merchandise next according to price, better as the designation that carries more moderate priced goods, and budget for the lowest price points.

In this way, customers are made aware that a wealth of different price points are available under one roof and that each will offer the necessary assortment to satisfy their needs.

In more specialized companies, there is generally only a single price point that is merchandised. Anyone entering the doors of The Limited or Banana Republic knows exactly what the price ranges will be. The popularity of the specialty chain underscores the practicality of limited price points and its inherent success in getting its products into the hands of the consumer.

MARKDOWNS

No matter how carefully the buyers and merchandisers plan their purchases, there are always some items that do not sell as well as had been expected. Whatever the reasons for their inability to attract customer attention, they must be disposed of in order to make room for new products. Markdowns, or reductions in the selling price, are the ways in which these items are sold.

Markdown Causes

The reasons for the failure of these items to bring the expected sales results are many and include buying errors, poor selling techniques, inadequate visual presentation, insufficient promotional endeavors, initial prices that were inappropriate, adverse weather conditions, and poor fit with the merchandise assortment.

Buying Errors

It is the professional buyers and merchandisers who are charged with the responsibility of stocking their inventories with the best merchandise that is available in the marketplace. These seasoned professionals utilize a wealth of internal and external sources of information before they make the buying decisions. Even with these preplanning procedures, errors are still made. It is safe to say that no amount of forecasting will guarantee success.

One of the errors that is often attributed to these professional purchasers includes **overbuying**. At the beginning of the season, especially in fashion merchandise, there is often an indication of a particular style or color that is expected to result in significant sales. In an industry where reorders of **hot items** are often slow in coming, some buyers try to anticipate the customers' reactions to such products and sometimes purchase more than they normally would so that their inventories will be adequately stocked to meet the anticipated demand. If the sales are significant, the buyer is a hero. However, if, sales do not materialize as planned, the markdown route is inevitable.

Where the merchandise is not fashion-oriented or seasonal, there is little need to dispose of it very quickly. **Staples**, or items that regularly sell throughout the year, will ultimately sell, making it unnecessary to take markdowns. Once the inventory of these slow sellers dissipates, they may be replaced with other items.

Another approach that could be troublesome, and lead to price reductions, is reordering too late in the selling season. When a particular style becomes a **runner**, there is temptation to continue it in the merchandise assortment as long as possible. With it being difficult to predict when customer interest will wane, sometimes the last shipments arrive too late, and must be disposed of via the markdown route.

Poor Selling Techniques

One of the problems that continue to plague retailers is poor selling. Many retailers do not adequately prepare their sales associates to handle the questions posed by would be purchasers and neglect to teach them the fundamentals of successful selling. When shoppers walk through the sales floors of many of America's leading retailers, they are often ignored by the sales associates. The mere presence of someone in the store is generally an indication that he or she is in the market to make a purchase. Even when there is a sales associate present, poor training may prevents him or her from bringing a sale to fruition. There might be an "I don't care" attitude or one that is too overbearing. While these are two extremes, the result is often the same—the shopper leaves the store without making a purchase.

Selling is required not only at brick-and-mortar operations. Catalog customers and e-tail shoppers sometimes also need to be sold a product. When a catalog order is being placed, often times there are questions that need answering before the transaction is completed. Without answers, the sale could be lost. Similarly, shopping on a Web site is not always automatic. Browsers may need to have certain concerns addressed in order for them to make the purchase. Many Web sites have interactive capabilities so that such problems can be handled and sales will be made.

Inadequate Visual Presentation

Even the best merchandise requires high level visual presentation if the company is to maximize its sales potential. Companies like Crate & Barrel, Pottery Barn, and Williams Sonoma continue to grow not only because of the products they feature but because of the manner in which they are visually merchandised. The merchant who fails to feature items in their best settings, risks shoppers bypassing them.

These visual presentations must be presented in outside show windows and in interior areas in a manner that motivates the passersby to make closer inspections. It is these silent sellers that often make or break the sale. In Chapter 15, Visual Merchandising, attention will focus on how retailers use these display techniques to their best advantage.

Insufficient Promotional Endeavors

Whether it is the use of advertising or a special event, sufficient dollars must be budgeted so that maximum exposure to the product will be the result. Today, with operational expenses at an all-time high, many merchants try to make up their costs by reducing the monies needed to promote their products. This is a shortsighted approach in retailing. At a time when competition is extremely fierce, it is the promotional endeavors that can bring the merchant's products to the customer's attention.

Inappropriate Initial Prices

When an overzealous buyer tries to capture early sales, he or she is sometimes likely to apply an extra markup. The thought is that early in the season shoppers are more willing to spend a little extra to get the latest merchandise. Of course, if the competition's prices for the identical merchandise are lower, the results could be disastrous. Not only may customers become wary of the store's higher prices, but the store could lose its patrons.

The result is often to take markdowns, making the products less profitable. High opening prices should be avoided unless the merchandise is private label or part of an exclusivity plan that the buyer has arranged with the vendor. In any case, it is risky business.

Adverse Weather Conditions

When the merchandise is of a seasonal nature, and its sale is dependent upon certain weather characteristics, any deviation from the norm can play havoc on the retailer. In the case of swimsuits, for example, a rainy summer could spell disaster. Similarly, a mild winter could reduce the demand for outerwear.

These conditions are no fault of the buyer. He or she must take the risks involved with such merchandise purchases or be caught short if the season's weather is typical. When the weather doesn't cooperate, the markdown route is inevitable.

Inappropriate Placement in the Assortment

As we have learned in Chapter 11, Buying at Home and Abroad, the buyer carefully plans the model stock to make certain that it contains the elements to make the selling season a successful one. The products that have been assembled bear some cohesiveness, whether it is style, price point, color, or size. Sometimes, a buyer will stray from this preplanned assortment and be tempted to bring in a few items that do not necessarily fit with the remainder of the inventory. It is these items that can be rejected by the customers. Unless there is some evidence that these items will tempt the shoppers to buy, their inclusion on the selling floor should be avoided. It might be a price point that is atypical of the other goods, a color that doesn't work with the rest of the palette, or a style that doesn't fit with the others.

Timing Markdowns

No matter what the cause of the markdown, it is necessary to determine when it is appropriate to take the reduction. As we learned earlier, it is generally unwise to carry the unsold goods to the next season, thus making the markdown the only viable way of its disposal.

When to take the actual markdown is a matter of concern for all retailers. Traditionally, the markdown periods have been around the fourth of July and after Christmas. Although most stores no longer use this time frame as a hard-and-fast rule, some do. Nordstrom, for example, especially in its men's department utilizes the semiannual approach. Others, including department stores and specialty chains resort more and more to reducing the prices of slow sellers after they have failed to bring positive results. It might be just a matter of a month or so that will warrant the markdown.

Early markdowns are favored by some because of the following:

- The selling season may still be at its peak, providing the retailer with a wealth of shoppers.
- The revenues obtained from these sales can be used to purchase other goods that might be better received by the consumer.
- The selling floor is emptied of slow movers, making room for new items.

Later markdowns also have their proponents, including the following:

- When markdowns are taken during the selling season, shoppers often learn when this will happen and wait for the reductions. This was a serious problem for Macy's during the 1980s when the Wednesday in the middle of the month was used for special sales events. Many customers waited until these days to make their purchases, thus affecting other shopping days.

- While waiting for merchandise to catch fire, it does sometimes take longer than expected. If this is the case, the early markdown will hamper profits.
- Some merchants, especially those with prestigious images, such as Nordstrom's, feel that the presence of markdown racks transforms their stores into places where value shoppers will make the shopping experience for their regulars less appealing.

Filene's Basement initiated the automatic markdown system, one way to sell off slow-moving merchandise.

Automatic Markdowns

Although the concept of **automatic markdowns** is not widespread, it does have a place in retailing. Most notably, Filene's Basement, who initiated the concept, and Syms, who has used it in its women's department, has made it work successfully.

The idea is to turn the merchandise as quickly as possible without day-to-day input from the merchandisers.

Focus on . . .
Filene's Basement

THE CONCEPT OF AUTOMATIC MARKDOWNS took place in the basement of Filene's department store in Boston, Massachusetts, in 1909. The idea was Edward A. Filene's way to rid the company of excess merchandise in the department store. Using the basement as his arena for these slow sellers and after-season leftovers, he priced everything to sell quickly, in fact, in a matter of 30 days.

Goods that came to the basement were attractively priced for this quick disposal. After a couple of weeks, if the goods still remained, the price was automatically reduced by 25 percent. The price was systematically lowered each week until the product was sold. In the event that there were no takers at the end of 30 days, leftover merchandise was donated to charity. With the success of the quick disposal of the merchandise from the upstairs store, other retailers and manufacturers soon joined the bandwagon and started bringing their unsold goods to Filene's. It is not unusual to see end-of-season inventories from prestigious retailers such as Neiman Marcus gracing the Basement's selling floor. Many consider this to be the birth of off-price retailing. Although it took 10 years for the Basement to operate in the black, it eventually went on to be one of the more profitable operations in retail history.

The popularity of the Boston operation can best be appreciated by the fact that it is considered to be the city's second most popular attraction. It is shopped by some 15,000 to 20,000 people a day. Its colorful history has made shopping there part art form and part sporting event. Shoppers line up before dawn for special sales, they engage in tug-of-war contests over merchandise, and some even try clothes on in the aisles. Celebrities often visit the store when they are in Boston.

Today Filene's Basement stores carry on the tradition in other cities. These stores operate under different management from the original Filene's Basement. Still, the lower level at the Boston store generates excitement for its faithful followers.

Determining the Markdown

The specific reductions that are taken by retailers to rid themselves of the unwanted goods are by no means uniform in the industry. Some believe in the concept of starting with a small markdown, such as 20 percent, and then waiting until sales falter to proceed to additional markdowns, continuing until the inventory is disposed of. Others are of the mind that it is better to drastically slash prices—say by 40 percent—so that quicker disposal of goods is accomplished.

It should be understood that minimal reductions in the selling price, such as 10 percent rarely motivate shoppers to buy merchandise that otherwise wouldn't interest them.

Whichever approach is taken, it is a general rule that not every item in the inventory is marked down, only those that need a little extra enticement. Some companies that wait for season's end to announce their clearances follow the concept that reduces the entire inventory in one felt swoop. The key to the success of any of these plans is to understand the needs of the retailer's clientele.

Markdown Recap Moderate/Better Collections

Month: Feb-2002

Dept.	Plan	First	Second	Third	POS	MUC	MKU/MKDR	Total
370	47.5	0.0	41.8	0.1	5.0	0.0	-1.6	45.3
373	115.5	77.2	26.9	1.3	0.0	0.0	-1.5	103.9
374	48.7	10.7	15.2	0.0	0.0	0.0	0.0	25.9
376	19.9	40.7	0.0	1.4	1.0	0.1	-1.3	41.8
Total	231.6	128.6	83.9	2.8	6.0	0.1	-4.4	216.9

This markdown recap form reviews markdowns by department.

```
DEPT: 370                          PRICE MANAGEMENT FACILITY                                    PMF65000
                        PRICE CHANGE ID: 9950015001194442 PERM MKD RELEASED          RUN DATE: 07/24/2001
                                                                                     RUN TIME: 14:12:52
EFFECTIVE: 05-30-2000 00:00:00  EXPIRATION 12-31-9999 23:59:00                        PAGE:       1

DESCRIPTION:  BUNGALOW BRAND TO 25% OFF SELECT STYLES




PARTICIPANTS: 0210


                                                          CURRENT   NEW                  TOTAL   TOTAL
CLASS  NUMBER   DESCRIPTION   NUMBER    DESCRIPTION   COLOR SIZE  PRICE  PRICE  ADJUSTMENT  UNITS   IMPACTS
3517  3200705  BUNGALOW/VIEWPO BK3845  PRINTED WOVEN              38.00  27.99    0.00      619    6196.19
3517  3200705  BUNGALOW/VIEWPO BK3846  PRINTED WOVEN              38.00  27.99    0.00      142    1421.42

                                           SUBTOTAL PRICE CHANGE IMPACT:                   761    7617.61

3521  3200705  BUNGALOW/VIEWPO BK2066  SCREEN TEE                20.00  14.99    0.00      456    2284.56
3521  3200705  BUNGALOW/VIEWPO BK2072  SCREEN TEE                20.00  14.99    0.00       50     250.50

                                           SUBTOTAL PRICE CHANGE IMPACT:                   506    2535.06

3528  3200705  BUNGALOW/VIEWPO BK2063  PRINTED OTTOMAN           38.00  27.99    0.00      418    4184.18

                                           SUBTOTAL PRICE CHANGE IMPACT:                   418    4184.18

                                       GRAND TOTAL PRICE CHANGE IMPACT:                   1685   14336.85
```

The price change printout shows the impact of markdowns on selected items.

▨▨▨ Markdown Percent Calculations

Today's computer programs enable retailers to reprice merchandise very quickly. With the simple entry of the appropriate numbers, the results are easily calculated. It is necessary not only to compute the actual reduction but to also figure the markdown percent based upon sales.

The following example, however, simplifies the computational aspect of markdowns, and shows exactly how it works.

A merchant determines that with sales far behind projections for the shoe department, it makes sense to mark down the entire footwear inventory by 30 percent. What is the markdown percent based on sales, assuming that all of the $100,000 inventory sells?

1. The dollar markdown must be determined.

$$\text{original retail} \times \text{reduction percent} = \text{markdown}$$
$$\$100,000 \quad \times \quad .30 \quad = \quad \$30,000$$

2. The actual sales are next determined.

$$\text{original retail} \times \text{reduction} = \text{new retail}$$
$$\$100,000 \quad - \quad \$30,000 \quad = \quad \$70,000$$

3. The markdown percent on sales is then determined.

$$\text{Markdown \%} = \frac{\text{Markdown}}{\text{Sales}}$$

$$\text{Markdown \%} = \frac{\$30,000}{\$70,000}$$

$$\text{Markdown \%} = 42.86\%$$

It should be understood that this is an extremely simplified illustration since it is virtually impossible for the retailer to sell the entire inventory and be left with nothing, no matter how drastic the markdown might be.

More involved calculations address what percent of the inventory sells and at what percents.

TRENDS FOR THE NEW MILLENNIUM

- In general, retailers continue to use larger markups in order to cover their ever-increasing operating expenses.
- More and more merchants are using private brands and labels as a means of dealing with the competition and enabling them to increase their overall profit margins.
- The continuous battle with internal and external pilferage will continue to result in higher markups so that the losses can be somewhat recovered.
- Except for a few diehards, the vast majority of retailers are resorting to markdown plans that address immediate needs rather than waiting for the traditional end-of-the-season time periods.

CHAPTER HIGHLIGHTS

- Markup is the difference between the retailer's cost and selling price, and may be figured as either a percent of retail or cost.
- The factors that affect the ultimate retail prices are numerous and include the buyer's judgment of the item's appeal, competition, the degree of exclusivity of the merchandise assortment, the nature of the goods, and the potential stock turnover rate.
- With the use of private brands and labels, retailers can pay less attention to competition than with products that are widely distributed.
- A company's image can contribute to the eventual prices it charges. Prestigious companies, for example, may take advantage of their name to charge higher prices while value merchants such as the discounters and off-pricers will charge lower prices.
- Since operating costs continue to escalate, many merchants are using larger markups than ever before in their histories to cover these expenses.
- Price points or ranges are essential in retailing in that the merchant can concentrate on a narrower wholesale market and tailor its operation to address this restricted price point.
- Markdowns are essential to moving slow sellers out of the inventory. By doing this, retailers are able to use the monies to buy new merchandise and to make room for incoming purchases.
- It is generally considered poor business practice to carry merchandise over to the next year since customers' needs usually change.

IMPORTANT RETAILING TERMS

inventory shrinkage

markup

markdown

maintained markup

dollar markup

markup percents

retail method of inventory

wholesale clubs

average markup

comparison shoppers

exclusivity

membership clubs

perishable merchandise

prestige retailers

pilferage

keystone pricing

keystone plus pricing

overall uniform pricing

department pricing

big box operations

individual merchandise pricing

negotiable pricing

average pricing

price points

price lines

overbuying

hot items

staples

runner

automatic markdowns

FOR REVIEW

1. What do consumers who patronize the more traditional types of retailers, and often pay full price for their goods, expect from the merchant in return for these higher prices?

2. What is the formula for dollar markup, and what does each of the three aspects of the calculation stand for?

3. Why do the vast majority of today's merchants use the markup percent based on retail concept?

4. How can the buyer's ability to judge the merchandise he or she has purchased affect the price the consumer will be charged?

5. Why does competition play such an important role when it comes to merchandise pricing?

6. In what way can a retailer avoid the pitfalls of competitive pricing?

7. What does the term *exclusivity* mean in retail merchandising, and how can it help the buyer achieve a higher than typical markup?

8. Which product classifications cause the retailer the most difficulty when it comes to pricing?

9. Can adverse weather conditions hamper the sale of merchandise? Give several examples.

10. Why does precious jewelry often warrant unusually high markups?

11. Does the retailer's image ever contribute to its pricing policy?

12. How does internal and external theft contribute to a company's pricing policy?

13. What is meant by keystone pricing? In what way is keystone plus pricing different?

14. How does average pricing differ from overall uniform pricing?

15. What is meant by the term *price points*?

16. Why is it necessary for retailers to maintain price points?

17. Can markdowns be avoided in dealing with fashion merchandise? Why?

18. What are some of the causes of markdowns?

19. When is the best time for retailers' to markdown their less desirable goods?

20. Under what circumstances is it appropriate to carry fashion merchandise from one season to the next?

AN INTERNET ACTIVITY

Using your favorite search engine, log on to a number of retail Web sites and determine whether or not they promote price in their online presentations. You should select three department stores such as Marshall Field's or Macy's, three off-pricers such as Burlington Coat Factory, Stein Mart, or Marshalls, and three specialty stores such as Gap or Banana Republic. Prepare your report in chart form with the following headings:

Company Name	Web site	Retail Classification	Emphasis on Price

EXERCISES AND PROJECTS

1. Plan a visit to three fashion-oriented brick-and-mortar operations for the purpose of determining whether they charge the manufacturer's list price. Often times, well-known vendors such as Perry Ellis, Liz Claiborne, Ralph Lauren, Jones New York, and others include their own price tags on the merchandise. Sometimes the retailers follow this price while at other times feature prices that are lower. Complete a chart with headings as shown below for the three stores you have selected. List at least five vendor names that have preticketed their merchandise with their own tags.

Name of Store	Labels with Vendor-Designated Prices	Actual Retail Prices

2. Plan a visit to any unit of a supermarket in your area as well as one of the wholesale clubs to see whether prices for the same products differ. Select ten

products that are considered to be staple items such as brand-name cereals, bottled water, soda, frozen items such as pizza, and so on. Make certain that the items you have chosen are of the same package size and weight so that you can compare prices fairly. Prepare a chart listing the products and their supermarket and wholesale club prices.

Using the information you have gathered, write a summary indicating the price differences that you have found. Indicate the names of the stores you visited.

THE CASE OF THE MARKDOWN DILEMMA

One of the more successful department store operations in the midwest is Finders and Wells which has been in business since 1925. It has been well-known throughout the midwest ever since it opened its first store which, as of today, is still its flagship operation. The recognition and loyal following it has always enjoyed is due to its wonderful merchandise assortment and the services that it offers to its clientele.

As the company entered the new millennium, it has grown to 23 units, all of which are located within several of the midwestern states. Their profit picture has been relatively steady, with economic downturns somewhat affecting the company as it does all of the stores across the country. Among the many pricing strategies that the company has used ever since its beginning is the one that addresses markdowns. Their approach has been the traditional one in which retailers take markdowns twice a year, once after the fourth of July and the other after New Year's

Day. Their belief is that the use of markdowns for slow sellers at any other time of the year would hamper sales. While the less desirable merchandise might sell more quickly, customers might wait to see if the other merchandise would also be marked down before the end of the traditional selling period.

Mr. Robert Hampton, senior vice president for merchandising, a position he has held for the past 15 years, believes that the status quo has served them well and that they shouldn't fool with success.

Ms. Janet Woods, divisional merchandise manager for the retailer's most important classification, women's apparel, and a member of the management team for the past two years, firmly believes that the use of more frequent markdowns would better serve the needs of the company. She feels that merchandise that doesn't sell in a predetermined time period should be reduced so that it might be disposed of more quickly, making room for newer products.

For the past six months, at the regular merchandising and management meetings, the topic has been discussed again and again. Each of the two managers have their own followers in the management team, with the split approximately 50–50.

At this point in time a decision must be made as to the type of markdown philosophy the company should take.

Questions

1. What are the advantages of each of the plans?
2. Which executive's approach do you believe should be taken? Why?

PART FIVE

Promotion and Customer Service

Having taken care of all of the decision making in terms of management, facilities design, and purchasing, it is imperative that the retailer's potential market be made aware of the company's existence.

Most professional merchants recognize that without the appropriate promotional endeavors, their companies will not attract the masses needed to make them successful. To that end, considerable sums for advertising are set aside by many retailers, as well as for special promotional events that will hopefully motivate customers to venture to the stores. Equally important is properly servicing those who are interested in patronizing the retailer.

In Chapter 14, Advertising and Promotion, the different types of advertising and special events projects that retailers use are discussed. From those that cost very little money to those that are extravagant in nature, this chapter shows how retailers of every size may subscribe to some form of advertising and promotion.

Taking an item and presenting it in the best possible light is the job of visual merchandisers. Their ability to transform the mundane into something exciting in a visual setting makes their role in retailing invaluable. In Chapter 15, Visual Merchandising, all principles and elements are carefully addressed so that even the novice can try his or her hand at it.

Today's merchant is totally aware of the competitive nature of the game of retailing. With many inventories similar from one company to the next, it is the service that separates one from the other. By carefully providing personal selling that instills a notion of confidence in the customer, and by offering a host of traditional as well as customized services that make the shopping experience pleasurable, it is likely that customer loyalty will follow. In Chapter 16, Servicing the Customer, the numerous services that are afforded by retailers are discussed, as is why they help to bring customers back again and again.

CHAPTER 14
Advertising and Promotion

After you have completed this chapter, you should be able to discuss:

- ► The various components that make up a retailer's sales promotion division.
- ► Advertising and how it differs from selling, visual merchandising, and publicity.
- ► The manner in which the major retailers organize their advertising departments and the functions of these departments.
- ► The different elements that comprise an advertisement.
- ► The effectiveness of single ads and ad campaigns in terms of the sales they generate.
- ► The role of the advertising agency.
- ► Media choices for retailers and the different benefits derived from each.
- ► Special events and how retailers use them to promote their products and images.
- ► How publicity helps promote the retailer's image without the costs of advertising.

Consumers from every walk of life are in need of products that run the gamut from the basic necessities to those that make living more pleasurable. Whether it is the food that sustains them, or the luxuries that some can afford, there is a multitude of retail establishments ready to offer this merchandise. Brick-and-mortar operations, catalogs, Web sites, and cable TV shopping channels all vie for the consumer's attention in hopes of turning a profit for their companies.

The merchants who make up these various retail outlets are many. In fact, there has never been a retailing climate in which so many have competed for the consumer's dollars. It might be one's favorite department store, a traditional specialty organization, a value operation such as a discounter or off-pricer, a wholesale club, a store-is-the-brand merchant, a franchise operation, an Internet Web site, a catalog, or a host of other outlets to whom the public turns to for their purchases. With all of these retailers competing for the sale, it is safe to say that choosing one is not generally an automatic response for the consumer. Of course, a percentage of the population regularly patronizes a particular supermarket for grocery needs, or a department store for apparel, but, by and large, much of the retail dollar is up for grabs.

Through direct and continuous efforts to make the public aware of their operations, retailers can be more assured that they will have a chance to capture a segment of the market to whom their products are targeted. These endeavors are primarily through **advertising** and promotion. Without regular notification to the public of their existence, few retailers would be able to maintain favorable sales volumes. It might seem that retailers, such as supermarkets, who supply the basic needs do not regularly expend large advertising budgets to call attention to themselves. However, by studying the number of print and broadcast advertisements these outlets place every week, it is obvious that these ads are a necessity to guarantee shoppers fill their stores.

Merchants spend untold hours making certain that they have focused their operations on sound retailing principles, and that their decisions are worthy of the clienteles to whom they are appealing. They establish strategies that help to achieve their goals, buy the merchandise that is appropriate for their regular and potential customers, and offer services that will bring the shoppers back again and again. While all of this planning is obviously necessary to develop a sound business, it is also imperative that merchants create advertisements and promotional tools that will encourage the consumer to choose their stores instead of the competition.

The matter of advertising and promotion is not a simple one. It requires experts to develop approaches that not only gain the attention of the consumer markets but convince them that the retailer will satisfy their needs better than other retailers.

It should be understood that these advertising and promotional endeavors are not restricted to the country's major retailers, but are also utilized by those small entrepreneurs who compete for the consumer's dollars. The depth and breadth of these undertakings are of course different for each of these players. Each must find the way that publicizes its existence with the dollars that have been set aside for this purpose. While the major retailer will have its own sales promotion division to oversee the **publicity** aspect, the small, independent merchant will either handle his or her own promotional endeavors or call upon an outside specialist such as an **advertising agency** for guidance.

THE SALES PROMOTION DIVISION

Given that a company is a major one in retailing, it is the rule that a separate division be established to oversee everything that is of a promotional nature. This includes the development of advertising approaches that are of a singular nature, campaigns that cover a wealth of media, special events that will create interest for customers, visual presentations that are attention getters, and publicity that will present their name in the marketplace.

To successfully carry out all these endeavors, the company must first establish its goals and organize its division so that the plans will be faithfully executed. In the largest retail organizations, the sales promotion division is a major function of the organizational structure, as we have already seen in Chapter 5, Organizational Structures. Its functions are generally divided among four major departments with each headed by a manager, as seen in the following chart.

A typical organization chart for the sales promotion division of a department store.

The overall operation is managed by a divisional leader who interacts with the other divisional leaders in the organization to make certain that the promotional plans best present the company's merchandise. Thus, the sales promotion division head regularly meets with the general merchandise manager whose responsibility is to supply the company with the most suitable products. With these two divisional leaders in sync, the ultimate sales goals are more likely to be achieved.

In this chapter, attention will focus on the advertising, special events, and publicity departments. Visual merchandising, since it has become such an important force in the brick-and-mortar operations, will be discussed separately in the next chapter. Of course, the coordination of all of these efforts is essential so that the greatest sales potential will be realized.

ADVERTISING

Many industry professionals are in agreement that aside from the merchandise itself, advertising is the lifeblood of retailing. As defined by the American Marketing Association, advertising is "any paid form of nonpersonal presentation of the facts about goods, services, or ideas to a group." Unlike selling which requires interaction between two people, or visual merchandising which requires the display of actual merchandise, advertising merely requires the use of artwork and **copy** to get its message across. Also, unlike publicity which is free, advertising is paid for.

In-House Advertising Departments

In companies with their own **in-house advertising departments**, its size is dependent upon the amount of advertising it undertakes and the types upon which it focuses.

Retailers who are more restricted in their advertising needs are likely to have a department that is organized along the lines of the one featured in the chart at the top of page 347. Whether it is for print or broadcast advertising, the advertising manager has complete control, and oversees each aspect of the program.

In the giants of the retail trade, a more segmented approach is utilized. With their involvement in every aspect of advertising, individual departments handle periodical, direct, broadcast, and sign (or mass) advertising. Each department has its own manager who is responsible only for his or her own particular media outlet, as depicted in the chart at the bottom of page 347. The actual copy and artwork needed by each of the departments, as well as the production requirements such as proofreading, are found in a common area that services all media departments.

This is by no means the only format that retail giants use. In actual practice, each utilizes a plan that best serves the company.

Whatever the organizational arrangement, the preparation of the advertisement requires several components. These include, but are not limited to, the following:

The main duty of a copywriter is to provide the written portion of the ad.

The copy and art experts develop the layout of the ad to make it visually appealing.

- *Writing copy.* The written portion of the advertisement alone may be used all

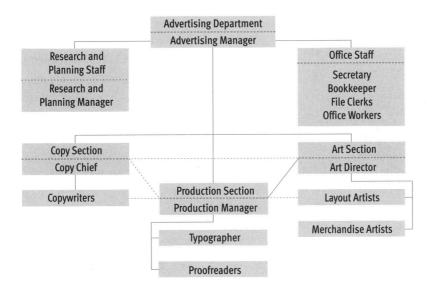

A division typical in-house advertising department.

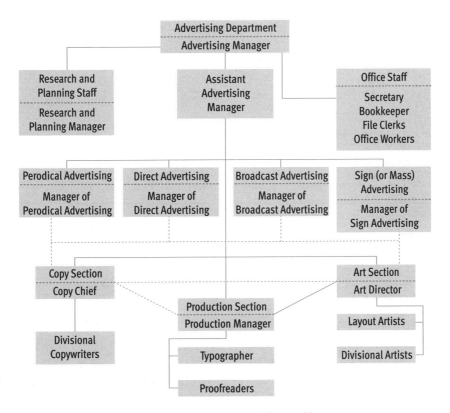

Many retailing giants organize their advertising department following this structure.

The advertising manager checks the copy for accuracy and appropriateness.

by itself in an ad or to augment any artwork.

- *Preparing artwork.* The illustrations that are in most ads are either photographs of the actual merchandise or drawings that have been created by artists.
- *Developing the layout.* The art and copy that have been created are then physically arranged in a layout that has significant eye appeal.

Not too many years ago, the vast majority of the work needed to create advertisements was hand-rendered. That is, layouts were a matter of creating pasteups which required a great deal of time and effort. Today, the traditional light boxes and other tools have become a thing of the past, replaced by computers that can more quickly and efficiently create effective advertising designs.

Belk - Southern Division
Advertising Requisition

BUYER	LOMBARDO
DEPARTMENT #	370 MODERATE COLLECTIONS
AD#/CIRCULAR	
RUN DATE	MARCH

EVENT	LAKE CITY GRAND OPENING	TODAY'S DATE	1/3/01
ITEM	IZOD SPORTSWEAR	AD SIZE:	ONE PANEL IN MEN'S BETTER MAILER

Reg.   18 - 52   or   Orig.
Sale Price   13.50 - 39.00   AND   % Off   25% OFF
Special Purchase   Value Priced

Feature [X]   Sub-Feature [ ]   Box [ ]   Other

VENDOR OR LABEL   IZOD
PERMISSION TO USE NAME?   YES [X]   NO [ ]
CO-OP: YES [X]   NO [ ]   % of Ad   Contract Attached   YES [X]   NO [ ]
Trademark (register mark R or TM):   n
Logo: YES [X]   NO [ ]   Prior Approval Required?   YES [X]   NO [ ]

25% OFF ENTIRE STOCK OF REGULAR PRICED IZOD KNITS, WOVENS, AND SHORTS FOR MEN

Fabrics/Materials:
Colors Available:
Style #:   (Must be provided for Ad List)

PHOTOGRAPHY

NEED TO SHOOT? [ ]   FROM BSS [X]   IF BSS, SPECIFY PICK UP FROM WHAT PIECE   Spring Sale Pick Up Large Book 2 Figure
SAMPLE PROVIDED?   YES [ ]   NO [ ]
CHROME PROVIDED?   YES [ ]   NO [ ]

PLEASE LIST ANY PREFERENCES YOU MAY HAVE CONCERNING THE MANNER IN WHICH THIS
SHOULD BE PHOTOGRAPHED. INCLUDE VENDOR REQUIREMENTS. IF THE ITEM IS A FORM OF
CLOTHING, (1) PLEASE SPECIFY HOW IT SHOULD BE WORN, (2) IF ACCESSORIES ARE NEEDED,
PLEASE PROVIDE WITH SAMPLE, (3) PLEASE SPECIFY TYPE OF SHOE REQUIRED AND (4) MODEL
SPECIFICATIONS (ie. AGE, LOOK, ETC.)

If R.O.P., Check/"X" the markets where ad is to run (must match co-op contract):

Citadel 202 [ ]	Summerville 566 [ ]	Dublin 238 [ ]	Hilton Head 534 [ ]	Moultrie 179 [ ]	Vidalia 547 [ ]
Northwoods 453 [ ]	Charleston 324 [ ]	Albany 484 [ ]	Aiken 554 [ ]	Bainbridge 269 [ ]	Spring Hill 121 [ ]
Mt. Pleasant 74 [ ]		Gainesville 496 [ ]	Valdosta 510 [ ]	Statesboro 284 [ ]	Lady Lake 226 [ ]
Avenues 141 [ ]	Regency 142 [ ]	Douglas 107 [ ]	Brunswick 514 [ ]	St. Marys 573 [ ]	Deland 234 [ ]
Orange Park 149 [ ]	Roosevelt 151 [ ]	Ocala 109 [ ]	Waycross 520 [ ]	Crystal River 563 [ ]	Lake City 204 [X]
Winter Haven 207 [ ]	Lakeland 535 [ ]	Walterboro 133 [ ]	Tifton 266 [ ]	Sebring 583 [ ]	Daytona 399 [ ]
Lakeland 473 [ ]	Winter Haven 248 [ ]	Beaufort 200 [ ]	Thomasville 274 [ ]	St Augustine 350 [ ]	
Oglethorpe 239 [ ]	Melbourne 505 [ ]	Cordele 522 [ ]	N. Augusta 299 [ ]	Leesburg 497 [ ]	
Savannah Mall 557 [ ]	Titusville 395 [ ]		Americus 528 [ ]	Leesburg 287 [ ]	

Buyers provide the product information that is the basis for advertising copy and artwork. In large firms like Belk, this information is generally recorded on a description form.

Belk
Aiken, SC Grand Re- Opening
March, 2001

ROP COMMITMENT FORM

We will use the Aiken Standard to deliver our ROP message. The circulation is 16,000 daily and Sundays. The Daily Rate is 8.86 and Sunday Rate is 9.38. A full page is 6 columns wide by 21 inches deep or 126 inches. A half page is 6 columns wide by 11 inches deep or 66 inches. A quarter page is 3 columns by 11 inches or 33 inches.
Full color is added at 395.00.

Ad Size	Daily Rate	Total Cost	Vendor Share 50%	Check Choices
Full Page	8.86	1,116.36	558.18	
Full Color Cost		395.00	197.50	
Half Page	8.86	584.76	292.38	
Quarter Page	8.86	292.38	146.19	

Ad Size	Sunday Rate	Total Cost	Vendor Share 50%	Check Choices
Full Page	9.38	1,181.88	590.94	X
Full Color Cost		395.00	197.50	
Half Page	9.38	619.08	309.54	
Quarter Page	9.38	309.54	154.77	

Date of Ad: SUNDAY, MARCH 4TH, 2001
Brands to be advertised: IZOD MEN'S SPORTSWEAR
Products to be Featured: SPORTSWEAR COLLECTION
Please specify any additional requirements for the ad (i.e. logo, sizes, fiber content, number of tear sheets, etc.
LOGO MUST BE USED, VENDOR PRE-APPROVAL.

Method of Payment: Check _____   Invoice Deduction X
Send Co-op Advertising Claim to:
Vendor   IZOD   Vendor I.D.#   3200468
Address 6065 Roswell Road, suite 510
City   Atlanta   State ____ GA   Zip   30328-4013
Attention   RICHARD WRIGHT
Authorized by: ACCOUNT EXECUTIVE

RETURN TO: Belk - Southern Division
5210 Belfort Road, Suite 400
Jacksonville, FL 32256
Attn: DONNA LOMBARDO
Fax: 904 296 7556

The retailer's advertising commitment form, like this one from Belk, spells out the cost of the ad along with other important details of the sale.

External Sources of Advertising Assistance

In the smaller retail operations, as has been mentioned, the luxury of an in-house advertising department is generally nonexistent. With the limited amount of dollars available for such promotional endeavors, the costs outweigh the need. This, however doesn't take the minor player out of the game. They turn to outside specialists to assist with their advertising needs. The following are just some of the routes taken by these merchants to help with their advertising requirements.

Advertising Agencies

These companies are the specialists in the field. They are in business to assist clients with a wide variety of services needed to make their companies and products better known to the public. They create single print or broadcast ads, complete campaigns, or anything else of a promotional nature. The remuneration they receive is often based upon a percent of the cost of the placement of the ad. That is, the media, rather than the retailer, pays them according to the space they purchase in a newspaper or magazine or the time purchased for the ad on television or radio. Sometimes, as in the case of the creation of a direct-mail piece, there might be a flat fee. It should be understood that advertising agencies service not only the smaller merchants but also the major retailers who have their own in-house staffs.

Vendors

Recognizing that without the success of the retailer product manufacturers would not be able to sell their merchandise, vendors are often willing to provide sample advertisements for their accounts to use. These computer-generated ads are complete in terms of illustrations and copy. The only elements that are omitted from these ads are the retailer's name and the retail prices. The user of these ads is at liberty to insert his or her own name or logo in the space that has been provided and the retail price that he or she is going to charge.

While this is a simple and cost-free approach to advertisement creation, it does run the risk of having others use the identical ad in the same print publication. This would take away from the exclusive nature of the advertisement, rendering it a me-too promotion.

Freelancers

In every aspect of advertising there are individuals who, for a set fee, will create an ad that is appropriate for the retailer. He or she might be a generalist who can develop every aspect of the ad, or a specialist who might create the layout and employ others to prepare the artwork and copy. Some **freelancers** specialize in one medium, such as direct mail, while others may plan each of the media. Using this approach to advertising assures the retailer that the ad will be developed exclusively for his or her business, without worrying about others utilizing it for their promotions.

Media Services

Most of the print and broadcast media maintain departments that offer **media services** including planning and actual development. These services are generally free, with the revenue coming from the actual ad placement.

The smaller, local, independent newspapers or shopping publications—which are predominantly used by small retailers—are heavily involved in these services. They recognize that these entrepreneurs can afford neither their own advertising experts nor the services of freelancers.

One typical promotion advertisement is the clearance sale ad.

Advertising Classifications

Retailers have choices in terms of what approach they would like to emphasize in their advertisements. The approach might center on specific merchandise, or to a lesser extent, the company's image. The former is known as **promotional advertising** and the latter, **institutional advertising**.

Promotional advertising

Most retailers want to get an immediate response to the ads or commercials they place in the print or broadcast media. To accomplish this goal they rely upon the promotion of specific products that they feature in their inventories. It might be an ad that features an item from a particular designer collection, a sale that announces significant price reductions, or, in the case of supermarkets, the specials for the week.

The intention is to tempt the shopper to make his or her way to the store to buy the advertised goods or order them from a catalog or Web site.

⋮ An Ethical Consideration

FROM TIME TO TIME, RETAILERS TRY TO BRING SHOPPERS into their stores by advertising merchandise that is in short supply, at very special prices. The intention is to entice the individual into the store, in the hope that other merchandise will be purchased. This practice, called "bait and switch," is unethical since the merchant knows that there will not be a sufficient quantity of the items to satisfy everyone's needs.

In an era when people have less time to shop than ever before, this practice is not only unethical but, in the long run, will dissuade the consumers from trusting the retailer.

Institutional Advertising

At the other of the spectrum is advertising that is intended to promote the retailer's image. It might be to tell of all of the services the merchant offers that make the shopping experience a pleasurable one, to show its dedication to American-made products, or to salute a particular event or charity. Such advertising depicts the retail operation as a humanitarian organization, and not one that is solely interested in profits.

Typically, institutional advertising is used more sparingly than is promotional advertising. The return on this type of advertising investment is difficult to measure, and it is only used as an adjunct to the other.

Combination Advertising

Sometimes, the retailer utilizes a format that combines both promotional and institutional advertising. By using **combination advertising** the company can implant an idea that is institutional in nature but at the same time helps to sell a product. Fashion merchants often use a message that brings attention to the fact that the store is dedicated to fashion merchandise (the institutional portion), while featuring a particular style (the promotional portion) that it wishes to sell.

Events like Macy's annual flower show attract shoppers to the store, but because they contribute only indirectly to the bottom line, the proportion of the advertising budget allocated to institutional advertising is relatively small.

Advertising Campaigns

The occasional use of an ad is not likely to bring the results that the retailer is seeking. If advertising is sparingly or irregularly used, it will not have an impact on the consumer. As we examine the wealth of print publications and broadcast media, we see that retailers advertise again and again to attract attention. A one-time ad might be missed by a whole host of readers or viewers at a particular day or time, wasting the dollars that have been expended for it.

By blitzing the media with a central theme or merchandising concept, the company's name, product lines, and image will soon be indelibly etched in the minds of the consumer. In this way, whenever shopping needs must be fulfilled, the customer might recall the retailer's name and head for that particular brick-and-mortar operation, catalog, or Web site to make a purchase.

The best **advertising campaigns**, if budgets allow, are the ones in which all of the media are used. This is especially true if the retailer is introducing a new prestigious line, announcing a major sales event, or refocusing its image. By using newspapers, magazines, direct-mail pieces, television, radio, or any of the local communication outlets, the company is certain to gain the exposure needed to make the event a successful one.

Cooperative Advertising

One of the concerns of many of those responsible for advertising in retailing is the continuous cost escalation. Buyers of print space and airtime are finding that their dollars no longer go as far as they once did. Always looking for industry support to promote their companies and the products they sell, buyers and merchandisers are generally involved in a concept known as **cooperative advertising**. It is an arrangement in which the vendor and the retailer share the expense of advertising.

The way it works is that a formula is developed that provides promotional funds to be used for advertising purposes. Generally, the amount that is arrived at is based upon the dollars that the retailer spends with the vendor. A portion of that amount, say 10 percent, will translate into promotional dollars. Once the actual amount has been determined, it is applied toward the cost of an ad—with each party paying for one-half of the ad, up to the predetermined amount.

The following example is typical of a cooperative advertising arrangement:

The vendor and retailer jointly sponsor the cooperative ad, and both receive exposure from it.

The buyer of menswear for Stewart's Department Store has purchased $100,000 worth of goods from Arlington Industries. Both parties have agreed to a cooperative advertising arrangement of 5 percent on purchases. The allowance would be as follows:

$$\$100,000 \times .05 = \$5,000$$

Stewart's would then be able to apply the $5,000 to an advertisement. Thus, if an ad costs $10,000, each party would be responsible for one half. It should be noted that if the ad were to cost more than $10,000, Arlington's responsibility would remain at $5,000, the percent based upon the purchase. If the ad cost $3,000, the vendor's portion would only be for $1,500, or one half, as originally agreed to. The remaining "unused" amount based on the $100,000, or $3,500 would be carried over for use in another advertisement.

The advantage of this type of arrangement benefits both the vendor and the retailer. The vendor gets the brand name out to the public, and the retailer is able to promote his or her store along with the featured merchandise.

Seasoned buyers and merchandisers are always in the market for these promotional dollars since it is a method of doubling the amount of money that has been allocated to them by management. One cautionary measure that needs careful attention is that purchases should never be made simply because of the advertising allowances that are offered. Once it has been determined that the goods are suitable for the buyer's model stock, then the cooperative advertising arrangement should be negotiated.

Crossover Advertising

The vast majority of the major brick-and-mortar retailers in the United States spend a great deal on advertising in the hope that it will encourage potential customers to come to their outlets. Today, however, in-store shopping is not the only game in town. More and more of these high-profile merchants are depending upon their Web sites to bring additional sales to the company.

In an effort to beef-up these off-site sales, merchants are using their print and broadcast ads to remind the shoppers who are unable to make store visits that there is a Web site for their purchasing pleasure. This is called **crossover advertising**. Somewhere in these advertisements the company's Web site is prominently featured. It is the merchant's way to remind the shopper that a Web site does exist for their use. The hope is that those who log on will eventually find their way into the stores where the selections are generally broader.

Advertising Media

Many different communication outlets are available to the retailer for use in the promotion of the company and the merchandise it sells. The nature of the retailing operation dictates which medium is best suited for putting the company's name and merchandise before the consumer. While one might be better suited to a specific retailer than another, this is not to say that each merchant should follow suit when choosing where to expend its promotional dollars. Some make use of all media, while others might restrict their advertising to just one. Department stores, for example, generally utilize a mix of newspaper, magazine, direct-mail, television, radio, and Internet advertising to reach their targeted audiences, while the small retailer may only subscribe to the direct-mail route.

Through an examination of each of the media in terms of its advantages and disadvantages, the retailer is able to choose one that is best suited to the store's needs.

The Stein Mart Story
Selecting the Media that Brings Results

LIKE MOST MAJOR RETAILERS, STEIN MART engages in a large advertising program that brings shoppers to the stores. The advertising efforts are the work of an in-house staff that creates the ads and makes the decision as to where they will be featured.

The program involves both print and broadcast media, with the former accounting for the lion's share of the advertising budget. Unlike many of today's merchants, the company is concentrating less on black and white ads and more on color inserts that are placed in the major newspapers in the cities where stores are located. Black and white is used sparingly and is mainly reserved to announce special sales. Color circulars bring the best results and are therefore the mainstays of the advertising program. Sometimes Stein Mart uses direct mail for its circulars, but this is only on occasion.

Broadcast advertising primarily takes place on the radio. Instead of the in-house team preparing the spots, Fry-Hammond-Barr, an ad agency, develops the campaigns.

In addition to the advertising program, the company participates in several promotional endeavors such as fashion shows and charitable events. One original approach uses the "boutique ladies" to visit large corporations to help teach the employees about fashion and correct dress. This generally results in getting these consumers into the stores and selling merchandise to them.

This ad for a small, single-unit retailer appeared in a community newspaper, whose advertising department prepared it for the advertiser. Using this medium enabled the retailer to reach its target market at a low cost per potential customer.

Newspapers

Although the use of television and direct mail by retailers has increased in recent years, the newspaper remains the leading medium used by the vast majority of the industry. Whether it is print ads in the country's biggest newspapers, such as *The New York Times*, or *Los Angeles Times*, or the small local publications that serve communities nationwide, the format is one that brings the best sales results.

Some of the advantages of print ads are the following:

1. The diversified offerings provide interest for every family member. Whether it is the sport's enthusiast, the teenager who often faithfully reads the advice columns, the would-be gourmet cook who seeks out new recipes, or the investor who religiously checks his or her stocks, there is potential for each of them to see the advertising.

2. When costs along with the actual number of prospective customers that can be reached are considered, the cost per consumer is lower than other media.

3. The life of the newspaper is relatively long. For the dailies it is 24 hours until the next edition is published; for the Sunday edition, which features the greatest amount of advertising, the life is often until the next weekend edition is produced. Compared to radio and television, where messages become fleeting moments, the newspaper has longevity.

4. The acquisition of the newspaper is often automatic. Through vast number of subscriptions, there is a guarantee that it will regularly be delivered to the household or office without the need to find a place from which to purchase it.

5. A newspaper can be read at any time—while commuting, during a break, or at the end of the day.

There are also some disadvantages to the newspaper.

1. The amount of time that is spent reading the newspaper has decreased in many families. Women, for example, are working outside of the home in greater numbers than ever before. Coupling this with their household chores, often there is limited time to enjoy the newspaper. Teenage readership has also declined, with more and more getting their news via radio.
2. A great deal of attention has been focused on the Internet where more and more families are logging on to buy merchandise, follow their investments, chat with others, etc. All of this replaces the time that was once spent reading the newspaper.
3. The limitations of the newsprint stock makes for poor reproduction quality.

Magazines

Primarily used by manufacturers of products that have significant market appeal, magazines are not the choice of many retail operations. With costs relatively high, and the trading areas covered by a majority of retailers generally smaller than the reach of the magazine's circulation, it is not usually a place where merchants expend their promotional dollars. There are, however, exceptions to the rule, with some of the giants in the industry utilizing the magazine to get their messages across. Companies like Sears and JCPenney, with outlets all across the nation, reach markets via magazine advertising. Fashion retailers, too, such as Saks Fifth Avenue sometimes enter the magazine arena even though their trading areas do not often cover the print publication's consumer market. These retailers use this format as a means of presenting their fashion image to the wealth of travelers who come to such places as New York City and Chicago, where they have flagships. By doing so, they are preselling the travelers on the idea of making in-store visits when they come to these cities.

In order to concentrate on narrower marketplaces, those retailers whose companies are in smaller geographic areas, and wish to advertise in magazines, often opt for **regional editions** of the publications. A home furnishings retailer that is based in the South, for example, and wishes to reach a market in that portion of the country, might choose a regional edition of *House & Garden* to do so.

The long lasting nature of magazines has no rivals. With the newspaper lasting but a day before it becomes obsolete, and the message on radio and television quickly vanishing, the magazine affords the advertiser continuous inspection that might last a few months. Further value is placed on this periodical since often times it is passed from one family to another, accounting for a readership than is greater than the actual circulation it achieves.

Because of the long life it offers to the advertiser, the ads featured are typically institutional rather than promotional. Readers' attention is sought over a long time period. In newspaper advertising, the opposite is true. Consumers are expected to immediately react to a featured product and come to the store to make the purchase while the supply lasts.

Unlike its print counterpart, the newspaper, the magazine requires a great deal of **lead time** for the publication of an ad. Where the closing date for the placement of a newspaper advertisement is often 48 hours, the same for a magazine can be a few months. Thus, when timely ads are the desire of the retailer, the magazine is not selected.

Television

Nothing else quite compares to the combination of sight and sound as does television. It brings realistic as well as stylized commercials into households all across the nation in a manner that no other medium can accomplish. Of course, its considerable expense limits usage to just a few of the major players in the field, with the lion's share of the advertising going to producers of consumer products.

The cost, however, is considerably reduced when the user limits his or her commercials to a narrow marketplace. This is possible because of the pauses that programs utilize during their shows to sell the sponsor's merchandise. While the use of one sponsor for an entire program has faded in the industry, more and more advertisers are resorting to **spots**. Many local advertisers, are taking it even a step further by contracting for only that part of the television audience that is within their trading area to see the commercial. The way it works is during specific time periods, such as those when the networks revert back to their local affiliates, a multitude of different commercials are aired. In this way, a midwestern chain might buy this local time to reach its audience, while a southern merchant might use the same time to make its appeal to potential shoppers. Winn Dixie and Publix, supermarket chains with stores limited to the south, will opt to show their commercial to those southern viewers.

Even with the regional option that reduces the cost of usage, and the incomparable messages it imparts to viewers, television, as a retail medium, is sparingly used.

Radio

When the Sony Walkman first came onto the scene, it opened an avenue for retailers to recapture the radio listening audience, which at the time, was in somewhat of a decline. The new device enabled joggers, walkers, exercise enthusiasts, as well as those who lounged at the beaches and poolside, to keep abreast of the day's happenings. Added to this was the ever increasing growth of automobile travel that holds motorists captive in their cars during gridlock periods and the regular driving times required of their daily commutes. Of course, a segment of the population still listens to the radio at home or in the workplace.

With all of these occurrences favorably impacting radio usage, its relevance to retail advertisers began to spiral upward. Consumers of all ages committed some of their time to tuning into their favorite stations and programs. In particular, the teenagers and young adults became less and less enthralled with the newspaper, became important listeners, and eventual purchasers, of products that were advertised on the wave lengths.

With costs relatively modest, particularly when compared to television and the print media, the radio became a viable means to reach targeted markets even for small retailers with limited budgets. Utilizing the regional approach, restaurants, department and specialty stores, entertainment centers, and others found this advertising niche a winner for their needs. Stations that featured rock and rap zeroed in on the younger market, while more serious listeners regularly began to tune in to the talk shows.

It is now considered by many merchants a perfect communication outlet for their needs, at costs that are affordable, and with little lead time necessary to place most advertisements.

Direct Mail

One needs only to look at his or her mailbox each day to find that he or she is being inundated with an abundance of mailers from retailers. Coming in such forms as catalogs, brochures, broadsides, pamphlets, and a host of other types, it is considered to be one of the more important media outlets.

With expenses that range from the lowest cost one-page flyers to the more costly, ambitious catalogs that run over 100 pages, direct mail has become an extremely important income producing outlet for merchants who are involved in multichannel retailing, as well as for those who confine their sales to direct marketing.

Department stores extensively use this form of advertising when they send customers their end-of-month billing statements. By enclosing a motivational piece along with the bill, they are able to appeal to a clientele who has been satisfied in the past. This captive audience regularly uses the enclosed order forms to purchase again and again.

Catalogs have become a vital outlet for retailers of every size. Hundreds upon hundreds of these sales booklets find their way into homes throughout the year. The competition in catalog retailing has become so keen that it rivals the experiences of merchants in their brick-and-mortar environments.

Direct mail catalogs are fast becoming a major advertising medium for multi-channel and retailers as well as direct marketers.

Production of direct mail requires careful attention to the quality of the printing because customers rely on the printed image for their impression of the appearance of the advertised products.

Through the use of store mailing lists, or those that have been purchased from marketing research companies, the retailer is able to zero in on a targeted market that can be customized for the store's own needs. Of course, the lists that are maintained by the retailer's own company features names and addresses, and now telephone and fax numbers, as well as e-mail addresses of the store's own customers. Those purchased from list houses may also be tailored to the retailer's needs. Such characteristics as family income, type of employment, level of education, size of the family, and other demographic and psychographic classifications are researched to deliver a list that will include those individuals who could become customers.

Finally, direct mail affords the retailer the opportunity to get the advertisement directly into the consumer's hands to be read at his or her leisure.

Web Sites

While still in its infancy in terms of the sales its produces for the retail industry, the Internet has become a medium that offers many advantages to the merchants who make use of it. With tens of thousands of retail Web sites, consumers can log on to many of them to find exactly what they need without leaving the comfort of their homes.

Whether it is a Web-only merchant such as Amazon.com, who only sells via this medium, or those who toil in the multichannel game, the outlets are often more diverse than the brick-and-mortar operations we have become used to patronizing.

A look at many of the Web sites reveals a variety of formats that retailers have chosen to use. Some merely advertise a brick-and-mortar or catalog operation and direct the motivated surfers to visit the store or obtain a catalog to make purchases. At the other end of the spectrum are those who maintain page after page that features a host of products that can be instantly ordered. Some are even interactive Web sites in which there is communication between the retailer's representative and the consumer.

As is the case with any form of advertising, Web site quality varies considerably. With more and more specialists using this medium to challenge their design abilities, the level of creativity is continuously improving.

These days, retailing industry professionals consider this form of advertising a necessity addition to the more traditional approaches to advertising.

Outdoor Advertisements

A wealth of **outdoor advertisements** are gaining popularity with retailers all over the nation. These types of ads include billboards, posters on public transportation vehicles, and backlit transparencies.

Billboards along interstates or major thoroughfares often bring drivers and passengers information about companies that will soon be in the vicinity. While this is by no means a major form of advertising, it does serve the purposes of some businesses. Restaurants, in particular, make their presence known to hungry motorists by this means. Other retailers, such as automobile dealers and shopping center groups are making steadier use of the billboard. Posters, which are smaller versions of the typical billboards, are regularly found on the sides and backs of buses, alerting pedestrians and those waiting to board these vehicles of retailers that are in the area.

Backlit transparencies are excellent attention getters. They are illuminated from within, and provide consumer coverage any hour of the day.

Outdoor advertising is relatively inexpensive, and offers the retailer the ability to capture the consumer's attention 24 hours a day.

Outdoor advertisements on backlit transparencies and signs on buildings, as well as transit ads on buses and at bus stops, are popular with retailers.

Advertising Cost Analysis

At the top of the list, in terms of expense, is television advertising, followed by magazine newspaper, the Internet, radio, direct mail, and the outdoor entries. The retailer must consider the expenses involved, and the return on investment that such costs could bring.

After studying the advantages and disadvantages of each, and deciding which would bring the most positive results, the merchant must choose from everything that is available in each classification that would best serve the company's needs. The consumer magazine category, for example, features more than 3,000 entries from which to choose. Each provides a different cost and readership profile that must be analyzed by the retailer to make certain that the best one is selected. The same is true whether it is a newspaper or broadcast medium that is chosen.

One of the easiest ways to make comparisons among all of the potential communication outlets is through the use of the **Standard Rate & Data Service (SRDS)**.

Focus on . . .
SRDS

SINCE 1920, THE STANDARD RATE & DATA SERVICE has provided media rates and data to the advertising industry. The company offers comprehensive coverage on the traditional media such as magazines, newspapers, television and radio, as well as today's alternative marketing opportunities such as online, out-of-home, and direct marketing. SRDS is a steady source of information for every segment of the business world, and helps individual clients to grow with high-quality data and advanced functionality.

SRDS is the leading information provider in the high-powered advertising industry. It is a member of the VNU family, a $3 billion international company with over 9,000 employees in the United States and 20,000 worldwide. Making SRDS even more valuable to the potential advertiser is the company's kinship to Nielsen Media Research, Bill Communications, and BPI Communications, publisher of the Adweek family of publications.

When merchants are researching potential outlets for advertisements, SRDS affords them the largest and most comprehensive database of media rates and data available in the world. The company catalogs more than 80,000 media properties and 30,000 direct marketing lists in all. To keep information current, SRDS verifies each listing 20 times a year and issues more than 25,000 listing updates every month. These updates keep subscribers current with changes in advertising rates, circulation information, and personal contacts. It also continually provides information on the many new and exciting advertising opportunities, whether they be new magazine launches or new alternative media options such as Web sites and out-of-home vehicles.

The importance of SRDS to the advertiser may be best realized by the fact that 95 percent of all advertising agencies, such as Ogilvy & Mather, J. Walter Thompson and McCann Erickson rely on SRDS products.

Some of the benefits of SRDS to retailers are

- More than 3,200 detailed listings for newspaper dailies and specialized papers.
- More than 3,400 magazine listings cover 85 subclassifications.
- More than 30,000 direct-mail listings organized into 223 market classifications.
- More than 4,000 TV and cable listings.
- More than 10,000 AM/FM station listings.
- More than 2,200 marketing vehicles for Spanish-speaking audiences in the Hispanic market listings.
- Thousands of online advertising possibilities in SRDS's sources.

Through SRDS's print publications or its Web site, a merchant can quickly compare his or her advertising opportunities and the cost of each.

Evaluation of the Advertising

Having carefully considered the alternative advertising techniques, and having made the decision to follow a particular route, the retailer must make certain that the expended dollars have been wisely spent. In order to decide whether or not the single ad or campaign positively impacted sales, an evaluation is in order.

For the smaller merchant with, perhaps, a one-unit operation, the task is relatively simple. Because of the personal contacts with their clienteles, these merchants are able to get verbal acknowledgements of the ads when consumers come into the store. While this is by no means a scientific approach, it does quickly let the entrepreneur know if it is the ad that has brought the customer into the store.

In larger companies, the evaluation process is approached more technically. Many have in-house research departments that can set up the evaluative procedures. One method that is extensively used is to compare the sale of the advertised products before and after the ad runs. If sales increase after the ad's publication, then it can be assumed that the ad was the reason for the additional sales. Additional research might also focus on the amount of the increase and whether or not the sales revenues offset the cost of the advertisement.

Another evaluative measure that is used focuses on store traffic, if indeed, the advertisement was placed by a brick-and-mortar operation. In some campaigns, the theme of the ad is not for specific merchandise, but to call attention to the store itself, or a particular department within the store. If this is the case, the research department could use an observation tool that measures customer traffic before and after the publication of the ad.

Advertising is a costly expense to the retail industry, and it must continually be evaluated to determine if the company's expenditures are appropriate in terms of the profits they generate or if changes must be made to maximize the profit potential.

PROMOTION

In addition to using advertising as a means of motivating shoppers to become customers, most retailers utilize a variety of promotional endeavors to augment the ads and bring greater attention to the company and the merchandise it offers for sale. A blending of a host of different promotional tools helps the retailer achieve the sales levels that have been established in order to bring a profit to the company. In addition to visual merchandising, an extremely viable promotional tool that will be explored in the next chapter, the vast majority of these endeavors involve special events.

Special Events

As the name implies, these promotional features are not routinely offered by the retailer, but are presented as limited occurrences that are both special and often, unique. Their creation and development generally lies with an in-house staff if the company is a large one or an outside agency if it is smaller one. In either circumstance, experts are called upon to lend their talents to the creation of events that will hopefully draw attention to the retailer's operation. The expenses involved in these promotional endeavors range from modest sums to extravagant expenditures. Macy's, for example, one of the world's major users of promotion, budgets huge sums for its special events programs. With such annual presentations as its Thanksgiving Day Parade, the fireworks display on Independence Day, and the springtime flower show, its monetary outlay runs into the millions. For the flower show alone, more than a million dollars is spent to transform the store into a botanical garden. With the in-store traffic that is generated by these events, and the sales that follow, it is safe to assume that the ends justify the means.

Special events are one way to get attention, and a major cost of a special event is advertising it.

Typically, retailers use a variety of formats for their special events programs. Included are fashion shows, celebrity appearances, **trunk shows**, special sales, demonstrations, sampling, charitable functions, holiday parades, community programs, and others.

Fashion Shows

For the fashion retailer there are few other special events that bring out the shoppers like fashion shows. Running the gamut from runway presentations to informal modeling, the sales results are usually worth the cost and effort of the productions. Most typical are the runway shows that take place somewhere in the store. It might be within the department of the featured merchandise, so that when the production ends, the attendees can closely examine the goods and purchase them if they like. Some merchants have special events centers in which the show takes place. These usually provide more room for customers, and thus, can bring greater sales. Another runway option is in the store's restaurant. While customers are enjoying their meals, the models are displaying the merchandise.

The runway production costs vary from presentation to presentation. If professional models are used, the costs could escalate. Some retailers make use of in-house employees, thus cutting the modeling expense. Other than building the runway and providing music, either in the form of live entertainment or tapes, there is little extra expense.

A fashion show in the mall at the store's entrance invites customers inside to try on the items that are modeled.

Retailers also use formal productions especially when they are part of fund-raising events. With the commitment to charities providing excellent public relations, this is a sound investment. Often times outside auditoriums or ballrooms are used to feature these events. There might be a large stage that is erected to show the models in their attire, along with a runway. These are generally the most elaborate shows that retailers are involved with. With professional models, music, commentary, and the like, these shows often cost several thousand dollars.

Informal modeling is not typically considered a fashion show, but rather a way in which apparel is modeled throughout the store. Live mannequins stroll throughout the store carrying signs and telling on-lookers where the merchandise may be found.

Companies like Nordstrom, Jacobson's, Macy's, Bergdorf Goodman, Marshall Field's, and other fashion image retailers make use of all of these fashion show formats.

Celebrity Appearances

A great number of consumers react positively when the announcement is made that one of the celebrities they admire will make an in-store appearance. The bigger the name, the bigger the crowd that assembles. It might be a particular designer, an entertainment personality, a sports figure, or anyone else with the potential to attract attention.

Belk Department Stores reaped the rewards of having Tommy Hilfiger appear in one of its locations when he was launching his new fragrance. Not only did the company enjoy record crowds, but fragrance sales produced enormous sales.

Trunk Shows

One of the fastest growing special events is the trunk show. Designers or their representatives visit the stores and bring with them their latest collections. Customers are

Trunk shows bring the manufacturer's latest collection to the store, often generating orders even before the store stocks the new merchandise.

notified by mail or by some media form such as the newspaper that the event will take place.

The concept requires the merchant to set aside space in the store where the trunks filled with merchandise will be featured. Some might be modeled, with others merely shown and described by the company representative. Customers are sometimes invited to have merchandise adjusted to their personal preferences, and thus customized. Others are there merely to be ordered, as shown, for future delivery. These events usually take place at the season's opening so that the customers will be the first to enjoy them.

Most retailers who participate in these events report that they generally result in significant sales.

Demonstrations

One of the ways in which the cosmetics industry, in particular, helps to generate business is through the use of makeup application. Leading manufacturers send cosmeticians to the major retailers who spend their time demonstrating the use of their latest products. Individuals are invited to act as models, and learn all about the company's offerings as the makeup is being applied. Not only do sales come from the participants, but from the on-lookers as well. When the names of the marquee brands are advertised in the newspapers, a host of consumers are likely to make their way to the store.

Other demonstrations that manufacturers offer to retail clients run the gamut from the use of vacuum cleaners to the latest entries in computers.

"How to" Clinics

One very effective promotional endeavor that brings immediate sales to retailers is the use of clinics that teach consumers how to solve their problems. Home Depot offers a host of different clinics of this nature ranging from how to install ceramic tile to maintaining a garden. Scores of different "how to" clinics are listed in the stores on a bulletinboard giving the dates and times of each event. The end result of these programs is the purchase of the necessary tools and supplies to complete each project.

Sampling

When one walks though the aisles of such vast warehouse operations as Costco or Sam's Club, they are likely to be treated to a variety of different food products that they sell. Stations that feature microwave ovens, and cooks who prepare the foods, are constantly serving samples for the passersby to taste. The intent is to motivate the shopper to purchase the products that they have just sampled.

Other sampling techniques involve the aforementioned cosmetics industry. Vendors supply the retailers with attractive items that are either given away free with any purchase, or are made available at nominal costs. This is a way in which the vendor can introduce the new product lines and help the retailer introduce it to his or her clientele.

Charitable Functions

Major retailers regularly use charitable functions as part of their promotional programs. These vehicles serve two purposes: first, they help to build the retailer's image as a leader who is interested in serving the needs of the community; and second, they provide a wealth of potential customers who frequent these events.

Retailers such as Bloomingdale's, Macy's, Nordstrom, Marshall Field's, and the like feature charitable functions that include fashion shows, dinners, dances, celebrity appearances, and other events.

Some typical charitable functions that have gained widespread attention are:

Charity events are widely sponsored by retailers; they allow a retailer to improve its image and achieve greater sales.

- Bloomingdale's benefit for colon cancer research that featured the *Today* show's Katie Couric, whose husband died of the disease.
- The annual Dayton Hudson sponsored Fash Bash that tours three cities and raises money for several charities.
- JCPenney's promotion to benefit the Susan G. Komen Breast Cancer Foundation.
- Nordstrom's various events on women's health issues.
- Bon Marche's in-house events that raise money for cancer research.

A major entry into the charitable fundraising arena is the approach taken by Neiman Marcus. Using their "Fortnight" format which showcases products, culture, and lifestyles of countries around the world, the company has again begun to use salutes to countries as part of the store's fund-raising efforts. Its tribute to Italy, Festa D'Italia, was featured at the Dallas flagship store and, in varying degrees, the other stores in the chain. Socialites and designers commingled to raise funds for The Dallas Center for the Performing Arts.

Focus on . . .
Macy's West

WITH A MAJOR FUND-RAISING EFFORT, MACY'S WEST has not only helped to raise funds and awareness for AIDS, but has also helped to vastly underscore the company's image.

Using megastars, sports champions, and marquee designers, the company raised yet another $2,000,000 for the ongoing fight against the disease. The event was part of a fundraiser that was initiated by Elizabeth Taylor. Such high-profile names as Sharon Stone, Magic Johnson (an HIV sufferer), Cindy Crawford, and Tommy Hilfiger marched down the runway to give this extravaganza the clout it needed.

The four-night event began in San Francisco, where the opening night featured a black-tie gala. The last night moved the spectacular to Los Angeles where the celebrity industry turned out to lend its support. When the monies raised from the event were counted, it brought Macy's West contribution to $10,000,000.

Macy's West was the first of the major American retailers to go public with AIDS research fund-raising. Started as a small men's fashion presentation in the staff cafeteria, with just a handful of employee devotees, it now is witness to a multitude of limousines that bring benefactors to the annual happening.

At the turn of the century, and the dawn of the new millennium, the 20th installment of this charitable event, labeled Passport, has not only made an indelible impression on the community, but has also served Macy's image as a concerned business entity.

* *

Holiday Parades

The most prominent of these parades are featured on Thanksgiving Day. While the Macy's extravaganza is the best-known, others are presented by major retailers throughout the United States. These events are used to signal the beginning of the Christmas selling season.

The Macy's entry, produced in conjunction with NBC, is a multimillion dollar event that features stars of stage, screen, television, and the sports world. Augmented with the now famous balloon characters that tower over the crowds and bands from every part of the country that have competed for the right to participate, the crowds that assemble number several hundred thousand. With television coverage, the

Macy's Thanksgiving parade brings throngs of shopping to the flagship store; broadcasting on national television provides institutional publicity far beyond the flagship's trading area.

happening also announces to the viewing audience that the time has come to begin holiday shopping.

So enormous is the commitment to these parades, and so successful are they in terms of promoting their stores, that the retail participants generally begin the next year's event immediately after the current one has been presented.

Community Programs

Many merchants recognize the need to either sponsor community events or participate in their presentation to the public in their retail environments. Educational institutions, for example, are often invited to promote their programs through these endeavors. One event that is typical of these community presentations is the fashion show. Either in a selling department that has been cleared to make room for the show, or in areas that are adjacent to the store, high school and college students participate in the modeling of the store's latest apparel collections. Not only does this bring good will to the company, but it also often introduces the store to new customers.

"Promoting" the Promotion

The creation and presentation of the special events, as we have learned, generally requires a large commitment of time and money. Their occurrence, however, does not guarantee that audiences will be there to appreciate them.

In order to assure that these happenings will be well attended, it is necessary to publicize them through newspaper ads, spot announcements on radio and television, and direct-mail pieces. The ads might offer additional motivation to attend through the description of prizes that will be offered or any other incentives that will bring in the crowds.

Promotion is one of the ways that retailers may use to show how they distinguish themselves from the competition. While merchandise offerings in many of the competing operations are identical to each other, the special events provide the impetus to gain in-store visits. With the proper "promotion" of the promotions, it is likely that store traffic will increase, giving the merchant the opportunity to distinguish his or her operation from the others.

PUBLICITY

Every major player in the retailing industry has in-house publicists whose jobs it is to present the company in the best light and attract shoppers. The people involved are public relations experts who know the ways in which to achieve these goals.

Unlike advertising, special events, and visual presentations, which all come about as a result of spending the dollar amounts that have been budgeted, publicity is a means of spreading awareness to the consumer without any direct cost.

Through means of contact with the editorial press, the public relations experts are able to get their messages to would be customers. Some of the vehicles they use are press releases and press kits. Where these had been typically sent via the traditional mailing route, today's publicity professionals use e-mail to instantly get their ideas across to those who might spread the word. Of course, whichever technique is used, the intention is to sufficiently motivate these "communicators" to relay the messages to their readerships and listeners.

TRENDS FOR THE NEW MILLENNIUM

- While newspaper advertising is still the premiere medium used by retailers, more and more are spending their promotional budgets on radio—especially if the targeted audience is the teenager—and direct mail.

- The Internet will continue to expand in terms of retailer advertising commitments and to reach those who have stayed away from the traditional media outlets, such as newspapers.

- Cooperative advertising ventures will also become more important so that retailers will be able to maintain better communication with potential customers without having to spend more money.

- Catalog usage will continue to increase as a means of getting a share of the customer's dollars and in the hope of motivating them to visit their brick-and-mortar operations where the inventories are larger.

- Special events will continue as vehicles to distinguish one merchant from another and gain a more loyal consumer following.

CHAPTER HIGHLIGHTS

- Through direct and continuous promotional efforts by retailers, the public will be aware of their operations and their merchandise, giving them the assurance that they will have a chance to capture a segment of the market to whom they are targeted.

- The sales promotion division of a major retailer is generally divided into separate departments that are responsible for advertising, special events, visual merchandising, and publicity.

- Major retailers have in-house advertising departments, while their small store counterparts use outside sources for their advertising needs.

- External advertising assistance comes from vendors, the media, ad agencies, and freelancers.

- Advertising takes two forms: promotional and institutional.

- Cooperative advertising is a joint venture between the merchandise suppliers and the retailers.

- Although some of the other media have gained in importance in retailing, the newspaper remains the most important communications outlet.

- With the advent of the Walkman, the radio has become an increasingly important advertising medium because it allows joggers, exercisers, and others on the go to tune in.

- Special events are activities such as fund-raisers, holiday parades, and celebrity appearances that retailers use to promote merchandise and improve their images.

- Publicity comes as a result of something that a retailer does that is newsworthy. It catches the attention of the editorial press who, in turn, pass the news on to their readers and viewers.

IMPORTANT RETAILING TERMS

advertising

publicity

advertising agency

copy

in-house advertising departments

freelancers

media services

promotional advertising

institutional advertising

combination advertising

advertising campaigns

cooperative advertising

crossover advertising

regional editions

lead time

spots

outdoor advertisements

Standard Rate & Data Service (SRDS)

trunk shows

FOR REVIEW

1. Which are the departments that generally comprise a sales promotion division of a retail operation?

2. How does advertising differ from publicity?

3. Generally, what four components make up the preparation of an advertisement?

4. From whom does an advertising agency receive its remuneration?

5. In what way does a vendor assist the retailer with his or her advertising endeavors?

6. What is the difference between promotional and institutional advertising?

7. Does the retailer ever combine promotional and institutional advertising in an ad? If so, what is it called?

8. Why is it often necessary for the retailer to use an ad campaign rather than a single entry?

9. How does cooperative advertising work?

10. Define the term *crossover advertising* as it is used in the chapter.

11. Which of the media generally commands the lion's share of the advertising budget?

12. Which types of retailers are more likely to make use of magazine advertising?

13. Why has the radio become more important to the retailer than it once was?

14. How can a direct-mail advertiser assemble a mailing list if he or she hasn't maintained his or her own mailing list?

15. In what way does the retailer determine the success of a single ad or an advertising campaign?

16. What is meant by the term *special event*?

17. Why do more and more merchants use charitable functions as part of their promotional endeavors?

18. Which segment of the fashion industry uses the demonstration technique to attract a passerby's attention?

19. Give an example of a community program that the retailer uses as part of its special events agenda.

20. What is meant by the term *publicity*?

AN INTERNET ACTIVITY

Many of the search engines that we use on the Internet are involved in promoting retail Web sites and help direct the consumer to them. Log onto five of them, and prepare a chart with the following heads to indicate the names of the merchants to whom the surfer is directed.

Search Engine	Retailers Cited

Write a summary that ranks, in order of completeness, the best to the worst of the search engines that directs the consumer to retail Web sites.

EXERCISES AND PROJECTS

1. Using one of the major newspapers that serve your community, select three advertisements that specifically address a promotional ad, an institutional ad, and a combination ad. Each advertisement should

be mounted on foam board and should be accompanied by your comments indicating why they fall into these particular categories.

2. Contact a major department store or chain organization that is within reach of your residence to learn about their calendar of special events for the next month. From the list, choose an event to attend for the purpose of evaluating its effectiveness. A report should then be prepared including the following:

   - advertisements that preceded the event
   - type of event
   - breadth and depth of the presentation
   - size of the attending audience
   - your evaluation of its effectiveness

THE CASE OF THE FASHION ENTREPRENEUR WITH LIMITED PROMOTIONAL FUNDS

Surrounded by a wealth of fashion-oriented retailers who seem to spend untold sums on special events that promote their merchandise, the owner of Amanda's Boutique is at a loss as to how her store can promote itself without spending large sums of money.

The merchant does a minimum amount of advertising in local publications as well as through some direct mailings that are sent to the customers who have frequented the store. While the results have been satisfactory in terms of the dollars that have been expended, they do not bring new customers to the store.

One of the promotional endeavors that Amanda Gallop, the owner of the business, is considering is the use of a fashion show that would be earmarked for women in the community. After running this initiative by some of her key employees, Amanda decided to plan a budget that would bring positive sales results to her boutique. When all of the costs were figured such as the expense of hiring professional models, using a trio to provide the musical accompaniment, program development, and the like, the costs were far greater than she could afford. She was now faced with the likelihood of canceling her fashion show plans and trying another means of promotion to better serve her business interests.

Questions

1. Should Amanda forgo her fashion show plans? Why or why not?

2. Would another special event be more cost effective?

3. If the fashion show was the only tool that would best serve her interests, how might she go about producing such a show with very little expense?

CHAPTER 15
Visual Merchandising

After you have completed this chapter, you should be able to discuss:

- ▸ The different approaches retailers take to assure themselves of the most beneficial visual presentations.
- ▸ How in major retail brick-and-mortar operations, the visual merchandising chores are left to in-house staffs.
- ▸ Why most large chain organizations utilize the concept of centralized visual merchandising.
- ▸ Why in any merchandise installation, the focal point is the merchandise and not the display props.
- ▸ How components such as lighting, signage, graphics, mannequins, props, and color are used to augment displays.
- ▸ The five design principles utilized by visual merchandisers— balance, emphasis, proportion, rhythm, and harmony.
- ▸ Why visual merchandisers must check on interior installations daily.

Capturing the attention of the passersby or the numerous browsers who comprise the traffic inside a retail operation is a formidable task, but when properly executed, these lookers are transformed into customers. While the merchandise on the selling floors is the result of the buyer's many hours of planning, its visual presentation often leaves much to be desired. Lackluster displays sometimes present a product in a manner that will not get the attention of the would-be customer. Of course, this is not true of every retail establishment. Some, by virtue of their visual merchandising teams, and their dedication to eye-catching presentations, are able to take what would otherwise be mundane offerings and enhance their presence with traffic-stopping results.

Although the department store has been the greatest proponent of visual merchandising, as can be seen in the sometimes extravagant downtown flagship stores, other retailers have joined them, creating interiors where magic is often performed giving excitement to the merchandise. A walk through stores like Crate & Barrel and Pottery Barn immediately reveals that everyday dinnerware, glassware, and household accessories take on a new exciting look that is bound to attract attention. Close inspection of many of the items that they feature

Lord & Taylor uses lavish Christmas displays to attract large crowds.

shows that these are just practical items that have taken on a special pizzazz because of the manner in which they are shown. In the gourmet retail cooking arena, another sense of excitement has been generated by the in-store displays of Williams Sonoma. Taking a variety of cooking utensils, dining elements, table accessories, and other items for the home, and featuring them in eye-catching table and countertop settings, makes shoppers stop in their tracks and significantly motivates them to make a purchase.

With the enormous amount of competition in retailing today, the need for individual approaches is great and none could better serve the merchant than imaginative visual merchandising. That is not to say that large budgets must be the only route to successful product presentation. On the contrary, some of the better visual efforts come at relatively low cost. At Pottery Barn, for example, the use of a particular color scheme that transcends many of the offerings, does not rely on a monetary investment. Instead the approach focuses showing items in abundance, giving them greater eye appeal. Whether it's the cobalt blue theme that regularly abounds its glassware department, or the emerald green that is often featured, the visual impact is striking. It doesn't cost a penny more to use color as a central theme; it only requires the attention of a professional to underscore its value as a visual merchandising tool.

Even supermarkets, at one time the least likely to engage in visual merchandising to promote goods, are now taking extra steps to improve their visual presentations. Chains like Harriss Teeter have made its premises more appealing with special displays that feature precooked meals and produce departments that present the products in visually enhanced settings. By doing so, customers are drawn to these areas and are motivated to buy what they see displayed.

Where budgets have been reduced in many of retailing's brick-and-mortar operations, the end result often results in unimaginative lackluster visual presentations. It is the creativity of seasoned professionals that can overcome this insufficient funding and deliver dazzling themes.

DEVELOPMENT OF THE VISUAL CONCEPT

In order to differentiate one's premises from others in the retail industry, merchants must carefully develop a concept that is unique to their operations. In the larger companies the task is left to the **in-house display staff**. The staff is supervised by a visual merchandising director, who at many retail operations enjoys the title of vice-president, and acts at the same level as merchandise and store operation executives.

The visual merchandising director, along with a team of display installers, signage experts, carpenters, and others, are responsible for both exterior and interior visual merchandising. Whether it is the exterior windows that need spectacular installations, or a department that requires product arrangements that will gain shopper attention, the tasks are carried out each and every day of the year.

In smaller retail organizations, the task is usually carried out by the owner or given to a freelancer, whose function is to primarily create window displays that will entice pedestrians to come into the store. By and large, it is these itinerant professional visual

Vitrines are used on selling floors to allow viewing from many angles.

merchandisers who plan and execute the display windows. In some cases they are also called upon to spruce up the interiors to make them more appealing to the clientele.

Whether it is the in-house team, or the professional freelancer, the overall goal is the same—to make the environment one that generates business.

The Department Store Approach

Compared to other retail classifications, it is the department store that has the largest visual merchandising budget. Department stores regularly change their display windows, especially in the downtown flagships where sizes and configurations are unrivaled. In addition, the staff is responsible for every visual presentation ranging from **vitrine** to countertop displays. Daily **walkthroughs** are also part of the routine to make certain that the selling floor is refurbished each day, and to also make the necessary adjustments to displays that might have been damaged by overzealous shoppers.

This task is not only for the flagship, but also for each of the branches in the organization. Their presentations must echo those of the main store, and be carefully executed.

The size of the visual team varies from company to company. The major players, especially those that are convinced that visual merchandising is truly the silent seller that many retail professionals believe it is, often have staffs that number more than fifty people, with specialists performing in every aspect of the department's endeavors. Companies like Lord

& Taylor and Neiman Marcus, for example, are indicative of the larger departments. Others, without the same commitment to visual merchandising, have in-house staffs that employ fewer people, with each performing several functions. Some of the department store visual teams have separate staffs for their flagships and branches. The former houses the director and those that create the actual props to be used in the installations, as well as display people who trim the windows. The latter generally has just a few installers who follow the directions that come from the company's main store.

In some department stores, in-house artists create unique display props.

The Stein Mart Story
The Role of Visual Merchandising

WHERE MANY OF TODAY'S RETAILERS HAVE ABANDONED their use of store windows to display their merchandise, Stein Mart believes that these showcases are still the silent sellers that bring the shopper into the stores.

The company has a twofold approach to its visual merchandising program. Most important, is the concept that assures some level of uniformity throughout the chain. To do so, the director of visual merchandising prepares a video for each season, which features the approach that the regional staff must use in the installation of displays. In it the director shows different types of props that are easily created to achieve effective eye appeal along with any messages the company is trying to get across to its customers. Props that are easily created are not only attractive, but also save the company the expense of purchasing costly materials. Along with this general approach, regional visual merchandisers are encouraged to develop displays that depict the communities in which the stores are located.

Each of the regions has visual merchandising personnel who go from store to store to install the window and interior displays. While other chains often use the services of store managers for display installations, Stein Mart believes that only professionals can create the perfect display.

Centralized Visual Merchandising

In the case of chain operations, there is generally a different approach to the visual merchandising procedure. Just as the buying, merchandising, and management functions are centralized, so is the one that deals with visual presentations.

Typically, the concept is developed by a team that is housed in the company's corporate headquarters. Headed by a director who creates the concepts, and a few individuals who provide assistance, sample display presentations are developed. It might be a window display, countertop presentations, props, specific signage, or any element that will be needed by all of the units in the chain. Once installed, the sample displays are photographed and, along with directions for installation, are forwarded to either regional visual teams or directly to the stores where they are created by managers, who faithfully follow the plans that have been sent to them. The key to this visual approach is uniformity. Each store in the chain must have the same appearance in order to give it a universal image. By relegating the creative aspect to the team at central headquarters, they are assured of having competent professionals carry out the developmental stage, and others, at the store level, who follow their instructions.

Williams Sonoma centralizes the management of its visual merchandising; presentations are designed at company headquarters and are duplicated in each store.

Companies like Gap, Pottery Barn, and Williams Sonoma utilize the centralized approach to visual merchandising.

Small Store Visual Arrangements

Just as small retailers cannot afford the expense of in-house specialists to perform their buying, merchandising, and promotional activities, neither can they undertake the cost associated with in-house staffing to carry out their visual presentations. Instead, they use freelancers to make their installations, or use simple approaches that they themselves can install. Sometimes a freelancer is used at the beginning of each season to create a design that can be adapted periodically by the entrepreneur. For example, it might be a spring or autumn theme that will remain until the following season. Only the merchandise is changed, not the background props. In this way a professional touch is given to the display area.

Freelancers

As has been discussed thus far in the chapter, the freelancer is a professional who has his or her own business specializing in developing visual presentations for retailers. This visual professional does everything from the development of the creative concept to the installation of the displays. They work on a one-time basis for their clients or on contracts that cover a full year's efforts. The better known of these individuals generally require a contract for their services.

COMPONENTS OF VISUAL PRESENTATIONS

Every seasoned merchant recognizes that there must be a balance between the merchandise that they offer in their model stocks and the backgrounds and props that are used to highlight them. First and foremost, the merchandise must be the primary focus of any visual presentation, never to be upstaged by any of the other elements. Display props should be used only to augment and enhance the merchandise.

Attention-getting props in Christmas displays draw the shopper's eyes to the featured merchandise.

Once the merchandise has been selected, except in the case of institutional presentations that center on image building ideas or community dedication and are generally void of merchandise, the other components must be selected to complete the display. Elements such as props, mannequins, lighting, color, signage, and graphics are employed as the enhancements.

Table 15.1 features selected suppliers of elements that are used in visual merchandising. Those unable to visit the showrooms may get a taste of the offerings though visits to the companies' Web sites.

TABLE 15.1 SELECTED VENDORS OF VISUAL MERCHANDISING PRODUCTS		
VENDOR	**SPECIALIZATION**	**WEB SITE**
Abbot Flag Company	Banners, flags, and pennants	www.eagleregalia.com
AdMart Custom Signage	Signs and graphics	www.admart.com
Bernstein Display	Display props	www.bernsteindisplay.com
Carol Barnhart	Display forms, mannequins	www.carolbarnhart.com
Clearr Corporation	Illuminated signage	www.clearrcorp.com
Display Boys	Custom displays	www.displayboys.com
Ferrari Color	Large format graphics	www.ferraricolor.com
Flynn Signs & Graphics, Inc.	Sign systems	www.flynnsigns.com
Greneker	Mannequins and forms	www.greneker.com
JustPedestals, Inc.	Display pedestals	www.justpedestals.com
LightBoxCity.com	Light boxes	www.lightboxcity.com
Meisel Visual Imaging	Graphic specialists	www.meisel.com
Opto International, Inc.	Display systems	www.optosystem.com
Patina-V	Mannequins	www.patinav.com
Rootstein	Mannequins	www.rootstein.com
Sachs Lawlor	Sign manufacturing	www.sachs-lawlor.com
Scenery West	Themed environments	www.scenerywest.com
Spaeth Design Inc.	Animated presentations	www.spaethdesign.com
Swirling Silks, Inc.	Custom soft signage	www.swirlingsilks.com
Visual Fabrics Inc.	Display fabrics	www.visualfabrics.com

Source: *VM+SD*, January 2002. Courtesy of VM+SD Magazine/ST Media Group International, Cincinnati, OH.

Props

Ranging from the elegant, professionally crafted entries to more simply developed items, a wealth of props are available to transform empty window shells and counter surfaces into environments that stop traffic.

The vast majority of the country's visual merchandisers visit trade shows each year that give them ideas for new themes as well as introduce them to the abundance of new props and materials available for use. At the ShopEast Show that is held twice a year in New York, vendors from all over the world exhibit scores of display props that range from simple to ornate. Many props are also tailored specifically by these resources for individual retailers.

The more creative of the visual merchandisers use their artistic talents to either create props themselves, refresh shopworn pieces that were initially used for other purposes, or use everyday items. In the shopworn category, old picture frames, chairs, rusted watering cans, and the like, when enhanced with a fresh coat of paint, make excellent props in which merchandise can be presented. Everyday items such as ladders, flowerpots, musical instruments and others make excellent choices when used in windows and interior displays. When any of these items are used in abundance, the impact that they make is particularly appealing.

 Focus on . . .
Spaeth Design

WHENEVER A MAJOR DEPARTMENT STORE OR REGIONAL MALL wishes to create dramatic excitement that utilizes an animated theme, it more than likely heads for the studios of Spaeth Design. In business since the 1940s, the company continues to captivate the public with its extravagant, artistic **animated installations** that are seen in many parts of the world. The company brings the ideas and dreams of visual merchandisers to life with its dramatic installations. A staff of creative and innovative designers, sculptors, model makers, welders, and craftspeople executes projects of any proportions.

Spaeth's client list includes overseas companies such as HarborCircus Mall in Kobe, Japan; Maykal Instaat Ve Ticaret A.S. in Istanbul, Turkey; Selfridges & Co in London, England; and Engelhorn & Sturm in Manheim, Germany. Domestically, it is best known for the magnificent windows during the Christmas season at Lord & Taylor, Saks Fifth Avenue, Marshall Field's, Macy's, and Nordstrom.

The designs the company has created have gained awards for many of its clients including *The Nutcracker* windows at Saks Fifth Avenue and *A Christmas Carol* at Lord & Taylor.

So involved are the development of the Christmas productions that the actual design and execution begin in July so that the installations can take place immediately after Thanksgiving. This early start means that each retailer will be assured of an individual design.

The success of these animated productions can best be appreciated by the attention they receive from the public. During the Christmas season, 90 percent of the company's designs are featured. The retailers install ropes to control the enormous crowds that wish to see them. Often times, the crowds wait more than half an hour to view the displays.

After they've seen the displays, a majority of the onlookers head for the store's entrances, making the expense of the display worthwhile for the retailer.

Mannequins

In the fashion arena, nothing presents a complete ensemble as dramatically and realistically as a mannequin. The mannequin choices are numerous ranging from those that faithfully represent the human form to the more **stylistic mannequins** that embody the latest in artistic expression. The price of mannequins range from a few hundred dollars to more than a thousand dollars for the state-of-the-art offerings.

In choosing the mannequins that are appropriate for their stores, the visual team must first determine if the budget mandates standard mannequins that fit every display situations or if it allows for a variety of different types. The major mannequin companies such as Roostein, Patina V, Silvestri, and Greneker have showrooms in many countries.

In situations where budgets are limited, and little is available for mannequin replenishment, alternative solutions may be

Dramatic mannequins show how apparel looks on the human form.

needed to solve the problem. One approach is the creation of one's own mannequins. With the use of a few basic elements, such as a coat hanger, wire, and some pieces of lumber, even a novice can produce a form that will satisfy a display's needs.

Signage and Graphics

A look into most brick-and-mortar windows or walks through most of their premises immediately reveals a host of different signs and photographic enlargements that are quite striking.

Signs are used for a number of reasons, including the identification of the particular departments in the stores and announcements of special events. They are featured in many different formats including poster boards, banners, backlit transparencies, and pennants. They are either temporary, to be used for short time periods in display windows or for special events, or permanent, used for lasting identification purposes in departments. The major retailers generally have in-house staffs that produce the signage. Others rely upon external companies that produce everything from simple paper products to the more extravagant types.

One of the mainstays of many retail operations are **hanging and framing systems**. These are installations that enable the merchant to quickly and easily make changes that will benefit his or her operation. They are particularly useful to retailers whose customers have a minimal amount of time to spend in their stores. Since the average customer spends only nine minutes in a store, it is essential that he or she know exactly where to go to make the purchase. Another fact that underscores the need for directional signage is that 80 percent of the shoppers entering a store know exactly what they would like to buy, but only 50 percent know where to find it. The hanging and framing systems are perfect to use for getting the customer to the point of purchase quickly.

Uptons, a Georgia-based retailer, installed such a system and found that it has not only brought positive results to the company, but also enabled it to cut signage costs.

Today, more and more retailers are using photography as a means to dramatize their display windows and interiors. Retailers like Abercrombie & Fitch and Gap regularly use these graphics in both their windows and internal environments. They are modest in cost, can be quickly and inexpensively installed, and may be changed with little effort. Often times they are made available by the vendors without cost to the retailer.

The most recent innovation in this aspect of visual merchandising is digital graphics. They can be tailored to fit the budgets of both large and small retailers. On the grander scale are the graphics that were used in the Polo Sport flagship on Madison Avenue in New York City. The project was coproduced by Polo Sport Services and Duggal Color Projects. They teamed up to design and fabricate eight high-resolution photographic prints that went on to stop pedestrians in their tracks. The images were output using Cymbolic Sciences' Lightjet printer, which produced prints that were actually sharper than traditional photography.

A combination of graphics and signage attracts attention and provides product information.

Backlit transparencies are being used in malls to present timely, informative messages.

For companies that are smaller, the result can be inexpensive and equally effective. Chiasso, a small regional giftware chain in Chicago, used a Mother's Day promotion that involved 20 fabric banners, each measuring about 30 by 60 inches, that were produced with the use of the computer program, Adobe Illustrator, and the Raster Graphics 5442 electrostatic printer. The end result was a show-stopping display that cost relatively little.

Of course, stock photos provide images that may be quickly obtained at modest prices. Retailers like Gap and Eddie Bauer, for example, use them in many of their visual presentations. Among the more widely used resources are Adstock Photos, The Image Bank, and FPG International. Samples are available either through catalogs, by logging on to Web sites, or from CDs that many of the companies provide.

 Focus on . . .
Clearr Corporation

ONE OF THE MORE EXCITING CONCEPTS IN SIGNAGE CENTERS on images that are illuminated in some manner. Ever since Clearr Corporation entered the signage business in 1959, its products captured the attention of a variety of retailers, as well as the consuming public. Today, the company is the leading manufacturer of backlit and edgelit graphics.

Featured in department stores, specialty chains, shopping malls, outdoor environments, restaurants, banks, and other retail forums, their quality is unparalleled. Central to its production is the backlit format. With the aid of a lightbox, photographic transparencies immediately come to life. The vibrancy that is achieved through this medium has not been duplicated by any other form of signage. What makes this type of presentation even more exciting to the retailers is the cost factor and simplicity of production. Any slide, transparency, or color negative can be converted to a large transparency that fits the requirements of the the lightbox. The film is placed in a fixture that houses fluorescent bulbs to uniformly light the image from behind.

Drawing on the success of the stationary fixture, Clearr Corporation has taken the process one step further with motion capability. Macy's, in the children's department of its New York City flagship at Herald Square, uses Clearr's 3-Message Internally-Illuminated Display, Graphic Revolutions, and Scrolling Backlit Displays, MOVING PIX, as a focal point. With vibrant backlighting and mesmerizing motion, they continue to captivate the viewer's attention. Through specially designed computer controls, all of the images change in unison.

Aside from the backlit entries that gained the company prominence in the signage industry, it is also the producer of simulated neon signs, edgelit displays, and outdoor illuminated signs.

Since many of its users report sales increases of 20 percent or more, it is obvious that this investment is well founded.

Lighting

As was discussed earlier in the text in Chapter 10, Designing the Facility, lighting is an essential part of facilities design as well as visual presentations. It is the dramatic effects that lighting offers that quickly transforms an otherwise routine visual presentation into one that is enhanced.

One of the trends that is used in display lighting is the hiding of the fixtures that house the bulbs. Fixtures were almost always exposed to the viewer as in the case of **fluorescent fixtures**, **track lighting** systems, and **spotlight cans**. The fixtures themselves were considered to be important design elements, as well as providers of sufficient light for the displays.

The hidden light sources offer a blend of ambient and accent lighting, both of which are essential to perfectly light any display area and the merchandise that is within it. Generally, visual merchandisers utilize strong focal lighting on the products they wish to sell. Also, a little ambient light is used on the walls so that the goods will be separated from the backgrounds. Often times, the formula uses halogen light sources to provide the dramatic intensity necessary to highlight the merchandise, and hidden fluorescent reflectors to wash the walls. In any situation, experts are essential to make certain that the right lighting choices have been made to maximize the display's effectiveness.

The antithesis of the hidden light concept is the use of customized light fixtures that identify a retailer's image. Such retailers as Old Navy effectively use such fixtures in both their exterior and interior environments. With the Old Navy tagline, "Old Navy Covers the World," the creator of the light fixtures designed globe wall sconces that feature stainless steel, laser cut continents with glowing white acrylic oceans. It is the unique fixturing that not only gave the store its own image, but dramatically illuminated the selling areas as well.

Track lighting can be easily directed to highlight merchandise.

An Ethical Consideration

IS IT A LEGITIMATE ENHANCEMENT WHEN VISUAL MERCHANDISERS utilize blue bulbs to illuminate diamonds on black velvet, or is it an unethical practice that makes consumers believe the quality of the stone is better than it really is? When the customer removes the gemstone from the store, it often seems to be lacking the same sparkle that was present in the store. The high intensity of blue lighting, and the contrast of the black velvet, gives the impression that the diamond is a better quality than it actually is. In daylight, the reality of the purchase will often be noticed, and customer dissatisfaction will result.

Retailers who resort to this type of misrepresentation, although legally permissible, are running the risk of losing future business. Customers who consider themselves duped may not return for other purchasers.

• •

Light Sources

No matter which approach to lighting is used, it is essential that the appropriate light sources be selected. There are several to choose from including fluorescents, **incandescents**, **high-intensity discharge lamps (HIDs)**, **halogen**, or **neon**. Each has its own specific advantages that must be considered by lighting specialists and visual merchandisers before they can be used.

TABLE 15.2 LIGHT SOURCES		
CLASSIFICATION	**USES**	**ADVANTAGES**
Fluorescents	General overall lighting, wall washing, display illumination	Low cost, long lamp life
Incandescents	Spotlighting, overall illumination (floodlighting)	Enhances true color and textures, heat reduction (low volt variety)
High-Intensity Discharge (HIDs)	Unusual lighting	Small in size but produces more light per watt than either fluorescents or incandescents
Neon	Outdoor signage, indoor sculpted effects	Relatively maintenance-free, vivid colors easily sculpted into shapes
Halogen	Extremely bright illumination	One-quarter the size of an incandescent, ideally enhances merchandise

Fixtures and Systems

There are numerous fixtures and systems from which to choose. Some of those that are typically used are recessed systems, in which containers that hold either fluorescents or incandescents are set into the ceiling, track lighting, a system that allows for the adjustment of lighting fixtures to the exact position needed for proper illumination, and decorative lighting, such as chandeliers, used to add a visual impact to the overall store design. The use of more than one of these types of fixtures and systems provides an aesthetic, as well as a practical means of lighting.

It is the type of retail operation that dictates which lighting is best for illumination purposes. Recessed fluorescent fixtures, for example, are extensively used in supermarkets where overall lighting is essential. At the other extreme is the upscale fashion emporium where chandeliers are often seen not only to provide sufficient, dramatic lighting, but also to serve as an enhancement of the store's elegant environment.

In the broad spectrum of retail operations, track installations are mainstays. Not only do they serve the needs of the retailer because of their adjustable capability, but, because of the multitude of styles in which they are available, they augment the style that has been chosen by interior designers in the company's fixturing.

Color

Without incurring any extra expense, color is the one element that can dramatically impact a visual presentation. Visual merchandisers are keenly aware of the excitement that color can generate, and how it can transform an otherwise routine merchandise display.

Color has a great effect on our emotions. This makes the skillful use of it a plus in any visual display. It not only generates interest, but it also may motivate us to buy. Different colors can create different moods, thus stimulating certain responses. Blue, for example, the favorite color of most people, suggests coolness and serenity, while red often generates excitement. While the perfect color selection is not a pure science, the professional visual merchandiser generally knows which one will provide that extra incentive to stimulate positive reaction from the observer.

Used in its purest form, color may not always provide the exact tone necessary to maximize display effectiveness. Different **values** (the lightness or darkness of the color) and **intensities** (the brightness or dullness of the color) must be determined to create the exact colors that will enhance the merchandise that is paramount to the success of a display.

One of the ways in which even the novice may select the best color combinations or harmonies for a visual presentation is by understanding the **color wheel**. This device is one that helps us to understand the relationships of colors and applying them in the most effective manner. Using the wheel, color schemes or harmonies can be quickly selected without the possibility of error. Arrangements that are monochromatic, analogous, or complementary, for example, can be determined and applied appropriately to whatever merchandise is being displayed.

The color wheel has six main **hues** from which the visual merchandiser may choose for arrangements—the **primary colors** which are red, yellow, and blue, and the **secondary colors**, orange, violet, and green. Mixing two adjacent primaries results in the secondaries, while mixing a primary and secondary results in a tertiary color. By also adding neutrals to the scheme, additional results can be achieved.

The six major arrangements are as follows:

Monochromatic Color Schemes. The use of only one hue in the scheme.
Analogous Colors. Colors that are adjacent to each other on the wheel.
Complementary Colors. Two colors that are opposite each other on the wheel.
Split Complementary Color Scheme. One color and the two colors that are on either side of its complement.
Double Complementary Color Scheme. Two sets of colors that are opposites on the wheel.
Triadic Color Scheme. Arrangement of three colors that are equi-distant from each other on the wheel. (The primary colors form a triad as do the secondary and tertiary colors.)

Examination of Table 15.3 gives some examples of these harmonies and their effects.

TABLE 15.3
COMMON COLOR ARRANGEMENTS

Color Harmonies	Examples	Effects
Monochromatic	All one color, such as red	Visual elegance
Analogous	Red, red-orange, and orange	Visual excitement
Complementary	Yellow and violet	Color intensity is heightened
Split complementary	Yellow, blue-violet and red-violet	Very creative visual impact
Double complementary	Yellow-orange, yellow-green, red-violet, blue-violet	Magnetic effects
Triad	Yellow, red, and blue	Intensive color effects

Color usage, of course, has no limitations. Professionals often come up with harmonies and schemes that defy the scientific approach offered by the wheel, but result in eye-catching arrangements that are at once dramatic. They may be taken from fabrics of which the merchandise is made, wallpapers that are used as backgrounds, or display fixtures. By concentrating on these colors, the display will achieve a harmony between the background and the featured merchandise.

Additional interest may be achieved through color by utilizing tints or shades of the hues, different intensities, and the neutrals such as black, white, gray, and tan.

DESIGN PRINCIPLES

In order for a visual presentation to achieve the results that it wishes to convey to the consumer, it must be developed keeping in mind the many design principles that constitute a good display. Balance, emphasis, proportion, rhythm, and harmony are the design principles that must be adhered to by the visual installers ensure the best results.

Balance

The assignment of exact weights on two sides is not exactly what visual merchandisers are trying to achieve in their presentations. Their goal is to give the illusion of equal distribution. To achieve this balance, an imaginary line is drawn down the center of the area that is about to be visually presented. It might be an exterior store window, a shadow box, a vitrine, an interior platform or any other setting that holds a display. If satisfactorily accomplished, the merchandise and/or props on one side of the imaginary line should equal those on the other side. This illusion or visual effect may be achieved in one of two manners. They are either symmetrical or asymmetrical.

Symmetrical Balance

Also known as formal balance, **symmetrical balance** is the easier of the two to accomplish. It involves the placement of identical items on either side of the imaginary line that has been envisioned. If a mannequin is used on one side, then another is used to balance it on the other. While this is relatively simple to achieve, it sometimes leads to unimaginative presentations. Except for novices who are uncertain in terms of more creative installations, this is type of balance is not typically found in stores.

Asymmetrical balance, as seen here, allows for creativity and informality while maintaining the stability of the presentation.

Asymmetrical balance

While the equal distribution factor is still essential in this type of balance, the proper use of **asymmetrical balance** leads to more creative and exciting environments. Often referred to as informal balance, it allows the professional to produce less structured display arrangements. While still requiring an equality of merchandise or prop distribution, the pieces need not be placed in a mirror-like setting. The sum of the different elements one side of the imaginary line must equal the sum of those on the other. If a mannequin is used on one side, for example, it might be balanced by prop such as an artificial tree on the other. The ingenuity of the installer is most evident in asymmetrically balanced displays.

Emphasis

When we approach a store window or an interior display of merchandise, the viewer's eye should be immediately drawn to a particular item, or one that is supposed to be dominant. The emphasis or focal point should be on the merchandise and not on the backgrounds in which they are being presented. If the props, for example, are the pieces that capture the shopper's attention, and his or her eyes remain focused there, the display is considered to be a failure. The purpose of any visual presentation is to sell the merchandise, not the materials that are used as enhancements.

In order to create design emphasis, a number of approaches are used. One might be to accent or highlight the item that is central to the theme with the use of a halogen spotlight that throws out an intense light and separates it from the rest. Another would be to place emphasis on a piece of merchandise by selecting it in a color that is different from everything else in the display. If a red sweater, for example, is surrounded by white merchandise, the red item will become the focal point.

Stores like Pottery Barn use color as their means of creating emphasis. In any of their stores there is a tendency toward featuring an abundance of one color to attract attention.

Proportion

It is essential that the size of the objects featured in a display be in **proportion** to the size of the venue in which it they are being featured. A case in point is mannequins that are too tall for small showcase windows. They immediately give the viewer the impression that the installation was not carefully planned. Similarly, very small items should never be placed by themselves in large showcase windows. Their presence is quickly lost is such settings.

Rhythm

When all of the elements of the display help to move the eye smoothly from one to the other, **rhythm** has been achieved. It is up to the installer of the visual presentation to make certain that this movement has resulted. There are several methods by which rhythm can be achieved including repetition, continuous line, progression, radiation and alternation.

Rhythm may be achieved with the use of multiples of the same item.

The arrangement of ties on the round table forms a rhythmic radial design.

Repetition. This is achieved through the use of multiples of the same shape.

Continuous line. Linear devices such as a garden hose coiled through the merchandise provide a continuous line that moves the eye from one element to another.

Progression. When there is a gradation of shape, size, or color, progression has been accomplished. For example, when one color such as red is featured in tints such as pink, and gradually progresses to deeper tones, the eye automatically moves from one to the other.

Radiation. When there is a prop that is rounded, such as a wagon wheel, often used to display small items, the observer's eye moves outward from the central point of the installation.

Alternation. When shapes or colors are used alternately, rhythm can be achieved. By using a background of black and white, for example, a design rhythm is the result.

Harmony

When the visual merchandiser has successfully incorporated all of the elements of the display to form a cohesive picture, the principle of harmony has been accomplished. It generally requires the use of a central color scheme, props that enhance and augment the merchandise, lighting that attractively and dramatically illuminates the presentation, signage that provides additional information, and anything else that helps to transform the ultimate effect into one that is eye-catching.

THEMES

Today's retailers subscribe to three approaches to setting a picture for the merchandise they offer. It is the traditional, standard approach that utilizes changing themes to depict different season, holidays or special events. Typically, department stores rely upon this concept to make the transition from one period of time to the next. It revitalizes a store and signals the shopper that the next season's merchandise has arrived.

Many merchants are refraining from the ever changing visual concept and are opting for one that identifies the store with but one theme throughout the year. This is known as the thematic approach. In such endeavors, retailers must make certain that the concept is a lasting one since it will be the centerpiece of their operations for a long time. The initiator of this idea was Banana Republic. When they began their business, the founders' merchandising approach centered around safari-type clothing with khakis as the main emphasis and a permanent set of props and fixtures that would enhance these products. (See Chapter 10).

Most department stores rely on changing themes like Mother's Day in their visual programs.

TABLE 15.4		
VISUAL MERCHANDISING APPROACHES FOR SELECTED STORES		
COMPANY	**APPROACH**	**EXAMPLE**
Macy's (New York City flagship)	Traditional	Transformation of main floor with $1,000,000 in flowers to introduce spring
Disney Stores	Thematic	Entire store embellished with Disney characters and props
Marshall Field's	Traditional	Huge Christmas tree with lighting ceremony in main hall
Banana Republic	Minimalist	No obvious display props, lighting is major visual enhancement
OshKosh B'Gosh	Thematic	Railroad depot utilizes a wealth of props to augment product line
Ralph Lauren (Madison Avenue flagship)	Thematic	Mansion setting with a multitude of antiques to enhance merchandise
Ann Taylor	Minimalist	Basic fixturing without help from seasonal props

Finally, there is a trend for many merchants to forgo a great deal of visual merchandising and design interiors that best reflect their product assortments. Even the use of temporary props have been abandoned with the merchandise itself the only means of attracting attention. While this approach might not be a visual merchandiser's dream, it does fill the bill for stores like the aforementioned Banana Republic whose premises are minimally designed and perfectly suited for the sophisticated merchandise it offers.

Table 15.4 features selected retailers and the visual merchandising approaches they have chosen for their stores.

STEPS TO ASSURE VISUAL MERCHANDISING SUCCESS

The dollar investment in visual merchandising is often enormous in some retail organizations. If we examine the efforts of some of the country's major department stores, we realize that the expenses are in the millions. Of course, the costs are well worth the expenditure if the expected results are achieved. In order to maximize the effectiveness of window displays and interior installations, a procedure must first be established and then strictly adhered to by the staff.

Some of those areas of concern that must be continuously addressed include refurbishment of the components that are imperative to sound visual merchandising, the removal of displays that have outlived their timeliness, cleanliness of the environment in which a new installation is ready to be presented, daily refreshing of in-store displays, attention to merchandise offerings that are on self-serve counters, and the regular moving of merchandise to other areas in the department so that each product may be sufficiently exposed to the shoppers who are merely passing by.

Component Refurbishment

Think of the carefully executed widow display that cannot satisfactorily impact those who pass by because the spotlights that are used to accent the merchandise have burned out, or the poorly coifed mannequin's wig that immediately detracts from the merchandise that has been selected. These are but a few of the distractions that can make an otherwise effective display one that is below par. It is essential that if it is an exterior window or a vitrine within the store, that the glass be perfectly clean. Light bulbs must be new enough to assure that they will last the time that has been allotted for the installation and mannequins must be free of chips or scratches so as not to present a shabby image. Every component must be carefully scrutinized before it can be properly used.

Timeliness of the Display

When Christmas has passed or Valentine's Day has seen its final hours, for example, displays of that nature must immediately be withdrawn from their venues. Not only is the use of such space wasteful, it prevents showing merchandise that is timelier to the company's merchandising efforts. Immediately after Mother's Day, for example, the summer season is in full swing and swimwear might be the product that should take center stage. Since no one is interested any longer in the Mother's Day items, sales will not be forthcoming as a result of that visual effort.

Cleanliness of the Environment

If you have ever looked into a store window you might have witnessed some pins or price tags strewn on the floor. Carpet floor might hold loose threads and wooden floors might be scratched. These might be considered minor details, but they do take away from the overall presentation. These are simple problems to correct and should be done so every time an installation is mounted. Image is a very important factor to the success of any retailer. Any disregard of cleanliness often gives the impression of slipshod retailing.

Refreshing the In-Store Displays

With customers regularly pacing through the store, there is a tendency for many to tamper with the merchandise that has been carefully placed in a visual presentation. If a

mannequin is used on the selling floor, often times the passerby feels the fabric, or closely inspects the different apparel pieces in the display. At the end of the day, the installation is no longer as fresh as it was at the start of the day, and it becomes less attractive as the days pass. To make certain that a fresh quality is still part of the presentation, daily walkthroughs should be taken by a member of the visual merchandising team to make the necessary adjustments. Care must also be exercised in supermarkets where self-service displays need continuous merchandise replenishment. The purchasing and handling of products like produce must regularly be cared for so that the displays are always fresh. In this way, the shopper will be treated to a feast for the eyes and might be motivated to buy something that wasn't initially planned for. If this is not a routine practice, the end result will be lower sales, and an impression of a poorly managed retail operation.

Displays, particularly in high-traffic areas such as store entrances, should be regularly checked for tampering.

Continuous Maintenance of Self-Service Fixtures

Many brick-and-mortar operations have severely reduced the size of their sales staffs. Instead, they are turning to open counters from which the consumers may make their selections. While this does significantly control expenses, the end result is often a counter that is left in total disarray.

Two of the stores that utilize the self-selection concept to are Gap and Banana Republic. Each uses a visual merchandising approach that revolves around islands where merchandise is abundantly displayed according to color. The items are carefully folded to add greater appeal and motivate shoppers to examine them. Of course, with this understood touch-me concept, the merchandise often ends up as a jumbled mess, with items no longer in their assigned places.

To make certain that this less than appealing situation is quickly corrected, it is essential that folders always be on the selling floor. It is really a simple matter to solve the problem. All it takes is a determination by management to address the problem and instill in those on the selling floor the need for a perfect look.

Merchandise Rearrangement

In every department in a store there are prime selling locations, as well as those locations that have less visibility. Merchandise that is featured in prime locations often catch the attention of those who are passing through on their way to another area. In this case, unexpected sales are often produced. In order to assure that each item in the inventory gets the benefit of the best location on the selling floor, it is essential that the different products be rotated. Of course, if one style is a hot number it should hold center stage until its salability wanes. Once this occurs, the items should be quickly replaced by others that have greater sales potential.

Gap is a firm subscriber to this philosophy, placing the newest items at the front of the store. They are replaced when that inventory is about to sell out. It then moves these items back onto the selling floor, making way to the new arrivals. The rotation always gives the shopper something new to look at and purchase.

VISUAL MERCHANDISING: THE LINK TO ADVERTISING

As those in retailing know, it is advertising that is supposed to alert consumers to a retailer's merchandise offerings. Through the use of each of the media, sales should come to the brick-and-mortar operation either by mail and telephone orders or through in-store visits. By and large, those merchants with stores would rather motivate the shopper to make personal visits because those sales are often greater than the ones that come from off-site outlets. With the assortments greater than any catalog or Web site can offer, the chances for bigger sales are greater.

Thus, advertising is designed to motivate the consumer to come to the store and satisfy his or her shopping needs. Once he or she makes the trip, it is up to the visual merchandising team to continue the effort.

The major department stores, who are the traditional proponents of advertising, use large parallel-to-sidewalk windows, especially in their flagships. These are the showcases that house the merchant's most important attractions. Often times the visual merchandisers take their cues from the buyers who have expended advertising dollars in the promotion of specific merchandise or special events. Buyers might be looking to promote the introduction of a new designer, the heralding of the new back-to-school collections, or the welcoming of spring. Once the ads have run, they are often tied into these show windows. The ads announce the event and the display presents the merchandise to the consumer who has been motivated to come to the store to see the advertised merchandise. Coupling the ad and the visual presentation gives the promotion the much needed one–two punch. The visual effort doesn't stop there, but merely is the vehicle to get the shopper into the store. Once in the department that sells the items, creative interior displays are there to further entice the customer. If all goes as expected, the team effort often results in a purchase and a satisfied customer.

Thus, promotional dollars are best spent when the various components of the retailer's promotion division act in unison. Many produce calendars which address the various events that the store is developing, the different media and visual components that will be utilized, and the dates of the presentations. In this way, the visual team has sufficient time to design the perfect installations that will not only make for eye-catching displays, but will also enhance the concepts that were laid out in the ads.

If the buyers have carefully chosen the merchandise, then these collaborative efforts will maximize sales.

TRENDS FOR THE NEW MILLENNIUM

- The use of the formal, extravagant window displays once commonplace in retailing has given way to more interior presentations. With the cost of retail space at an all-time high, merchants are opting to use their square footage for more selling space rather than for exterior windows. A look at the mall entries, whose stores have limited window space, indicates that this traditional visual merchandising endeavor has seen better times.

- All types of graphics, including the stationary and in-motion types, illuminated externally or from within, will continue to play a major role in visual merchandising. With its relatively modest expense, and its ability to attract attention, retailers will spend more of their promotional budgets on this visual aid.

- There will be an even greater place for stylized mannequins rather than the traditional realistic types because they tend to cost less and serve the same purpose.

- More and more retailers will opt for basic environments with less attention paid to seasonal displays that utilize a great deal of props. The merchandise itself will be carefully displayed to provide the focal point.
- Lighting will continue to be of the low voltage variety to save energy.
- The visual merchandisers role will continue to expand in the area of store design.

CHAPTER HIGHLIGHTS

- In large retail organizations, the visual concept is developed and carried out by a team of in-house visual merchandisers.
- Many chain organizations subscribe to the concept of centralized visual merchandising. Displays are developed and photographed at the home office, and then sent to individual units for the installations to be carried out by the store's manager.
- Small retailers who are unable to have their own visual merchandisers either use freelancers to carry out the display installations or develop their own plans.
- The most important component of any visual presentation is the merchandise. All the other elements used are enhancements.
- Lighting is a very important part of any visual display. It highlights the merchandise by setting the appropriate mood for the viewers.
- Graphics are becoming more and more important to today's visual environment. One of the leading types is called the backlit transparency, which is illuminated from within to provide an exciting image.
- Color is one element that is free to the user. If properly utilized it can create eye-catching displays that motivate purchasing.
- There are several design principles that are used by visual merchandisers in every installation. When all of them are correctly applied, the end result will be a display that is totally harmonious.

- If a display is to achieve its maximum potential, care must be exercised and it must be carefully scrutinized to make certain that it is free of imperfections.

IMPORTANT RETAILING TERMS

in-house display staff
vitrine
walkthroughs
animated installations
stylistic mannequins
hanging and framing systems
fluorescents fixtures
track lighting
spotlight cans
incandescents
high-intensity discharge lamps (HIDs)
halogen
neon
values
intensities
color wheel
hues
primary colors
secondary colors
monochromatic color scheme
analogous colors
complementary colors
split complementary color scheme
double complementary color scheme
triadic color scheme
symmetrical balance
asymmetrical balance
proportion
rhythm

FOR REVIEW

1. Who is generally responsible for the visual merchandising concept in a department store?
2. How does the centralized visual merchandising concept work?

3. Since most small retailers cannot afford their own in-house visual design staff, how do they utilize the services of display professionals?

4. Which component of a display is the most important and why?

5. In addition to store-bought props, what others can a visual merchandiser use to create effective presentations?

6. How do stylistic mannequins differ from the traditional types?

7. What is a backlit transparency and how does it differ from the traditional signage found in retail operations?

8. What are hanging and framing systems?

9. Define the term *hidden light sources*.

10. In what way do fluorescents and incandescents differ?

11. Why do most visual merchandisers turn to halogen lighting for their installations?

12. What purpose does the color wheel serve in visual presentations?

13. How do monochromatic and analogous color schemes differ?

14. How can a monochromatic color scheme be expanded to make window and interior displays more interesting?

15. What is the difference between symmetrical and asymmetrical balance?

16. Distinguish between continuous line rhythm and rhythmic radiation.

17. What is meant by a thematic approach in visual merchandising?

18. Why must the display components be continually refurbished?

19. What is visual merchandising's link to advertising?

AN INTERNET ACTIVITY

One of the challenges of visual merchandising is to select the appropriate components to enhance the merchandise that is being featured. With so many sources available, it is often difficult and time-consuming to select the best vendors to satisfy a retailer's display needs.

The advent of the Internet has made this task an easier one. Retailers need not make endless vendor visits to find products for their display installations.

Using the Web sites listed in Table 15.1, Selected Vendors of Visual Merchandising Products, choose one display component such as lighting or mannequins to find out the breadth and depth of vendors' assortments. Prepare a chart with the following heads, using the information you have obtained on the Internet. If you find any other Web sites, they may be used in place of the ones listed in this table.

Vendor	Web Site	Product Line

EXERCISES AND PROJECTS

1. The most important silent seller that a retailer uses to entice consumers to enter their premises is the exterior display window. Ranging from the very large parallel-to-sidewalk types to those that are more like shadow boxes, the retailer is able to put his or her best foot forward. Plan to visit three of the most important brick-and-mortar operations in your area to evaluate the effectiveness of the displays in these exterior windows. The following should be used in a report that will be delivered orally to the class:

    - photographs of the displays
    - concept that was used to attract attention
    - the types of signage and graphics, if any, that were used
    - the effectiveness of the lighting
    - the attention paid to the various design elements
    - the cleanliness of the venue in which the display was featured

    Upon completing each visit and addressing each above point, mount the photos on three individual foam-boards. In addition, your evaluation of each of the displays should be presented.

2. Today's supermarkets are using a good deal of visual merchandising to present their products. In fact, many are using new fixturing, lighting, and other enhancements to better display their goods. Visit three supermarkets to determine the level of visual merchandising being used in the stores. List your findings on a chart with the following heads:

Company Name	Fixturing	Lighting	Unique Display Features

Compare all three stores to determine which one was best suited to attract customers and sell more merchandise. Be sure to list the reasons for your selection.

THE CASE OF CREATING A VISUAL ENVIRONMENT TO REFLECT A NEW COMPANY DIRECTION

When Home Décor opened their first store, it decided that the best approach in terms of visual merchandising would be to build a facility that would be strikingly simple. Not knowing exactly what would dictate their future merchandising needs, store management believed the minimalist approach would be best.

The stocking of basic accessories for the home such as traditional glassware, dinnerware, tableware, and the like seemed to perfectly fit into this type of environment. As time passed, the company began to open other units, and today has a total of 28 stores in the chain. Remaining faithful to their original merchandising philosophy, the company continued to carry a wide assortment of sterling silver and silver-plated tableware, crystal glassware, and china.

During the past few years, the buyers and merchandisers began to see that fashion had come to home furnishings. The same designers who created apparel were now crossing over into this aspect of retailing. The product mixes invariably took on a fashion-forward look, with a great deal of the items having a contemporary look. Instead of the basic neutral colors that were the mainstays of the home products' industry, new collections were replete with bold colors and imaginative designs. Besides management's awareness of this new trend, the customers also became more cognizant of it and began asking for these items. Little by little, the new items were added and eventually filled more space than the traditional wares.

One of the glaring deficiencies at Home Décor centered upon its their visual presentations. The lackluster visual presentations no longer seemed appropriate for this new look. The problem confronting the company was how to transform the present store appearance into one that visually enhanced the new merchandising direction without adding considerable expense.

Questions

1. Which physical components might be used to transform the premises of the stores to give them a more contemporary flair?
2. Without adding any expense and retaining the same fixtures, how can the overall look of the store be updated to create more visual excitement?

CHAPTER 16
Servicing the Customer

After you have completed this chapter, you should be able to discuss:

- ► Why personal selling is imperative in a wide variety of retailing establishments.
- ► The reasons why many stores that once subscribed to the self-selection concept are recognizing the importance of the sales associate and are now expanding their sales forces.
- ► The rules of the selling game, which include a positive appearance, motivational skills, enthusiasm, knowledge of the product and the company, communication skills, and tactfulness.
- ► The manner in which retailers are training their sales staffs to better service customers.
- ► The importance of selling in the various off-site retailing ventures that are becoming more important than ever before.
- ► The different types of charge accounts and credit card services that are provided to consumers.
- ► How retailers are servicing customers through the use of traditional as well as customized services.
- ► Why call centers are playing an important role in retailing.

As we closely examine the retail playing field, we recognize the vast number of different operations that are vying for a share of the consumer's dollar. Whether it is the brick-and-mortar companies, catalogs, Internet Web sites, or cable television shopping networks, there is a wealth of opportunity for the shopper to have his or her needs quickly satisfied. How a consumer decides which of these merchants he or she will patronize is, of course, based upon merchandise assortments, pricing, ease in making the purchase, and, in the case of the brick-and-mortar operations, their design and physical layout.

With the enormity of the competition, another factor that often plays a significant role in motivating the customer to select one merchant rather than another is service. All too often, retailers have neglected to satisfactorily address the needs of the customer. They spend considerable sums maintaining management teams that direct the businesses operations, and train them to meet the challenges needed to be produce sufficient revenues. However, those who interface daily with the company's clientele are not as carefully trained. When one enters a store, it is often difficult to find a sales associate, and when one does appear, he or she is sometimes ill prepared to answer the simplest questions. The problem of properly servicing the customer doesn't rest with brick-and-mortars operations alone, but carries over to the off-site retailers as well. It is hard to understand why merchants spend so much on advertising and other promotional endeavors to bring the shopper to the store only to let him or her get away without making a purchase.

An inattentive salesperson can lose a sale even though shoppers seem interested in the products.

It is a relatively simple matter to correct. Through proper orientation of new employees, meaningful training, and competitive remuneration to attract above average personnel, the problem can be quickly resolved.

The other way in which merchants can distinguish themselves is through the offering of services that go beyond the attention offered by sales associates. There is a wide disparity among retailers in terms of the services they offer to the shoppers. Of course, the breadth and depth of these services must vary according to the different retailer classifications. The traditional department store, for example, will be more likely to offer services that the discounter will not be able to. The former, with the benefit of larger markups will have the funds necessary to make the shopping experience more pleasurable than the off-pricer whose customers are more interested in bargains than extras.

Each merchant, in order to remain competitive in his or her classification, must examine the plusses and minuses associated with providing services to customers, and utilize those to distinguish itself from the others in their class.

The material that is presented in this chapter focuses not only on selling but on the broad spectrum of services that are offered by retail operations.

PERSONAL SELLING

In the not too distant past, when one entered a store, he or she was routinely greeted by a sales associate who was ready and able to guide the shopper to the right merchandise, assist with the purchasing decision, and transform the shopper into a satisfied customer. It was not unusual to find a large percentage of consumers who would be considered loyal customers. In the 1970s and 1980s, the era of this type of personalized service began to give way to the concept of self-selection. Retailers began to alter their environments with the newer open counters from which shoppers may help themselves. In many retail operations, gone were the traditional counters that necessitated sales assistance. This concept enabled retailers to reduce the size of their sales staff, and in turn, the expenses associated with **personal selling**.

While the cost of doing business was reduced, the relationships between customer and sales associate waned. Many customers preferred this type of shopping, but others felt they weren't properly attended to, especially if questions needed to be answered.

At this point in time, the selling phenomenon is once again resurfacing. Merchants are finding that sales associates not only help make the sales, but often are also responsible for bigger sales because of their ability to suggest additional merchandise to the shoppers who seek their assistance. Even those who opted for the self-service route are turning to personal selling so that they can satisfactorily compete in today's overcrowded marketplace. Even stores that pride themselves as off-pricers, offering the best for less, are hiring sales associates to interface with the shoppers. One such retailer is Stein Mart. While many of Stein Mart departments have a **skeleton sales crew** on hand to assist shoppers, its boutique department offers personalized service to any one who wants it.

Many chain operations such as Ann Taylor and Banana Republic approach selling in a less formalized manner. Shoppers are greeted as they enter the store and are asked if they need assistance. The level of the seller–buyer relationship is determined by the customer. If close attention is wanted, full assistance is available.

 Focus on . . .
Nordstrom

STARTING ON THE SITE OF AN OLD SHOE REPAIR SHOP, John Nordstrom invested $5,000 to establish a shoe store in Seattle, Washington, in 1901. With $1,500 to fix up the store and $3,500 for inventory, he was on his way to introducing American consumers to one of the most prestigious retail ventures in retailing history. From his very first day in business, when he had to take a pair of shoes from the window to sell to a customer, he hit upon the principle of doing whatever it takes to take care of the customer. It is this principle by which Nordstrom still runs today. In the 1960s, the company, now with other units, expanded into apparel.

The centerpiece of the operation is service, with personal selling, in particular, at the forefront. Its attention to customer needs remains unparalleled in retailing. While others continue to capitalize on the Nordstrom approach, few if any have reached the heights of personal selling as has Nordstrom.

Unique to the company is the concept that sales associates may sell merchandise to their customers from any department throughout the store. That is, they take care of the customer from start to finish. If, for example, a shopper has purchased a dress and is in the market for a pair of shoes, a handbag, and hosiery, and requests that the sales associate in the dress department help her with her other needs, that salesperson takes her from department to department helping with the other selections. Nordstrom believes that once the sales associate has established a rapport with the customer, that associate should be able to help with all of the customer's wardrobe needs.

The company is one of the few in the United States to pay its sales employees on commission. In this way, those who are self-starters and sufficiently motivated will be paid according to their ability. Commission sales, along with bonuses, enable the sales staff to work harder and establish their own customer followings. Those who meet or surpass preestablished sales volume goals achieve the status of Pacesetter. Target figures are adjusted annually, with about 8 to 12 percent of the people in each division reaching Pacesetter goals. Those who achieve this level are recognized with a special certificate, an event or an outing in their honor, business cards designating their Pacesetter status, and an increased employee discount for one year.

Those who are at the top of the selling game at Nordstrom do not wait for the customers to come to the store to serve them. Most of the Pacesetters make great use of the telephone in order to keep in touch with the clientele that they have established. Asking for permission to call the clients makes their relationship even stronger. It might be to chat about some new item that seemed perfect for the customer or perhaps about a special sales event. The concept seems to work perfectly in that customers come to rely upon these calls to keep them abreast of what's happening at Nordstrom.

Once these relationships have been established, future sales come as a result of a number of different circumstances. It might be a call from someone's private plane or an overseas venue with a request for a suit that will be needed in a couple of hours. Knowing the client's measurements and tastes from previous meetings, the order can be quickly filled.

Recognizing that personal attention is the key to success for both the merchant and the sales associate, Nordstrom goes the extra mile in making the sales staff feel special. It supplies them with thank you notes that may be sent after a sale has been completed, postcards, personalized letters, and address lists to help them follow up with customers.

In an industry that is often characterized by low salaries, Nordstrom is the exception. With sales associates salaries often reaching $100,000 or more, it indicates that special attention to servicing the customer brings monetary rewards usually reserved only for management personnel.

The Rules of the Game

When a salesperson greets a shopper, he or she must first carefully prepare for the meeting. First and foremost, it must be understood that the sales associate represents the company. The initial dialogue is extremely important. If successfully mastered, it can mean the difference between a sale and a walkout. Of paramount importance for the sales associate are appearance, enthusiasm, communication skills, product knowledge, company knowledge, tactfulness, and self-control. All attributes but appearance are relevant to those employed in the brick-and-mortar operations as well as the off-site venues.

Appearance

A sales associate's appearance is very important. Many retailers, in orientation sessions for new employees, stress appropriate dress and grooming for saleseople. Some retailers don't address this issue, and take the risk of having someone on the selling floor that doesn't foster a proper image for the company. What is appropriate dress? Each of us has his or her own standards that may or may not fit into the image that the merchant is trying to impart to the customer.

Appropriate dress is an essential part of working on the selling floor.

Today, retailers require far less structured attire than they did years ago. In the not-too-distant past, pants for women were taboo and bright colors were frowned upon. A more cloned look was the order of the day. At this point in time, many merchants subscribe to a more relaxed manner of dress much the same as various business environments, such as investment banking and law. In fact, more and more retailers are encouraging their staffs to wear the merchandise that is featured in the store. Very often a shopper admires a salesperson's attire and this helps make a sale. In the Ralph Lauren flagship in New York City, sales associates are given monthly dollar allowances to purchase the store's merchandise and wear it on the selling floor. The sophisticated dress of the Lauren sales associates often inspires shoppers to buy the same items. At chains like Gap and Banana Republic, the sales staff is also encouraged to wear their company's offerings. While those at Gap are casually dressed in appropriate attire for that store, in other retail venues that mode of dress might not be considered appropriate.

The rule of dress must be spelled out at the time of employment. Once it has been clearly established and understood by the new employees, a positive appearance will more than likely follow.

Enthusiasm

Having an enthusiastic attitude should not be confused with the hard-sell approach. Shoppers should not be overwhelmed, as in the case of the stereotypical used car salesperson, but should feel that the seller has a real feeling for the merchandise. The lethargic approach will often dampen the spirit of the shopper and discourage purchasing. A warm, friendly smile, along with a bright, cheerful greeting, will sometimes transform a looker into an interested customer.

If we examine two reactions to the same film, we will better understand the value of enthusiasm. When two friends are asked about the same movie, each might have a different way of displaying their enthusiasm. One might say it was really good. The other might describe it as a film with fabulous acting, great scenery, and a must see. Of course the latter example will more likely motivate the individual who asked the question to buy a ticket.

Enthusiasm seems to transfer from one individual to another. If properly used on the selling floor, the sales associate has a better chance to make the sale.

Communication Skills

Using the right language and proper diction are extremely important when first greeting the shopper and while trying to make the sale. It doesn't mean the language usage should be extraordinary, but sufficiently simple and clear so that a seller–shopper dialogue is the result.

The use of slang should be avoided. While this is appropriate in personal discussions, there is no place for it in the business world. Learning to speak correctly is a matter of study.

Through courses, videos, audiotapes, and CDs, those interested in mastering the language will be able to do so and become better sales people.

Product Knowledge

Over the course of any selling day, some shoppers are likely to inquire about the specifics of a product. This is especially true for companies that sell electronics. Living in a technological society requires the sales associate to know all the nuances of the latest technology. Whether selling a computer, television, VCR, camcorder, DVD, Palm Pilot, or any other device, the details of the product should be known.

Product information is not solely necessary in electronics' world. It is also essential to know about fabrics, styles, silhouettes, and color harmonies in the world of fashion. A shopper might want to know if the item being considered for an overseas trip will require ironing, or if a particular garment's shape will remain in style for more than one season.

Product information is available to the salesperson from a variety of sources. Colleges and universities offer specialized courses that concentrate on a host of products. Videos are also very popular way to learn about products. Many of these videos are available from vendors who wish to make the retailer's employees better informed. Information on specific merchandise classifications is available through trade associations and business groups. Those interested in learning more about gems, for example, can obtain a booklet produced by the Gemological Society. Online resources are also other places where such information can be obtained.

When a sales associate is adequately prepared to answer any merchandise questions, the sale is more likely to be achieved.

Company Knowledge

One should never have to call upon a manager to answer questions concerning company policies. A sales person should be well-informed about return policies, credit availability, merchandise returns, alterations, special order merchandise, and the like. Not only will this give the shopper an understanding of the company's policies and philosophies, but it also helps to establish confidence in the store and its sales staff.

This information is generally available in new employee orientation sessions as well as through ongoing discussions with the management team.

The Stein Mart Story
Satisfying the Shopper through Courteous Selling

MANY OF TODAY'S MERCHANTS HAVE PUT SELLING last in their organizations. Except for the few who sell upscale merchandise, or items that require a great deal of technical information before the sale can be made, the art of selling has become a rarity on many selling floors. In particular, the value merchants rely on their pricing structures to motivate shoppers to buy without the assistance of sales associates.

Although Stein Mart is a value retailer, the company strongly believes that personal, courteous selling is a major factor in its success. Stein Mart's sales associates are well trained before they are allowed to go onto the selling floor.

As mentioned earlier in the chapter, of particular note are the selling endeavors of the boutique ladies, a mainstay in all of the company's units. These sales associates are trained treat each shopper as a special client, and to help shoppers make selections that range from a single item to an entire wardrobe. Each boutique lady is actually a fashion consultant, offering a service that is generally unheard of at off-price ventures. The efforts of these individuals have resulted in repeat business year after year, bringing greater sales to the company.

Many of these women, through their courteous and professional demeanors have developed their own clienteles and have helped Stein Mart maintain the image of a service retailer.

• •

Tactfulness

With knowledge of psychology, the seller is more likely to approach sensitive problems more easily. If an overweight shopper, for example, is deciding between two outfits, the sales person should "sell" the shopper on the most flattering one. Only if there is persistence by the shopper for the wrong item should the seller acquiesce. By allowing the "wrong" purchase, the sold merchandise more than likely will be returned. Not only will the sale be voided, but the end result could be a dissatisfied customer.

Leading the customer in the right direction without implying that he or she is making the wrong decision requires care. If carefully approached, and the right words are used, the appropriate merchandise will be bought and the chances of that individual becoming a regular patron will also improve.

Tact is something that is second nature to some people, but others need continual training to get it right, as discussed in the next section.

Self-Control

Even the most mild mannered salesperson has come across a situation in which he or she is ready to verbally or even physically react to a customer's demands. Bearing in mind the **customer-is-always-right concept**, this reaction must be avoided at all costs. Losing one's temper will not only result in the loss of the sale at hand, but also might affect future business for the company as well.

Those with short fuses shouldn't consider a career in sales. They will be wasting their time, and not only will not be up to the challenge, but might quickly find themselves unemployed.

Perfecting the Persona

The proper sales training is very important. All too often, except for a small percentage of retailers, sales training is either accomplished during a brief time frame, or not at all. The arguments for not giving adequate training include the cost, the probability of rapid employee turnover, and the lack of trainers to accomplish the task. Of course, ill-prepared sales associates will lose many sales and even discourage shoppers from returning to the store.

Merchants who do properly train their sales staff can accomplish the task several ways, including through role-playing, videocassettes, on the job training, vestibule training, and online training.

Role-playing

No other sales training technique parallels an actual sale as does **role-playing**. It is a methodology that involves two individuals; one poses as the buyer, and the other the shopper. The typical situation may take place in the retailer's premises or at an off-site professional training venue. Whichever location is used, it is essential that a trained evaluator oversee the performance. At the end of the presentation the evaluator rates the level of selling concentrating on a number of areas such as the customer approach, communication skills, and the ability to handle the customer's objections. Recording the session makes an indelible impression on the trainee. By playing the video back, the trainer and trainee are better able to discuss each aspect of the presentation and amend those that need improvement. By reviewing the video again and again, the newly hired sales associate will be able to hone his or her selling skills.

To make the session even more meaningful, the evaluator should design a form that addresses each of the essential elements of a professional sale, and provide the trainee with a copy of it. This will serve as a future reference point, which, like the video, may be referred to many times. In addition to the written evaluation, a careful verbal assessment should be delivered to the new seller. In this way, any constructive criticism can also be used in real selling situations.

Professional Videocassettes

Today, more than ever before, a wealth of professionally prepared materials are available to retailers for use in training their sales associates. High on the list are the videocassettes that instruct the viewers on everything from preparing to sell to the actual stages of a sales demonstration. The advantages of these tools are numerous and include low cost, the ability to use the tapes over and over again, off-premises use, and limiting the time necessary for in-person training.

On the Job Training

While pretraining is generally an essential aspect of sales personnel readiness, it alone doesn't always place the trainee in a real-life situation. Often times, human resources managers who are training specialists use one of the pretraining techniques in conjunction with **on-the-job-training**.

The best of these arrangements involves a mentoring system in which a retailer's seasoned sales associate closely watches the new employee as he or she makes his or her way through an actual selling situation. The mentor is given the responsibility of evaluating the sales attempt, making suggestions for improvement, and in general, providing the little extras that would improve the performance.

If this approach is used it is imperative that the mentor not be involved in the actual sales situation, but be close by to be able to assess the performance. Interference during the sales attempt could not only give the shopper the impression that the salesperson was ill-prepared, but also could cause a drop in the employee's morale.

Vestibule Training

It should be understood that selling is not merely a conversation between the seller and the potential customer. It generally involves a host of other responsibilities. Learning to use the company's systems, especially the computerized sales terminal, is essential to the organization's inventory and sales recording controls. If not properly handled, the problems that arise could hamper the proper recording of the sale, giving either the customer or employer an unwarranted disadvantage.

The vast majority of today's retailers find that credit card purchases significantly outdistance cash sales. Even supermarkets, the last of the cash-and-carry merchants, are finding that many of their customers are opting for credit or debit card transactions. Proper training in the use of "plastic" assures that only those customers who have been approved will get the merchandise.

Even the task of properly packing merchandise should be carefully taught. It will ensure the safe arrival of breakables and the arrival of soft goods as perfectly as when they were purchased. This procedure can be quickly and easily accomplished by a seasoned professional and need not take endless hours to perfect.

The use of any number of forms can be easily taught in this **vestibule training** venue. Today's merchants are busy satisfying the customer's needs by making available special order goods, arranging for alterations, enabling goods to be delivered to the home, or trying to locate merchandise from another store. It becomes a problem on the selling floor if the sales associate is ill-prepared to handle these tasks. An otherwise simple task can take unnecessary time and result in the cancellation of the purchase.

Online Training

One of the newest sales training methods is **online training**. Many companies recognizing the need for such training and the retailer's inability to always adequately perform this function have made a variety of training approaches available. In addition to specific course packages that are available in an Internet format, some training groups also provide CD-ROMS if that is a company's preference.

One leader in the field is MOHR Learning, a division of Provant, America's leading performance solutions company. One of its more popular products is Quick-Start, a tool that is available either as an Internet course or a CD-ROM. It involves a sports themed selling game that challenges the user in the art of selling. It concentrates on four key areas such as greeting the shopper, product knowledge and selling benefits, handling objections, and closing the sale. One of the advantages of the program is the ability to tailor it to other merchandise classifications such as clothing, electronics, and housewares. The programs can also be personalized for each retailer by providing MOHR with the merchant's specific policies and responsibilities. Retailers can access its Web site at www.mohrlearning.com.

The Selling Experience

While some people have a natural instinct for selling, there are no sales short cuts. Of course, if a shopper enters the store, selects his or own products, and brings them to the sales associate to finalize the sale, this is a simple sale to complete. On the other hand, when a shopper is moving through a department without giving an indication whether he or she is really there to buy, it is a challenge to the seller to transform the shopper into a customer. By arming one's self with the proper approaches, needs assessment, and product information, a sale is more likely to be forthcoming.

Basically, the selling experience involves a number of different stages such as greeting the customer, determining what his or her needs are, presenting the merchandise that will hopefully satisfy those needs, handling any objections that might prevent the sale from being realized, and closing the sale.

Greeting the Customer

Unskilled sales people often use the approach that begins with, "May I help you?" The danger of this approach is that the response might be, "No." If the shopper replies negatively to the sales associate, there is nowhere else to go. Questions that might bring negative responses should be avoided at all costs.

The correct approach might begin with just a smile. This could be followed with, "Good morning. If there's anything I can help you with, please let me know. If you need any sizes, I'll be more than happy to help you with that. If we don't have the size or style you want, please let me know and I'll do my best to accommodate you." This

A pleasant greeting can set the stage for a successful sales presentation.

type of greeting is basically the treatment that sales associates themselves would like to receive when they shop.

Service-oriented retailers like Nordstrom teach this type of approach during training sessions and have learned that they work best when trying to begin a sales presentation. It helps put the shopper at ease, and takes the hard-sell overbearing attitude out of the selling mix. The dialogue needs to begin on a positive note, and carry through until the sale has been consummated.

Needs Assessment

When a salesperson has been successful in approaching the customer, often times a specific item will be requested. In these cases, it is irrelevant to try to determine the customers needs. This, however, is not always the case. Often times an associate needs to question the customer to determine what he or she is looking for. In the case of the individual who has accepted the seller's offer to help with the purchase of computer, the first question might be, "Is the computer for your home or office?" Once this has been established, it might be followed with, " What types of tasks are you expecting to perform on the computer?"

In a fashion operation, where the customer is looking for a dress, the first question should be, "Is there any special occasion that you need the dress for?" If the response is for a party, it could be followed by "Is it a formal affair or one that is semiformal?" Next, the question might be, "Do you have any color preference, or would you like me to show you the popular colors for this season?" Once the needs have been established, the time is ripe to bring the appropriate merchandise to the customer.

Merchandise Presentation

Merely showing an item or two doesn't often motivate the customer to make a purchase. This art of the sales presentation might warrant a demonstration or at least a discussion as to why the specific items were chosen to bring to the customer's attention.

In the case of electronics, a demonstration is generally in order. If the purchase in question is a television, the comparison of two would be in order. In this way the prospective purchaser would be able to assess visual clarity, sound, and other features such as picture in picture. Offered two choices, the customer is able to make a comparison that could lead to a sale.

If a customer is interested in a particular line of cosmetics, then an *application* could immediately reveal which products were better suited to the individual. It might be a matter of color choice or ease of use. For fragrances, applying a few different products could provide the customer with choices.

Some products need to be tried on, including apparel and footwear. In these situations, the sales associate should lead the customer to the fitting room, and inquire whether or not assistance is necessary.

In every case, a continuing dialogue should occur. This will help the seller assess the purchaser's acceptance of the items, and determine which of them have a chance to be purchased. Sometimes it is a matter of reinforcing the customer's own decisions, or suggesting an alternative which would more than likely be the one that best serves the individual's needs.

It is most important that a positive attitude be maintained at all times by the seller. Not every shopper is a pleasure to serve, and some might need more attention than others. Often times, objections pertaining to the merchandise will be forthcoming and must be professionally handled to close the sale.

Handling Objections

When a customer is not ready to commit to a purchase, it is often necessary to find out the reasons why. It is not necessarily that he or she is disinterested in buying, but that more time might be needed before the final decision is made. Whatever the circumstances, the sales associate must be able to handle the objections and try to turn them into selling points.

There are several techniques that are standard for overcoming objections in retail. One might be to use the **agree and counterattack method**. In this methodology, the seller agrees with the objection, but uses some selling points that refute it. Sometimes it is called the **"yes, but" technique**. In a selling situation that involves the purchase of an automobile, the customer might object to the leather seats, stating that they are too cold in the winter. The seller, using this technique, would agree only to further respond with, "Heated seats are standard on this model and will provide excellent comfort during the cold months."

When a shopper professes that the price of the dress is higher than expected, the seller's response might be, "Yes it is a little more expensive, but it is so basic that it could be worn for many occasions."

Another approach to customer objections involves the asking of questions. This must be carefully done as to not put the individual on the defensive. If, for example, a customer is not in agreement with the type of sofas that have been suggested, the sales associate might ask, "What period of furniture would your prefer?"

Unless you are absolutely certain that the customer's objections are ill-founded, you should never disagree with him or her. When you are positive that the objection is incorrect, then denying it is in order. Of course, care must be exercised when using this methodology. In the case of price, for example, if the customer states that your competitor sells the identical item for less, and you are certain that this is not true, the objection might handled with, "No, I believe that are prices are the same, but I will be willing to check to make certain."

It should be noted that not every sale can come to a satisfactory conclusion even if all objections are carefully handled. Not everyone can be sold, but by keeping the discussion on a positive level, the customer might come back at another time.

Closing the Sale

When the seller believes he or she has satisfied all of the preceding stages of the presentation, the time could be ripe to attempt concluding the sale. The time selected is not always going to bring the sale to a favorable end. Choosing the right time is often a matter of trial and error. The first attempt, if unsuccessful, is considered to be a **trial close**. That is, others should be tried until every approach has been exhausted.

Sometimes the customer gives a clue that will signal the willingness to buy. It might be, in the case of a furniture purchase, "Will I be able to buy the set on credit?" For a dress, the clincher could be, "How quickly can I have it altered?" Another clue might be "I'm buying this as a wedding gift. How long does the couple have to make another selection?"

In every situation, even when all closing attempts do not result in the culmination of a sale, there comes a point in time when the seller either stops trying, or in certain cases, might suggest that a manager take over. In the case of automobile sales, it is common practice that when the salesperson hasn't been able to close the sale because of price, the manager is brought in. He or she might be able to offer a better deal and satisfy the customer's demands.

Whatever the end result, courtesy is imperative so that future business might be forthcoming.

The Follow-Up

In many retail operations, especially those that are prestige or service-oriented, it is common practice for the sales associate to write to customers thanking them for the business. Companies like Nordstrom and Neiman Marcus, for example, provide their associates with notepaper so that they can communicate with satisfied customers. It is a gesture that takes a little bit of time, but the payoff could be significant. People in the retail sales arena often build up clienteles that ask for assistance each time they enter the store. In many cases, a rapport might be established that brings future business in ways other than in-store appearances.

At Nordstrom, for example, one Pacesetter revealed that a regular customer rushed to get to a flight to Washington, D.C., for a wedding only to discover that he packed the pants from one suit and the jacket from another. Knowing the customer's measurements and style preferences, he had a new suit, which was perfectly altered, waiting as his car arrived. It is this type of seller-customer relationship that brings sales to the retailer.

An Ethical Consideration

ONE OF THE SALES METHODOLOGIES THAT SOME RETAILERS use to sell merchandise is known as **bait and switch**. This is a practice whereby merchants run ads that feature goods at unusually low prices as a means of motivating shoppers to come to the store. When the customer gets to the store, the featured goods are sold out and the retailer tries to sell them something else that is more profitable. While this is unlawful in most states, it nonetheless is still a practice.

It is not only illegal, but unethical as well. When merchants resort to these tactics they are running the risk of discouraging shoppers from future patronization. Advertised items should be readily available to those who have been motivated to come to the store, and the seller should make every effort to tell the customer of that product's benefits. If the profit margin for such items too little, then the company shouldn't feature it.

OFF-SITE SELLING

Selling to the consumer via means other than in the brick-and-mortar operations is nothing new to retailing. Companies like Sears established themselves as catalog merchants, serving the needs of those who were unable to visit its stores. As the population continued to grow, and people not only lived too far from the stores, but were too busy at work to make those time-consuming trips, more and more merchants offered catalogs to their customers. Numerous catalog-only retailers joined the fray. With the availability at an all time high, it has become a successful way in which consumers can satisfy their needs.

At this point in time, the Internet continues to increase in importance as a means of selling. Merchants with store operations and catalog divisions are opening Web sites in record numbers to sell to a wide consumer market. Known as multichannel retailers, their task is to sell by any means possible.

Finally, a great number of merchants have developed programs for cable television that regularly attract huge numbers of viewers who buy their products.

In each of these formats, there is a need to sell to the consumer. Much as in the case of traditional in-store retailing, questions often have to be answered before any sale will be consummated. Of course, much of the business is transacted on an impersonal level, without the need for personal interaction. In cases where direct communication is needed, it should be handled in a professional manner.

Catalog Selling

When a potential customer wishes to place an order by telephone, often times the decision to buy is not a straightforward one. Just as in the case of the in-store shopper, questions about the merchandise often need clarification. Those who handle these orders have an advantage over their brick-and-mortar counterparts, in terms of customer approach. The catalog purchaser initiates the sale, and doesn't need the personal approach that is necessitated with face to face contact. The catalog representative, however, must be able to answer any questions that the customer might have. Since these sales reps do not generally have the merchandise on hand to discuss their benefits, they must carefully study the merchandise in the catalogs, the company's philosophies in terms of pricing, and any rules and regulations regarding such aspects as returns.

Like those who work in the store, these people are not merely order takers, but company representatives who are often called upon to answer questions and satisfy the customer's needs. If this role is performed satisfactorily, the shopper might become one who will patronize the retailer again and again.

Internet Selling

While much of the ordering is automatically accomplished on the Internet, some purchases require interaction between the customer and the company representative. Any number of questions may be on the shopper's mind before he or she makes a final decision. Many companies address this possibility by establishing an interactive mode where the buyer and the seller can communicate. One user of this concept is Lands' End. In addition to having a very carefully organized Web site that addresses a host of potential inquiries, they also feature a service called "Lands' End Live." By accessing this feature, customers are able to communicate with company representatives either by way of the telephone or through an online chat. It is at this point that the seller must be able to answer any questions that might be posed and then try to bring the sale to a successful conclusion.

As in the case of in-store and catalog selling, the more professionalism that is utilized the more likely that repeat business will follow.

Home-Shopping Selling

Whether it is QVC, HSN, or any of the other cable networks that sell merchandise, there is a great deal of interaction between the show's personalities and those who wish to purchase. In this case, unlike the catalog and Internet venues, the sellers are seen by the viewers. Thus, appearance is an essential factor, along with the ability to answer the caller's questions. Often times these chats are lengthy and require the same selling process as those who sell in the stores. Not only is this a one-on-one presentation, but, in reality, it might involve thousands of silent viewers. The vast majority of those who shop via these home shopping networks call in their orders without the need to have a direct communication. They are, however, often listening to the interaction of those who actually make the calls and the show's representatives who offer the answers. A motivating response to one caller might not only close that sale, but in fact, might be responsible for the closing of numerous others.

Whether it is an in-store presentation, or one that is made through an off-site venue, it is imperative that the company rep be fully knowledgeable, courteous, forthcoming, and sufficiently enthusiastic.

CUSTOMER SERVICES

When a customer enters a brick-and-mortar operation, logs onto an Web site, telephones a catalog company, or interacts with one of the many home-shopping cable channels, there is an expectation that these companies will provide a host of services to make the shopping experience a pleasurable one.

As has been underscored over and over again throughout the text, the new millennium challenges every merchant to do the best he or she can to gain his or her fair share of the consumer's disposable income. While merchandise assortments are often the key to the success of every retailer, often times, with identical or similar merchandise available in many places, it is the little extras that motivate the individual to buy from one retailer rather than another. Often times, the key to success is based upon the services that these merchants offer to the clienteles.

Easy to locate customer service areas make shopping more convenient, thereby encouraging customer loyalty.

Many retailers have emerged as service leaders and have reaped the rewards from this image. Nordstrom, the ultimate service provider, has set a standard in the field for upscale, fashion emporiums, and has made enormous numbers of people regulars because of their service. Not only have the traditional retailers such as Nordstrom benefited from their service, but so have

This child cart pick-up and return is a service to shoppers accompanied by children.

many other merchants, such as the off-pricers and discounters. Each company makes a determination on how to best serve their customer base, and offer the necessary services to bring them back on a regular basis.

The services offered in the retail arena are numerous. Many are free, while others carry a charge. Some of them are typically found in most retail operations, with others less frequently employed.

Traditional Customer Services

There are numerous services that are offered by brick-and-mortar operations, as well as off-site retailers. These are made available to the customers in order to make their shopping experience a well rounded one.

Gift Registries

Stores of almost every type offer **gift registries** for couples who are about to be married or those who are expecting a child. The individuals either come to the store to examine the offerings or make selections online. They complete a wish list, and then wait for their friends and relatives to purchase from it. The purchasing may either take place in the store, or through the retailer's Web site. The benefit to the celebrant is that no unwanted gifts will have to be returned. For the purchaser, it is a quick way to provide the recipients with their own choices. It is especially valuable for those who do not reside in the same city as those who are celebrating the upcoming event. Through the use of the retailer's Web site or by way of telephone or fax, the purchase can be simply accomplished.

The merchants themselves are less troubled with gift returns because the choices have been preselected. It also often introduces new customers to the company.

Merchandise Alterations

Most full-line and specialized department stores offer merchandise alterations to their customers. Sometimes the service is free, while at other times it carries a nominal cost. In either case it relieves the customer's need to find a professional tailor to perform the alterations.

More and more smaller retailers are offering this service as a means of competing with larger stores. The availability of having a professional tailor on hand is often the difference between making a sale and losing it. Uncertain shoppers sometimes need the assurance that the garment can be perfectly tailored to fit their figures before they will make the decision to buy.

Personal Shopping

Most major department stores and upscale specialty organizations that have a significant fashion orientation provide a service known as **personal shopping**. It is especially suited to the needs of those who have little time to shop, or for those who need special assurance that the purchases they are about to make are appropriate.

In most of the companies that offer personal shoppers to customers, it merely takes a phone call to get this special help. A shopper, for example, might need a suit for an important business meeting, but doesn't have the time to go through everything available in the store. By phoning ahead, the shopper gives the store's shopping specialist her preferences in terms of color, price, and style, and the time she is available to come to the store. When she arrives, she is met by the consultant in a special place where the merchandise has already been assembled for her to look at and try on. Bergdorf Goodman, one of New York City's high fashion emporiums, has numerous private rooms in which the customers are shown the preselected merchandise. Food and beverages are also made available in these private surroundings so that those with time limitations can make the most of the shopping experience.

Sometimes personal shopping is used not only for a complete ensemble but for a particular item that would enhance the outfit that the customer already owns. Macy's encourages such clients to call in their requests, and when he or she appears, a selection of the appropriate items will be on hand.

In Nordstrom, the personal shopping role is the practice of every sales associate. Each is ready to take a customer through the store to suggest merchandise, or provide this service via the telephone. It is not unusual for a Nordstrom employee to receive an emergency call that warrants delivery of merchandise directly to the customer' place of business, home, or hotel. It is through this accommodation that Nordstrom has benefited.

Credit Accounts

While these programs, for the most part, bring additional revenues to the company, they are nonetheless considered to be services for the customer. Most large retail operations offer a variety of plans ranging from those that are interest free for customers who pay their bills in 30 days, to those that require interest and are payable over a period of time.

Customers tend to spend more when purchasing with credit cards.   Comp USA offers a proprietary card.

TABLE 16.1
PROPRIETARY CARDS

TYPES	EXAMPLES	FEATURES
Charge accounts	Most department stores	Customers are given lines of credit and must pay their bills in 30 days.
Revolving credit accounts	Most department stores and chain organizations	Lines of credit are established. Customers make monthly payments and can make additional purchases as long as the total doesn't exceed the established line of credit.
Installment credit	Most major department stores, electronics, and furniture chains	For major purchases, the store sets up a monthly payment plan that must be paid in full at the end of the prescribed period.

TABLE 16.2
THIRD-PARTY CARDS

TYPES	EXAMPLES	FEATURES
Travel and entertainment	American Express, Diners Club	Unlimited credit, but user must pay off entire bill at the end of the billing period.
Bank cards	MasterCard, VISA	Cards are issued by banks and are usable at most retail operations. Credit limit is established for each account. Minimum payment is due every month until balance is paid. Users can buy and pay as long as they remain within their credit line.
Cash reward cards	Discover Card	Similar to bank cards, except that the user receives a rebate at the end of the year based upon his or her spending.

The purpose is not only to provide shoppers with extended times in which to pay their bills, but also to increase the size of the purchase. When compared to cash purchases, the credit card transactions are generally larger.

Living in a world of plastic makes the offering of charge plans a must for most retailers. Without them it is likely that the vast majority would not be able to remain in business.

The types of retail credit that are offered are the **proprietary credit card** and **third-party card**. Tables 16.1 and 16.2 feature each classification and their features.

Dining Facilities

Many large retailers offer dining services to their customers. These include the upscale types as well as the self-service ventures. Most department stores feature one or more of these eating venues. Even companies like Sam's Club have food counters at which patrons may purchase food and beverages.

The concept not only provides the retailer with a profit, but also encourages the shopper to stay in the store for a longer period of time. If the store doesn't feature dining facilities, when hunger strikes the shopper will more than likely leave the store and not return for additional shopping.

Leased Departments

Many major retailers have **leased departments** in which they rent a portion of their premises to outside companies who specialize in services that are not typical of the store's offerings. These include travel services and beauty salons.

These departments often carry the names of established companies and sometimes motivate the consumer to come to the store to avail themselves of their services. Frederick Fakai, for example, the world famous hair stylist, operates a leased department in Bergdorf Goodman. It is the retailer's plan that once inside the store for these services, the shoppers will also purchase the company's own goods.

Customized Services

While many retailer services are typically found in the large companies, and serve an important need for their clienteles, others are unique to individual companies. The intention is to distinguish one store from another, and hope that these special services will sufficiently entice shoppers to patronize the stores that offer them. One of the retail organizations that offers some customized services is Marshall Field's, the Chicago-based merchant.

 Focus on . . .
Marshall Field's

BASED IN CHICAGO, ILLINOIS, AND A DIVISION OF TARGET, INC., Marshall Field's has long been considered one of the premiere department stores in the country. The premises of the downtown flagship, in particular, immediately reveals a breathtaking arena. The fixturing, lighting, and visual presentations significantly enhance the merchandise that has been selected by the company's buyers and merchandisers.

Recognizing that the competition is keen, Marshall Field's uses customer service as a means of attracting shoppers to the store, and hopefully motivating them to become regular patrons. It, like all of the other department stores in its trading area, offers the traditional customer services including gift registries, merchandise alterations, delivery, credit, gift wrap, in-store dining, and beauty salons. While these do help to improve its overall bottom line, management is always looking to customize their service offerings to make them unique in the field.

Recognizing the value of making its regular customers feel special, they have instituted two programs, Regards Reward and Regards. Each rewards the loyal clientele with special savings. The first provides any shopper who has accumulated $500 or more of new purchases on his or her Marshall Field's charge card with a sales certificate good for a 15 percent discount on a sale day of the customer's own choosing. No matter how many items are purchased on that particular day, merchandise is discounted 15 percent. The second program, Regards, recognizes its most loyal customers by extending a special membership to them. When $2,000 has been charged annually on the Marshall Field's card, the customer is eligible to receive complimentary signature gift wrap, complimentary coffee or tea whenever he or she is in the store, special offers, members-only mailings, and guest service toll-free lines.

When a new Marshall Field's charge account is opened, the shopper receives a 15 percent discount on any purchases made that day. Recognizing the importance to spread its appeal to markets that are not regularly served by it, the company offers a 10 percent discount to any out-of-town visitors to their flagship and major branch in the Water Tower. It also offers these visitors complimentary cake and coffee in their food emporiums. Not only will many of these shoppers call on the store whenever they are in town, but often times they open credit card accounts that enable them to buy from the catalogs they will receive. Having been provided with this special treatment, many also use the Marshall Field's Web site for purchases.

Keeping the customer happy is very important to Marshall Field's. It invites customers to complete comment cards in which its merchandise and services may be evaluated. This tool helps them to upgrade services, and makes each customer feel that he or she has played a part in the company's improvement.

● ●

Special Shopping Times

Some merchants set aside specific hours periodically to cater to a particular segment of their market. It might a few hours before the normal shopping day for handicapped shoppers to come to the store to purchase; or a special time when only men can enter the store to make holiday purchases.

Henri Bendel, the upscale fashion emporium in New York City has a Girls' Nites program that features exclusive workshops on beauty, weddings, and other fashionable subjects. Recognized authorities such as national makeup artist Eric Jimenez, designers such as Diane Von Furstenberg, and *New York Magazine* editor-in-chief Caroline Miller are just a few of the invited guests who make the Girls' Nites special.

Interpreters Programs

The continued influx of visitors from all over the globe has created a demand for people who are able to communicate in foreign languages. Often times it is these shoppers who spend considerable sums in the stores on themselves, as well as on gifts that they will bring back home. Harrods, perhaps the world's most famous fashion retailer, provides interpreters for just this purpose. Just about any foreign visitor can have an individual assigned to him or her who is perfectly able to communicate in the necessary language. Macy's, in its New York City flagship, also provides a host of language experts who can communicate in most any language. Without any charge to the customer, he or she will not only assist with purchases, but will also arrange for immediate alterations, assist with currency exchanges, and provide anything else that will make their shopping experience more pleasant.

Special shopping night themes help attract a desired audience.

Corporate Gift Service

Many retailers, particularly those that are located in the major commercial cities, provide special services that accommodate businesses that regularly need gifts for their employees and clients. At Christmas, in particular, some companies spend enormous sums on gifts to thank their customers for past patronage. Macy's provides a **corporate gift service** in which expert consultants help in the selection of client gifts, incentive offerings, and retirement awards. Through the use of a special Macy's corporate account, the user is entitled to volume purchase incentives and other service amenities.

The 10 Commandments of Customer Service

Put Your Customers First
Retail stores cannot exist without customers ... so welcome them and make them feel valued.

Make It Easy ...
for shoppers to get into and out of your store, to find a sales associate, to gather merchandise and to locate fitting rooms, restrooms and the return desk.

Know Your Customers
Embrace every opportunity to notice them, listen to them and remember them.

Keep It Simple
Discount store shoppers don't expect piano music, and commissioned sales help won't fly in a warehouse club, but a friendly smile, a bit of empathy and a willingness to help work in every environment.

Cultivate a Service Culture
Passion for customer service must be part of the culture, not just part of the mission statement.

Be Consistent
Multi-channel is industry jargon. Customers expect customer service, prices and return policies to be consistent, regardless of whether they shop your store, catalog or website.

Play Fair
Do what you say you'll do, when you say you'll do it, at the price you promised.
If you advertise something, have it in stock. If it's out of stock, provide comparable alternatives.

Empower the Front Line ...
to make decisions and deliver results, and counsel them when mistakes arise.
Take care of the people who are charged with taking care of your customers and they will take care of your business.

Use Technology ...
to aid and abet customer service, not to replace it.

Recover Quickly
Mistakes will happen. The true measure of good customer service is how quickly you can turn a negative into a positive.

The ten commandments of customer service.

Choosing One's Own Sale Day

In order to reward customers for their patronage, Bloomingdale's has developed a program that focuses on the faithful. Shoppers receive notification through the mail of special days that have been set aside for them to receive a 15 percent discount on everything that is purchased for one day. The particular day is left to the consumer since the company is aware that not everyone may be available at the same time to take advantage of the offer. When entering the store, the shopping pass that has been sent, is taken to any Bloomingdale's sales associate who will activate it. All day long the discount can be taken on merchandise.

Child Care Facilities

Shopping is necessity for consumers, but many face the problem of finding free time to accomplish this task without interruption from others. In particular, children often prevent parents from spending the time needed to make their selections. Retailers recognize that the more time available for uninterrupted shopping, the more likely the sale will be greater. To accommodate shoppers, IKEA, the furniture and housewares chain with branches throughout the United States, has solved the problem by offering a fully protected fun environment in which parents may leave their children while shopping. This specially designed area is managed by trained people who have complete responsibility for the children left in their charge. Each child is marked with a special tag for identification and is only released to the parent when matching identification is shown.

Each retailer must assess his or her own clientele's needs and develop those service programs that bring greater sales to its company.

Call Centers

Recognizing the need for customer service is obvious by the number of different types retailers offer. While the addressing of customer problems is a necessity, the expense involved in handling these concerns continues to escalate. Many merchants are finding that not only is the expense often becoming prohibitive, but finding the right people to perform this service is becoming more and more difficult.

The answer for many retailers has been the use of call centers, centralized facilities that are operated by external companies. One of the global leaders in corporate networking solutions and services is Avaya, Inc. Among the many retailers it services, in terms of interfacing with consumers and handling problems, is Home Depot. Through web chat, email, voice-over IP, and telephone, all of which originates from a call center managed by Avaya, Home Depot is able to relieve their in-store personnel from handling problems and pay more attention to making sales. Home Depot gets the information about all of its products to Avaya, who in turns uses it to satisfy customer inquiries and complaints. In addition to the problem solving nature of these and other call centers, the information that is gathered from the consumer may be used to better understand buying patterns and preferences. In this way, Home Depot and other retailers may better tailor their operations to satisfy customer needs.

TRENDS FOR THE NEW MILLENNIUM

- Customer relationship management (CRM) is a business strategy in which everyone in the retail enterprise is focused on the customer. More and more retailers are developing programs of this nature which will reveal all the needs of the customers.

- As competition continues to upwardly spiral, retailers, whether they are the brick-and-mortar operations or off-site ventures, are regularly developing customized service programs that will distinguish them from the others in the field.

- Many retailers who have used straight salary as a means of sales associate remuneration are moving in the direction of providing incentives to encourage better selling. These motivations are taking the form of commissions in addition to regular salary, commissions only payment, or bonuses that are based upon the achievement of predetermined quotas.

- The use of prepackaged training programs that can be tailored to the company's needs will increase because they have proven to be effective and cost considerably less than maintaining a training staff.

- Many retailers who decreased the size of their sales staffs and turned to self-selection as a means of selling are recognizing the need for personal selling. Many will be providing better-prepared sales people to address the needs of their clienteles.

CHAPTER HIGHLIGHTS

- Customer service is not only important in brick-and-mortar operations, but in the off-site organizations as well.
- When some merchants changed their selling formats from service to self-selection, sales began to decline.
- Nordstrom has set the standard for excellence in retail selling as well as in customer service.
- The rules of the selling game include proper appearance, communications skills, tactfulness, motivational expertise, and enthusiasm.
- Product knowledge can be acquired by taking courses and through technology.
- Sales training may be achieved through role-playing, professional videocassettes, on-the-job training, vestibule training, and online training.
- Proper selling involves appropriate customer greetings, needs assessment, merchandise presentation, handling objections, and attempts at closing the sale.
- Some Web sites are providing online help so that a customer's questions can be answered directly.
- Retailers provide a wealth of traditional services to make shopping more pleasurable.
- Customized services are provided by retailers who wish to go the extra mile to make their customers feel special.
- Retail credit is provided either by the merchants themselves or through third-party creditors.

IMPORTANT RETAILING TERMS

personal selling
skeleton sales crew
customer-is-always-right concept
role-playing

on-the-job training
vestibule training
online training
agree and counterattack method
"Yes, but" technique
trial close
bait and switch
gift registries
personal shopping
proprietary credit cards
third-party cards
leased departments
corporate gift service

FOR REVIEW

1. Why are many retailers improving their customer services?

2. In the 1970s and 1980s, what changes took place in terms of service on the selling floor?

3. Which retailer is said to epitomize personal selling and customer service?

4. Why is appropriate appearance such an important part of the salesperson's preparation?

5. How can a sales associate learn proper communication skills if in-house training is unavailable?

6. What are the areas of company knowledge that a sales associate should be familiar with in order to make a better sales presentation?

7. Describe how tactfulness helps generate future business.

8. Why is role-playing considered by many to be the best way to learn selling techniques?

9. What is meant by the term *vestibule training*, and what purpose does it serve?

10. Upon greeting a customer, what is important to remember?

11. Discuss two techniques that are typically used to overcome customer objections.

12. Is it always possible to close every retail sale? Why or why not?

13. Why do some upscale retailers use follow-up techniques for customers who have just made purchases?

14. Does any actual selling take place in the off-site retail environments? Explain.

15. What are some of the traditional services offered by the major retailers in the United States?

16. What is the difference between typical department store charge accounts and the revolving credit accounts these stores offer to customers?

17. Distinguish between bankcards and cash reward cards.

18. Why do some retailers offer interpreter services to their shoppers?

19. How does the corporate gift service differ from typical gift registries?

20. Why do some merchants set aside space for child care facilities in their stores?

21. In what way do call centers improve upon in-house customer servicing?

AN INTERNET ACTIVITY

Along with brick-and-mortar enterprises and catalog companies, retailers with Web sites are now offering a host of services to their users. Once a venue where automatic purchasing was the primary focus, many of the Web sites offer different services to augment purchasing. These companies may be divisions of multichannel retailers or merchants who use the Internet as their sole means of selling.

In this assignment, you should access a number of different retailers who sell merchandise on their Web sites. Companies who operate brick-and-mortar operations as well as Web sites should be explored, along with companies that are solely Internet based.

Select one multichannel and one e-tail retailer to compare the services they offer online. Prepare a report using a form with the following heads to list each of the traditional and customized services offered on the Web. Sum-

marize your conclusions about why one retail source is better than the other in terms of customer service.

Retailer	Traditional Services	Customized Services

EXERCISES AND PROJECTS

1. Visit two stores that are in the same retail classification, for example department stores, chain organizations, or supermarkets. Each of the chosen companies should then be assessed in terms of the services provided to their customers. Once you have recorded your findings, a comparative analysis should be written addressing these services, along with your conclusion as to which company is more customer-oriented and why.

2. Pretend that you are in the market for a consumer product that requires some personal selling. It might be a computer, a television, receiver, a camera, or any other high-ticket item. Visit two stores and assess the selling assistance that was provided. When finished, write a one-page paper describing the approaches used in each of the selling presentations, and select the one that you think was handled best, along with the reasons for your choice.

THE CASE OF DEVELOPING A CUSTOMER SERVICE PROGRAM THAT BEST SERVES CONSUMERS

Ever since the rush for off-price merchants to enter the retail arena, the consumer was continuously given more and more places in which to find bargain merchandise. Joining the fray in 1980, was Paramount Specialty Shops, with a wealth of fashion-oriented items that paralleled the inventories of the most sophisticated, traditional fashion emporiums. Collections that included names like Ralph Lauren, Anne Klein, Perry Ellis, and other marquee labels were commonplace at Paramount. The success of the operation can best be measured by the number of new units it continued to open. There are now 125 units.

Taking its cue from the early entries into this value-shopping format, the company built its facilities as barebone environments that were void of any services other than the acceptance of third-party credit cards. With the success continuously spiraling upward, the company envisioned a chain that would ultimately double its present numbers. During the past two years, however, other companies that catered to value shoppers began to open, competing with many of Paramount's units. Not only did these competitors offer the same type of merchandise mix at bargain prices, but some designed facilities that were more consumer-friendly and offered a host of services.

While business in most of the Paramount stores continued to be successful, management was worried that the new competition might result in the loss of some of its regular patrons. Through informal research Paramount learned that while customers were most interested in price, more and more expected some level of customer service.

David Michaels, the company's CEO, was not in favor of introducing any services since he believed it would affect the bottom line. Price, he stated, was the only real reason for the clientele to patronize the stores in the chain. Amy Alexander, the company COO, was in total disagreement. While she agreed with the fact that price was most important to shoppers, the need for some customer services was imperative because of the new competition in this arena. She argued that even though the cost of these services would hamper the profits at the present sales levels, the new approach would attract more customers, increase sales, and the same or a better profit picture would prevail.

Questions

1. With whom do you agree? Defend your position with sound reasoning.

2. If some services are offered, what method would you use to introduce them to the company?

3. Which services might be appropriate, as well as cost effective, for Paramount to offer?

APPENDIX
Careers in Retailing and Related Fields

After reading this book, it is obvious that many different types of roles must be played in order to manage any retail operation. Those who are motivated to enter the field, and some of those that are directly related to it, will have the opportunity to involve themselves in the areas that seem most appropriate for their skills and motivations.

Whether it is a small or large brick-and-mortar operation, or one of the off-site ventures that are significantly impacting the industry, there is wealth of opportunity ahead. With its promise for greater globalization, retailing is one of the few careers that does not restrict its participants to a rather limited geographic region. Small towns and big cities and domestic and foreign venues, each provide ample opportunity to make a significant contribution to the field.

Working as a team member in retail operations of any size has its own rewards, as does the starting of one's own business. Each offers a degree of excitement and monetary remuneration that is based upon individual ability, knowledge, and the determination to achieve success. It is a career that doesn't require the ultimate educational achievements demanded by other professions, but a level of competency and individual motivation. Those who enter this arena with a willingness to work diligently, and play by the rules of the game will undoubtedly have the opportunity to reach the top.

Before anyone enters the field it is imperative that an exploration of the field be undertaken so that one's abilities and desires can be best matched to the specific positions within the field.

JOB CLASSIFICATIONS

One need not look further than the pages of the numerous chapters in the text to become familiar with the wealth of jobs that are performed in retailing. Each brick-and-mortar operation, catalog, Web site, and home-shopping service is home to every level of management, merchandising, and product development. Even those off-site ventures that seem to focus on self-selection often require a certain degree of personal selling. Of course, it is the stores that require the greatest degree of professional salesmanship.

Bearing in mind that retail careers cross over into these different arenas, the reader should carefully examine each of the career classifications and eventually pursue the specific venue that appears to bring the greatest excitement and potential for success. Thus, whether it is a department store, specialty chain, supermarket, franchise, discount operation, off-price venture, catalog, Web site, or home-shopping service, the jobs offered by the organization are more or less the same.

It also should be noted that many of today's merchants are participants of multichannel retailing in which different divisions vie for the consumer's dollar. By seeking employment in this type of company, there is even greater potential for the individual to explore the various types of opportunity without having to move from one company to another.

Typically, careers in retailing are centered on the areas of *merchandising, management, operations, promotion*, and *finance*. Parallel careers, such as those that are available in resident buying offices, marketing specialist groups, and fashion forecasting services, feature a host of opportunities, many of which are similar to those found in the retail operations, and others that are exclusive to their particular types of businesses.

The following discussion will focus on the management and mid-management levels of employment that are open to those who have satisfactorily fulfilled the obligation of entry-level positions.

Brick-and-Mortar and Off-Site Job Opportunities

Each offers a potential for advancement and salaries that are commensurate with educational background, experience, and a willingness to perform at the highest possible level.

Merchandising

If the excitement of purchasing merchandise that appeals to the consumer and brings a profit to the company is the goal, then merchandising is the most appropriate career to pursue. In major retail organizations, this division is comprised of a host of line and staff positions. In smaller companies, the limited amount of business dictates fewer positions and the absence of staff or advisory people. Table A.1 is based upon the needs of the major retailers in the industry.

TABLE A.1	
MERCHANDISING CAREERS	
POSITION	**DESCRIPTION**
General Merchandise Manager	Heads the merchandising division; oversees the company's entire merchandising budget; leads management team in determining company product mix, pricing strategies, and merchandising philosophy.
Divisional Merchandise Manager	Heads several related divisions in the company, oversees buyers, allocates budgeted dollars to individual buyers, sets tone for division's merchandise assortment, and assists buyers in the division with major purchasing decisions.
Buyer	Develops model stock, visits wholesale markets, buys merchandise, and is often involved in product development of private label merchandise.
Assistant Buyer	Often purchases staple goods, reorders merchandise, places special orders and assists the buyer with purchasing decisions at home and in the wholesale market.
Fashion Director	In companies with fashion orientations this is most often a staff position in which specialists advise the merchandising team as to the present status of the new collections and the trends in the market.
Comparison Shopper	Another staff position, the role is to compare prices of merchandise at competing companies.

Management

Those who manage the retail operations are in areas that cut across the entire organization. Some of the positions are included in Table A.2.

Operations

This division is generally maintains the physical plant and the management of its employees. Table A.3 lists several careers in operations.

TABLE A.2
MANAGEMENT CAREERS

POSITION	DESCRIPTION
Store Manager	Overall management functions which include services and management team selection. Also responsible for carrying out company policy.
Department Manager	Responsible for individual departments and personnel in each, scheduling, and employee evaluation.
Assistant Department Manager	Aids the department manager in running department, sells, handles complaints, and is responsible for end-of-day receipt tallying.
Human Resources Manager	Provides company with competent employees, and oversees all aspect of human resources management.

TABLE A.3
OPERATIONS CAREERS

POSITION	DESCRIPTION
Operations Manager	Responsible for areas such as security, plant maintenance, traffic, receiving, supplies purchasing, and workrooms.
Security Chief	Develops loss prevention systems and manages the security team.
Maintenance Manager	Responsible for housekeeping, construction and facilities alteration, ventilation, and maintenance of mechanical equipment.
Receiving Manager	Oversees incoming merchandise, checking and marking, and invoicing.
Purchasing Manager	Buys equipment and supplies for the company's operation.
Workroom Manager	Responsible for clothing alterations, merchandise repairs, and restaurants.

Promotion

The company's promotional and publicity endeavors are imperative to informing the consumers and press about their latest innovations. Managers who fulfill these responsibilities head a number of different areas of expertise, some of which are included in Table A.4.

TABLE A.4	
PROMOTIONAL CAREERS	
POSITION	**DESCRIPTION**
Director of Promotion	Oversees and coordinates all of the promotional efforts of the company and the managers of each promotional department.
Advertising Manager	Responsible for all of the media planning, development of campaigns, and management of personnel in division.
Visual Merchandising Manager	Develops window and interior visual concepts, oversees installations, hires artists, and trimmers, coordinates efforts with other promotional managers.
Special Events Manager	Creates concepts for company's special events including fashion shows and in-store celebrity appearances.
Publicity Manager	Prepares press releases and interacts with the press.

Finance

The success of any retail operation in terms of profit comes from close control of its financial expenditures and the manner in which it offers credit to its customer base. Those who manage these endeavors are included in Table A.5.

TABLE A.5	
FINANCE CAREERS	
POSITION	**DESCRIPTION**
Accounting Manager	Responsible for formulating accounting procedures and practices, and hiring subordinates.
Payroll Administrator	Develops and coordinates payroll procedures and practices.
Credit Manager	Manages every aspect of credit, oversees credit policies and credit authorization.
Inventory Controller	Develops methods for inventory taking and management of the procedures.

▆▆▆▆ Careers That Parallel Retailing

Aside from those who work directly in any retail organization are those who have careers in external companies. Whether the company is comparatively small or a giant in the field, outside resources are often necessary to get an impartial handle on what is taking place in the industry. In the fashion arena, for example, marketing specialists, the largest of which are the resident buying offices, continually feel the pulse of the wholesale industry through research, and make their findings known to their clients. In this way, the merchants are able to better understand what is ahead of them in terms of merchandise availability, trends, and the like. Reporting services also serve the retailer's needs, apprise them of the competition's merchandising focus, and the general state of the marketplace. Others such as fashion forecasters assist the retailer's buying and merchandising team through predictions of the styles that will be coming to the forefront so that the proper purchasing plans can be developed.

In each of these parallel industries there are careers that may attract those who are enamored with retailing but would like to pursue a challenge that is not directly focused on consumer interaction. Some of the careers in this category are listed in Table A.6.

TABLE A.6	
MARKET SPECIALIST CAREERS	
POSITION	**DESCRIPTION**
Resident Buying Office Merchandise Manager	Oversees a wide product classification, prepares programs for market weeks, and manages buyers in division.
Resident Buyer	Assesses wholesale market, advises retail buyers on merchandise availability, prepares buyers for market trips, and prescreens merchandise collections.
Assistant Resident Buyer	Follows-up retail orders, handles retailer adjustments and complaints, prescreens lines, and accompanies buyer to marketplace.
Product Developer	Develops private label items.
Fashion Forecaster	Predicts the direction up to 18 months before the season so that buyers may plan their needs well in advance of the market weeks.
Reporting Service Manager	Studies the sales of current merchandise and reports the hot items to clients for possible inclusion in their inventories.

PLANNING FOR THE CAREER

Anyone who wishes to pursue a career either in a retail operation or in one that parallels the industry must be fully prepared. The preparation involves any number of areas including educational background, learning about the company, developing materials such as résumés that will help to gain an interview and refining the qualities needed for the interview. A significant preplanning effort will bring the best results.

Educational Background

The better educated one is for any career, the more likely he or she will excel. Some industries, such as law and medicine, require substantial formal education before entry is permitted. Retailing, on the other hand, is considerably less stringent in its educational requirements, but nonetheless, those who are better educated will more than likely be the candidates of choice.

For entry-level positions such as sales, most merchants do not look for special diplomas or degrees, but rather a desire by the individual to meet the challenges of face-to-face interaction with the consumer. For those who perform diligently at this lower-level position, often times promotions to more responsible positions are likely. Many a department manager has risen to that level by showing the dedication necessary to meet the company's standards.

Those who wish to enter at a more professional level will need to have completed a particular course of study that culminates with a degree. Some companies require associate degrees as their minimum requirements, while others opt for baccalaureates. Some seeking managerial material to eventually run the companies often require master's degrees. In most retail operations with mandatory educational requirements, retailers typically enable employees to work and attend college at the same time so that they can complete the necessary degree. Many will pay for the credits, making schooling less burdensome on the employee.

Introduction to the Company

In order to learn about educational expectations and other company information, those seeking positions should do a thorough investigation not only to learn if the company is appropriate for their consideration, but also to fortify themselves with the necessary knowledge for the interview.

Such information may be obtained by writing to the company or, in today's world of advanced technology, through the Internet. By and large, most retail organizations have sections on their Web sites that invite potential employees to learn about employment opportunities. By logging on to them one can quickly come upon an employment application that can be transmitted to the company and evaluated. In Chapter 6, Human Resources Management, an overview of such employment information is offered.

If the company that is being considered for employment is within close proximity to the interested party, then an in-person visit is in order. In particular, brick-and-mortar operations may be entered with complete anonymity. The visit allows the candidate to assess the work environment and the types of employees that are already in place, along with the mode of dress. These can be simple, yet invaluable sources of information that help determine whether or not the company should be pursued. If these indicators seem appropriate to the job seeker's needs, then a trip to the employment office would be in order to learn more about the company. It might be a time when the setting of an interview appointment will be in order.

Gaining an Interview

Being granted an interview is dependent upon the concept of supply and demand. As we entered the new millennium, there were considerably more jobs that needed filling then the number of applicants seeking them. Of course, this is not always the case. In times of a recession, or during downturns in the economy, the reverse is true; more people are seeking positions than are available. With the conditions ready to change all the time, there must be a plan to secure the interview that best meets the goals of the individual seeking to initially enter the field.

Different approaches are used to break into a new company. These include examining the classified ads in the newspapers, visiting employment agencies that specialize in retailing, and networking. Networking involves calling on friends or relatives to discover which ones have access or connections to the retail organizations. Doors often open to those who come with recommendations.

No matter which route one takes to gain an interview, significant planning must be undertaken to make certain that the candidate is well prepared for the meeting. Part of this preparation involves writing a résumé and a cover letter to accompany it.

Résumés

A résumé gives the individual responsible for hiring a general picture of the potential candidate. It is this document that either gives the go ahead for an interview or the reason to deny the candidate the opportunity. Thus, the development of the "perfect" one is extremely essential to the candidate's potential employment with the company.

Résumé writing requires total competency. It may be accomplished by the individual if he or she has the writing skills necessary to succinctly present the appropriate information. Often times it is best to employ the services of a professional who has mastered résumé writing and is able to present the individual's characteristics in the perfect format.

There are numerous resources from which to obtain information about résumé writing on the Internet. Free assistance is available quickly and easily by logging onto www.askjeeves.com and then clicking on to The Resume Dolphin. To search for a professional résumé writer, go to www.jobsearchpro.com. At www.resumerservice.net, the user can view a step-by-step procedure that will help one write his or her own résumé. On the same Web site help is also available for a fee. One can also e-mail a résumé preparation company, such as info@resumedotcom.com, and get advice as well as a complete résumé for a nominal fee. These are but a few of the hundred professional services available to job applicants, it is just a matter of examining many of them and deciding which one provides the service for a cost that is appropriate.

Additionally, numerous books on résumé writing are available at the libraries and bookstores. These written materials provide a wealth of forms that can be used to tailor a résumé to one's own needs.

Cover Letters

Accompanying each résumé should be a cover letter that states why the potential candidate is submitting a résumé to the company. The letter might include information on your desire to work for that particular company, or the name of someone familiar who has recommended you as a potential candidate. It is unnecessary to include any of the information that is already part of the résumé. This would only be redundant and too time-consuming for the company representative to read.

The Interview Follow-up

Once the interview has been completed, it is always appropriate to thank the interviewer for his or her time. Not only is this a courtesy, but it shows a candidate's level of interest in the position.

This thank you should come in the form of a letter that should be as painstakingly prepared as the résumé. The resources that were used to prepare the résumé are also available to provide the necessary formats for professional follow-up letters.

The proper use of these documents will help make the impression necessary to gain the interview, and then perhaps, employment with the company.

Index

FIGURE CREDITS

Chapter 1: Courtesy of Ellen Diamond: 6-9, 12-13, 18, 21, 24-25, 29; Harrods, 2002: 16.

Chapter 2: Courtesy of Ellen Diamond: 36, 40-41, 43, 45-46, 48, 51, 53; Courtesy of Charter Oak Partners, an affiliate of Rothschild Realty, Inc.: 52.

Chapter 3: Courtesy of America Online, Inc.: 59; Copyright 2001-2002 The Excite Network, Inc. All Rights Reserved.: 60; ©2002 Amazon.com, Inc. All Rights Reserved.: 61; These materials have been reproduced with permission of eBay Inc. Copyright ©eBay Inc. All Rights Reserved.: 63; Courtesy of Fairchild Publications, Inc.: 66 (Photographer: Jason Cohn); Courtesy of Ellen Diamond: 67-68; ©Lands' End, Inc. Used with permission. The My Virtual Model™ Dressing Room is courtesy of My Virtual Model Inc.: 71; Courtesy of Lillian Vernon Corporation: 73; HSN/ hsn.com: 78.

Chapter 4: Courtesy of Ellen Diamond: 89-90, 100, 107; Courtesy of Fairchild Publications, Inc.: 91 (Photographer: D. Achard), 96 (Photographer: Jan Jarecki); Courtesy of Sheri Litt: 92; SRI Consulting Business Intelligence: 93.

Chapter 5: Courtesy of Ellen Diamond: 115, 117.

Chapter 6: Courtesy of Monster®: 139 (top); Courtesy of Ellen Diamond: 142; Reprinted with permission of Best Buy Co., Inc.: 143; Courtesy of Fairchild Publications, Inc.: 147 (Photographer: Tom Iannaccone).

Chapter 7: Courtesy of Sensormatic: 162-165; Courtesy of Ellen Diamond: 166, 171, 176-177; Copyright 2002 US Search.com, Inc.: 169.

Chapter 8: Courtesy of Ellen Diamond: 183, 186, 188; Paxar Monarch: 195.

Chapter 9: Copyright ©2002, ESRI BIS. All rights reserved. ESRI Business Information Solutions.: 207; Courtesy of Fairchild Publications, Inc.: 208 (Photographer: Robert Mitra); Courtesy of Ellen Diamond: 210, 213-215, 219, 222; The Mills Corporation: 216; Courtesy of The Rouse Company: 217; AP/Wide World Photos: 220.

Chapter 10: Courtesy of Ellen Diamond: 232-234, 238, 240, 248; Courtesy of FRCH Design Worldwide: 237; Courtesy of Fairchild Publications, Inc.: 245.

Chapter 11: Courtesy of Sheri Litt: 258, 271; Courtesy of Ellen Diamond: 262, 265, 277-278, 286; Courtesy of The Doneger Group: 263, 280; Courtesy of Fairchild Publications, Inc.: 266, Courtesy of Belk, Inc.: 267; Courtesy of Donna Lombardo, Belk, Inc.: 275.

Chapter 12: Courtesy of Ellen Diamond: 293-294, 305-306, 308; Courtesy of Fairchild Publications, Inc.: 296 (Photographer: Donato Sardella); Courtesy of The Doneger Group: 307.

Chapter 13: Courtesy of Sheri Litt: 321; Courtesy of Ellen Diamond: 324, 327, 334; Courtesy Fairchild Publications, Inc.: 326 (Photographer: Donato Bardella); Courtesy of Belk, Inc.: 329.

Chapter 14: Courtesy of Ellen Diamond: 346, 348 (top), 358, 359, 363-365; Courtesy of Belk, Inc.: 348 (bottom), 350, 352; AP/Wide World Photos: 351, 366; Courtesy of Supermud Pottery Studio: 354.

Chapter 15: Courtesy of Ellen Diamond: 372-375, 380, 382, 386, 388-389, 391; Courtesy of Sheri Litt: 376; Rootstein Mannequins: 379.

Chapter 16: Courtesy of Ellen Diamond: 398, 407, 413, 415 (left); ©Jauques M. Chenet/CORBIS: 401; ©Copyright 2001 NRF Enterprises, Inc. Used with permission.: 420.

Color Plates: (1) Lee Snider/Corbis: a; Phil Schermeister/Corbis: b; Courtesy of Shook™: c. (2) Courtesy of Lillian Vernon Corporation: a; Copyright ©2002 Scholastic Inc. All rights reserved. Used by permission.: b. (3) Courtesy of The Rouse Company. (4) ©The Art Institute of Chicago. All Rights Reserved.: a; Arizona Diamondbacks: b; ©The Kingston Hospital: c–d. (5) AP/Wide World Photos: a; Jennifer Graylock/Fashion Wire Daily: b. (6) Courtesy of Fairchild Publications, Inc.: a–b (Photographer: Jenna Bodnar/Oya Photography), c–d. (7) Courtesy of Fairchild Publications, Inc.: a (Photographer: Eric Weiss), b (Photographer: Stephen Lourin), c (Photographer: Dan D'errica). (8) Courtesy of Fairchild Publications, Inc. (Photographer: Steve Eichner).